CONTENTS

2	
4	
12	
20	Niklas Maak
62	**Rif Revisited** Samir Bantal
70	**Great Plan for the Transformation of Nature** Alexandra Kharitonova
80	**Future Food** Louise Fresco interviewed by RK
84	**Food Insecurity** Samir Bantal
90	**Ocha: African Avant Garde** Dr. Linda Nkatha Gichuyia & Etta Madete
104	**Botscape** Keigo Kobayashi
118	**Sea Lovers** Ingo Niermann
124	**Villages with Chinese Characteristics** Stephan Petermann
148	**Thaw** Janna Bystrykh
170	**Gorilla Politics** Johannes Refisch interviewed by NM & RK
172	**Gorilla Theory** Niklas Maak
210	**Off-(Jefferson's) Grid** Anne M. Schneider
224	**Industrial Farming Blues** Janna Bystrykh
252	**Buying = Saving** Federico Martelli, Cookies
272	**TRIC: Post-human Architecture** RK
274	**Descartes Was Here** Clemens Driessen
300	**Pixel Farming** Lenora Ditzler
324	**?** RK

Ignored Realm
RK

While today, the countryside is largely off (our) radar, an *ignored realm*, considering its condition and future was a priority as recently as the last century—the Soviet Union, the New Deal, Nazi Germany, Mao, and the EU were experimenting with vast efforts to improve its accessibility and efficiency, and to shape its politics. The dialectic between city and countryside fundamentally defined the meaning of each. Today, we have neither a dialectic—a real, mutual relationship—nor a definition. In the 1960s and 70s, the status and condition of the countryside were crucial too for post-colonial and revolutionary thinkers, from Fanon to Malcolm X; the first presidents of recently independent African countries, Arab leaders like Nasser, Gaddafi, Saddam Hussein, and Hafez al-Assad—all published agricultural tracts that were important components of their proposed and actual revolutions.

Countryside was a canvas on which every movement, ideology, political bloc, and individual revolutionary projected their own intentions. The past two decades—or maybe the entire period since 1991—has been characterized by a complacent expectation that one kind of civilization—metropolitan, capital-oriented, agnostic, western—would remain the template for global development, possibly forever. Meanwhile the "model" ignored drastic developments in the Middle East, Africa, Asia, China, and has been oblivious to climate change and the environment. At most, "we" have appended politically correct sensitivities about colonialism, race, and gender to its basic premise, which we have now allowed to morph into Silicon Valley's ever more grim recipe for the Smart City as the ultimate outcome of History. The combined systems of airline hubs, highways, fast trains, (self-driving?) cars, internet, and mobile phones hold us in a self-imposed prison of the urban where the "experience" economy tries to hide the fact that there is nothing fundamentally new to experience in urban life... Today, even a "new" city is familiar: a predictable accumulation of roads, towers, icons... but as soon as we leave the urban condition behind us we confront newness and the profoundly unfamiliar. Inadvertently, this outcome was set in motion by the UN's 2007 announcement that 50 percent of mankind already lived in cities, and that this percentage would increase to 70 percent by 2050. That statistic alone became an alibi for our almost exclusive focus on the city. Are we really heading to an absurd outcome where the vast majority of mankind lives in only 2 percent of the earth's "overpopulated" surface—and the remaining 98 percent would be inhabited by only one-fifth of humanity, staying there to service them? Total Urbanization requires that a large part of the countryside would be claimed as a back of house for urban civilization, a residual, enabling domain, where all the needs, demands, impositions of the urban can be orchestrated and implemented at will. Is it any coincidence that since our fixation on Total Urbanization, crucial ecosystems have, possibly, slipped past the point of no return? In 2020, two blatant tasks stand out. The inevitability of Total Urbanization must be questioned, and the countryside must be rediscovered as a place to resettle, to stay alive; enthusiastic human presence must reanimate it with new imagination. *Countryside* is not a polemic against the city. For that we should imagine Zola on Brands, Dickens on gated communities, Whitman on Facebook, Tolstoy on Zuckerberg, Proust on the Smart City...

Countryside collects global samples from all ideologies and all continents to construct a composite picture of the current condition of "countryside"—a glaringly inadequate term for all the territory that is not urban, 50 times bigger than all our cities combined. Given countryside's enormity, this portrait can only be pointillist. This catalogue collects evidence of "progress" in the countryside—even within the gloom of Warming—but also detects alarms that have never even reached the city. Currently, countryside discourse is polarized between attempts to keep "as is" and to change "everything." What we wanted to collect is evidence of new thinking, new ways of paying, new ways of cultivating, new ways of building, new ways of remembering, new ways of exploring, new ways of acting, old ways of contemplating and being, new ways of using new media, new ways of owning, renting, new ways of protecting, new ways of planting, new ways of farming, new ways of fusing, new ways of harvesting, that are taking place beyond a metropolitan consciousness and that ultimately could make it possible that we all don't end up unhappily huddled together in cities, and would enable us to experience a realm that we have ignored at our, and its, peril.

A base from which to make the world a better place.

Director's Foreword
Richard Armstrong

Countryside, The Future offers our principally urbanite audience a close inspection of rural conditions across the globe. It includes no design work, no examples from the personal or corporate archives of Rem Koolhaas. Rather, it marks a turn in trajectory following a career-long focus on cities. This exhibition of research presents the curious encounters, the stories, phenomena, conditions, fears, and hopes discovered and refined by RK and his cohort—Samir Bantal, Niklas Maak, and many others—from their travels around the world. Installation as *gesamtkunstwerk*, it transforms the architecture of Frank Lloyd Wright's rotunda with a paper-thin layer marrying information and spectacle, all choreographed to the spatial idiosyncrasies of one of the world's most iconic buildings. Of the five exhibitions mounted in the Guggenheim on the work of an architect, this is the second that features RK. About the same time as his now-seminal treatise on modernity and the city, *Delirious New York*, landed on bookshelves in 1978, the museum dedicated the top ramp of its rotunda to *The Sparkling Metropolis*, an installation of drawings and paintings by Madelon Vriesendorp and Elia and Zoe Zenghelis, RK's partners in the fledgling Office for Metropolitan Architecture (OMA). Subsequently, OMA designed the Guggenheim's exhibition spaces in Las Vegas, which were operated with the State Hermitage Museum from 2001 to 2008. In the mid-nineties, RK initiated the Project on the City at the Harvard Graduate School of Design to research mutant forms of urbanism. AMO, a three-lettered agency named by reversing the acronym of RK's professional practice, was begun. Its considerable brain power and imaginations fuel such projects as Countryside. Collaborating with established architects to create something without precedent reflects the ambition that Artistic Director and Jennifer and David Stockman Chief Curator, Nancy Spector, and I had for the position of Curator, Architecture and Digital Initiatives. Shortly after being appointed in 2014, Troy Conrad Therrien invited RK and AMO to develop their inquiry into the countryside, which then triggered several Harvard GSD studios under RK's leadership. With architecture saturated by urban interests, this inversion of attention has since proved prescient. The rural populist reshaping of democracies around the world has brought a daily onslaught of new information, actors, dynamics, and innovations from non-urban frontiers into the light. Responding to the need for an agility not typically afforded exhibitions wedded to the long lead times of borrowed works, Therrien relocated to Europe to keep pace with the active reappraisals as the stakes increased and discourse surrounding the inquiry accelerated. Assistant Curator, Architecture and Digital Initiatives, Ashley Mendelsohn remained in New York as the other half of a transatlantic curatorial team that helped steward this shifting, complex, and ambitious exhibition. Our gratitude goes to them both.

RK and AMO likewise worked in close collaboration with many of the museum's talented experts: Associate Director of Exhibition Management, Michael Sarff; Director of Exhibition Design, Jaime Krone; Director of Graphic Design, Jae-eun Chung; Head of Media Arts, Piotr Chizinski; and Publisher, Diana Murphy. They creatively contributed to everything from concept to logistics, from programming artificially intelligent factory robots that roam the ramps to installing a working tomato farm outside. I thank them all and the gifted teams that helped realize this project. As longtime patrons of RK, Sheikha Al-Mayassa bint Hamad bin Khalifa Al-Thani and Qatar Museums have generously supported this effort. We also extend our sincere gratitude to the many institutions and individuals whose support has made this exhibition possible. We acknowledge generous funding provided by Lavazza, American Express, IKEA Foundation, Sies Marjan, Northern Trust, and Hong Kong Design Trust. The Leadership Committee, chaired by Dasha Zhukova, is gratefully acknowledged as well, with special thanks to the Blavatnik Family Foundation, Rachel and Jean-Pierre Lehmann, Naomi Milgrom AO, The Durst Organization, Robert M. Rubin and Stéphane Samuel, and an anonymous donor. Our great thanks also go to Creative Industries Foundation NL, the Dutch Culture USA program of the Consulate General of the Netherlands in New York, and the Netherland-America Foundation. For their support of this catalogue, we salute Elise Jaffe + Jeffrey Brown and the Graham Foundation for Advanced Studies in the Fine Arts. The Carnegie Corporation of New York, and its president, Vartan Gregorian, deserve appreciation for support of the exhibition's extensive programming. I also wish to thank RK, Samir Bantal, David Gianotten, Jeremy Higginbotham, James Westcott, Rita Varjabedian, Sebastian Bernardy, Anne M. Schneider, Aleksandr Zinovev, and their collaborators from around the world. And for her contributions to the design of the exhibition and the book you currently hold, I extend admiration and gratitude to Irma Boom.

Countryside, The Future
is made possible by Qatar Museums.

Global Partner

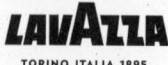

TORINO, ITALIA, 1895

Lead Sponsor

AMERICAN
EXPRESS

Major support provided by

IKEA Foundation
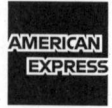

Sies Marjan

Additional support provided by

NORTHERN
TRUST

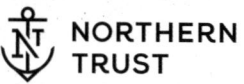

DESIGN TRUST
信言設計大使
AN INITIATIVE OF THE
HONG KONG AMBASSADORS
OF DESIGN

The Leadership Committee, chaired by Dasha Zhukova, is gratefully acknowledged for its support, with special thanks to the Blavatnik Family Foundation, Rachel and Jean-Pierre Lehmann, Naomi Milgrom AO, The Durst Organization, Robert M. Rubin and Stéphane Samuel, and an anonymous donor.

Additional funding is provided by Creative Industries Foundation NL, the Dutch Culture USA program of the Consulate General of the Netherlands in New York, and the Netherland-America Foundation.

Additional support is generously provided by Ministry of Foreign Affairs of the Kingdom of the Netherlands, Planet Labs Inc., Volkswagen, Gieskes Strijbis Fonds, and AMO B.V.

In-kind support for this exhibition is provided by

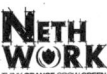 **DEUTZ-FAHR**

World Horti Center, Priva, Koppert Biological Systems, and Koppert Cress.

The exhibition catalogue, *Countryside, A Report,* is supported in part by Elise Jaffe + Jeffrey Brown and the Graham Foundation for Advanced Studies in the Fine Arts.

THANK YOU

Countryside was "literally" a journey along continents and landscapes, communities, systems, cultures, vernaculars, experts, animals, the citizens of the countryside. HARVARD UNIVERSITY's Graduate School of Design's Project on the City, past and current Deans Mohsen Mostafavi and Sarah Whiting, supported a four-year research effort in Rotterdam, involving five generations of students from the Architecture, Urbanism and Landscape departments. To penetrate the Chinese countryside, President Fan Di'an of the CENTRAL ACADEMY OF FINE ARTS invited RK and Stephan Petermann to explore, in detail, the transformation of China's countryside with their students, guided by Vice-President Lv Pinjing and Dean Zhu Pei to share their insights into the complexities of China's commitment to a living hinterland. President Louise Fresco of WAGENINGEN UNIVERSITY enabled us, with researchers Lenora Ditzler and Clemens Driessen, to participate in our first real engagement with plants—even agriculture—opening up a deeply fascinating world that we will certainly continue to explore... Niklas Maak and RK encountered 100 students from the UNIVERSITY OF NAIROBI on the invitation of Musau Kimeu, Chairman of the Architecture Department, and traveled with Etta Madete, Dr. Linda Nkatha Gichuyia, and Adnan Mwakulomba to the Kenyan countryside by the new Chinese train to experience a Kenya (and Africa) that is now at a unique moment of leapfrogging, where internet and mobile phones enable constantly new forms of interaction and technological progress... Keigo Kobayashi of WASEDA UNIVERSITY drove us through Fukushima's "new" countryside in search of evidence of a Japanese commitment to AI, robots, and other forms of automation, testing their ability to eventually take over territories abandoned by human beings altogether, forced by Japan's extreme demographics. In the end, the DESIGN ACADEMY EINDHOVEN offered invaluable support for the transformation of raw material into actual exhibits. Johannes Refisch, Lance Gilman and Rob Roy of Switch, citizens in Camini, informed Qataris, the Dutch agricultural sector, Siberian curators, midwestern experts, Westland thinkers, Rob Baan, Meiny Prins, Tisha Livingston, and Ed Smit generously shared their insights, ready to teach us subjects we were ignorant of.   We were solidly supported in this enterprise by David Gianotten, my partners, Jeremy Higginbotham, and Shaun M. Palmer at OMA. Troy Conrad Therrien, Nancy Spector, and Richard Armstrong were our constant partners at the Guggenheim Museum.   Benedikt Taschen for once again supporting an implausible initiative, Marlene Taschen, Julius Wiedemann, and Meike Niessen for bringing it to fruition.   The writer Niklas Maak for helping create this kaleidoscopic overview with his unique talents as a witness. Samir Bantal for sharing the sheer weight of responsibilities for countryside with stamina and insight, and to all the essay writers in the catalogue. The support and personal involvement of Sheikha Al-Mayassa bint Hamad bin Khalifa Al-Thani, Sigrid Kaag, Dasha Zhukova, Louise Fresco, Irma Boom, Fatma Al Sahlawi, Patricia Atkinson, Kayoko Ota, Rita Varjabedian, and Petra Blaisse have considerably stimulated the realization of this catalogue. RK

AMO

Conception
RK
Samir Bantal

With
Niklas Maak
Janna Bystrykh
Stephan Petermann

Curator
Troy Conrad Therrien

Design & Art Direction
Irma Boom

Book Editor
James Westcott

Assistant Editor
Rita Varjabedian

Book Contributors
Samir Bantal
Janna Bystrykh
Lenora Ditzler
Clemens Driessen
Alexandra Kharitonova
Keigo Kobayashi
RK
Niklas Maak
Etta Madete
Federico Martelli
Ingo Niermann
Linda Nkhata Gichuyia
Kayoko Ota
Stephan Petermann
Anne M. Schneider
Troy Conrad Therrien

Exhibition Design
Sebastian Bernardy
Yotam Ben-Hur
Lucas de Ruiter
Anne M. Schneider
Marvin Unger
Rita Varjabedian
Aleksandr Zinovev

Graphic Design Assistants
Severin Bunse
Emma Gregoline
Julia Neller
Countryside font:
IBO: So-Hyun Bae

Proofreader
Thea Miklowski

Special Thanks
Jenny Acker
Omar Al Ansari
Patricia Atkinson
Fahad Al Attiya
Esra Aydin
Valentin Bansac
Rebecca Bego
Petra Blaisse
Joana Cidade
Michiel Eijlders
Gizem Erbas
Fabrizio Esposito
David Gianotten
Petra Hans
Jeremy Higginbotham
Sigrid Kaag
Juha Kosonen
Alan Lo
Victor Lo
Benita von Maltzhan
Sander Manse
Rafael Mason
Paul van Meeuwen
Shaun M. Palmer
Erietta Panteli
PPS Imaging B.V
Nuria Ribas Costa
Isabella Rossen
Fatma Al Sahlawi
Ed Smit
Denys Tkachenko
Dongmei Yao
Marisa Yiu

AV
Eelko Ferwerda
Hans Wessels

HARVARD GRADUATE SCHOOL OF DESIGN

Dean
Mohsen Mostafavi (until 2019)
Sarah Whiting (2019–)

Studio
RK

Seminars
Sebastien Marot
Niklas Maak
Veronique Patteeuw
Irenee Scalbert
Carolyn Steel
Lea-Catherine Szacka

AMO Instructors
Janna Bystrykh
Stephan Petermann

Students Spring 2016
Stephanie Conlan
Matthew Gindlesperger
Bradley Kraushaar
Christian Lavista
Shiyao Liu
Yuyangguang Mou
Davis Owen
Qun Pan
Sophia Panova
Jiayu Qiu
Xiohan Wu
David Zielnicki

Students Spring 2017
Astrid Cam Aguinaga
Ximena De Villafranca
Yan Ma
Yumiko Matsubara
Liana Nourafshan
Wenyi Pan
David Pilz
Demir Purisic
Stefan Sauter
Anne M. Schneider
Jianing Tao
Eric Zuckerman

Students Fall 2017
Peiying Ban
Hannah Cusick
Aranzazu De Arino Bello
Gideon Finck
Woo-Young Kim
Lindsey Krug
Nicholas Lynch
Remus Macovei
Hayden Minick
Yina Moore
Noelle Tay
Yiting Xi

Students Spring 2018
Andrew Bako
Yotam ben Hur
Meredith Chavez
Chen He
Han Jin
Charlotte Leib
Minzi Long
Khorshid Naderi-Azad
Maoran Sun
Justin Tan

AMO Instructors
Sebastian Bernardy
Yotam Ben-Hur
Anne M. Schneider
Rita Varjabedian
Aleksandr Zinovev

Students Fall 2018
Charles Burke
Seo Won Choi
Tsz Hung Hu
Zhixin Lin
David Ling
Mark Pantano
Andres Quinche
Jingyuan Huang
Luisa Respondek

CENTRAL ACADEMY OF FINE ARTS, BEIJING

President
Fan Di'an

Vice president
Lv Pinjing

Dean
Zhu Pei

Studio
RK
Stephan Petermann

Contributors
Prof. Peter Ho
Jiang Jun
Li Shao Jun

Prof. Karl Otto Ellefsen
Vivian Song
Prof. Wen Tiejun
Shi Yang

Students 2017–18
Zhang Cunji
Erdene
Qin Hong
Lv Sixun
Song Ying
Guo Yixin
Song Yu
Cao Yue

Students 2018–19
Qin Jiachen
Zhang Lin
Zhu Ruohan
Zhang Shilin
Zhang Xinrui
Mi Yifei
Xu Yile
Yin He Ziqian
Ziyi

Students 2019–20
Li Dijin
Zhang Huoying
Na Mila
Qi Qianyan
Zhang Ziqi
Zhuo Zishun
Tong Zixiao

Construction Program, 2018
Sun Ce
Liu Dongling
Lv Jian
Wang Keliang
Zou Lisha
Teng Minghao
Zhang Tingting
Li Wengteng
Tian Ye
Peng Yinghui
Zhu Yingli
Wang Yongshuang
Ou Yucong

WAGENINGEN UNIVERSITY

President
Louise Fresco

Project Leaders
Clemens Driessen
Lenora Ditzler

Contributors
Mark Aarts
Dirk van Apeldoorn
Janna Bystrykh
Gerlinde de Deyn
Wim van Egmond
Jochem Evers
Sofia Koutsenko
Rogier Schulte

Students Summer 2018
Jorrit Becking
Zwanet Herbert
Ton Kaarsgaren
Stefan Verweij
Emily van Wakeren
Bernice Wesselink
Moritz-Ivo Will

Design Interns
Lukasz Bakowski
Dirco Kok
Nahid Aghaie Tabrizi

Special Thanks
Ernst van den Ende
Eldert van Henten
Corne Kempenaar
Lammert Kooistra
Janne Kool
Machiel Lamers
Joop van Loon
Bert Lotz
Ard Nieuwenhuizen
Stephan Mantel
Meghann Ormond
Marielos Pena Claros
Stijn Schreven
Esha Shah
Jonas Steinfeld

UNIVERSITY OF NAIROBI

Chairman, Architecture Department
Musau Kimeu

Instructors
Asya Essajee
Etta Madete
Adnan Mwakulomba
Geoffrey Mosoti
Nyakiongora
Dr. Linda Nkhata Gichuyia
Brek Yassir

Students
Catherine Kerubo Angwenyi
Wambui Gitau
Isaac Hiuhu
Kipleting Brian Kemboi
Sonam Kerai
Mark Kiarie
Faith Kimeli
Kiplelgo Symon Kipkemei
Saitabau Kiunga Kumary
Faith Chelangat Kurgat
Mark Masita
Kelvin Francis Mmbando
Kimberly Molo
Viva Mugambi
Malcolm Mwathi
Benson Mwaura
David Kibera Nduta
Margaret Ng"ang"a
Edward Ngugi
Iminza Audrey Onamu
Clinton Makhuka Opati
Joy Ouma
Charlene Wabwille
Julie Waweru

WASEDA UNIVERSITY, DEPARTMENT OF ARCHITECTURE

Instructor K2LAB
Keigo Kobayashi

Students
Alexandre Chanson
Wataru Nakanishi
Asato Nishida
Kentaro Nomura

DESIGN ACADEMY EINDHOVEN

AMO Interns
Paul Gruenenwald
Nele Hartmann
Lucas de Ruiter
Marvin Unger
Jasper Zehetgruber

GUGGENHEIM

Advancement
Leah E. Heister
Mary Anne Talotta
Brooke Affleck
Brady Allen
Corinne Godsall
Pamela Eisenberg Taite
Andrea Petrini
Lori Camilleri
Judy Cuker
Kelly Kramps
Chris Messer
Alyxandrea Ouellette
Shayna Goodman

Art Services and Preparations
Paul Bridge
Derek Deluco

Curatorial
Nancy Spector
Troy Conrad Therrien
Ashley Mendelsohn

Director's Office
Richard Armstrong
Lindsey Cash
Lydia O'Connor

Education
Sharon Vatsky
Jennifer Yee
Rachel Ropeik
Emily Rivlin-Nadler
Alan Seise
Laili Amighi

Exhibition Design
Jaime Krone
Lucie Rebeyrol

Exhibition Management
Clare Bell
Michael Sarff

Exhibition Services
Mark Argue
Mary Ann Hoag
Piotr Chizinski
Jocelyn Chase

Fabrication
Christopher George
Peter Brayshaw
Peter Mallo
Ross Caudill
Steven Ott
Marcel Walker

Facilities
Peter Read
Michael Zall
Richard Avery

Finance
Elizabeth Duggal
Marcy Withington
Lesley Lana
Anna Shadbera

Global Communications
Sarah Eaton
Stephen Grant
Cassandra Dagostino

Graphic Design
Jae-eun Chung
Janice I-Chiao Lee
Michael Enten

Information Technology
Josh Meehan

Interactive
Laura Kleger
Caitlin Dover
Maria Slusarev
Miriam Weiner
Clara Boesch
Stephan Kneusel

Legal
Sarah G. Austrian
Dana Wallach Jones
Marianna Horton Mermin
Elena Kyriakides

Marketing and Social Media
Holly Campbell
Lauren Van Natten
Alex Barber
Essie Lash
Alexa Revans
Elizabeth Cosgrove

Photography
David Heald
Allison Chipak
Susan Wamsley
Vida Lercari

Publishing
Diana Murphy
Melissa Secondino
Elizabeth Zechella
Ryan Newbanks
Virginia Gresham

Registrar
Christina Graham
MaryLouise Napier

Security
Emily Schluter
Kevin McGinley
Jonita Luti
Mathew Mantsch

Theater
Brenda Gray
Julia Hahn

Visitor Experience
Trevor Tyrrell
Emily Johnson
Brian Wilson
Nicole Fernandez
Kai-Ti Kao

Along for the Ride: Curator's Introduction
Troy Conrad Therrien

In the past five years, I've test-driven the back seats of many BMWs. Prioritizing performance and design—for those up front, at least—Rem Koolhaas has been partial to the brand since the late 1990s. It's how he shuttles between his home in Amsterdam and his office in Rotterdam. His path cuts past the Westland, a drive-by vista of horticultural sprawl: unassuming, largely uniform, single-story glass boxes that are as impressive as they are easy to miss. RK first pulled off the road to investigate them sometime in the last decade. The Pied Piper of metropolitanism—founding partner of OMA, the Office for Metropolitan Architecture, author of *Delirious New York: A Retroactive Manifesto for Manhattan,* instigator of the Harvard Project on the City—since being deracinated to Indonesia as a child, he has largely lived in a constellation of cultural density. As a student, he toured the Iron Curtain while his classmates sunbathed in Roman grandeur. At the height of the postmodern diaspora, as the Bronx was ablaze and New York City teetered on bankruptcy, he migrated here as other architects fled. London, Berlin, New York, Tokyo, Singapore, Lagos... always cities, always hopping over the oceans of water and landscape and infrastructure and flora, fauna, and humans that connected them. Cities were the locus of modernization, the no-nonsense frontier where academic notions surrendered to cold hard fact, where reality ran roughshod over good intentions. In Manhattan, he found an archetypal metropolis that carved the landscape up into a Cartesian carpet of illuminated steel-alloy machines running north-south, east-west, and vertically from the dirt to the sun-catching canopy in an endless scan for the next best idea, a decentralized dance of survival of the fittest form. In the Westland, the same, but moving plants instead of people: Countryside of the Captive Globe. Under the magenta glow of an optimized artificial sun, gantries sort parceled crops through a tightly calibrated obstacle course for the precision cultivation of cress: an infrastructural jungle with the complexity of a metropolis dedicated entirely to harvesting a single perfect species of garnish. Because humans are excised from the environment, pesticides are rendered superfluous. Robots make GMOs unnecessary—artificial organics: a Cartesian triumph. A fully controlled atmosphere means anything can be grown: Amazonian sprouts that taste like almonds, Patagonian shoots that sting like battery acid. Farther down the way at the world's foremost agricultural research institute, Wageningen University & Research (WUR), a miniaturized version plays out on a flatbed as a robotized laser scans the leaves of infant plants in search of nature's best algorithm for photosynthesis. WUR-Westland forms a tight feedback loop, a lab-to-farm-to-table agro-scientific-industrial-complex that has helped the tiny Dutch nation hold court as the world's second-largest food exporter.

Delirium had come to the countryside of RK's commute. Under the gossamer thin veil of frosted glass, it had crept up to the side of his road and could no longer be unseen. And as the sublime images of these alien landscapes have since gone viral—pink light already a tired trope of eco-conscious exhibitions around the world—RK and his think tank, AMO, led by Samir Bantal, and an army of conscripted intellectuals, scientists, experts, and students have been feverishly trying to sort out what's beyond the aesthetics. The Guggenheim exhibition, *Countryside, The Future*, distilled and extrapolated in this book, presents the preliminary results: demonstrative but still questioning, a freeze-frame of an obsession that continues to pick up steam.

A manifesto more pithy than a haiku, its title alone is a dense compression engine of meaning. Comma, not colon: *The Future* is not a subtitle, it's not subservient; it's a player, a dance partner for *Countryside*. Together, they form a twosome: not beginning and end but two sides rotating in constant tension, two magnets that instinctively repel but become electric when brought near. Eschewing nostalgia for the unknown and upcoming is the dynamo that propels this project. RK is not retreating to the wilderness in his twilight; he, AMO, and their collaborators are pressing on to yet another frontier.

Countryside, The Future is not an art show but it's also not a science exhibit. Nor an architecture exhibition. It's a collection of stories told through case studies, global zooms into an assortment of episodes, scientific and cultural, historical and futuristic, that could seem random to a casual visitor. Intuition often drives, but nothing is accidental. This is the first pass at connecting a thread through the countryside, even if the rationale is not always declared.

The approach is transhistorical, intercultural. Facts supersede etiquette. Academic taboos don't apply. Theirs is not a mission to placate, it's a quest to know, to unpack the inner workings of entirely alien territory. RK is an urbanite urbanist, a lifelong provocateur world-famous for dressing down the myopia of his home discipline in its attempts to make sense of modernization through the very object over which it claims providence. This mission is related but different, a new operation in a new theater of war against the not-sufficiently known. Theory is verboten. It may be forthcoming or, possibly, forever in abeyance: infinite foreplay, the relentless courting of a previously "ignored realm." Ignored by whom? RK, for one. But the rest of us as well. To say so is not a crime of hubris, but a declaration of method. A journalist before going to architecture school, RK told me when we began working together that his mentor had taught him to "approach every situation like a Martian, completely foreign and amazed, and write it all down deadpan." The countryside has long—always?—been chock-full of experts, overflowing with opinions, flooded by interpretations. But Martian strategy is necessarily unimpressed. Even the duly-picked-over can be a rich harvest. Calling it ignored is not ignorant, it's strategic. It's an opening.

COUNTRYSIDING

And now is the time to pry. Trump, Brexit, and the wildfire of other global populist movements stoked by demagogues pander precisely to those ignored by the very forces of capital that enslave them in its supply chain, galvanizing a motley coalition that favors nationalism over neoliberalism, insiders over outsiders. The spotlight is a grow light: the ignored are nurtured into pawns. The Countryside Bloc is shifting the way the world is organized, but recognition is not representation. Nor is a shift a revolution. Populism is the ritualistic swamp-draining through mass-media misinformation so a new group of speculators can make an unreported killing under the cover of red-pilled zealots pitted against blue-pilled zombies.

In a mind war, the countryside is the flatland of the imagination. It's the mass grave of those cognitively poisoned by junk—food, media, space; the disenfranchised many coerced into pointing fingers and guns at each other instead of at the perpetrators. *Countrysiding*, funneling populations into the countryside of the mind, is the fundamental doctrine of tyranny. Countrysiding manufactures small-mindedness, bigotry, tribalism, parochialism, nostalgia, ideological inbreeding, and all the other smears urbanites use to slander the rural as if they don't apply equally well to city-dwellers. Countrysiding is as racist as it is classist, but it doesn't discriminate whom it afflicts: rednecks and blue bloods; reds and the red, white, and blue. It's what the deep state does to the deep mind. A red pill is a glimpse of the mechanics, but it isn't a vaccine and it can be a poison. Countrysiding is the officially sanctioned dirty war that wants to turn us all into Flat Earthers. Countrysiding systemically flattens consciousness. It collapses the capacity to parse complexity, to respond to volatile, uncertain, ambiguous social scenarios with measured responses. It makes docile subjects, willing cannon fodder easily triggered into enlisting in culture wars, cold wars, world wars. Its tactics are numerous, from ideological gerrymandering to precision gaslighting at scale, but to ascribe its effects entirely to conspiracy is too generous to its architects. Countrysiding is as much a product of design as it is a by-product of the digitization of discourse to a binary spectrum of black and white, us and them, in-group and out, "city" and "countryside"—divisions exacerbated by reinforcement algorithms and machine-learned biases. Looking with alien eyes at the ignored realm is a step toward identifying and undoing the invisible infrastructure of countrysiding.

POLITICALLY CORRECTED

Hitler, Stalin, Mao: master countrysiders. But for AMO, their darkness wasn't just deep; they left a playbook for resurfacing the countryside. Bloodshed and genocide was their wheelhouse, but their politics was also capable of landscaping. AMO calls it "political redesign." The EU did it by consolidating farmland; Charles Fourier fantasized about it with sexy communes. Most megalomaniacal is Atlantropa, a plan to partly drain the Mediterranean and suture together the continents it splits. Now, as climate change threatens an unimaginably bleak future for unimaginable generations, the shining cities on democratic hills so adept at neutering their populations on the sly feign futility and impotence against the horrors of ecocide.

In the midst of a cancel culture that threatens a blitzkrieg of online outrage for even modest transgressions of politically correct tripwires, AMO has the guts to put its politics, literally, on the wall. "I want to wean the West off of its hubris," RK tells me over lunch in Shanghai. From a discipline to a hemisphere: countryside is a scaling-up. Bigger bigness. The only contemporary example of political redesign comes from Qatar. Under blockade, Qatar had to spin up a farm industry overnight. Now it exports milk. *Food, Security* could have been an alternate title to much of this exhibition. While AMO sounds the alarm on permafrost thaw—something like twice the amount of carbon currently wreaking havoc on our climate is precariously sequestered in the once-perennially frozen earth of Siberia and its northern neighbors—its prodding for innovation in WUR-Westland is its brand of climate activism. Food security is not a question of celebrity pleas but, possibly, engineering science.

AMO has taken up pixel farming with the same enthusiasm RK showed for Manhattan's grid, doubling down on the same Cartesian fetish of the vast data farms extolled in his paean to "post-human architecture" in this volume: an ever-telescoping matrix of compatible crops and culturally woke "eco-feminist" bots to harvest them. OMA's unbuilt plan for Paris's Parc de la Villette, a horizontal skyscraper of layered vegetation strips—too provocative for its time—has finally met its telos: a fully Cartesian food forest, a vegetal matrix with pixels the size of plants. From WUR we learn that much of the Amazon may have been planted. Borrowing indigenous strategies of cultivation, a fully automated armada of robotic insects trained on their knowledge may be on the precipice of completing the takeover. Perhaps this is the XXL that was always looming: architecture at the scale of satellite imagery, an automated agriculture of congestion, the detailing left to drones.

In place of a defining essay, a question mark. RK's text, "?," is a glimpse of the Martian's notepad: a litany of all the ways the countryside has been ignored. Yet another assault on unearned hubris: still paranoid but more critical. Thanks to American convention, the intended simplicity of a single punctuation mark will often be molested by a comma. Question mark and comma, an arranged marriage. The comma is along for the ride but it doesn't hesitate to agitate. It takes the back seat but claims to have a map. It's humble but refuses to be ignored. It's another source of animating tension. The comma is the curator: a persistent unsettler picked up along the way.

The ultimate trajectory of RK and AMO's foray out of cities is not an exhibition. The Guggenheim is just a stop, but one long in the making. It's the conspicuously missing block in the City of the Captive Globe, the blackballed, white-walled masterpiece of the countryside architect who perfected his organic architecture in the city just before he passed. The fusion of an inverted ziggurat and an earlier design for a canceled drive-through planetarium—a modern star temple looking for a patron—Frank Lloyd Wright's Guggenheim was commissioned by the museum's founding director and first curator, Hilla Rebay, to be a "temple of spirit" for "non-objective art." As if foretold, its most successful exhibition to date was the recent display of the work of Hilma af Klint, a Swedish mystic who channeled the inspiration for her work. The first abstractionist, she painted altarpieces for just such a temple. Over a century later, they were exhibited in the architecture they forecast, the white spiral for time-traveling artists to close loops in time over a twisted line in space: *Guggenheim, The Future*.

Up at the top of Wright's iconic circular form, the metallic inlays throughout the terrazzo floor that reveal the overriding geometry of the building cede to a Cartesian grid. Since the museum opened, this space had been used for back-of-house support functions; its walls were later recessed, opening up another sequence of display surfaces. Here, in 1978, as part of the Guggenheim's first architecture exhibition, *The Sparking Metropolis*, OMA's City of the Captive Globe was first hung. Four decades later, that space hosts WUR's lab equipment. RK's top-shelf Cartesian interests have migrated to a new "technology of the fantastic": from an image of the urban unconscious to archetypal agriculture.

The exhibition poster featured OMA's fictional floating pool, an allegory of time dilating Russian Constructivist architects swimming backward to propel the vessel slowly forward across the Atlantic. By the time they arrived, 40 years later, their American counterparts had turned against modernism, "ignoring the spectacular decline of their profession, their own increasingly pathetic irrelevance, their desperate production of flaccid country mansions." Still, they gathered to present the Russians with a medal: "It said, 'THERE IS NO EASY WAY FROM THE EARTH TO THE STARS.'" This time, the Europeans have gone country. Instead of reflections in their pool, their stars have become satellites.

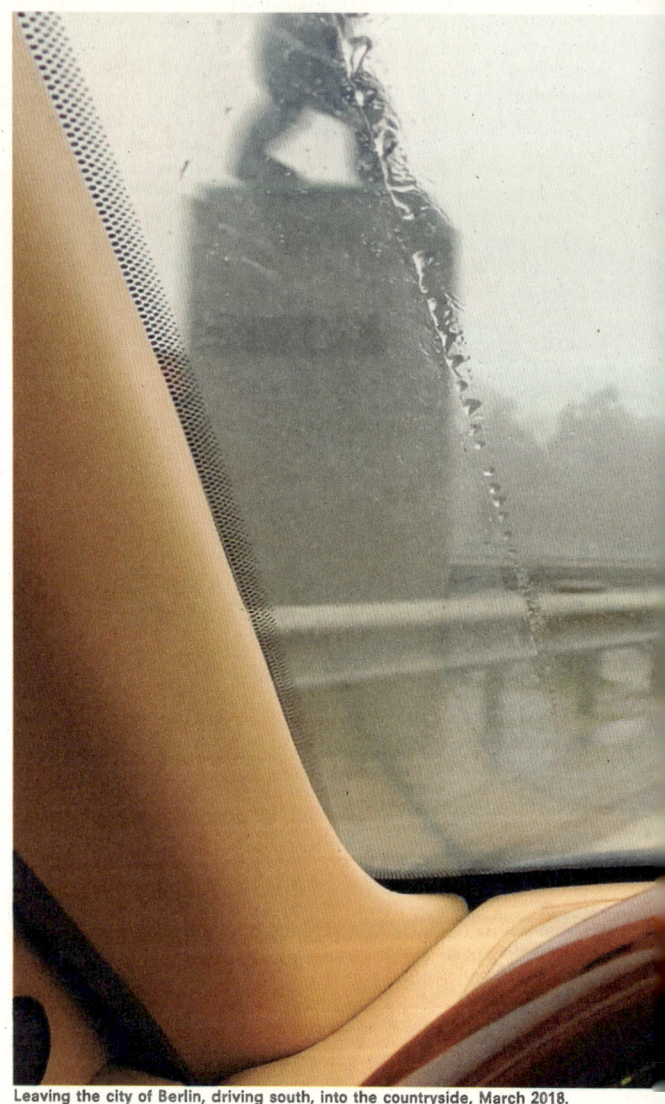

Leaving the city of Berlin, driving south, into the countryside, March 2018.

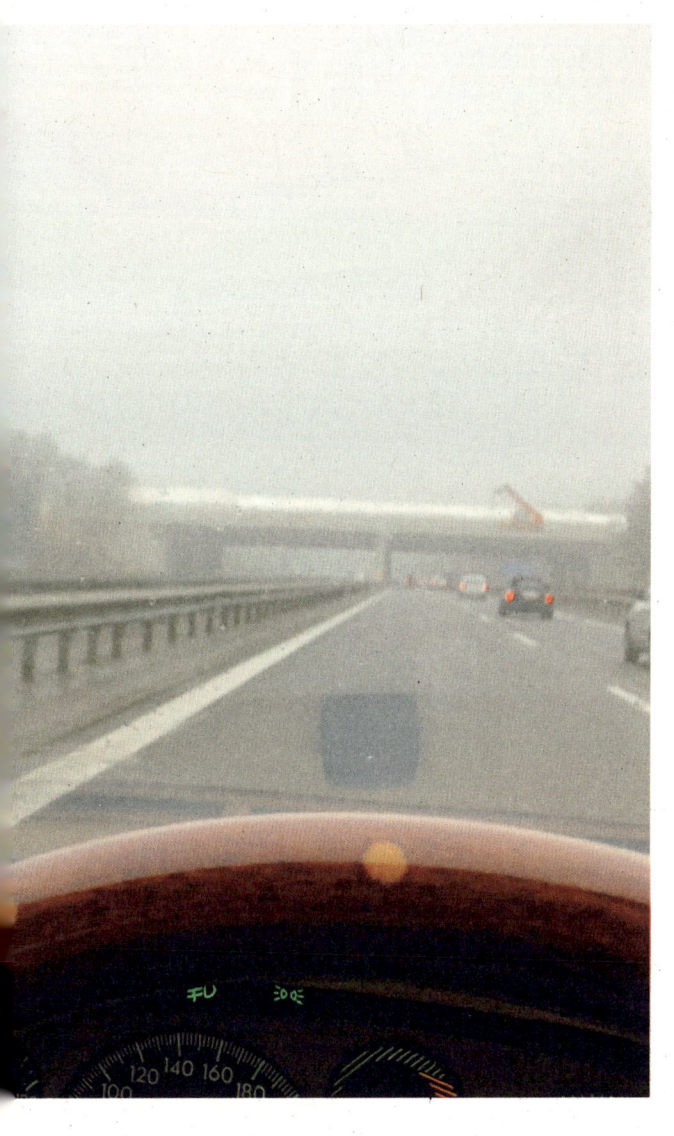

Eurodrive: Repopulation Utopia
Niklas Maak

It was the autumn of *Wir schaffen das* ("We'll make it")—late 2015, when millions of refugees were on their way to Europe. They walked. They came by train. There was a moment of euphoria when Germans, determined to help, gathered at Munich's train station, equipped with soft toys, homemade apple juice, and bavarian pretzels, to welcome the new arrivals. There was a strong moment of confidence, sparked by Angela Merkel's statement *Wir schaffen das*, a kind of cover version of Barack Obama's 2008 mantra "Yes we can." The welcoming scenes looked like a reenactment: they resembled those of the 1989 fall of the Berlin Wall, when the Ossis—Easterners—who crossed the former inner-German border, were welcomed with schnapps and loads of bananas, which made the westerners look like a benign exotic tribe visited by expectant, slightly confused anthropologists. Even though many Germans wanted to host a refugee at least for some days at their home, space quickly became scarce. Shipping containers were sold out, sports halls occupied. Then, someone came up with the idea to accommodate the refugees in some of the empty houses of dying villages in the countryside—and there were many. The emptiest of them was Manheim, a half-hour drive west of Cologne.

I. MANHEIM, GERMANY

When I came to the village of Manheim for the first time in early 2016, the doors were boarded up, streets empty, shops deserted, blinds lowered; moss grew on window frames. The village looked as if it died a long time ago. I parked my car in front of a shut-down pizzeria. In a garden, the sails of a white miniature windmill squeaked in the wind, a poster on a bus stop said "Welcome Home," but there was nobody home. For half an hour, I did not see a single human being. Manheim is more than 1,100 years old: Its first appearance in historical records came in the year 898 AD in a land grant from King Zwentibold. The village is made up of farms and a neo-Gothic church, as well as sooty, reddish-brown houses.

From the 1950s onwards, the farming village became a commuter town. Bungalows were built; the new residents worked in the nearby open-pit mines, or at the Ford factory in Cologne. Not so long ago, more than 1,700 people lived here. But all the while, the mining pit was growing larger and coming closer. Manheim abutted the biggest lignite mine in Central Europe, with a projected mining area of 21,000 acres. The hole in the ground continued to expand, dragging large parts of the Hambach forest with it, approaching the former A4 motorway, which was closed and dismantled. Without its asphalt, it looked like a surreal band of sand, a shore without the sea; under the road, the beach. It was clear that Manheim too would be swallowed by the expanding mine. Resettlement efforts started in 2012. Many took energy company RWE's compensation, and built a new house in New Manheim, five miles east. A few Manheimers hoped the opencast mine would not expand as planned. But when Angela Merkel proclaimed the end of nuclear power in Germany after the Fukushima disaster, they knew coal would be needed and their village would collapse. Old Manheim became a ghost town. But then things changed: As a consequence of another large-scale decision by Angela Merkel, hundreds of refugees arrived in the dying village. Someone appeared in front of one of the houses. His name was Hussein Balo. He was holding a toy tractor that someone had given to his children. He was 53 years old, born in northern Iraq, owner of a chicken farm near Mosul. When ISIS arrived, he said, 37 people from his family were shot. Balo escaped, at the last moment, with his children and grandchildren, to Turkey, then across the Mediterranean. They all survived. Balo pulled out his iPhone and showed me a film, a group of people huddled in a dinghy: blue water, gently smiling people busy with their mobile phones. It looked like a vacation video, except this film showed their flight across the sea: little children lying in the middle of the boat, spray blowing overboard; there's no hint that this is a life and death situation. That same year, thousands of people drowned trying to make the Mediterranean crossing.

Another film on his phone, shaky pictures, a farm in the dust, a man singing, laughing, racing against a goat. Shortly after, ISIS killed him, Balo said. The story of their escape is told by the pictures on his phone: They fled in three cars. Balo shows a photo of a silver Hyundai with bullet holes and bloodstains on the door. ISIS shot at them, but they were lucky, Balo said, no one died. They fled to Sinjar, where the conditions in the refugee camp were catastrophic; one of his nieces died there. The Balos—father, his two wives, seven sons, five sisters, their husbands and children—drove on to Kirkuk and to Turkey, bought a boat, a six-meter Zodiac, and crossed the sea. They were lucky: there was no storm, the boat had no leaks.

They came to Germany in November 2015, and were assigned a house in Manheim in January 2016. Another film shows his children building their first snowman, with a scarf, and a carrot as a nose: Welcome to the cold, safe world. Two hundred and sixty refugees were accommodated in Manheim's deserted homes. The situation was odd: The Germans exiled from Manheim had moved to new buildings that were as white and naked as a pre-fab container village, while the refugees moved into ancient German farmhouses and small family bungalows from the 1960s that made the village look like an idyllic, optimistic, heterogeneous, utopian Germany. A Syrian family with six children in a bungalow, 30 people from Eritrea in a farm-house... Later at night, I went to the pit. Giant excavators stood in the sand, like grazing dinosaurs. They moved forward in an endless, continuous movement, almost too slow to be perceived. They ate up the land, swallowing forest and eventually village to meet Germany's demand for energy. Behind me, a group of refugees showed up. They sat silently at the border of the pit, contemplating the vast sandy panorama. One told me it reminded them a little bit of the desert in their homeland. I walked back to the intersection of Germania- and Esperantostrasse; street names like a manifesto. The village of Manheim is also a museum of a vanishing life-form, a built document of the prosperous federal republic's postwar welfare state. Even tiny villages offered a stable infrastructure for what the German sociologist Helmut Schelsky coined, in 1953, the "leveled middle-class society." "Our village life was attractive for young families," said Wolfgang Esser, a former soldier, village resident and soccer trainer, who took care of the refugees' children. "Cheap rents, a kindergarten, an elementary school, an indoor pool, two grass pitches, easy highway access. That's a hell of an infrastructure for such a small place." The old village's bungalows show an astonishing love for detail and perfectionism. Their architecture mirrors the wealth and care of the West German postwar welfare state, while the buildings in New Manheim, the new resettlement village, sketch a portrait of the effects of a shareholder value-driven market economy. Façade materials and details could not be cheaper, the naked village shows that everything has been done to reduce building costs and make the houses more profitable for the building industry. No bar, no bakery, no shops. A commuter suburb rather than a village.   Still today, over 80 percent of Germany's area is used for agricultural and forestry purposes. According to the latest Farm Structure Survey, around 940,000 people (including seasonal workers) produce food and commodities worth more than €50 billion every year on some 275,000 farms. About 47 million people live in the German countryside, more than half the country's population. The countryside gets a good €2.4 billion a year in EU funding for rural regions. But depopulation is a big issue, as people can't find work in the countryside.   For a brief moment, Manheim looked like a new rural utopia: Suddenly half the population was younger than 30, children were playing in the village square again. A house with four units became an experimental commune – a "whole house," as it was called in premodern days. While cities had no space to accommodate refugees, the village became a permeable ecosystem, like a reef, a porous, inclusive, open, undefined space with niches and nooks, a deep surface that allows new forms of life to embed themselves in it or dock onto it. What if the Iraqis reopened the old bakery? What if Syrian doctors reopened the old medical practice? Could this kind of village, reconnected by rapid transit systems, even attract dissatisfied urbanites, and show that life in the country does not have to mean loneliness and abandonment; that the village is not just a trap for the unemployed and the elderly, but, especially in the light of technological change and the revolution in work, an alternative to living in overpriced, overregulated cities?   In a way, I thought, the transformation of dead, empty Manheim into a bustling refugee village could serve as a case model for other dying villages. I could not foresee that only two years later, the village of Manheim and the adjacent forest would be one of the epicenters of a global youth moment.

When I came back in 2019, the situation had changed. Soon after the refugees arrived, more and more protesters had started camping out in the forested area in a bid to prevent the forest from being cleared by the energy company RWE. William Blake once reduced the basic problem of human perception and coexistence thus: "The tree which moves some to tears of joy is in the eyes

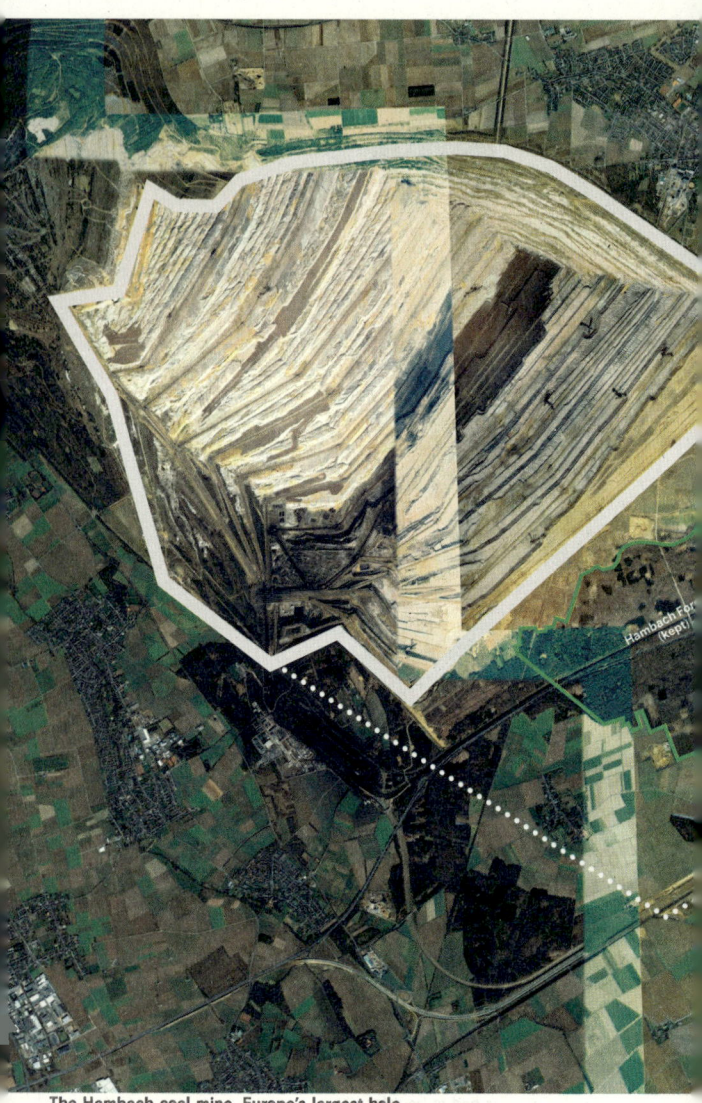

The Hambach coal mine, Europe's largest hole.

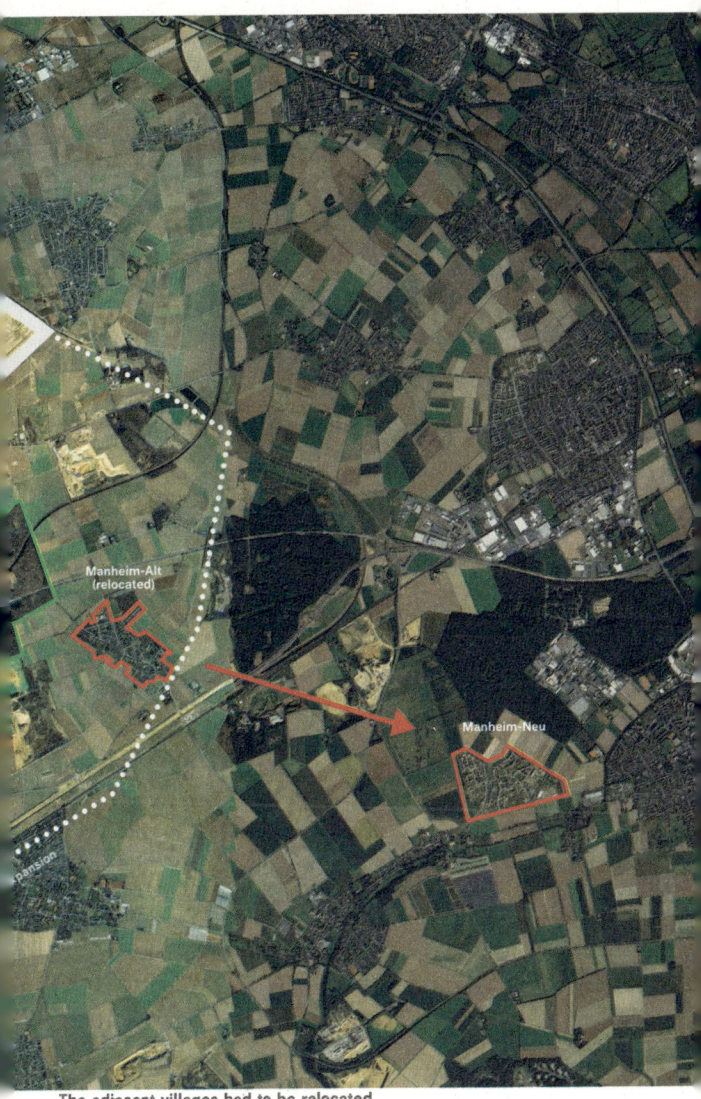

The adjacent villages had to be relocated.

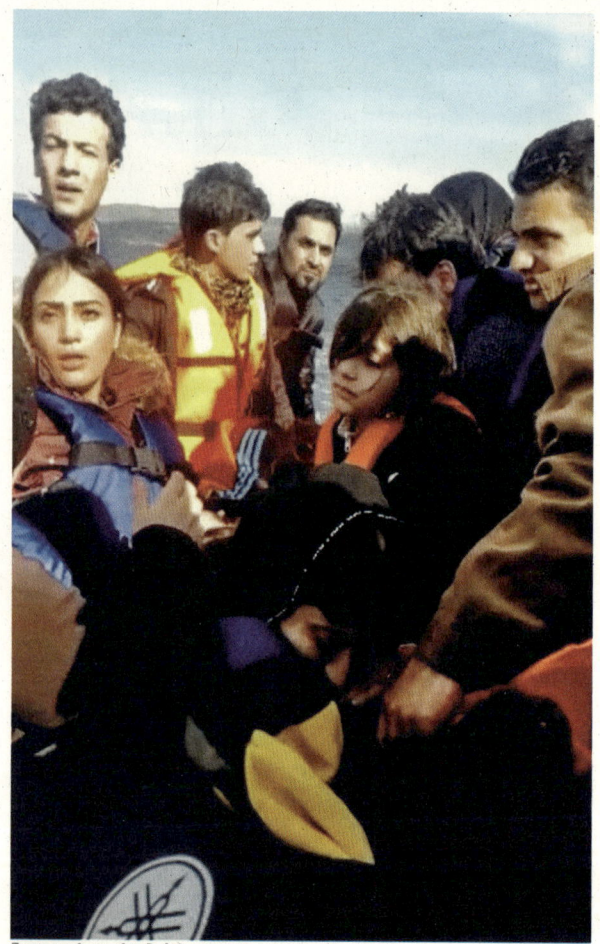
Footage from the Balo's escape, crossing the Mediterranean on a Dinghy.

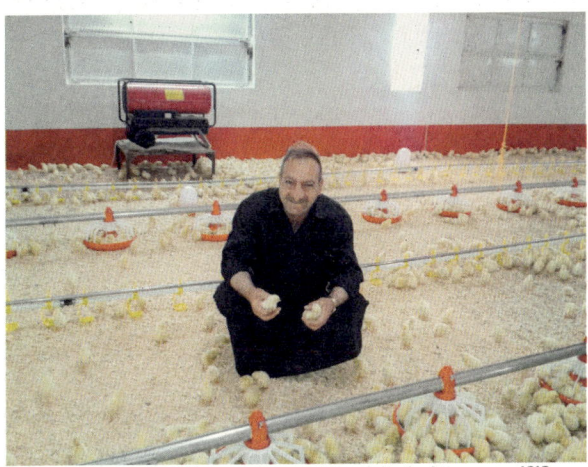
Hussein Balo owned a chicken farm near Mossul. He had to escape ISIS.

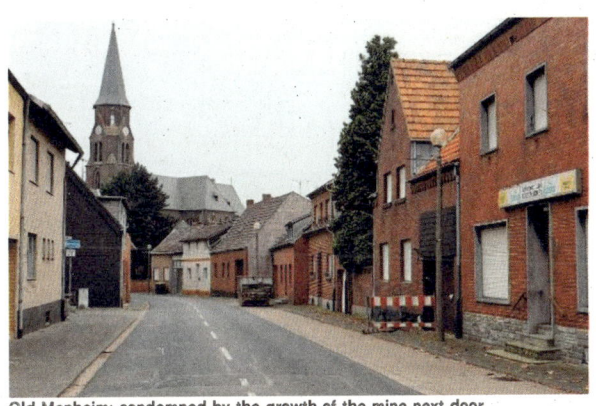
Old Manheim: condemned by the growth of the mine next door, the local population leaves the village.
(Norbert Ganser, "Cat Invasion in the Ghost Village," *Bild*.)

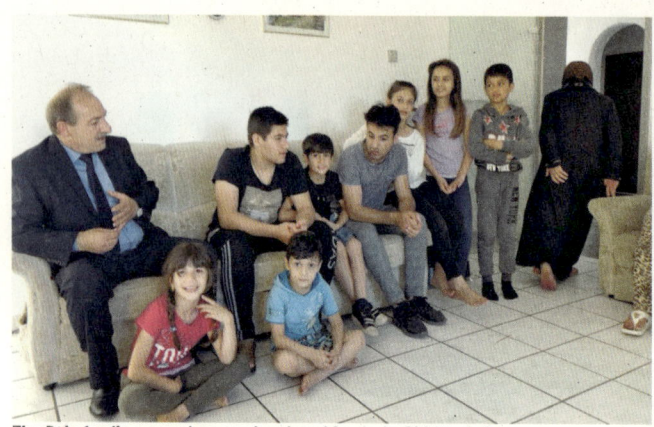

The Balo family moves into an abandoned house in Old Manheim...

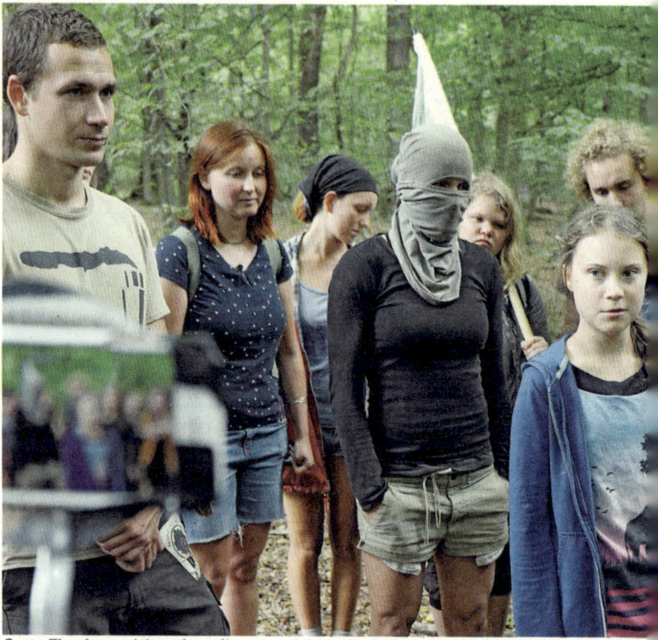

Greta Thunberg visits other climate activists who built treehouses in the Hambach Fore

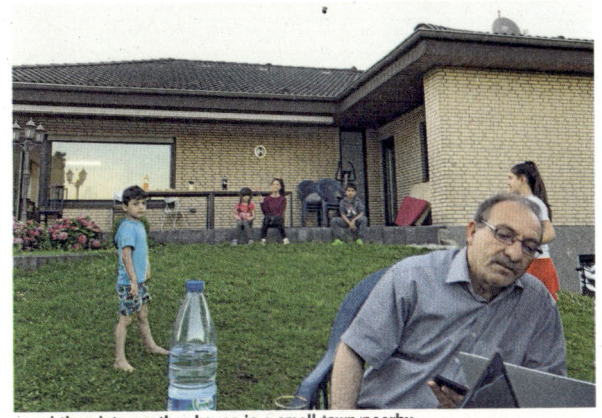

...and then into another house in a small town nearby.

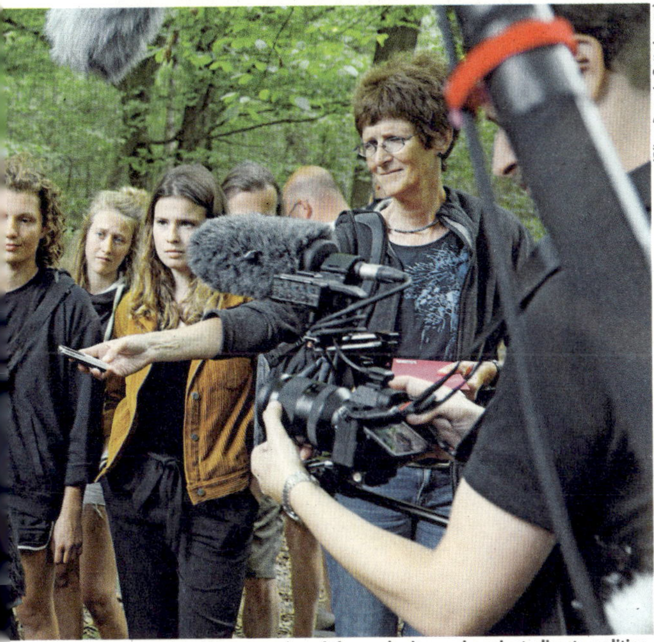

...to protest against the expansion of the coal mine and against climate politics.

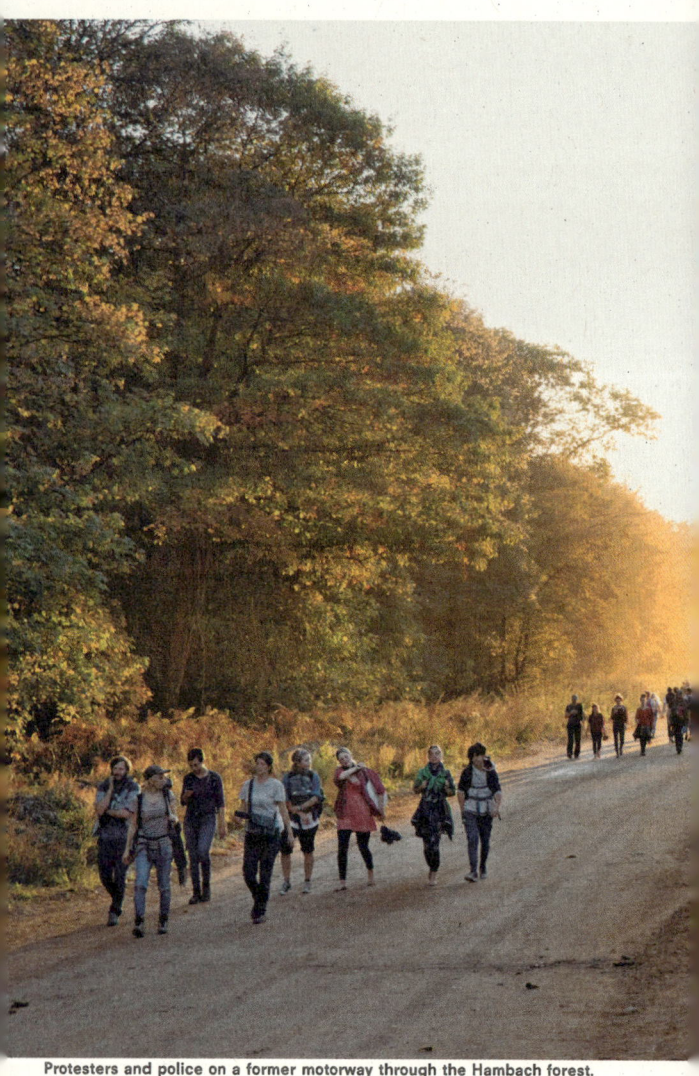
Protesters and police on a former motorway through the Hambach forest.
(Miriam Juschkat)

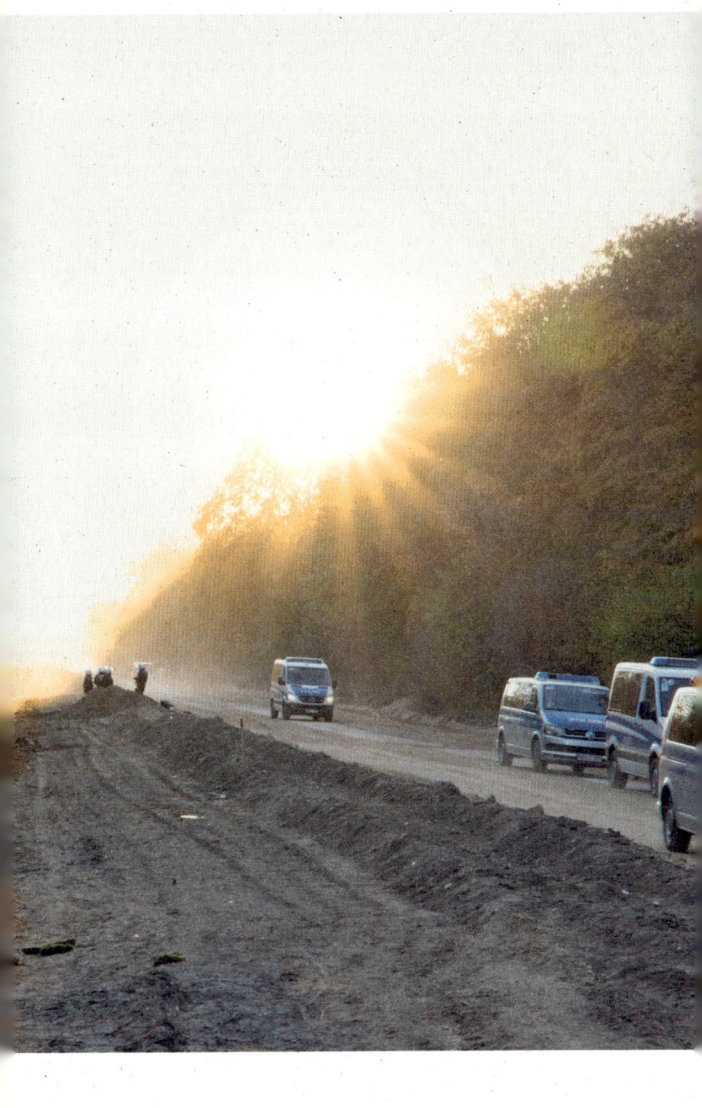

of others only a green thing that stands in the way." The same goes for the Hambach Forest: The activists called it *Hambi*, while RWE spoke, more technically, of a *Forst*. The word *Forst* sounds like something that can be taken down with chainsaws if necessary, while Hambi sounds like a defenseless animal with wide-open eyes, a creature that you should not hurt. An international environmentalist movement of previously unseen scale occupied the woods that served as a crumple zone in front of the moribund village of Manheim. Even Greta Thunberg visited the squatters in their tree homes. Someone sprayed an awkward, oddly hesitant slogan "Fuck the system, at least a little bit"—on the garden wall of a deserted 1970s house. In the forest, tree houses and road barricades were erected. RWE hired private security firms to patrol the forest and the village. Riot police tried to remove the environmental activists from their tree houses. People were arrested and jailed. Several days later, the deforestation stopped. The Higher Administrative Court had issued an injunction: Hambach Forest, with its common oak, hornbeam and lily of the valley populations, but most of all with its strictly protected Bechstein's bats, is a habitat of type 9160 of annex I of the European Habitats Directive.

The pit and the forest became the symbols of a fundamental dispute over the general direction of the country. Herbert Diess, CEO of Volkswagen, publicly declared that there is no point in building electric cars if the electricity comes from coal. RWE's managers were outraged: such statements by other companies were "highly unusual," they complained. If the Hambach Forest is not cleared, the economic damage will run to €5 billion, and put at least 5,000 jobs at risk, threatened RWE, which also owns the forest.

I went to the camp near the village. Hundreds of activists from all over Europe had built an encampment of temporary huts and tents, trailers and caravans, with an almost urban array of supply stores and shops. When I entered the protest camp, I saw an "awareness tent" and a "relaxation area" where you could do yoga and get massages. It looked like a mix of a luxurious safari camp and classic protest culture. Bakunin would have rubbed his eyes: Before you occupy the pit, first a little bit of reflexology.

From afar I could hear a shattering sound. The bulldozers had started razing houses in Manheim. Simultaneously, there was another sound: hammering. A group of activists was building new tree houses in the forest.

The sun sank over the pit. The hammering stopped. The

forest, or what was left of it, stood dark against the evening sky. Suddenly, I heard the sound of two fairy voices. Two young women sat on the ground and painted a protest poster with little flowers; a young man the same age sat with them. The song the women sang was called "Sommervise." It was a strange moment: Three people sitting close together in the German countryside for completely different reasons. Mustafa Balo, age 19, from Iraq, who wants to become a farmer in Germany; and two Danes, Freja and Kirsten, also 19, who wanted to travel south later, and spend the winter on the pleasant shores of the Aegean Sea that Mustafa's family had just crossed in the other direction. The German village, once the epitome of a stable local population, had become a space of unlikely amalgamations, a transitory zone where benign middle-class Danish girls, Iraqi farmers, underpaid Polish security guards hired by German electricity companies, depressed German car factory workers, anarchists, anti-terror brigades, environmentalists, yoga teachers, and gay Iranian piano players intersect. Only a few refugees remain in Manheim now. Among them is Saheb, 23 years old, from Najaf. His family had a garage there; he can fix cars, a skill he learned from his father. He would love to work, but his access to the labor market is highly regulated. The Balos now live near Kerpen. Rana, Hussein's daughter, hopes her husband, who is still in Iraq, will be allowed to join the family, although the family reunification policy has been suspended for political reasons. Rana's daughter Yasha says she wants to become a doctor. Manika says she wants to become a police officer, Mohamed a firefighter.

Manheim could still become a model for reviving rural areas. But to see how the village of the future, and the future of the countryside could look, you have to go to Italy. A few days later I drove to Catania, to see the villages of Riace and Camini, which had just been revived with the help of hundreds of refugees.

II. RIACE AND CAMINI, ITALY

I left in the early morning. Berlin's Luisenstrasse and Invalidenpark went by outside my side windows. At first sight, the city still looked OK. My radio (actually, it was Spotify's random song thing) played Petula Clark's 1964 song "Downtown," where a dissatisfied suburbanite is encouraged to "listen to the music of the traffic in the city, linger on the sidewalk where the neon signs are pretty."

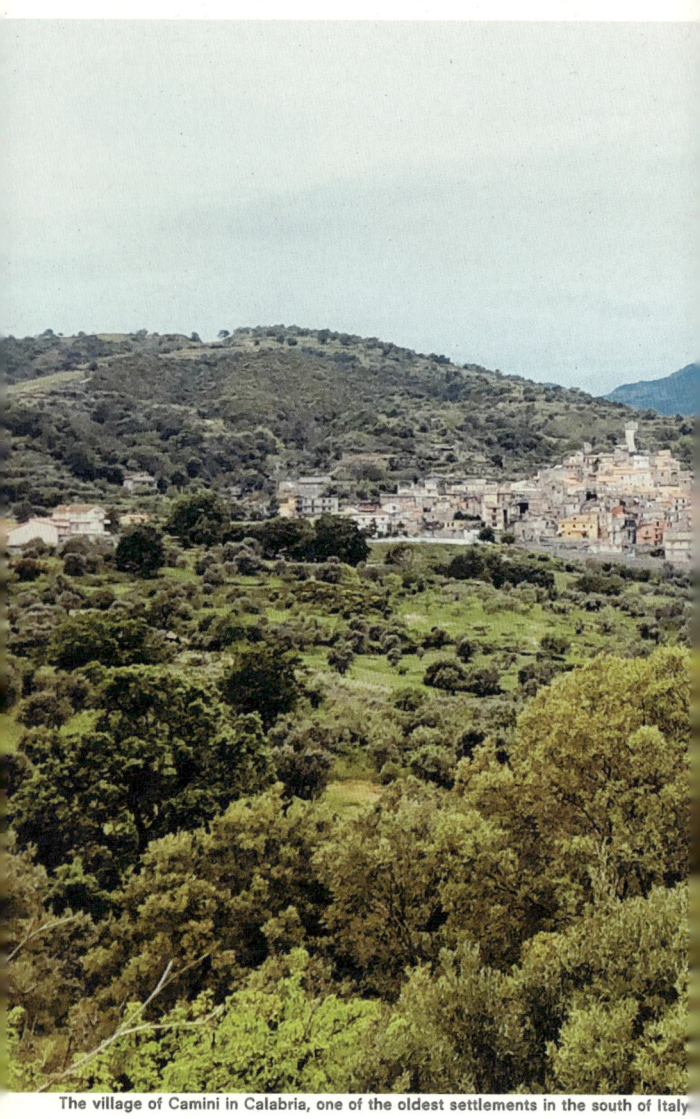
The village of Camini in Calabria, one of the oldest settlements in the south of Italy

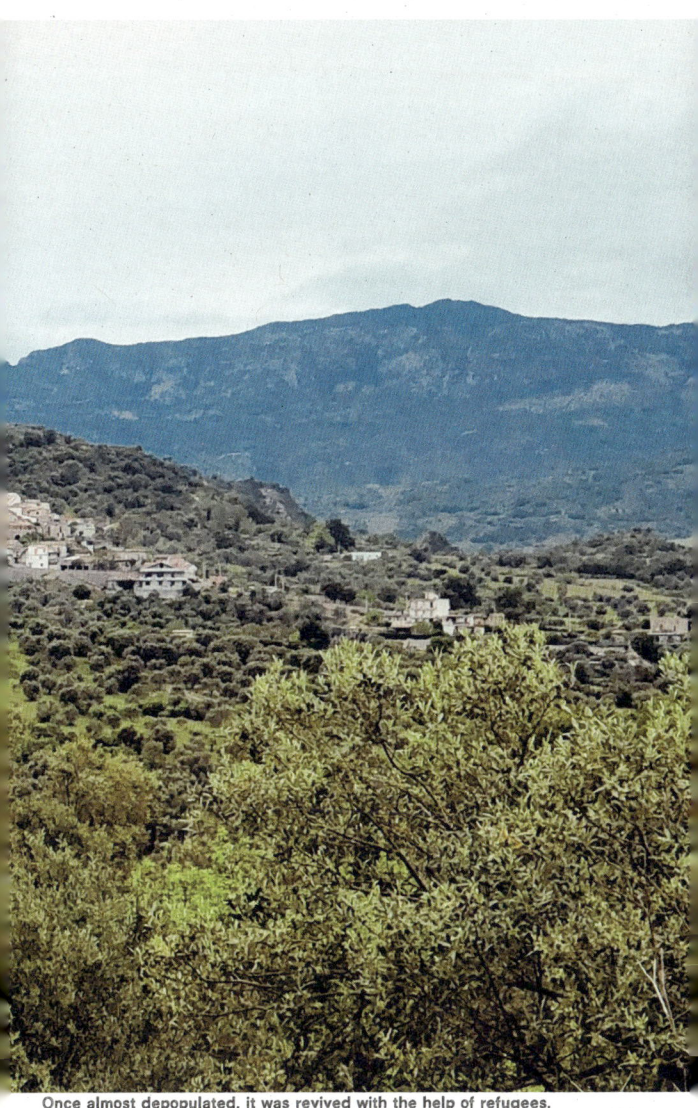
Once almost depopulated, it was revived with the help of refugees.

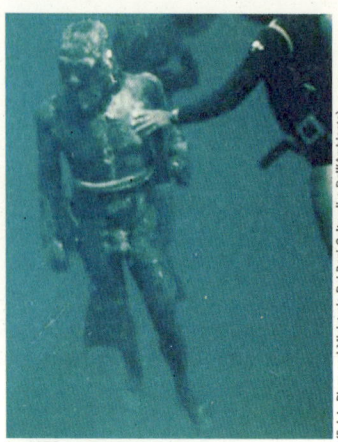
In 1972, two antique statues of warriors were found in the sea near Riace.

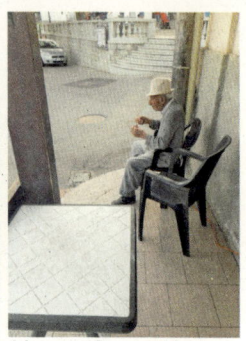
A longtime Riace resident.

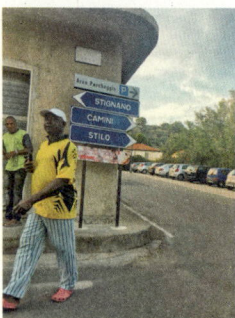
A street corner in Riace, 2018.

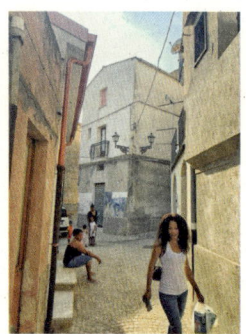
New populations for old Riace.

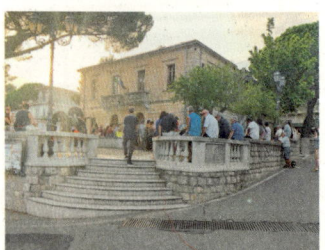
The village coming to life again.

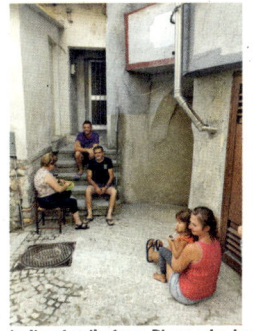

Italian family from Riace who had migrated to Germany: the father worked in construction, the son teaches engineering in Karlsruhe; they returned to help the refugees.

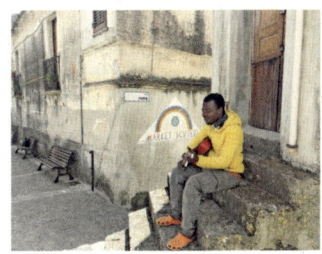

A Nigerian songwriter.

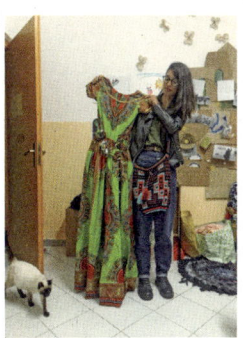

London artist showing Nigerian fashion in Camini.

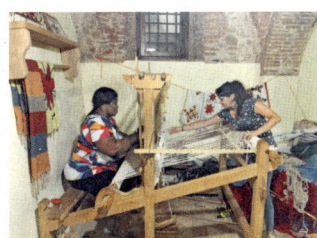

A refugee and a local working on a loom in Riace, Italy.

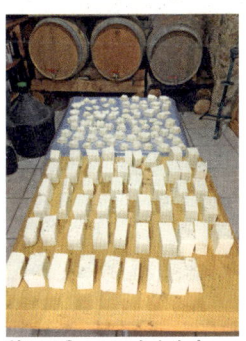

Aleppo Soap, made in Italy.

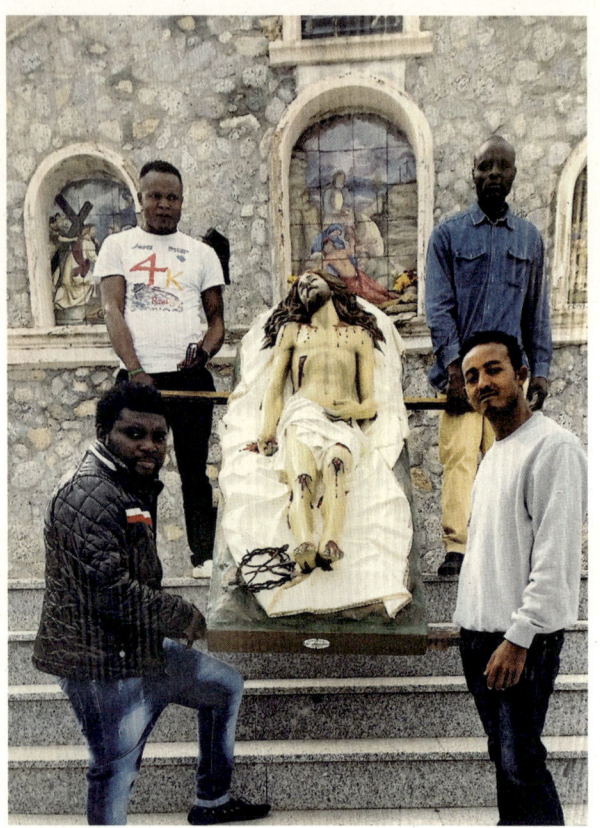
Refugees helping out in a Catholic ceremony in Camini.

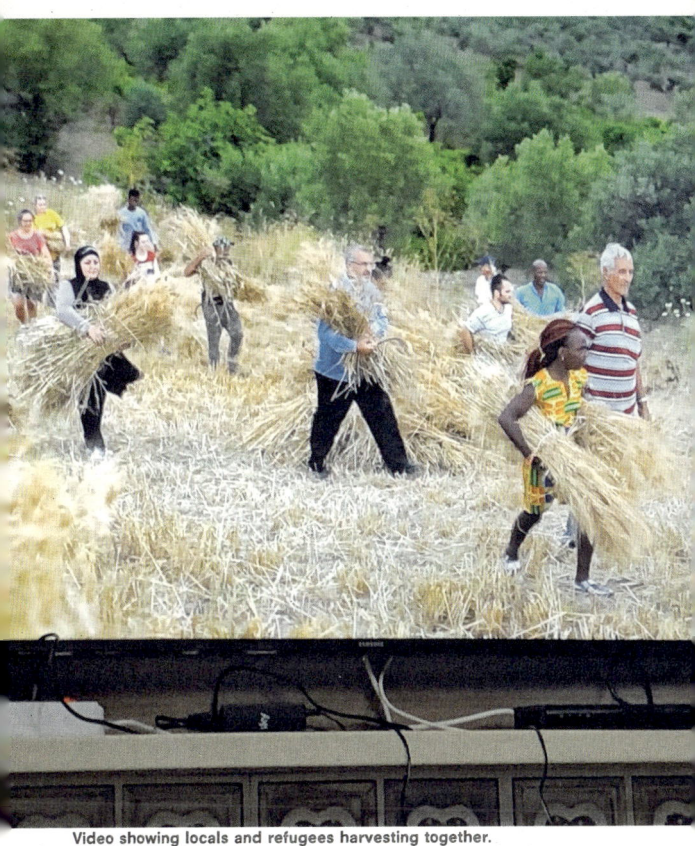
Video showing locals and refugees harvesting together.

Outside, there was no neon and none of that music, and thanks to electric vehicles, the "music of the traffic" will soon be reduced to the modest whoosh of tires on pavement, the "bright lights" dimmed by an ecologically responsible AI... I drove by a dead mall behind a shiny art-deco-ish IM Pei façade, apartment blocks with ambitious Anglophone names ("The Upper East"), a defunct e-scooter.

Could it be that the contemporary big city center appeals mostly to wealthy retirees and tourists? Could it be that we're the last generation to see the big city as a promise? But if cities are increasingly becoming overpriced, overly controlled, security-obsessed, data-extracting, tourist-friendly Potemkin villages alluding only to the bygone, faded glory of the chaotic, lively, dangerous metropolis, then could the countryside become a space of freedom, experimentation, and self-responsibility?

There was a discussion on the radio: Reint Gropp, the president of the Leibniz-Institut für Wirtschaftsforschung Halle (Institute for Economic Research), demanded that the government give up on rural areas, which have received €42 billion in subsidies since 1991. Gropp called for a 180-degree change of policy: Subsidies should go to productive companies in cities, and be used for digital infrastructure for young service providers in metropolitan areas, instead of spending it on life-sustaining measures for old rural industries. "We neglected the cities," Gropp claimed. What would that mean? Would bus lines be shut down, factories closed, old people forced to settle in the vicinity of still operational cities, as villages decayed and became biotopes for rare species—would eastern Saxony become a kind of northern Serengeti, a post-human safari paradise with wolves instead of lions, where humans would only enter now and then as respectful observers of a new wilderness? I traversed Germany, drove over the Brenner Pass down to Florence, Rome, and Naples. The countryside consisted of hills, fields, wind farms, and long, generic white boxes: delivery centers, storages, home improvement stores, factories, sometimes the silhouette of an old village which on closer inspection turned out to be an outlet center.

I stopped over at Naples, then drove to Calabria. The motorway was empty. It was a warm day, with a light breeze from the Mediterranean. I stopped at a gas station. The car in front of me was a chunky beige SUV that looked like a mixture of a depressed cat and an obese toaster staring with twisted headlights at a palm tree; its name was Renegade. Since when did people want to drive around on a warm Italian autumn day in an armored thing rather than in a convertible—and was it the same moment when cities started to be expensive, overly controlled, and unappealing too? The car looked as if it could vomit at any moment. After two hours, I reached the Ionian Sea. A small mountain village appeared in front of my windshield. This was Riace, one of the oldest villages in southern Italy, and maybe a model for the future of the countryside. The place had been inhabited since antiquity. For over two millennia, the villagers lived here in the foothills of the Apennines, from agriculture, olive-growing, and viticulture. But after the Second World War, in Riace and the nearby village of Camini, many young people left in search of employment, migrating to the wealthier north of the country or to Germany. Of over 1,000 inhabitants, there were less than 250 left. The houses fell apart. The shops and the schools closed. Then something unexpected happened. In 1998, a boat with Kurdish refugees got stranded on the shores of Riace Marina. Domenico Lucano, a young professor and later mayor of Riace, applied for money to renovate the derelict buildings and accommodate the refugees and to offer them job training. All of a sudden, there was life again in the narrow alleys. The success of Riace served as inspiration for many other villages. In Camini, Rosario Zurzulo—the returned son of Calabrians who, in the 1980s, had migrated north to find employment—and his wife Giusy Carnà founded a cooperative, called Jungi Mundi, financed with the aid of the Italian Ministry of the Interior. They created employment opportunities for refugees, but also for Italians. Some of the original villagers, themselves migrant laborers, returned from the north. The village rose up again.

Over 150 refugees, from Syria, Sudan, Eritrea, Ivory Coast, Iraq, Bangladesh, and Afghanistan, among other countries, helped rebuild the old houses. Rosario had made a deal with the owners —their houses would be renovated and in exchange let to the refugees, and later rented out. Local shops reopened. The school went from eight children up to 50. The bar reopened and became a popular meeting point for locals and new arrivals. Syrian women started to produce Aleppo soap and cooked jam, while Eritrean potters merged their knowledge with Calabrian ceramicists, creating new forms of pottery. I spent two weeks in the Calabrian villages. Ruins had been rebuilt with incredible craftsmanship. Children played in the church square. In the reopened kindergarten, Arabic and African name tags hung next to Italian ones. A Nigerian guitarist sat under an arch and rehearsed a love song he had written for someone far away. In the mayor's office hung an image of four refugees carrying a statue of Christ out of the local church to the beach, a ritual that had not been practiced in decades, as none of the elderly residents was able to carry it all the way down to the coast. I met an artist who used to live in London but was fed up with city life. She was in her late 20s and did not want to reveal her name, because she wanted to start a new life after what she called an emotional deception. I met a Nigerian fashion designer who was almost forced into prostitution before she made it to Camini, where she created the most beautiful dresses. I met an old local guy in a geriatric green Fiat Panda who sold oranges on the market square. He said with pride that he was a fascist and saluted. But even he seemed to like the mayor who brought the refugees to Riace and resurrected the village. The Calabrian experiment gave the lie to gloomy predictions that an existing society can only accommodate a certain number of migrants. At its peak, about 800 migrants, refugees, and asylum seekers from 20 countries populated Riace, whose population had been down to 600. Criminality was still lower than in most parts of Italy. Ten years after the process of rebirth started, the villages of Riace and Camini are, at the same time, something completely new—African-Arabian villages in the hills of southern Italy—and a rebirth of the all-Italian village, as it still haunts the memories of the Italians and the dreams of the tourists, with the smell of fresh pastries in the alleys and children playing in the village square. For many inhabitants, the village is not a thing of the past; it became a space of rediscovery of societal practices long submerged by the market economy and its demands, and in particular, a space of experimentation with alternative life models and possible future scenarios for dissatisfied urbanites who could work from there, and only occasionally go "to town."

III. TARNAC, FRANCE

From Calabria, I drove to France. I wanted to see the famous anarchist's commune of Tarnac, a small village in the heart of France's Limousin. In Tarnac, I wanted to meet Benjamin Rosoux and Guillaume Maigron, members of France's most-talked-about intentional commune. Some months ago, they had given a talk about their village at the architecture faculty of Marne-la-Vallée. Tarnac became world famous in November 2008 when helicopters circled over the village in the early morning hours, and special forces captured 20 men and women. The accusation was terrorism, at least according to President Sarkozy and criminologist Alain Bauer, who had stumbled upon a radical leftist, anarchist tract on the internet drafted by an anonymous collective, entitled *L'insurrection qui vient* (*The Coming Insurrection*). The book argued that French society is caught between consumerism, divisive selfishness, and a fundamental lack of perspective. The only hope, the authors argued, was to broaden the uprising that had already happened in the *banlieues*. The last chapter of the treatise is a kind of revolutionary guidebook, as well as a call to steal food from supermarkets and paralyze high-speed trains, servers, and the entire infrastructure of modern capitalism. When unknown people really did sabotage high-speed train lines in Limousin, authorities initiated a months-long investigation into suspicious activity, focusing on students from Paris, Bordeaux, and other cities who had settled into the old village to work, discuss, and live out a mixture of Black Mountain College, Monte Verità, and a kibbutz. But no evidence was found that the arrested people were linked to the book, or to the sabotage. Still, after Fox News presented *The Coming Insurrection* as a call to violence, a terrorist pamphlet and an attack on Western societies, the book became an international best seller among *altermonialistes*, and the village attracted hundreds of curious visitors who felt attracted by the mysteries of the supposed anarchist commune. The "Tarnac Nine" had reopened the local store and the local bar and made a living from sheep herds and a sawmill they owned in the forest. That was all I knew when I went there. I had been told that once in the village, I would be picked up by someone and be taken somewhere. I arrived at dusk. The village was quiet; the ancient stone houses crowded together like taciturn creatures. Some men showed up in a 1970s Peugeot, followed by an old German police truck with a Berlin license plate. I was told to drive onto the Route Départementale 109 eastward, and to wait at a crossing. I did. The sun sank. An old Ford stopped, the driver, dressed in a black and gold sweater, cranked down the window and asked me the way to a discotheque. Dissatisfied by my ignorance, he raced away, tires smoking.

After a quarter of an hour, a generic new

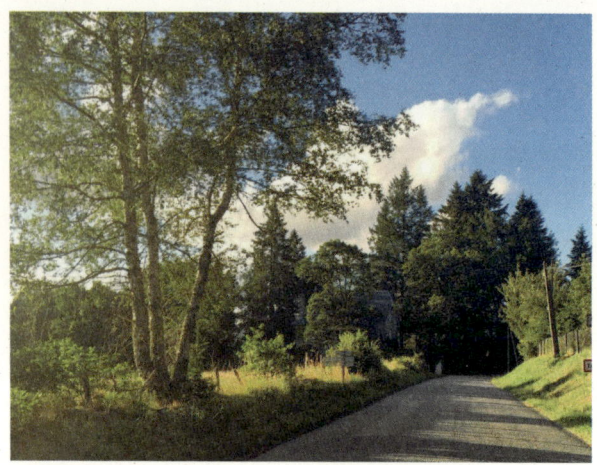
Arriving in the village of Tarnac, France, where an anarchist's commune experiments with alternative living models.

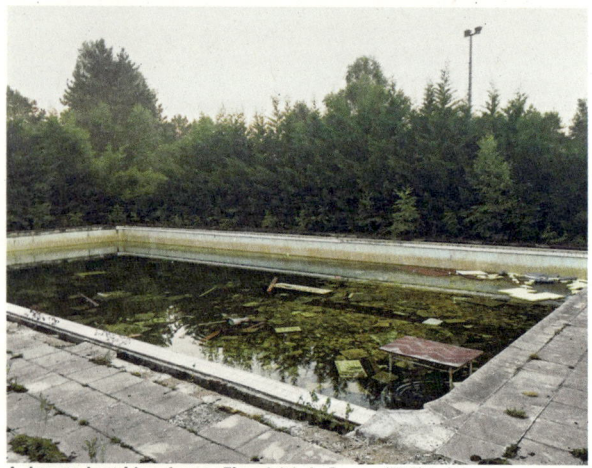
A deserted pool in a former Electricité de France (EDF) holiday village, now one of the commune's bases.

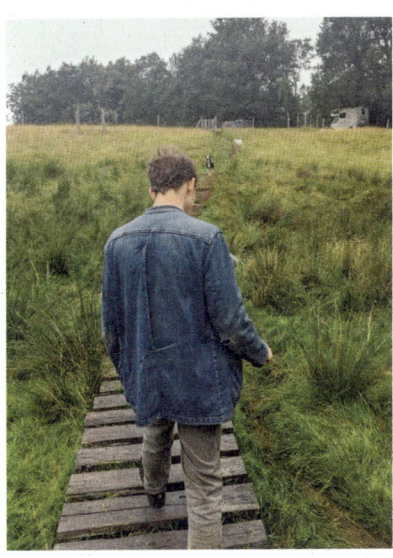

Local architect and shepherd, now commune member.

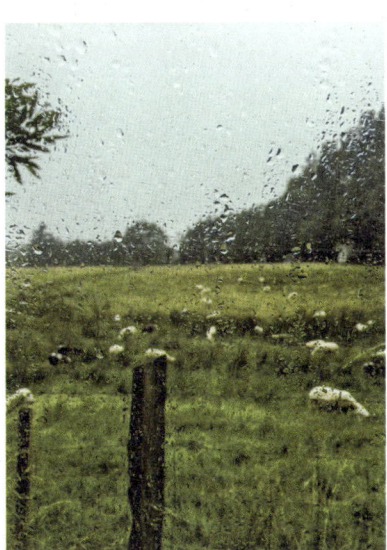

View from one of the communard's houses.

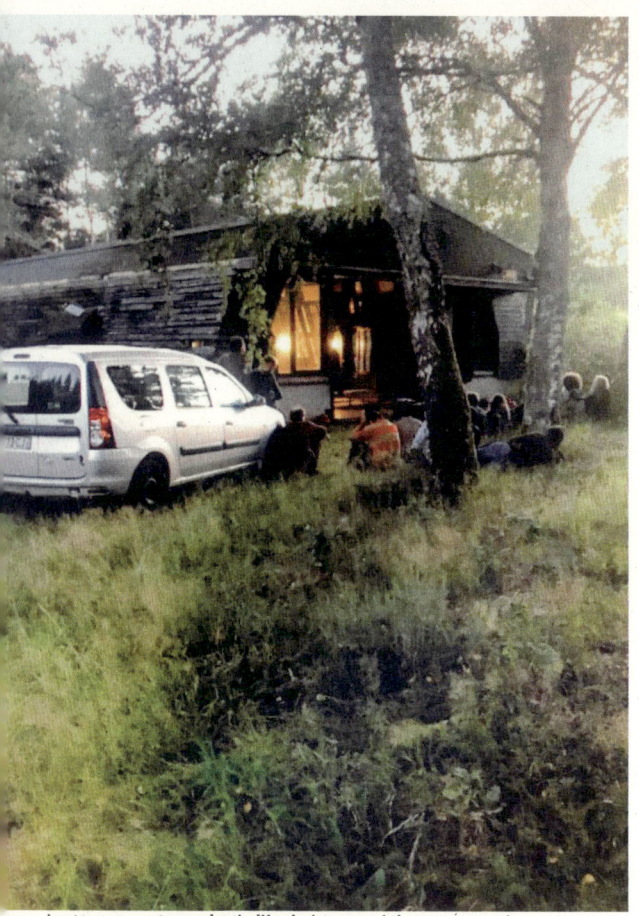
Lecture on postapocalyptic life during one of the commmune's gatherings in the vicinity of Tarnac.

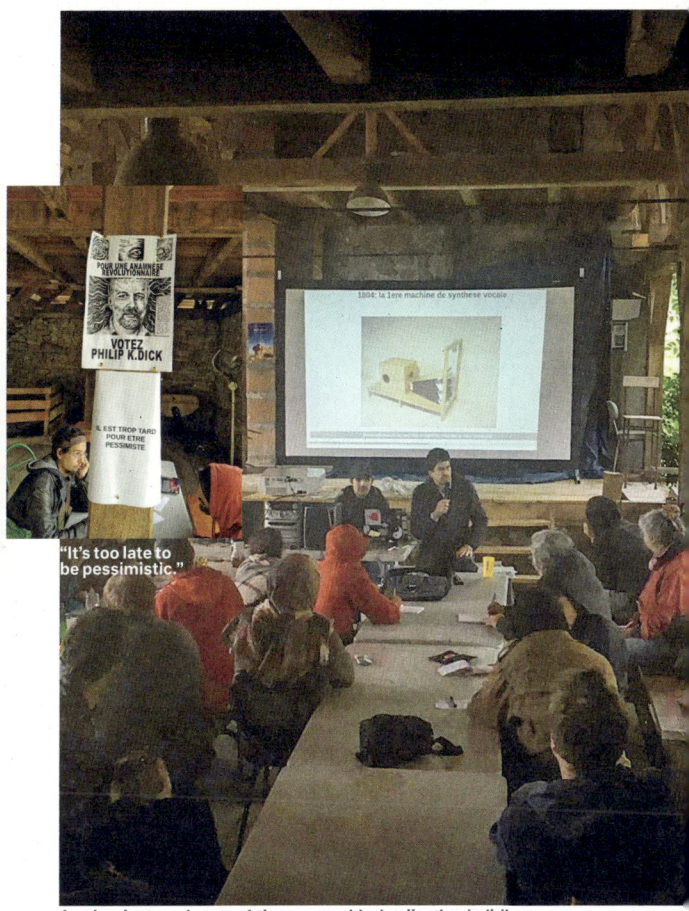

Another lecture, in one of the communities' collective buildings.

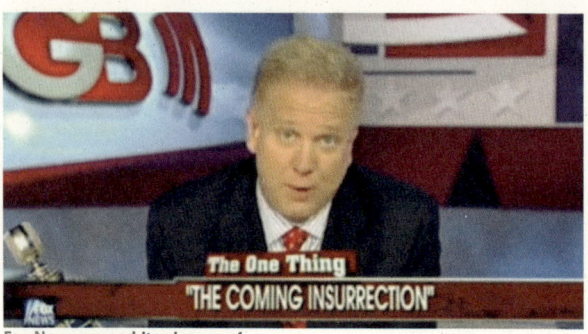

Fox News warned its viewers of "The coming insurrection."

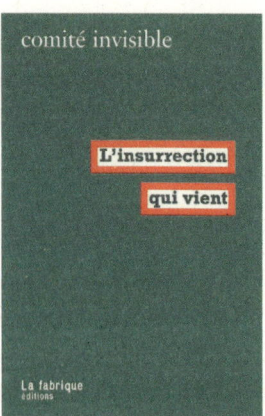

The Coming Insurrection, an anarchist treatise and guide to a revolution. Members of the Tarnac commune were suspected to be the anonymous authors but continue to deny it.

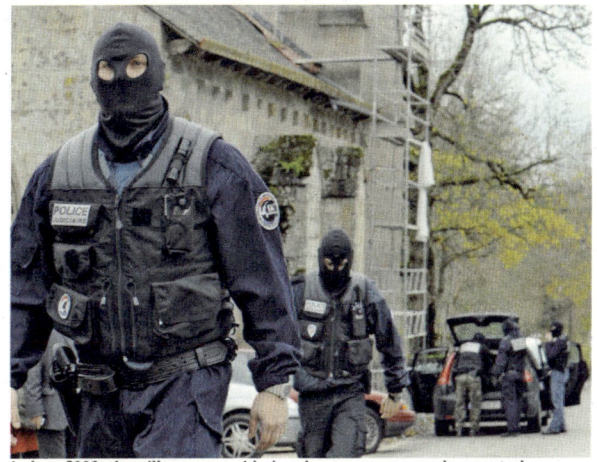
In late 2008, the village was raided and some communards arrested under claims to have been involved in the sabotage of a high-speed train, considered a "terrorist act" by the French government.
(Tierry Zocolan / Getty Images / AFP)

REPORTAGE

Tarnac : «Nos "terroristes" c'est des gentils !»

Par Guillaume Gendron, Envoyé spécial à Tarnac (Corrèze) — 8 février 2017 à 19:26

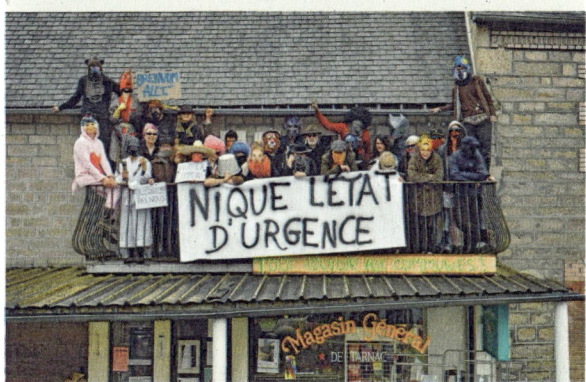
Later, all of the accused were acquitted, and all charges were dropped.

Renault appeared in my rear mirror. The driver, a dark-haired woman, nodded at me. I followed her car. We drove into the woods. After some kilometers, she parked under an oak tree. We walked past an old holiday camp formerly run by EDF, France's electricity company. There was an empty swimming pool, a wooden table floated in a muddy mix of rainwater, leaves, and debris. Tonight, the woman explained, there was a scientific lecture and a game-performance. We walked through high grass. A group of maybe 70 people gathered in front of a wooden barn. A man gave a lecture; he said that the apocalypse had already happened, that we were actually wrestling with a postapocalyptic situation. Some of the men greeted me and gave me a key to one of the houses in the village. Someone put on music. Someone filled some plastic cups with wine. Then the game began. You could choose to be either a human, or a zombie. You were given a stick to turn humans into zombies. The crowd swarmed out to the forest. It was dark and cold. The tips of fir tree branches looked black in the moonlight. There was a distant sound of laughter. Two students from Latin America stood silently beside me. They had come to Tarnac because they had heard that Julien Coupat, one of the Tarnac Nine, was friends with the Subcommandante Marcos. Almost no one I talked to came from the countryside. They all escaped big cities, universities, jobs to use the most remote countryside as a platform to question the predominant, late-capitalist, urban way of life.

    I drove back to the house. Someone had made a bed for me. A cat jumped down the steep stair. The next day, I followed some of the *communards* (who asked me not to reveal their names, as they had helped illegal refugees to find a place to hide in France, until their legal situation was solved) to another place in the forest. Tarnac apparently was just a placeholder name for a *reseau* of places. The one we went to was a sawmill. With the help of the German guys with the old police van, they had erected a large barn with a kitchen and benches. It felt like an informal, secret anarchist university. Mostly young people gathered in front of a projector as someone gave a scientific lecture on the history of artificial voices. Someone else was preparing a meal. Someone discussed the role of architecture in a resistance movement: Could barns like this be a new stage for politicization, for education and self-organization to counter the predominant societal narratives and players in the field of politics and economics? It was a unique blend of postapocalyptic theatre, rural tradition (the architect of the place is also a shepherd), and revolutionary teaching. Tarnac was not a village, but a forest that became a university. What is the countryside? To the Tarnac commune, it's an area full of mountains, meadows, deserts, and savannahs—an area that is hard to control, and therefore a space of liberty and experimentation. Their futuristic counter-model to the nostalgicization of country living can be described as an open game with existing technologies: one of the most important aims of their endeavors will be the creation of networks to sidestep large data collectors. Still, they live from small-scale, subsistence farming, from trading wood and from unknown donors. It's a life lived between sheep and communal film screenings in the local bar, far from the turbulent revolutions of contemporary life. Is Tarnac a model for the masses—or could other forms of an experimental existence, beyond the current organization of city and countryside lives, be imagined? There is one, 125 miles northeast of Paris. It's called the Familistère. It's a Phalanstery. It's over 150 years old, and still looks like an idea for the future.

IV. VERSAILLES

I drove north. Before going to see the phalanstery, I stopped over at Versailles, to visit the most momentous fake village in the history of modernity, the Hameau de la Reine, or the Queen's Hamlet. It was erected between 1783 and 1786 inside the vast park of the Château de Versailles as a place of leisure, and an intimate retreat for Marie Antoinette. While tensions rose outside the confines of the Park of Versailles, the queen's architect Richard Mique had created an idealized surrogate of a typical French hamlet. The queen reenacted the simple life she knew from the paintings of her time: The Hameau was 18th-century virtual reality in the French countryside; "simple people" like milkmaids and shepherds were invited to populate the tableau. The hameau was a fully operating farm with a farmhouse, cows and sheep maintained and cleaned by the servants, a dairy, a dovecote, a barn (mostly used as a ballroom), a mill and a tower that resembled a lighthouse, vineyards, orchards, fields and vegetable gardens were food for the royal table was produced. The Hameau was not the first, but the most accomplished and radical version of fake rustic model farms in aristocrats' parks, a simulacrum of the countryside in the countryside.

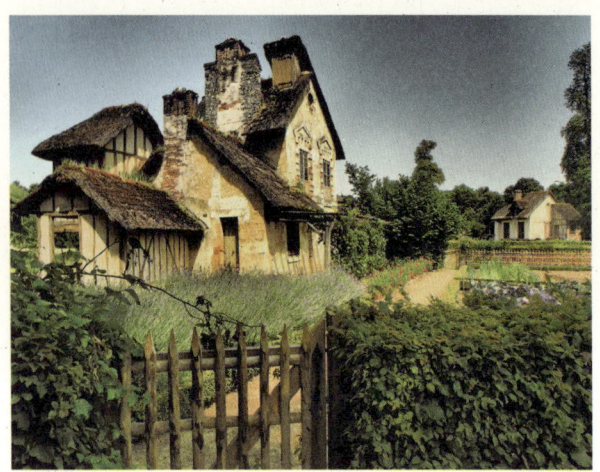

Le Hameau de la Reine, artificial Village in the park of Versailles, 1783–1788.

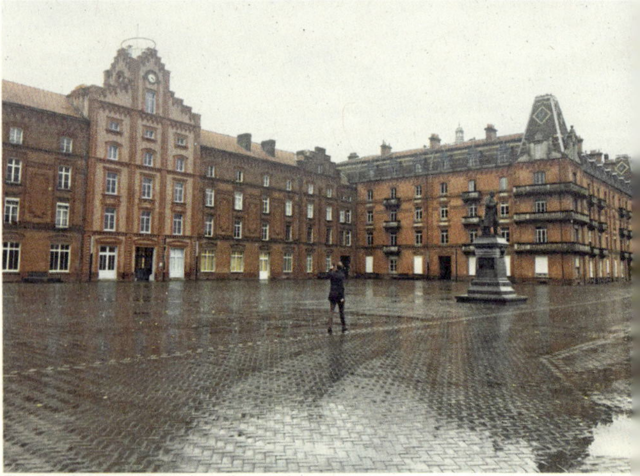

The Familistère in Guise, a collective housing utopia,
built in the 19th century.

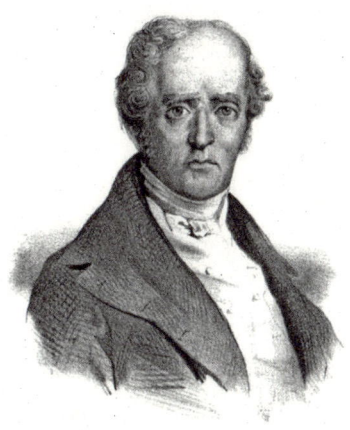

Utopian thinker Charles Fourier (1772–1837).

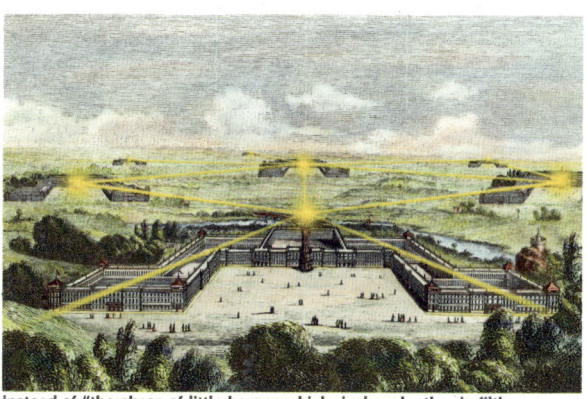

Instead of "the chaos of little houses which rival each other in filth and ugliness in our towns," Charles Fourier wanted to build a network of "phalansteries," designed to house around 1,600 people, working together for mutual benefit in agricultural communities.
(Background image: Granger)

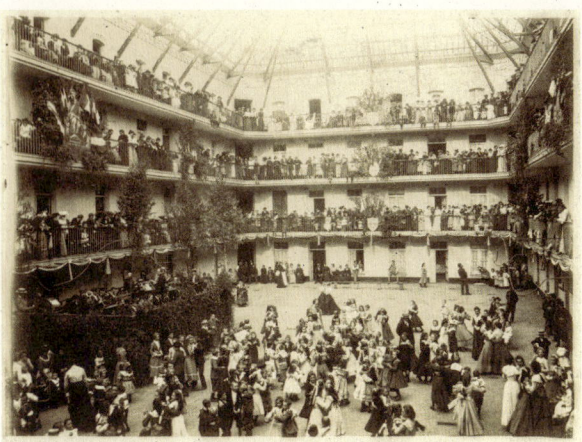

The Familistère was built from 1859–1884 by stove factory owner and philanthropist Jean-Baptiste André Godin.
(Collection of the Familistère de Guise, inv. no. 2006-33-1)

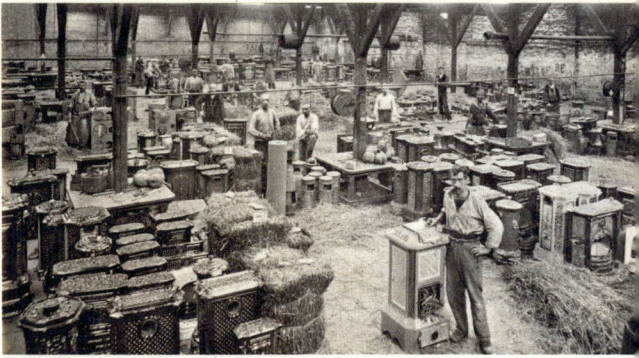

Factory workers in Guise, wrapping stoves with hay.
(Jongh Brothers. Collection of the Familistère de Guise, inv. no. 1976-1-490)

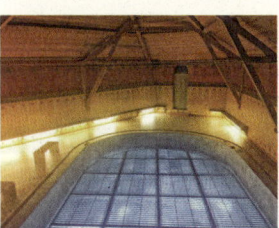

Hot water from the factory was used for a public pool where workers and their families learned to swim.

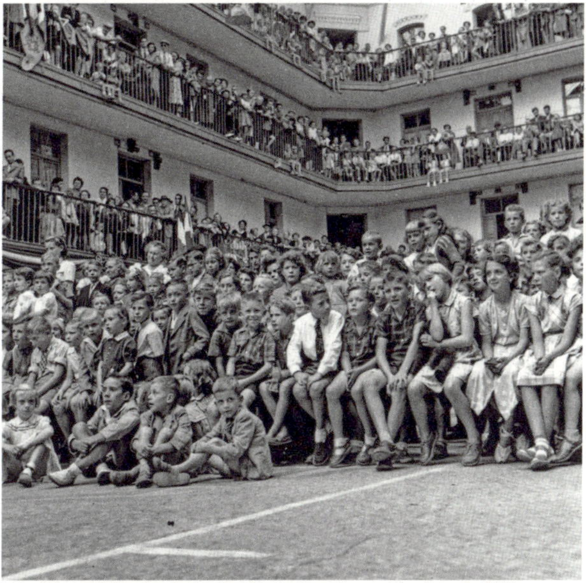

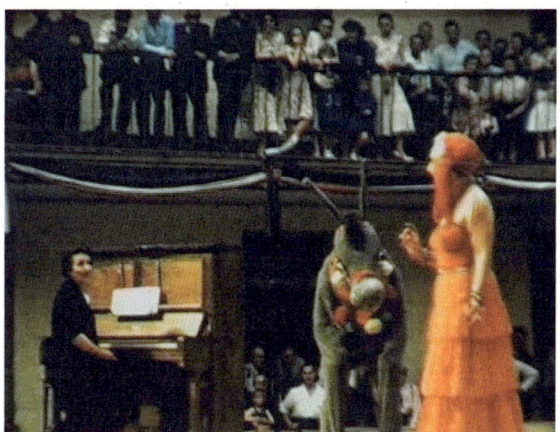

Labor day celebration in the Familistère's main courtyard, early 1960s.
(Roger Foret. Collection of the Familistère de Guise, inv. no. 1999-1-86)

A piano and a donkey: theater performance in Guise, late 1960s.
(Collection Familistère de Guise)

The terrain of the hamlet was completely enclosed by fences and walls: A bucolic prison that made its residents forget about the confines of the park. The Hameau was, on the one hand, a frivolous reenactment of the peasant's life. Historians claim that it was perceived as unintentional mockery of the peasants and in parts even sparked the French revolution. On the other hand, it was a rural utopia: A critique of the moral, societal, and religious values and rules of court life, a field of experimentation with new physical sensations, deviant sexuality, a redefinition of gender and role models, and a liberation of the body beyond court etiquette. In her village, the queen would wear light shepherdess dresses, have affairs with countless counts, but also with women; "Guilty of the other great sexual transgression: She is homosexual," Michel Foucault later wrote, and the dominant theme seems to be sexual debauchery. In the artificial nature of the Hameau, the idyllic and the incommensurable meet, like in a painting by Hubert or Fragonard, where the ruins of men's striving for control and order are overgrown by an exuberant, chaotic, hyper-fecund nature, where hypertrophic trees are shaken by gigantic storms, and bodies are exposed to the forces of nature. While divine order, symmetry, geometric harmony, patterned gardens, and an almost pathological rectangularization of nature were the predominant obsessions of the park's and the Château's design, the Hameau was the immoderate counterpart to the king's Cartesian, measured world: A paradoxical mise-en-scène of calm and turbulence, small-scale idyll and panorama of nature's unbound forces, serenity and sinuosity, simplicity and complication, production and debauchery, domestication and wilderness. If the Hameau was an ideal farmer's village without farmers, its true counterpart is to be found almost a century later and 125 miles northeast: The Familistère, a Versailles for the working classes.

V. FOURIER IN GUISE

From Paris, I drove to Reims, then headed north to Guise. The *Familistère* dominates an old stove factory. The four-story red-brick-building was erected by Jean-Baptiste Godin (1817–1888), a manufacturer of cast-iron stoves, as a revolutionary new habitat for his workers; it was operational for almost 100 years and largely influenced the history of modern collective and communal housing, from Le Corbusier's Cité Radieuse to more informal hippie communes.

With the Familistère, Godin embarked on building his own "Social Palace," to improve the living conditions of his workers and turn his factory into a laboratory for a different form of communal dwelling.

Each family had a three-room apartment, still a luxury at the time; education was free, and hot water from the factory used for a public swimming pool. Children were taken care of in two kindergartens, an infant school for toddlers and children up to age four, and a *bambinat* for children four to six, allowing their mothers to work. Each of the three buildings had a roofed courtyard, where the children could play in all weather and reunions, concerts, and festivities could take place year-round.

Godin's Familistère was the most successful realization of the phalanstery, a revolutionary building typology, imagined by the social theorist and utopian thinker Charles Fourier (1772–1837). Fourier disliked the city as much as he hated the village. An ardent critic of the exploitation of workers and farmers in early capitalism, he argued that the nuclear family home contributed to the oppression of women and that collectivization of farming would emancipate farmers from the confines of small-scale agriculture. He wanted to reconstruct society through a new typology of collective buildings that would radically reshape the countryside: His phalansteries were designed to house around 1,600 people, working together for mutual benefit in agricultural communities. "Instead of the chaos of little houses which rival each other in filth and ugliness in our towns, a Phalanx constructs for itself a building as perfect as the terrain permits," Fourier wrote. "The edifice occupied by the Phalanx bears no resemblance to our urban or rural buildings. ... The possibility of associating two or three hundred families in agricultural and manufacturing industry depends upon a system so entirely different from what now exists, that it will open to the reader a new social world."

Fourier's phalanstery was more than a collective farm. Also called Harmony, it was a revolutionary counter-model to the exploitation of farmers and workers, and a fundamental critique of the fragmentation and the dismemberment of the working class in nuclear family homes. The Phalanstery was a fantasy that made every worker and farmer a Sun King. With a central part and two lateral wings, the design of the Phalanstery evokes a "Versailles for the people" where everyone would have access to the formerly exclusive joys of a privileged aristocratic elite: Education, childcare, collective dinners, feasts, and the "liberation of human passions." These liberated passions, rather than capitalist efficiency, should be the foundation of work and relationships, Fourier claimed. His phalanstery was also an attack on the moral hypocrisy of an emerging bourgeoisie: "Love in the phalanstery," he claimed, is no longer "a recreation which detracts from work; on the contrary, it is the soul and the vehicle, the mainspring, of all works." In the illustrations to his texts, the Phalanstery is, like Versailles, always depicted as a single building, a unique, highly dense concentration of people in the middle of nowhere. But this largely ignores one truly revolutionary aspect of his plan: The phalanstery was not an architectural object or a prototype, but a massive attack on the social and spatial logics of both city and village, a strategy to reprogram the countryside by superimposing a structure of potentially endless networks of phalansteries. Fourier did not want one phalanstery; he wanted the whole world to be reorganized by an all-encompassing network of interconnected phalansteries—essentially microcities in the countryside—in which humanity, like a true phalanx, was thought to march forward as one entity. Credited with coining the word "feminism," Fourier was among the first to demand the right to work for women, and wages for reproductive work. He criticized the nuclear family for its exploitative character, "engrossing women in the complicated functions of our isolated households," and demanded that all sexual preferences, including androgyny and homosexuality, should be lived out unless others are abused. Jobs would be assigned based on interests and desires; unpleasant work would either be automated or merit higher pay.

In a way, Fourier also predicted modern dating apps: a card index in the phalanstery would propose suitable men and women for causal erotic encounters.

Besides these theories, Fourier irritated his readers with fierce attacks against any form of trading, often with anti-Semitic undertone, and with his fascination with desalinating the oceans: "It will be easy to remove the saline and citric particles from the water and render it drinkable, which will make it unnecessary for ships to be provisioned with barrels of water," Fourier wrote. "This breaking down of seawater by the boreal liquid is a necessary preliminary to the development of new sea creatures, which will provide a host of amphibious servants to pull ships and help in fisheries"; in his most far-fetching visions, he dreamt of turning the ocean into a giant underwater countryside.   Still, Fourier's writing—most notably the *Theory of the four movements* (1808) and his *Treatise on Domestic Agricultural Association* (1822)—inspired a whole movement of Fourierists who tried to realize his ideas in intentional communes and agricultural settlements all over the world.   Guise was the first Fourierian utopia that worked. By 1872, 900 female and male workers and their families were housed in the Familistère; in 1880, Godin turned it into a cooperative society, owned by the workers. Produce was sold at purchase price in a shop run by them. The Familistère stayed operational until 1968 when, some years after the takeover of the factory by another manufacturer, the cooperative association for the Social Palace was dissolved, and the apartments were sold. Today, the building complex, which is still partly inhabited, is protected as a historic monument and can be visited.

VI. PHALANSTEROLOGY: COUNTRY LIFE BEYOND THE RUINS OF LATE URBAN CAPITALISM

What could be the relevance of a phalanstery today? In the near future, city life might drastically change—and not in the way smart city developers advocate it. Today, almost every industrialized country in the world is facing a shift: the accelerating development of the technological revolution and the streamlining of robotics is reshaping labor practices. Speculations in economic theory range from systemic optimism (some forms of labor will disappear, but digitization will create even more highly qualified new jobs) to job apocalypse (digitalization and robotization will trigger a wave of mass unemployment). In many future laboratories, we find a paradoxical technophoria—everything will change—paired with an assumption of a harmonious stability in the overall distribution of work. The axiomatic question is not addressed: If cities, their topography, their collective rituals, and their socio-psychological rhythms are built around the idea of work and the concentration of human labor, then what would happen to the city if work as we know it disappeared? What kinds of spaces would a society need if it shifted its main goals from productivity and accelerated economic growth at any price to new forms of occupation, education, communication, and reproductive work? How would the countryside and the city—their spaces, rhythm, and collective rituals (lunch breaks, after-hours drinks, holidays)—change if work as we know it vanished? If the nature of work changed beyond the fake amalgamation of wage labor with "fun" and "hanging out" in the creative industries, everything would change: how we organize our days (with the kids at daycare and long commutes to office buildings), how we prioritize relationships (we spend most of our time with colleagues rather than with friends and family members), and where we dwell (now ideally "near work"). This shift would open up new possibilities also for the relation of city and countryside. The hailed smart city would not handle these changes adequately. Its incapacity to imagine new spaces for new demands makes it just a more efficient eco-version of the existing urban model. The changes of work, in demographics, technology, and social rituals would require new strategies and typologies beyond today's factories, office buildings, apartments, and houses —spaces that encourage different ways of spending time together, bringing up children, taking care of loved ones; education, loving, communication, the production of knowledge, and research could be organized differently. But where would these spaces be found?

Maybe they are already there. Many building typologies of late modernism will soon look like ancient ruins. The disappearance of human labor from the service sector has led to the evisceration of office parks and towers. The success of online retail, digital communication, and inverted mobility has killed a remarkable number of post offices, and has triggered a rising number of "dead malls"—hundreds of them. So, what to do with them? They are costly to destroy, and given the fact that building is a very carbon-intense practice, there are better solutions for reusing dead malls. They could be easily turned into a collective housing complex with a shared jungle in the former main arcade, small shops becoming units for families and larger stores spaces for co-housing, communes, co-working spaces, and other forms of collective, communal life. The dead mall could be turned into a 21st-century phalanstery. For Fourier, the Phalanstery was a form of spatial encouragement, a built frame that would enable people to experiment with and question the predominant social constructions, role models, power structures, and definitions of race and gender, turning depressed and exploited workers into "lovers & wild enthusiasts."[1] Today, for the first time, the technology required to realize this utopia is within reach. What started as a speculation 200 years ago, with Fourier's assumptions about post-nuclear family constellations, and a conceptual dissolution of the countryside-city divide in micro-urban rural Phalansteries, may become a reality. Unpleasant work could be robotized, and if the gain is not privatized but at least partly shared, former low-wage employees will benefit from this job loss by qualifying for other, more pleasant work or by dedicating themselves to other occupations in the field of previously unpaid reproductive labor, as Fourier predicted. The Phalanstery could serve as a thinking model for an architecture that fosters community, experimentation, new role models, new gender relations, post-familial constellations, and new forms of love, education, and production. A re-evaluation of the rural phalanstery might lead to a model that counters the overly controlled, labor-obsessed, exploitative, socially and aesthetically immobilized city; it could help develop a new narrative that goes much further than the depressively blunt, only mildly smarter urbanism, that is sold to us as the future of the city.

1 Hakim Bey, *The Lemonade Ocean & Modern Times* (1991).

Rif Revisited
Samir Bantal

My mother, Mimouna, was born in 1952 in Iksane, a Moroccan village close to the city of Nador and the Spanish enclave Melilla, in the region also known as the Rif. It was the same year the term "Third World" was coined by French economist Alfred Sauvy, as the global drive for independence formalized global inequality as a whole category of countries emerged that were not part of the Soviet Bloc or the Western Bloc.

My father was born in Beni Sidel, a village not far away from my mother's. Both my grandfathers were farmers; my father's father settled in Douar Leghriba, where he would be close to the plots of land he inherited from his father. The farm was a square adobe house with two long quarters on opposing sides that functioned as barns for the livestock. An orchard of olive trees surrounded the once isolated farm. Occasional almond and fig trees provided more shade and added color and scent to the farm. Surrounding the land was a thicket of cacti that not only provided a rocky, colorful fruit, but created a clear impenetrable border. This is where my parents spent their first years as a married couple, working on the farm, even though, unlike many of their peers, they were both educated. Occasionally, they'd spend time in Melilia, Nador, or Fes, bringing back urban fashion, music, and literature.

The research undertaken by several studios of the Harvard Graduate School of Design for the Countryside exploration that you are holding in your hand casts an unexpected new light on my family history. The Romans developed a philosophy and practice they called Otium: in order to enjoy beauty, one must restrain from work in the city and retreat to the beauty of nature. What my parents practiced was a reverse form of Otium, where they made sorties into urban areas in order to pursue self-exploration and contemplation, a rhythmic retreat from the drudgery of work in countryside. Maybe there's something about a nation's stage of development that determines where the most salutary retreat can be made: in the city or in the country. We discovered that in classical China, a philosophy flourished that was comparable to the Roman Otium: Xiaoyao. What the Chinese and the Romans held in common, perhaps, was a geographical and topological method of activating the task-negative part of our brain: the Default Mode Network. An idle running part of brain tissue associated with self-exploration, inward contemplation, and contextualization, DMN takes over when we retreat from focused tasks like work and business. The commodification of our modern free time has replaced philosophy with dopamine, catering to the part of our brain that relishes quick fixes. Wellness and a pinch of Yoga is the trillion-dollar mutation of Otium, and does not require ever leaving the city. Beige its ultimate color scheme.

Tourism is an effort to retrieve the primal mobility and rhythm of Otium, bringing us closer to nature, but the result is often the opposite. Even capped visitor numbers can't help us avoid overcrowding the Himalayas; no way up, no way down. Floating behemoths, cruise ships, covered in daybeds, glide smoothly along exotic shores; the equivalent of a small city, including the associated control, comfort, and safety, as we try to capture the last glimpses a glacier that soon will be history. Not a single nook on this planet is safe from our curiosity. Should we now retreat from nature, in order to save it? Or will the outdoor escalator become our inevitable fate? Can we still reverse back to Otium, and find meaning in isolation?

When I was young, every summer we would travel from the first world to the third world, from a Dutch town to the Moroccan countryside; "home," back to the farm. Every summer we would move from grey to actual beige. The blistering sun, sharp bushes, ticks, background manure smell, free-roaming chickens, and the deafening noise of cicadas, were replaced at night by a host of inconveniences. A far cry from the parental promise of rest and peace away from the city. But something had changed. We'd been away too long. We had been replaced by the farmhand. We had become city people, tourists in the countryside.

Before my father left for Europe to help build up the Dutch economy, I spent my first years partly on the farm and partly in Selouane, the town where I was born. In the 1960s and 70s, Morocco sent abroad its most hard-working and healthy men, especially from the Rif, a region that was not able to profit directly from global prosperity and was still recovering from decades of French-Spanish double exploitation. Once in the Netherlands, the newly imported workforce found itself confronted with urban life for the first time. The effects of this unanticipated—also by Western Europe—influx still echoes in many metropolitan areas. Rural social ideals did not align with urban volatile transactional dynamics. What would the Rif have looked like if German architect Hermann Sorgell—another revelation of our countryside research—had been even more convincing with his Atlantropa? Dammed and drained, would the Mediterranean have become the sce-

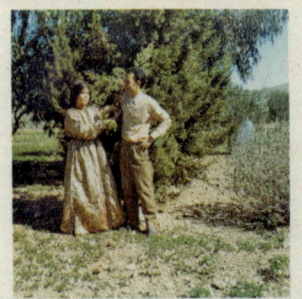

Mimouna & Mustapha Bantal, Laghriba, 1974

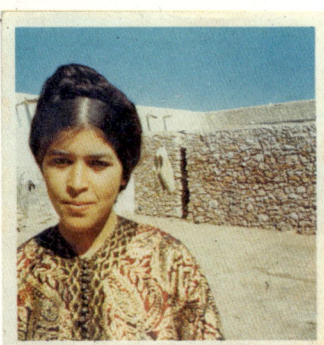

Mimouna, Laghriba, 1974

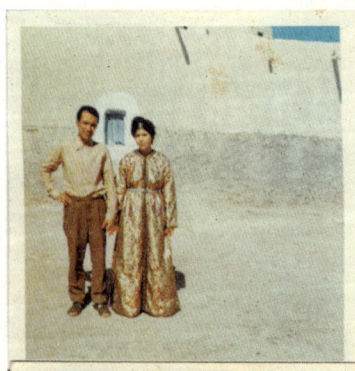

Mimouna & Mustapha Bantal, Laghriba, 1974

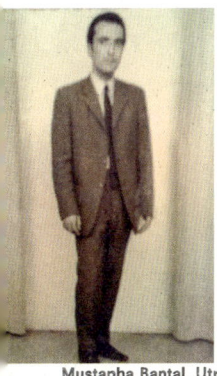

Mustapha Bantal, Utrecht, 1977

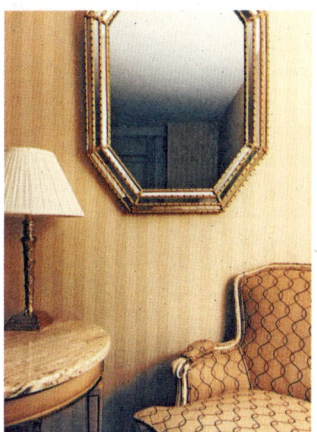

Beige hotel room, New York, 2017
(Samir Bantal)

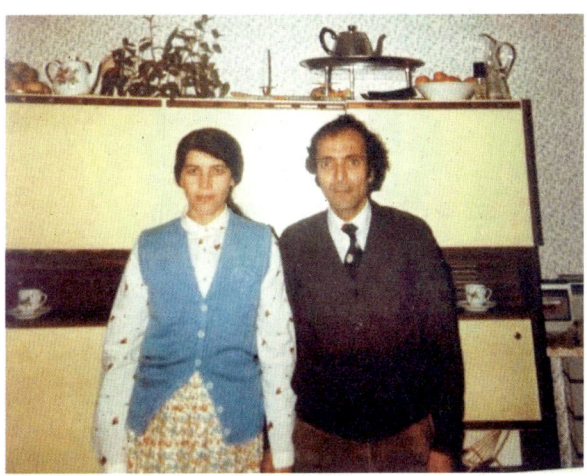

Mimouna & Mustapha Bantal, IJsselstein, 1980

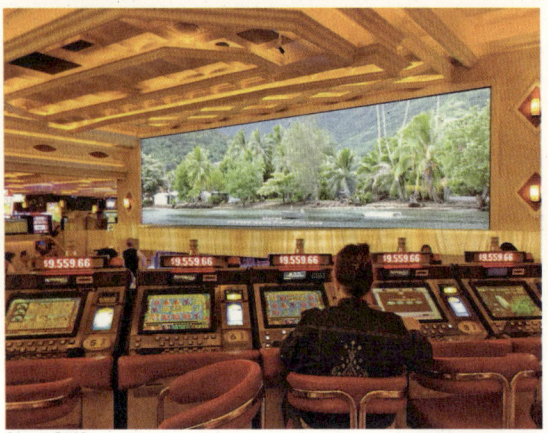

Reno, 2016

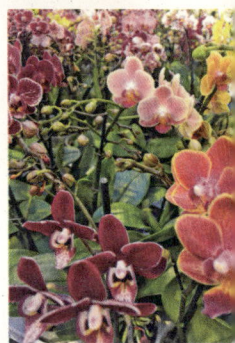

Westland, 2019

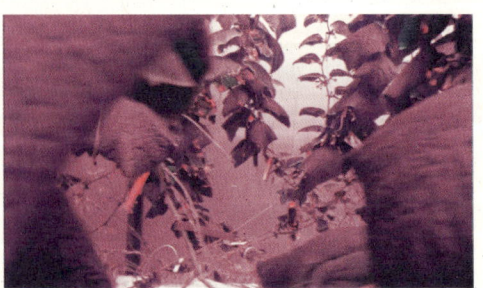

Westland, 2018

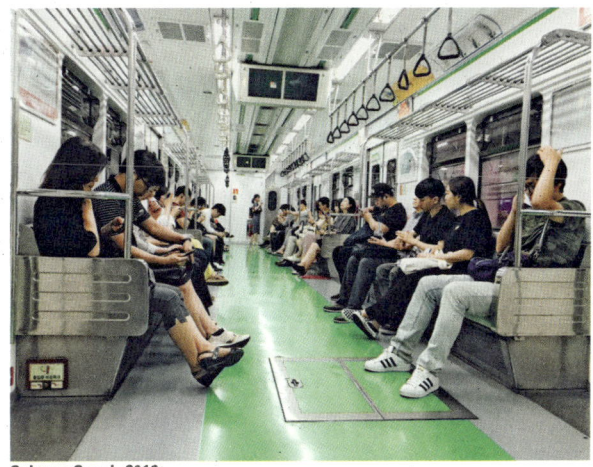

Subway Seoul, 2018

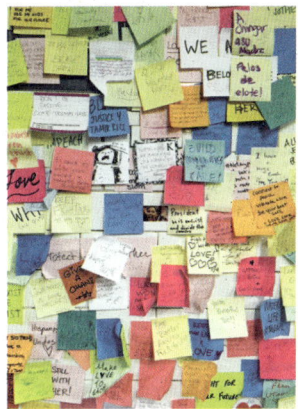

Subway New York, 2018

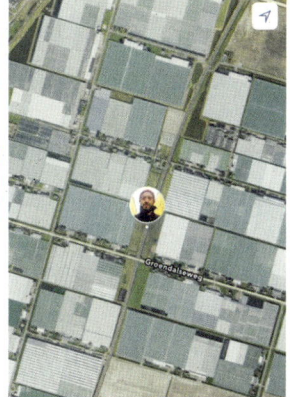

Westland, 2017

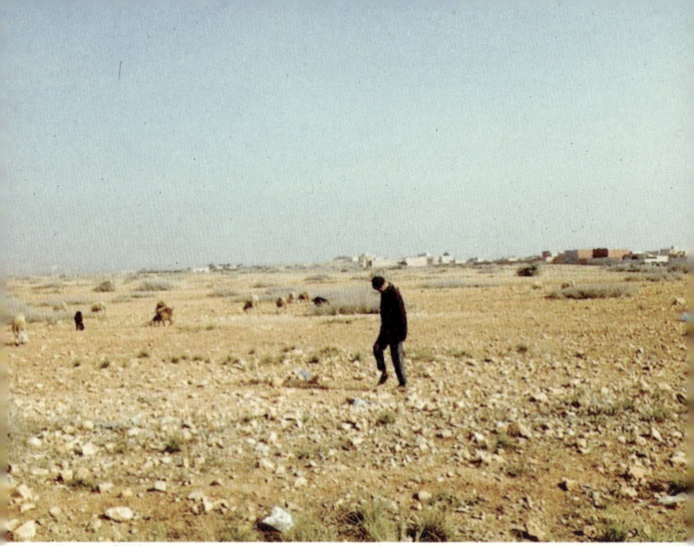

Iksane, 2018

TRIC, Reno, 2017

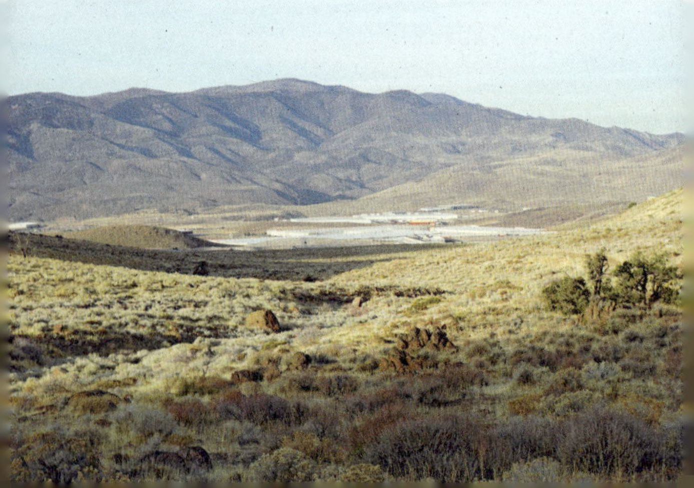

nic conference table of the nations that surrounded it, or simply a drastic increase of Lebensraum, achieved through engineering? From Rif to Riviera. Sorgel's flowcharts and diagrams depicting the unification of Europe and Africa reveals a delusional, optimistic confidence in (Western) planning to address imminent energy crises and European overpopulation. Under Sorgel's scheme, Europe would offer industrial riches to complement Africa's natural resources. Only as a new entity would Europe and Africa survive the pressure from the East and the Americas. These past five years of research into the countryside have brought us to unexpected places. Places we had never imagined existed, places that predict a certain future that awaits us. Reno's back office of the internet; the Midwest's mega farmscape; Chile's natural capital; Westland's regimented abundance, Wageningen's food algorithms; Germany and Italy's countryside emptying out and filling up again; Kenya's prototype villages and abruptly planted cities; Russia's history of megaprojects; China's villages as fulfillment centers; robots to maintain Japanese agriculture and infrastructure after natural or demographic disasters. Countryside appears to be our frontier for humanity's transitional challenges regarding nature, climate, energy, politics, technology, and culture. If the city is the engine of modernity, the countryside is its bodywork. Political leaders competing across the globe used the countryside to spread their ideologies to new uncharted territories. We masterplan our future, whether on continental scale or cellular level, and its architecture is manifested more and more by anonymous grey boxes. Amazon fulfills Santa's wish list from the same type of box where antimatter is fabricated or humanity's back-ups are archived. TRIC looks exactly like the Rif. The countryside has proven to be humanity's imminent future. But unexpectedly, the photographs by Sergei Mikhailovich Prokudin-Gorskii, one of which is on the cover of this book, brought back a personal past. His photographs show us a stable situation of three women, steadfast, full of confidence. A scene grounded in local tradition while distant global forces—even fashion—slowly approaching. Yet, the scene captures the vulnerability of a place unlikely to withstand the force of these (urban) trends. Trends that are unable to sustain local structures. The scene and dress of the three young women reminded me of the pictures my parents took at the farm in Morocco in the 70s. My mother wore a dress decorated with goldthread and floral patterns, like the ones from ancient Roman paintings, as they posed on what they saw as stable ground beneath their feet.

Great Plan for the Transformation of Nature
Alexandra Kharitonova

"God didn't build cities, he made the countryside."
—Michel Houellebecq on his novel *Serotonin*, August 2019.

Does Houellebecq mean that cities are hellish and the countryside idyllic, divine, "natural," an escape from human designs? But in the 20th century, countryside in the Soviet Union, more than anywhere else, became an instrument of political redesign on a Promethean level. From the revolution in 1917 forward, the enormous territories of the Soviet Union were, according to Lenin and subsequent leaders, in need of immediate modernization, at any cost. Large-scale agricultural projects, driven by Stalin and Khrushchev, were fundamental for maintaining independence from the West. Every campaign they pursued was not only for tangible economic and political goals, but was also accompanied by multilayered ideological projects, creating new ethical and aesthetic codes, projected by art and mass media. By the mid-1970s under Brezhnev, the USSR suffered an era of "stagnation." Great agricultural transformations faded into the background. The economy gradually shifted to the development of natural resources, mainly oil and gas. Temporary measures to save the economy turned into chronic dependence.

STALIN'S GREAT PLAN FOR THE TRANSFORMATION OF NATURE, 1948–1953

The political upheavals from the late 19th to the early 20th centuries—wars, revolutions, forced industrialization and collectivization of the 1930s—were intensified by droughts, crop failures, and mass famines. The biggest cataclysm was the Second World War—it ruined the agricultural sector of the USSR. In 1948, following another drought and mass famine, Stalin initiated a "plan for planting of shelterbelts, introduction of grassland crop rotation and construction of ponds and reservoirs to ensure high crop yields in steppe and forest-steppe areas of the European USSR." The project intended to remedy food shortages and climatic misfortunes, and to avoid reliance on foreign supplies. It was "great" in terms of scale, aiming to protect against hot southeastern winds, droughts, dust storms, and to "improve" the climate, creating new ecosystems, spanning a territory of 1.2 million square kilometers in the Volga region, Western Kazakhstan, the Northern Caucasus, and Ukraine. The ultimate goal was the solution to the problem of Soviet food supplies: increasing the yields of grain crops, vegetables, fruits, and the productivity of livestock. The idea of the shelterbelt originated in the late 19th century—after the mass famine of 1891–1892. To battle the drought, N. Genko, V. Dokuchaev and later G. Morozov experimented with a system of forest shelterbelts in the steppe zone, in Voronezh (Kamennaya Steppe), Samara and the Donetsk region (Velikij Anadol, Ukraine). Mixed planting of trees and shrubberies helped to improve the environmental conditions and served as protection against soil erosion caused by wind.[1] Stalin's project was developed by a group of scientists, based on scientific and practical tests to improve the microclimate around individual fields, but it grew into a grandiose concept for changing the climate across the whole of Russia.[2] As a result of political intrigues, Trofim Lysenko and his team were put in charge of the Great Plan. The project became a confrontation between "technocrats" (professional foresters, the Ministry of Forest Management) and "Prometheanists," Lysenko's group, the Main Administration for Field-Protective Afforestation.[3] The name Lysenko is still synonymous in Russia with cheating. The basis of his theory was the denial of chromosomal heredity and genetics, which he called "pseudoscience." Lysenko rejected Darwinism and natural selection, instead believing that certain features of plants were not determined by heredity, but could change under the influence of external factors. DNA was discovered in 1953, but at that time genetics was almost a forbidden science in the USSR. A populist agronomist "from the people," he didn't possess any academic degrees, but was well-known for his boisterous claims about diversification of a new types of wheat in record time. Lysenko's rise started in 1935, when he first attracted Stalin's attention with a fiery ideological speech at one of the Communist Party congresses. Later, at exactly the right moment—the beginning of the Cold War in 1947—he managed to convince Stalin of the possibility of an agricultural miracle by suggesting simple, labor-saving agricultural techniques.[4]

Lysenko was appointed Soviet head of agrobiology in 1948, after his public trashing of genetics.

In the period from 1949 up to 1965, Lysenko's plan called for the creation of eight state shelterbelts, 5,300 km long, combined within an extensive network of smaller strips along the boundaries of collective farm fields. The entire surface of the shelterbelts would make up more than 60,000 square kilometers. It was planned to magnify the effect with more than 44,000 small reservoirs and also the restoration of fertile layers of soil, using alternate sowing, by alternating cycles of grain crops and perennial grasses.

A complex bureaucracy was created to develop the plan, including a network of protective forest stations, but the realization of the project on-site was entrusted to local collective farms, with no experience in forestry. Methods and types of plants were assigned for each region by "technocrats" and "improved" by Lysenko's signature nest-planting method. The nest is a square meter with five holes, four in the corners and one in the middle. In each hole there should be planted seven or eight sprouted seeds. Lysenko believed members of the same species would not compete, but would "help" each other, sacrificing themselves for the strongest seedlings, so there would be no need for humans to take care of them. The nest should be surrounded by barley or wheat or the local crop, which would provide protection for the nest, as the combination would be effective in fighting weeds so that trees would grow with minimal maintenance.

As one of the foundational state projects, Stalin's shelterbelt plan became a central theme of postwar socialist realist art. In Dmitry Nalbandyan's iconic 1949 painting *For the Happiness of the People*, Stalin looms over an enormous map of forest shelterbelts with a pencil in his hand. He appears as a superhuman, demiurge, capable of transforming reality and controlling nature.

In Mikheil Chiaureli's epic film *The Fall of Berlin* (1949), Stalin is not only depicted as a victorious general, but also emerges as "the gardener of people's happiness." The film features music from avant-garde composer Dmitry Shostakovich, who was obliged to write the oratory *Song of the Forests* in 1949 to compensate for earlier accusations of "formalism" and "subservience to the West." The image of shelterbelts was reproduced on postage stamps, posters, and in propaganda filmstrips. It also appears in the vestibule of the Paveletskaya Koltsevaya station of Moscow's metro.

The apotheosis of the "Product Paradise" is central in the film *Kuban Cossacks*. The action unfolds at the agricultural trade fair, where the tables are bursting with a plentiful harvest. The movie is a virtuoso depiction of the future abundance of products, the Soviet food industry would deliver a beautiful dream of wishful thinking.

The choice of Lysenko as leader guaranteed its failure; more than 50 percent of the seedlings died, the first two shelterbelts were near-total losses.[5] Suggested methods were ineffective: plants competed for water and light, most of the trees didn't have a chance. But the fiasco did not cost Lysenko his life. Stalin died just before the failure became known. In 1953, the shelterbelt plan was aborted, only 46 percent of the project completed. In the end, 573 fields ringed with forest strips had improved yields,[6] but their planting had been based on earlier techniques. In 1967 there was a decree "On urgent measures to protect soils from wind and water erosion," but this was about local forest zones around fields; a large-scale return to Stalin's plan never happened. Fragments of the state forest shelterbelts exist to this day. In 2018, Olga Dyukova, senior researcher at the Russian Forest Museum in Moscow, visited the area near the major shelterbelt, Voronezh-Rostov-on-Don (920 km). "After 400 km, the forest steppe begins, followed by the steppe zone," Dyukova told me in an interview. There you can see the green barriers of the protective shelterbelts, dividing huge yellow fields into cells. The fields look beautiful, sunflowers and wheat grow in abundance—a lively and working agricultural system flourishes before our eyes. In the Krasnodar area, the shelterbelts are in fairly good condition, old and new plantings are visible, all post-Stalin, when a similar strategy was adopted but with improved techniques. I asked Dyukova if the shelterbelts plan was a failure. She said not completely. "We see branching, reduced sizes, other problems, all this needs constant care. But keeping in mind the scale—about 80 square kilometers—it looks decent. Without shelterbelts, the fields would no longer exist, everything would have been washed away."

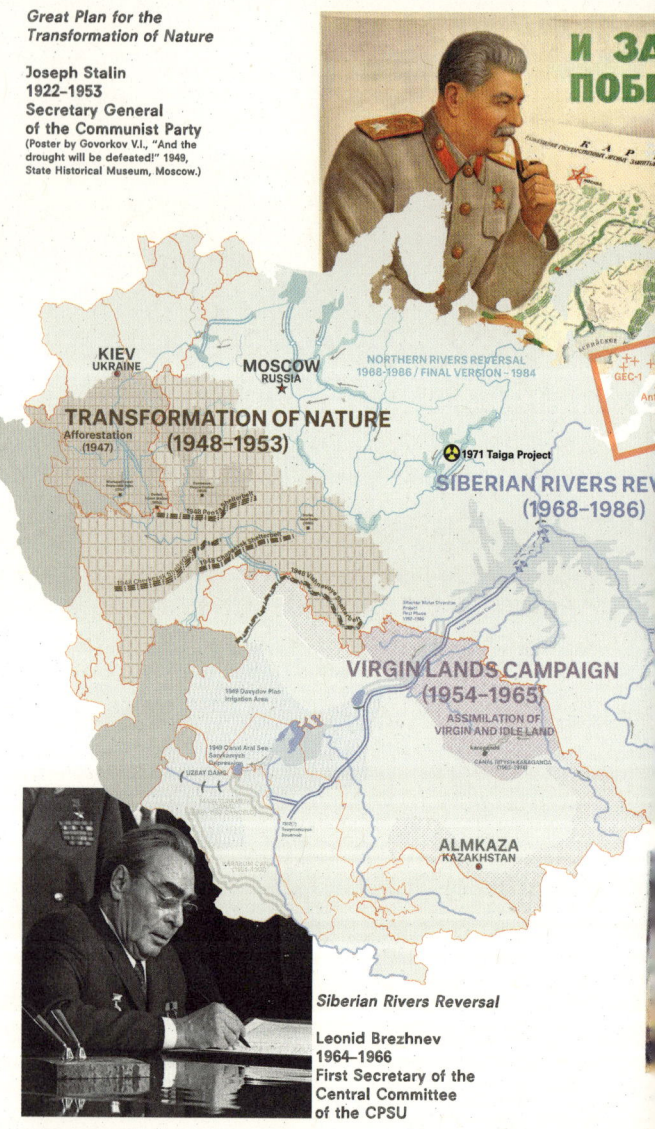

Massive Soviet investments the traces of which are still identifiable in Russia and now-independent Ukraine and Kazakhstan.

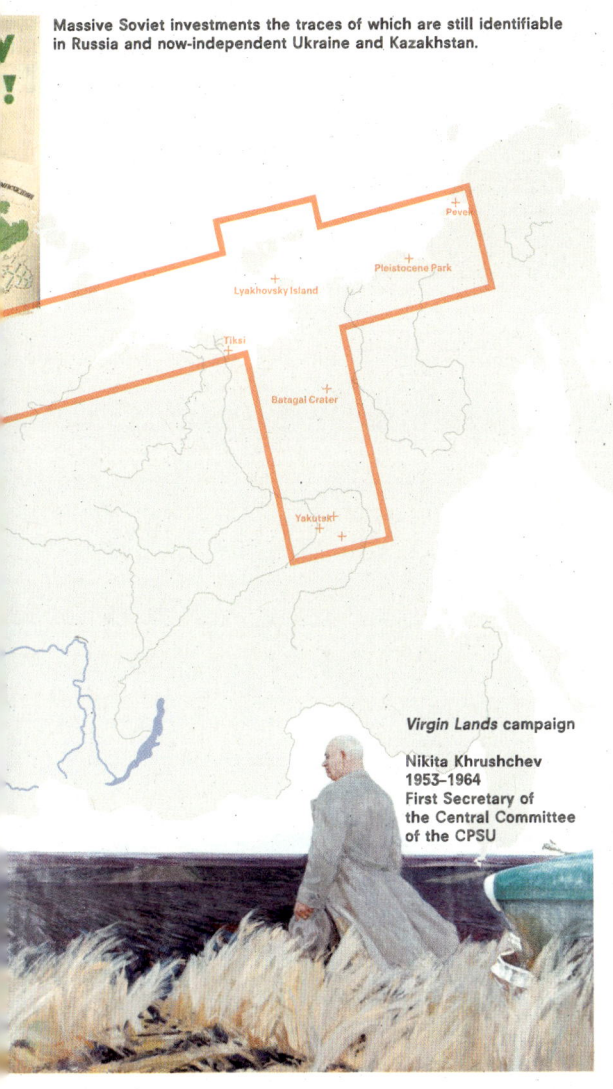

Pevek
Pleistocene Park
Lyakhovsky Island
Tiksi
Batagal Crater
Yakutsk

Virgin Lands campaign

Nikita Khrushchev
1953–1964
First Secretary of
the Central Committee
of the CPSU

(Uke Azhiev with M. Kenbaev and A. Moldabekov, *The Birth of the Virgin Lands*, 1960. Oil on canvas, 210 x 400. The Kasteev State Fine Art Museum of the Kazakhstan Republic)

THE VIRGIN LANDS CAMPAIGN, 1954–1965

Nikita Khrushchev succeeded Stalin in 1956 and was eager to initiate his own megaproject. During the 20th congress of the Communist Party that year, he read a report on Stalin's "personality cult and its aftermath," which marked "The Thaw," a certain easing of the regime. Khrushchev criticized Stalin and his repression, but not the cornerstone of the communist regime, the "socialist path of development" or the planned economy. Despite the postwar recovery and the promise that "the grain problems in the USSR are solved once and for all,"[7] the food supply problem had not disappeared—a grain shortage was imminent. Khrushchev oversaw the closure of more than 570 forest protection stations, possibly as a form of revenge.[8] He focused on his own countryside project instead: the development of the "virgin lands," a plan to cultivate around 450,000 square kilometers of steppe zones further east in Kazakhstan, Siberia, the Volga region, and the Urals. The campaign was an older proposal but it had been rejected by party leaders Malenkov, Molotov, Voroshilov, and by "specialists" such as Lysenko because of unfavorable climatic conditions, risks of soil erosion, and problems with irrigation. But Khrushchev was impulsive with a tendency to accept adventurous and haphazard solutions.[9] Increasing productivity was to be achieved by the "broadening" of plantation areas. Young Komsomol members were recruited to the labor force. Nationwide, an agitprop campaign targeted the young generation. In the late 1950s, documentaries and romantic comedies were released, showing volunteers conquering the steppes and finding love and happiness in the Virgin Lands (*The First Echelon*, 1955; *Ivan Brovkin on the State Farm*, 1959; *The Horizon*, 1961, to name a few). In fine art, the pathos of Stalin's heavy classicism was replaced by an impressionist aesthetic: socialist realistic paintings were now full of color, light, and air. Instead of a didactic depiction of the bright communist future, artists turned their attention to the individuality of the working-class heroes, including those working on the Virgin Lands.

The project demanded enormous investments in the agricultural sector and huge human and technical resources, but it was misconceived. Neither the specific nature of the soils nor the climate had been taken into account. Grain types appropriate for local conditions were not carefully selected. The soils were overfertilized to force results in the shortest amount of time. Part of the harvest was lost due to inadequate storage.

New settlers were offered incentives, like credits for residential construction and free transport, "a ticket to a new happy life." Around 1.7 million people were sent off to cultivate new territories. State farms were constructed but in the absence of any infrastructure for transport, machine maintenance, or grain storage—volunteers and their families stayed in tents and field wagons in the middle of nowhere. Yet, the Virgin Lands produced record harvests, initially, but in a few years the pessimists turned out to be right—another ecological catastrophe had been triggered. The overdose of fertilizers in the unsuitable territory caused the soil's salinization and oxidation, plowing and intensive soil exploitation accelerated erosion, fertile layers of soil disappeared; dust storms did the rest.

Immediately after the resolution of the Cuban Missile Crisis in 1963, Khrushchev humiliatingly was forced to import grain from the United States. In 1964, Khrushchev was replaced by Brezhnev, who had been a supervisor of the Virgin Lands campaign in the late 1950s. Brezhnev halted the project. The area was still cultivated until the 1980s, but eventually 90 percent of the Virgin Lands became unprofitable and were abandoned after the collapse of the USSR in 1991. However, in Kazakhstan the framework of modern agricultural and industrial infrastructure survived—337 state farms are now active in a section of former Virgin Lands.

THE SIBERIAN RIVERS REVERSAL, 1968–1986

The idea of reversing Siberian rivers—which emerged under Brezhnev—tried to avoid the mistakes of previous megaprojects by addressing the source of their problems. The goal was to avoid poor climate conditions and improve irrigation by cultivating promising territories in Central Asia. The systematic development of a unified project to reverse northern rivers into the Volga watershed, and the Siberian rivers (Irtysh, Tobol, Ob, Ishim, and others) into the southern regions was initiated under Brezhnev's decree in 1968. One hundred and sixty organizations were set up for the developments. The engineering proposals were presented in 50 volumes of technical drawings, with 10 albums of maps and sketches.

The core of the project was the construction of the "Siberia-Central Asia" canal, 2,550 km long, which had the potential to be the most important geopolitical transportation artery, connecting the Cara Sea with the Caspian Sea and eventually with the Persian Gulf. The digging would have to constitute 27.7 cubic kilometers per year to increase arable territories by 4.5 million hectares. The project had to be finalized by 1989. For the rapid construction of the channel, the possibility of using 220 underground nuclear blasts was considered, but after two experiments that plan was rejected. The project lasted 18 years in a situation of economic stagnation. Eventually it was closed down when Gorbachev came to power, after much public debate and criticism from writers, scientists, and ecologists. Stalin's, Khrushchev's, and Brezhnev's projects embody the pathos of unconditional faith in the possibility of a rebuilding of the world, inherited from the avant-garde movements of the early 20th century. Today, visionary elan gives way to economic pragmatism and ecological awareness. Recent statements by scientists that the planting of one trillion trees will be the best solution for natural carbon sequestration suggest that Russia is among the countries with great potential for reforestation; perhaps Stalin's Plan will gain relevance once more.

---

1 In 1933, such experiments became the basis of the afforestation program initiated by Franklin D. Roosevelt to battle the Dust Bowl in the American prairies.
2 Stephen Brain, *The Great Stalin Plan for the Transformation of Nature*, Environmental History, vol. 15, #4, October 2010, p. 680.
3 Brain, p. 670.
4 Brain, p. 682.
5 Brain, p. 690.
6 Brain, p. 693.
7 Remark by G. M. Malenkov, member of the Politburo at the 19th congress of the CPSU in 1952.
8 Нильс Иогансен. Как Хрущев отомстил Сталину. Газета «Культура», 26.02.2014.
9 Гвишиани А.Д. Феномен Косыгина. Записки внука. Мнения современников. Москва, 2004. Стр.96.

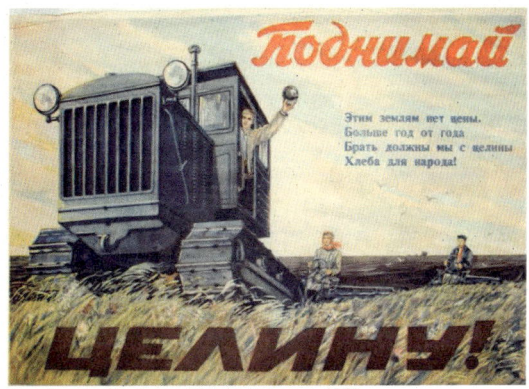

Develop the Virgin Lands! V. M. Livanova, 1954.
(National Museum of the Republic of Tatarstan, Russia)

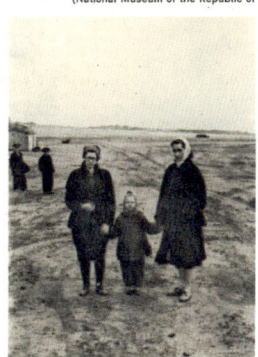

On the Virgin Land, Kazakhstan, 1954–1958.
(Elena Orekhova's archive/The History of Russia in Photo Archive, Russia)

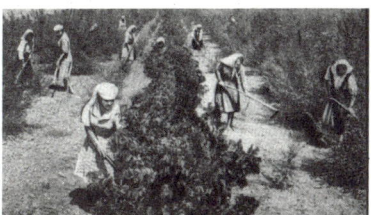

Komsomol Youth team of Anastasia Borisiuk at work at the Ural shelterbelt station of the State Protective Forest Shelterbelt, Vishnevaya Mountain–Caspian Sea, 1952.
(Russian Forest Museum, Moscow)

Future Food
Louise Fresco interviewed by RK

RK You are President of Wageningen University, what is radical thinking about food today?
LF When we talk about food, we need: carbohydrates, fat, and proteins. Fat and carbs are to an extent interchangeable. In the 1950s and 60s people thought astronauts could simply take a pill, but there's another important element: fibers. And as soon as we say fibers we need plants. You could also use fibers from wood chippings, reuse food leftovers, make them into fibers and vitamins, even retrieve proteins. We also have to find a way to produce amino acids. Theoretically they can be made in a factory— it's not that expensive. But the goal is mass production. One way to achieve this would be to improve the way plants convert solar energy into amino acids. That can be done using other types of plants, which are far more creative, biologically speaking, than the ones we have today. The second way of doing it is getting bacteria to produce amino acids. Bacteria are also able to produce sugars and fats; that has to be done in a controlled environment. The future is less outdoor agriculture and more factory agriculture, which is more like factory chemistry. The basis is going to be chemistry and biology more than mechanization.
RK Your main concern is looking at alternative sources of food, beyond the question of pleasure?
LF There's a whole other level to technology and biology, and that's pleasure, identity, history. Today, most of the nostalgia attached to food relates to it being authentic, local. Generations after us might be more in tune with artificial intelligence, become more interested in the high tech side of food. Solutions now are still a substitution of animals by plants, but you could also imagine things like a 3-D print-out of something bacteria-based, you could probably do that at home in the kitchen. If you look at agriculture and food production as an ecosystem, we don't use anything from the waste system. That is certainly going to change. Nutrients can be re-used. Next to the apples, there would be food composed of leftovers from earlier versions of food, which could be organized in

a cascading system, with as little nutrients as possible added to it, and with very few losses, also in terms of water.

RK How did you become an expert in agriculture?

LF When I was about 15, I saw pictures of the famine in Biafra. It was in *Paris Match*, and it made an enormous impression on me. I realized I could easily have been born in Biafra or Calcutta, and my life would have been completely different. I wanted to study medicine and become a kind of Doctor Schweitzer, then I realized that it's one thing to treat people medically, but when they go back home, they may not have enough food. So I decided to study agriculture as well as nutrition. My father was a professor of philosophy at Wageningen University, where I now work. I studied tropical agriculture and nutrition, and I went to Africa, Asia, my first concern was food security but I realized it's not just about calories or tons per hectare. It's about quality, identity, and diversity. Today, I push myself to think not just about food as the outcome of a biological process but as a conscious decision of mankind—how we can use technology to get the safest, most reliable, and most nourishing possible food.

RK Can you give an example of this kind of technology?

LF Food tracking will improve: we will know every single piece of food, every package of protein, the quality. And we'll ingest sensors to monitor our health, to tell us if we need more proteins, etc. That interconnectedness of food, agriculture, technology, and human beings is going to dramatically change the way we look at food.

RK In that scenario we'd lose all anonymity...

LF The worry I have is not that high tech is bad for us or that it makes food impersonal, but that you'll only care about reading your sensor, and potentially lose the idea that food is about sharing and enjoying as well as precision nutrition. I can imagine that when people come to my home, in 10, 20 years' time for a meal I would already know from their sensors exactly which nutrients they need, and I would only be allowed to make food with those nutrients and in the "correct" quantities. But no, I want to make lots of food. Sharing is about abundance, it's not about the functionality of nutrients. So while I moved from quantity to quality to high tech, I am now concerned with how to keep a balance between the cultural side and the high tech side of food.

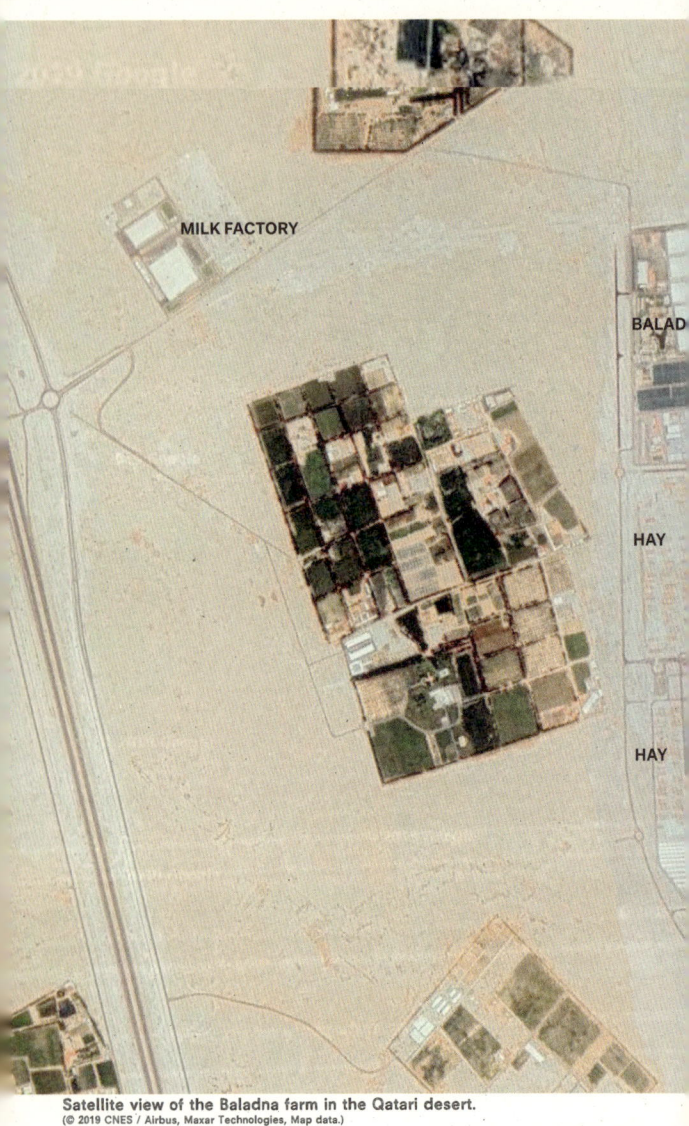

Satellite view of the Baladna farm in the Qatari desert.
(© 2019 CNES / Airbus, Maxar Technologies, Map data.)

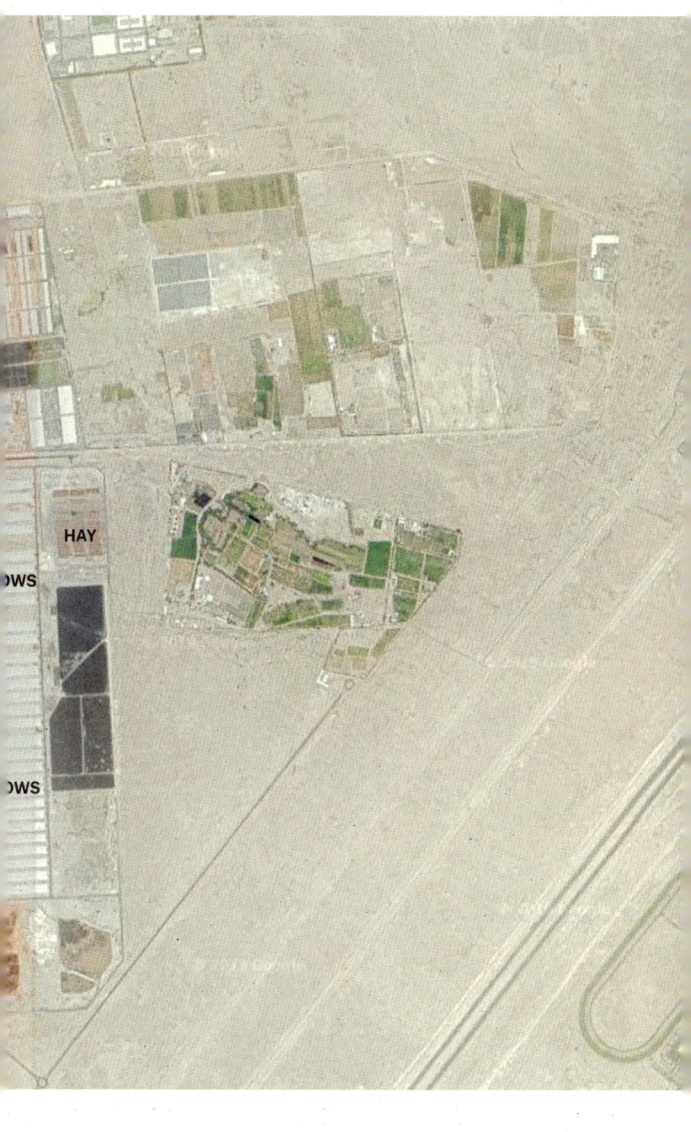

Food Insecurity
Samir Bantal

While 20th century Europe transitioned from agriculture to industry, 21st century Qatar still had to invent its own agriculture. A political crisis served as a blessing in disguise. First of all, Qatar is one of the richest nations in the world. Ninety percent of Qataris live in Doha, where hypermarkets magically restock themselves on a daily basis, and no one questions the origins of food. With a desert climate unsuitable for most forms of agriculture, Qatar imported almost all of its food, including dairy, from its neighbors.

Two weeks after Trump's visit to the region in 2017, signing the largest arms deal in history, a blockade was announced on Qatar by its neighbors, taking the world by surprise. Panic and disruption was smothered by an almost instant milk reboot. What happened? Did Qatar strike milk in the desert? A crisis action plan, silently in the making for almost ten years, had been activated. In 2008, the current emir of Qatar and his confidant Fahad Al Attiya questioned the nation's risky dependence on imported food. Al Attiya put together a task force swelling up to 200 people, meticulously dissecting the peninsula, constructing what became the country's Food Security Program. Qatar's biggest hurdle was its lack of water. The country used to have vast aquifers, but fodder grown only to feed racing camels had depleted the nation's natural water reserves to an alarming minimum.

The task force challenged current trade networks and fresh food sources, crafting the ultimate plan B: farming for resilience. Corporate consultants, consisting of engineers, economists, and agricultural scientists, performed a risk analysis similar to those made by insurance companies, showing a 46 percent probability of a blockade at the border. The first building blocks of an agricultural industry were placed outside the city. Under strict water regulations and the challenge to grow food in the desert without using underground water reserves, Qatar's desert became a test bed for efficient greenhouses, water retention capturing moisture from the hot air, and immense desalination plants. Unnoticed, the blueprints were taking shape. On June 5, 2017, the predicted blockade began, triggering the Ministry of Trade to take over the task of providing food for its people;

current stocks would only last 48 hours. That night, a team of 10 met in a situation room decorated with whiteboards and screens to monitor the public's panic trough social media. Food consumption had been precisely monitored, providing insight to the people's weekly demand. While diplomacy did its work in the public and international domain, excel spreadsheets were shared among the crisis team that flew out the next morning. Like a brain that reroutes its neurons instantly in case of trauma, the team had found new sources in Jordan, Oman, Turkey, Lebanon, Kuwait, Iran, Morocco, and Azerbaijan. Cows were flown in, with thousands at a time housed in huge state-of-the-art barns, boxes all connected by a wind tunnel that cools and humidifies the air. Outside, a Manhattan of hay, flown in from Australian grasslands, sits guarded by fire extinguishers. Next to the endless milk factory, a small theme park for the undisturbed urban visitor. The expected chaos did not erupt; instead, confidence and trust in the leadership increased. "Bring more than we need," said the emir. When, after two weeks people started to complain about the lack of tabbouleh, Qatar knew it had countered the blockade successfully.

Blocks of hay outside Baladna Farm, Al Khor, 2018.

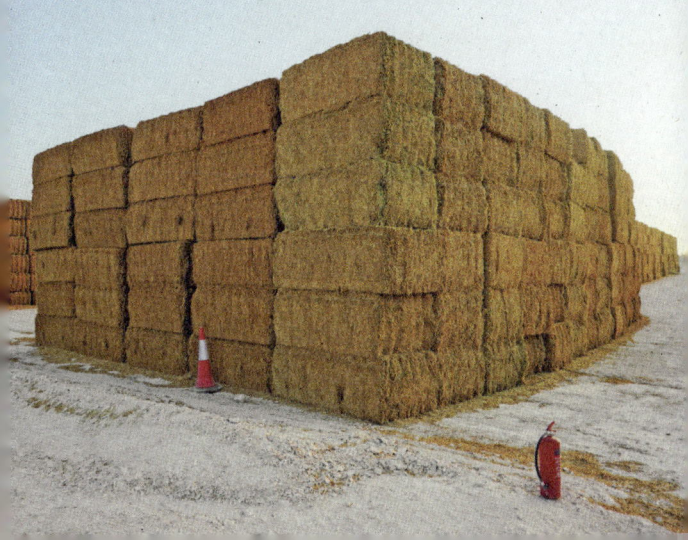

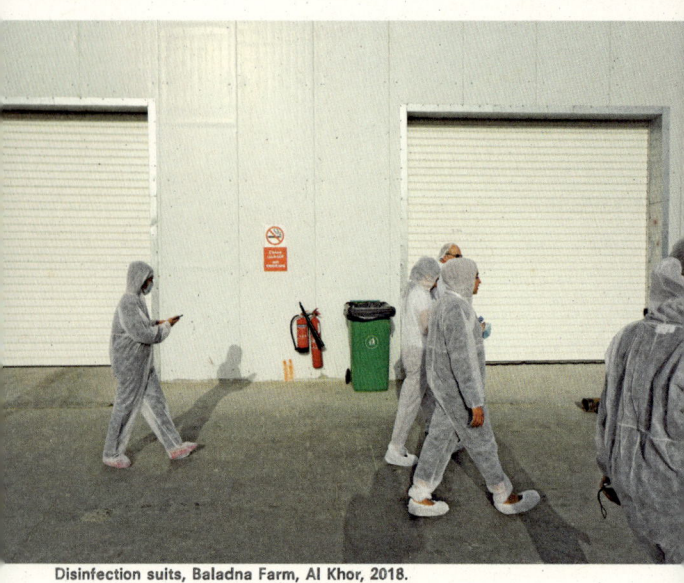

Disinfection suits, Baladna Farm, Al Khor, 2018.

"In late 2007, the deputy Emir called me and asked what happened to my father's dairy farm. He was worried that we didn't produce our own food anymore... he was receiving reports of dissatisfaction in Qatar. He asked me to investigate the state of our food security. My only qualification was my proximity to the farm of my childhood. At the time, the government had 11 bureaucracies related to food, directly or indirectly... did not help with my research... So the Emir wrote a letter: 'The task of this project is to submit a report in six months.' Six months flew by and I was still only scratching the surface. I needed another six months, more money, more people. In fact, the project lasted another four and a half years, eventually involved hundreds of collaborators. I questioned every assumption, traveled to Arizona, the Netherlands, Germany, Los Angeles, Florida, Malta, Texas, Japan. I checked systems, studied war, planned for worst-case scenarios... I had the biggest number of economists any governmental agency ever had. And I said to them: "What is the whole purpose of this project called Qatar?" You have money you have transferred from the ground, from oil and gas, into cash. Now you want to invest that cash. What do you want to get out of it? Do you want a return on investment? And you want the risk to be mitigated? I said to them, 'You put that amount of money into your local economy here, and then you have to import a population!' The irony is that Qatar engineered its own vulnerability. This would not necessarily diminish the country's standing."

His Excellency Fahad Al-Attiya, September 2019

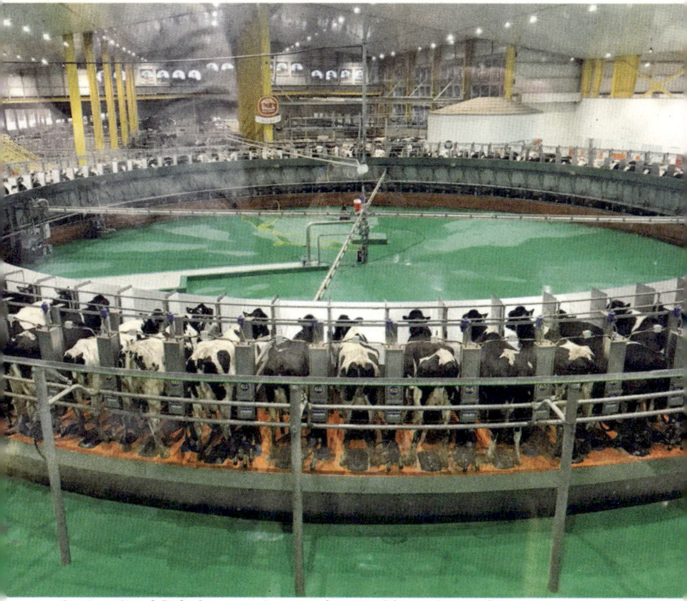

International Baladna cows' general assembly at the world's largest rotary milking machine, holding 100 cows.

"To define food security, you first have to define food insecurity. We started risk assessment and analysis to understand is there such a thing as food insecurity. We realized that there are different conditions of food insecurity and we split them in two categories: a) normal times and b) times of crisis. During normal times we do have problems in Qatar: we import 90 percent of our food. Half of it comes through Saudi Arabia, the other half through the Strait of Hormuz. This is OK for rice and sugar, which don't perish, but not for fruits and vegetables. Our fruits and vegetables are actually very poor quality. What comes from Holland is good quality, but expensive. So we have expensive high-quality food, and food that is very low quality but cheap. So in normal times, we already have a problem, because we don't have a domestic agriculture sector. The majority of the farms that exist in Qatar today are growing fava beans, and they make a lot of money. The fava is used for feeding racing camels. Where does the water come from for the fava beans? From underground. So we're growing something we don't need that has almost completely exhausted our only source of natural water."

Omar Al Ansari, September 2019

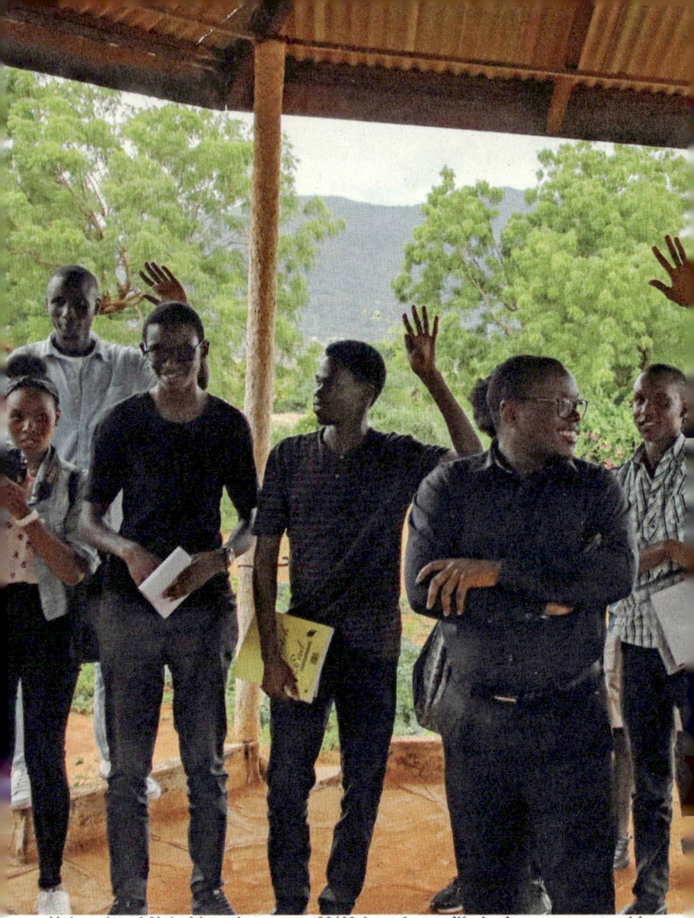

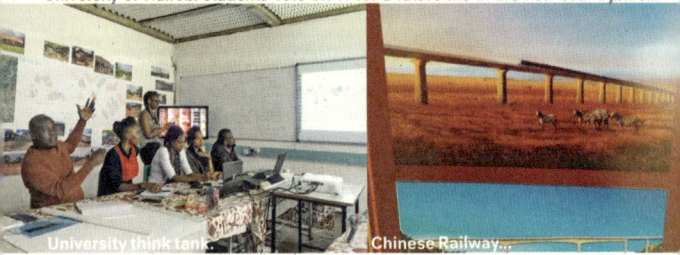

University of Nairobi students vote 60/40 for a future life in the new countryside...

University think tank.

Chinese Railway...

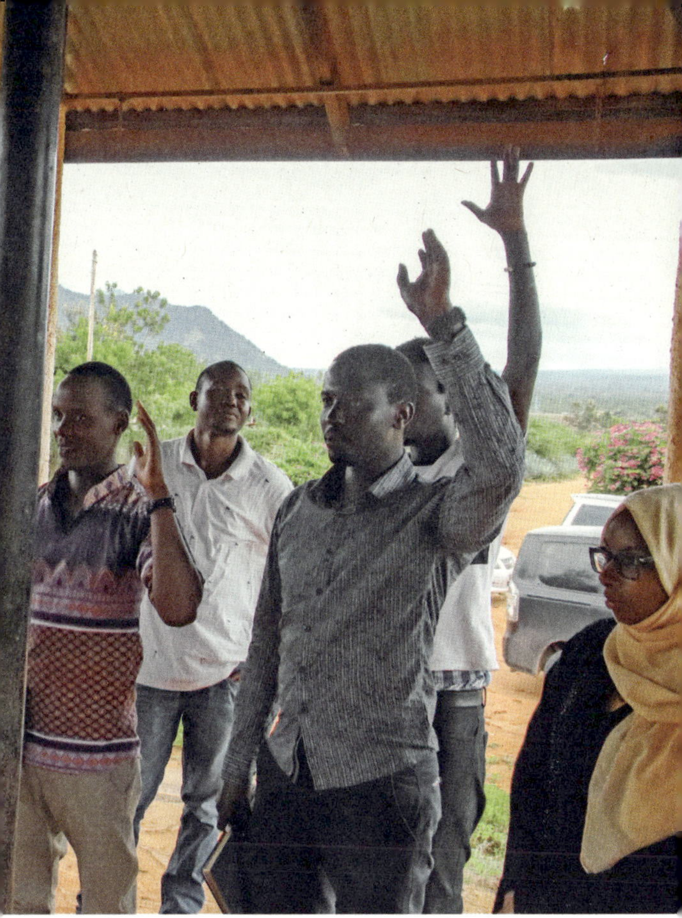

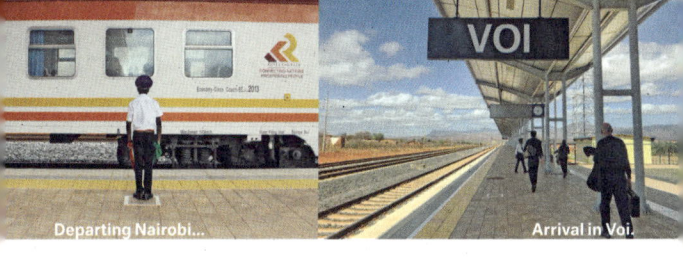

Departing Nairobi... Arrival in Voi.

Ocha: African Avant Garde
Dr. Linda Nkatha Gichuyia
& Etta Madete

Etta Madeta and Dr. Linda Nkatha Gichuyia, lecturers in architecture at the University of Nairobi, discuss Kenya's countryside, which isn't following the script set for it by the UN, colonial legacy, or contemporary Chinese influence...

PROJECTIONS VS. REALITY

LINDA NKATHA GICHUYIA Are mega-regions, mega-cities, urban agglomerations the inevitable fate of East Africa? These terms monopolize current discussions and definitions of emerging futures all over the world. The UN says over 50 percent of the world's population currently lives in cities and that over 70 percent of the world's population will live in urban areas by the year 2050. And according to this data set, by 2050, African cities will double in population. We are bombarded with statistics on the propagative effects such urbanization will have on all aspects of our lives. These and many more related "urban this and urban thats" currently colonize our urbanized mindsets. I wonder whether this status on the "inevitability" of urbanization is robbing us of a chance to "see with innocence" what is actually happening in the leftover space, the countryside regions of East Africa?

ETTA MADETE I totally agree. A few key statistics on the countryside of Kenya show that a false sense of density, brought about by the intrinsic nature of urban compaction, masks the true importance of the countryside as a key factor of development. We must be clear what we mean by a city. Is it merely the place with a lot of people all hud-

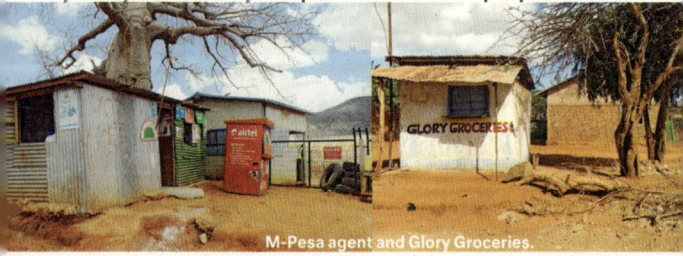
M-Pesa agent and Glory Groceries.

dled together around a hypothetical concentration of opportunity? If so, then the changing nature of opportunity will inevitably change the nature of our cities. In 2016, the World Bank reported that 74 percent of Kenyans live in rural areas. Furthermore, work by Deborah Potts shows the rate of urbanization in Africa is far slower than is usually reported. UN habitat research indicated that the proportion of Kenyans living in urban settlements shrunk from 34 percent in 2001 to 22 percent in 2010.

COUNTRYSIDE COLLAGE

LNG So how do you see the Kenyan countryside, Etta?

EM For myself and some of my peers, we see the countryside as an opportunity to plant seeds of a new life, different from the generation before us but rooted in old ancestral grounds. From the Universal Basic Income experiment, and wind and solar farms, to the agri-tech innovations that can only be cultivated in the diversity and contradictions found in the freedom, space, and seclusion of the countryside, there are so many trends bubbling to the surface. No longer are we confronted with the mundanity, deterioration, and "backwards" notion of farm life and the rural village. The village is becoming the voice of reason on how to move forward. Urban areas are a threat financially—everything you earn is drained by the high cost of living—a threat socially—all the work you do keeps you at your desk until nightfall when you get home and crash or get to your night time job/side hustle—a threat emotionally—because of the traffic, pollution, and psychologically unhealthy urban environment. Yet with technology, there is actually no need to live in the city at all. With clarity of mind and the elimination of threats, you can think, create, and innovate. You can grow your own food and stay connected to the wider world.

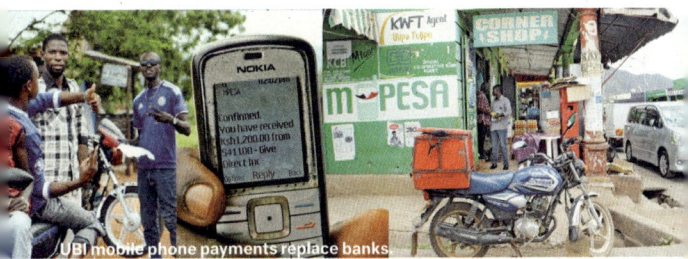
UBI mobile phone payments replace banks.

LNG I definitely relate to the imposed stresses of working in urban areas. It makes me want to go luxuriate in our countryside, also called *Ocha* or *Gishagi* in Kenyan slang. It is here where I'm shielded from the draining city hustle. The countryside is where I normally go to stop time and reset. All the projects you have mentioned, Etta, and others, show a lot is happening in the Kenyan countryside that needs to be understood and unravelled. I think three main features influence its current forms and spatial extents. First, the seemingly unrelated, mutually exclusive activities and spaces—like UBI experiments and renewable energy—that form a collage in the Kenyan countryside. Second, the shared and enabling functions, services, and visions across the country, almost like a mesh linking the discontinuous countryside activities through digital technology, financial systems, and shared government agendas. M-Pesa, our mobile money transfer service as well as the Equity bank model, which promotes the idea of financial inclusion even for the most remote rural folk, have revolutionized our way of life both in the city and in the countryside. Physical infrastructure being laid down by the government, like the Standard Gauge Rail and the LAPSSET (Lamu Port, South Sudan, Ethiopia Transport) corridor are physically opening up the countryside hinterland. Thirdly, Kenyan countryside regions are not at all shielded from global market influences, such as Airbnb and Uber, and shared global challenges, including terrorism and climate change.

EM Can you give an example of how these three features intersect?

LNG It's amazing how even in the remotest parts of Kenya, you can still book an Airbnb and pay for it using M-Pesa after withdrawing money from Equity bank using your phone's M-Pesa app. I can do all this in a matter of minutes maybe as I Uber to go give a lecture at the University of

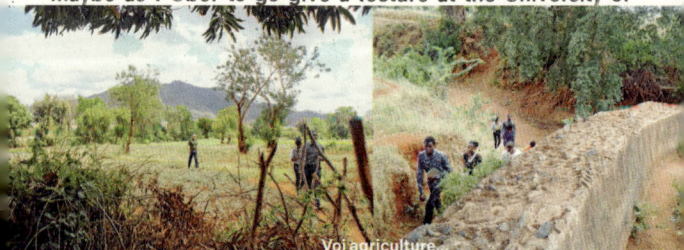
Voi agriculture...

Nairobi. And, before getting to my class, I have to go through two security screenings, a common condition in all public spaces post-9/11 and the terrorist attacks Kenya has suffered. All these three aspects mentioned form a kind of countryside tapestry.

EM Within this tapestry, I think the invisible links, such as the flow of money, are what makes the countryside accessible. There's an unmistakable green tinge to the urban and rural landscapes; you can't turn around without seeing a green-painted Safaricom M-Pesa agent shop. You can use M-Pesa with the most simple GSM phone, meaning it's accessible to almost everyone. Having money circulating at the grassroots level has created a new form of 'corner shop,' with people huddled in a particular spot, transacting. With M-Pesa you can send money, receive money, and pay for goods and services without once stepping into a bank. And in the countryside, banks are few and far between, and charge high fees, imposing colonial structures and long due-diligence processes that most people don't understand. M-Pesa, with low fees, easy accessibility, tax and regulatory anonymity, has connected the countryside—the farmer, the laborer, and the businessman.

HOME

LNG Kenyans have a peculiar sense of home and belonging. We tend to identify with our rural and tribal countrysides as our main reference to "home," whereas we see urban areas as just our workplace houses. Most Kenyans, including myself, working in the urban centers, travel back to their countryside homes often to visit family. We find ourselves constantly straddling modern life in the city and traditional life at home—our Gishagi, our Ocha. The movement between urban centers and countrysides reinforces the formation and fragmentation of scaled

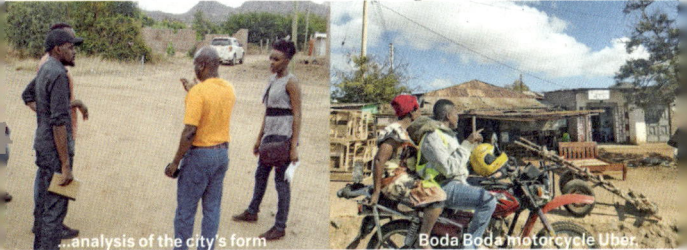

...analysis of the city's form   Boda Boda motorcycle Uber.

neighborhoods. It's expected that urbanites graft things urban onto the countryside, but the opposite is also happening: We're seeing the 'ruralization of the urban' as the main selling point of masterplanned live-work-play cities like Tatu City, Northlands city, Konza City, etc. They're designed to replicate a rural experience inside our fast-paced urban centers.

EM It's so true—as a Kenyan, I identify with two homes: where I live, which is typically close to income-generating activities and opportunities for education, health services, and entertainment; but I also identify home as where my family is from, the ancestral home. I have travelled home to western Kenya every three months or so since I was born, and still make the 10-hour bus journey today. I look jealously at my coastal friends whose commute has been made significantly easier through the 2010 Chinese-funded railway (the SGR), and I secretly cross my fingers that we may bury ourselves in more Chinese debt trying to reach my village in the west by the "red dragon" train too. As someone constantly moving between the urban and rural frame, I experience the reality that the urbanization of African cities is not as extreme as some statistics make out. As cities have grown and the population becomes more educated, this advancement breathes life, hope, and growth into our rural homes. Many of my generation are starting to invest back into their homes due to the high cost of living in cities, other urban pressures, and rural nostalgia. In the countryside, there are more opportunities, land is available, and they can have alternative sources of income. My home has developed and has services, Wi-Fi, and good roads, so I have no need to be based in the busy, noisy, and expensive city anymore.

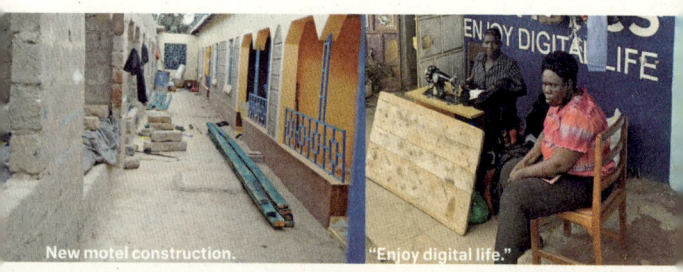

New motel construction. "Enjoy digital life."

A TALE OF TWO KENYAN VILLAGES

EM Voi is a town in Kenya that is fermenting a sort of rural urbanization. Partly due to its history and location, Voi has become a hotbed of consolidated growth, with a new China-funded train station and county government devolution-fueled development projects. The town is named after Chief Kivoi (born in the 1780s), a long-distance trader who guided missionaries into the interior of present-day Kenya. During the colonial era, the construction of the Kenya–Uganda railway in 1898 brought growth to the village—it became the main stopover for the colonialist moving between the Kenyan coast inland to Nairobi as well as south to Tanzania. Voi is still a key developmental node today, locally and internationally, as a gateway for tourists to the Tsavo National Parks.

LNG And Voi today looks very different as different countryside forces intersect there.

EM Exactly. In Voi the invisible systems you were speaking about are actually materialized with the Bodaboda (motorcycle taxis) zipping across the narrow village streets. You can play "Spot Waldo" with the Bodaboda as you move through the town. It's almost the only way to navigate through the sometimes narrow, uneven, and rain-worn streets. This transport revolution not only changed the way people move through the village but also how the youth navigate life. It's their main source of income as they become more tech-savy and seek ways to move beyond the stigmatization of rural life.

LNG Samburu on the other hand, at least the part I visited last summer, can be visually imagined by assuming that we have peeled Voi several development layers back to 1780 during Chief Kivoi's heyday. I collaborated on a study of the Samburu region with a team from University College

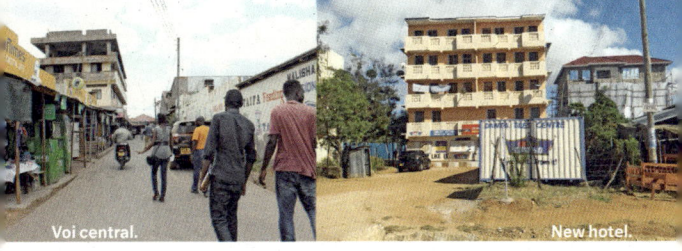

Voi central. New hotel.

of Dublin, mainly to learn from the locals and to document how to build a low-land style Samburu house. Lengusaka region in Samburu, like so many regions in Kenya, is extremely remote from any urban center. Their strong culture has shown little or no transformation compared to other regions in Kenya. However, their way of life has been enhanced by the invisible mesh of digital technology like M-Pesa and Equity Bank.

EM A lot is changing in countryside towns, inducing the breakdown of agricultural systems. Begha, a brick worker in Sofia, a district in Voi, told us: "Bricks sell better than growing food. So instead we grow bricks to buy food." The irony of this statement troubles me as I see most agricultural countrysides being transformed into construction fuel for cities. The dried-up Voi river basin now features an extraordinary brickyard almost 500 meters in length, with over 400 workers making burnt bricks every day. Perhaps this is the vision of the future of the countryside we ignore, the one whose stone is quarried away until depleted and whose soil is burnt away to build the cities of the future. The concentration of climate change initiatives in the city ignores the much larger problem of countryside exploitation, deforestation, quarrying, and mass destruction of natural and cultural ecosystems in rural areas.

CITY PLANTING

EM The government has initiated a "city planting" movement, using the countryside as a canvas for new cities like Tatu City and Konza Techno City, which are rendered as miniature New York Cities filled with glass skyscrapers and people walking around in suits. This elaborate government control of the countryside is just one part of a much larger operation for the commercialisation of rural landscapes. Another is the vast lands taken from various tribes in the name of conservation. Mordecai Ogada spoke

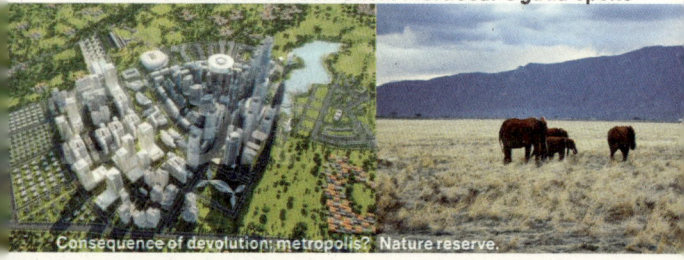

Consequence of devolution: metropolis? Nature reserve.

out about this in their seminal work, *The Big Conservation Lie*, saying, it's "a far-fetched thought that one can presume to celebrate, conserve, and value any culture or heritage while uprooting or otherwise dislodging people from their ancestral origins." This conflict of big economies versus community heritage begs the question: What is the future of human-wildlife conversation, and who will be the ones speaking? I am in conflict because on the one hand, we rely on these government projects to open up the countryside and make it accessible, and we rely on tourism as one of our biggest revenue sources, but I contest the imposition of a top-down narrative in which we have no say.

LNG For the past 10 years, there has been a mad dash for every county government to champion a model of development with the tall glass towers, spaghetti road networks, and busy-looking streets. Open most of the county government websites, and you're met by utopian masterplans, often quite alien to the region. Do you get as anxious as I do when I read newspaper headlines like: "China to put up Sh 65 billion 'Dubai' in Machakos"!? Machakos is one of the towns that has grown gradually over the years. Then boom! A plan to plant a 'Dubai' deep in the region's countryside. Voi and Samburu regions could give a window into the patterns of the bottom-up growth of regions.

AFRO-FUTURISM

EM Imagining the future is not only the remit of the urban planner, but is deeply ingrained in the Afro-futurism movement that has revolutionized art and culture in Kenya. Some use the term to refer to a radical and almost sci-fi form of African progress; others, like photographer and digital artist Osbourne Macharia, embrace it as a means to represent ourselves in an honest and un-nostalgic way. The tribal cyborgs in Jacque Njeri's *Maa-Sci* series of digital images, picturing the Maasai tribe exploring space,

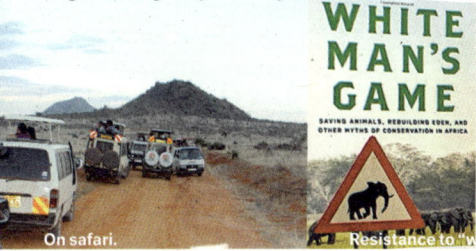

On safari.

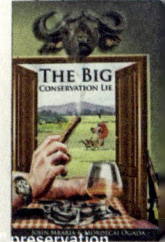

Resistance to "white" preservation

stands in beautiful contrast to the government-led "city planting" movement and wildlife commercialization. The artists take a ground-up and far more radical view of the future; the government imposes a predictable, discordant image of the future from above. I think the contrast will merge over time, like the socialist cities imagined by hippies in the US that became Silicon Valley today.

LNG Jaque Njeri's and Osbourne Macharia's work, and by extension the craft and sculptural works of Mutuma Marangu on Afro-cubism, for instance, demonstrates artists fighting to create alternative African narratives. These narratives draw inspiration from deep African roots and fuse them with influences from the rest of the world. Even with this "city planting" movement that is driving our county governments, I think in their own way, our officials are struggling to understand and decide what development means in the Kenyan context.

UBI

EM Speaking of experiments, the countryside is Kenya's laboratory for sure. A prime example is the Universal Basic Income experiment happening a stone's throw from the village I'm from. Starting in October 2016, the NGO GiveDirectly launched its Universal Basic Income experiment, based on the premise that aid should not be prescribed. Recipients are given cash—either a small amount over a long period, or a lump sum—and how they use it is up to them. I see it as a project that will change the way we think about aid and giving, not only at a global scale but at the human one. There is no visible trace of the experiment when you visit the villages in the program, as there are only 99 participants in Magawa village and 55 in Sinyanya. One participant remarked, "The main change I have seen with this village is that we have a lot more visitors." The change happens at an individual scale as a

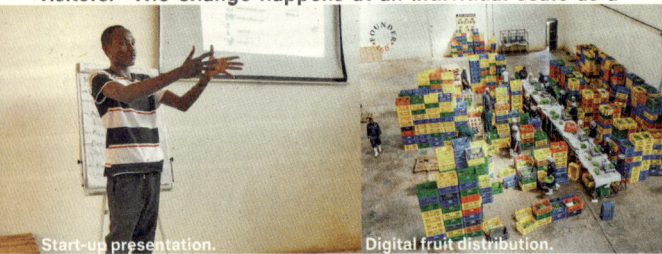

Start-up presentation. Digital fruit distribution.

mama mboga, the street vendor who sells vegetables for a living is now able to build a new home and comfortably send her children to school without being a victim of, for example, fluctuations in climate that impact her farming. What were your thoughts on the experiment, Linda?

LNG I think UBI is a very welcome experiment whose results could provide a model for contextual solutions that take into account unique local socio-cultural environments. The question is how we define income poverty, absolute poverty, and relative poverty in the Kenyan rural ecosystem, separate from the widely known international understanding of these terms. Can Kenya afford to fund a welfare system? Is financial aid or targeted programs by donor countries sustainable? The UBI experiment is an opportunity to reveal and unravel rural socio-economic conditions without making homogeneous assumptions across cultures and social scales. Hopefully, the results will enable us to "see" certain inevitabilities, opportunities, and possible threats, as well as trends associated with different rural regions of Kenya. This could lead to better tailor-made development solutions that are more socio-culturally sensitive.

CHIN-AFRICAN NEO-COLONIALISM

EM As an architect in Africa, the presence of Chinese influence cannot be ignored—from the emerging Chinatowns in cities to the massive infrastructure projects such as the $3.6 billion Standard Gauge Railway Project, the $32 billion Thika superhighway and the $7 billion affordable housing scheme, to mention a few. Recently, I visited the Chinese-built affordable housing in Ngara, and its sheer contrast to the way we live made me feel like the future's not ours—the dizzying verticality there, combined with the sweeping horizontal transport projects slicing through our landscape. Not to mention the free Chinese

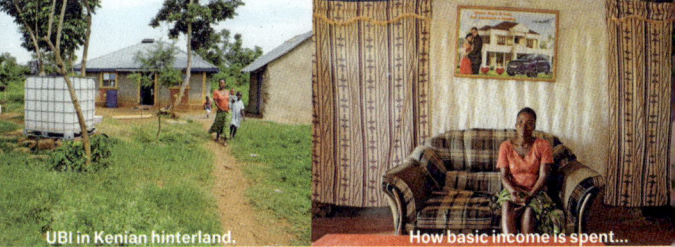

UBI in Kenian hinterland.   How basic income is spent...

being taught in our institutions. Despite the invasion of our sensibilities, I actually agree with this functional neo-colonialism, which brings with it lost freedom and debt we can't afford but also brings actual improvement to the people of Kenya. Even if the chains of British colonial rule are barely shaken off, accepting these invisible Chinese shackles seems to be in our best interest, for the time being.

LNG This makes me so anxious, Etta. I think we are blindly attracted to China's contrasting approach to international relations compared with the EU and US model of human-rights, the donor-recipient relationship, and interventionist and aid-based approaches. Then, along comes China, offering multilateral and equal partnership goodies without the nasty colonial baggage and with a "trade and invest-ment" promise to sweeten the deal. Before long, lo and behold, China is Kenya's largest creditor. We owe China 72 percent of our bilateral debt and 21.3 percent of our external debt. With what we know now, we need to take a beat and review this relationship because I don't think it's working. We did not sign up for this neo-colonial treatment. Is it too late for a divorce? Can we legally ask for full custody of our funded projects?

KENYAN MEGAPROJECTS

LNG Reminiscent of the Silk Road effect, urban centers and new neighborhoods may develop along these financial pathways. Have you heard that the 60-square mile wind farm in Turkana is now operational?

EM Yes I have, and the sight of those windmills eclipsed by the barren Turkana landscape is a contrast that gives me goosebumps. Not because of the sheer humor of seeing camels rubbing their necks on the 330-foot-high turbines, but because of how the vast expanse of the non-

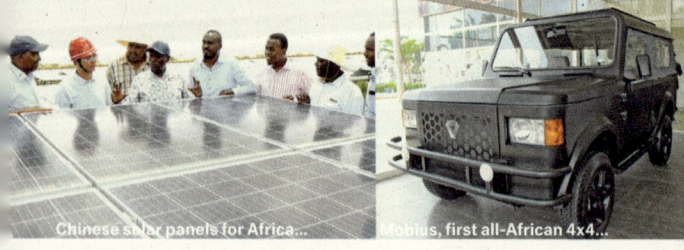

Chinese solar panels for Africa... Mobius, first all-African 4x4...

city is feeding the city. Traditionally, the city was fed through agricultural fields. Now, the city is like an overfed and yet still-hungry bear that relies on the countryside not just for food but for energy. Historically, Kenya, is well known for renewable energy, with 690 megawatts of installed geothermal capacity from the Olkaria geothermal station opened in 1981. The new Turkana wind farm provides 310 megawatts, or 17 percent of our installed electrical capacity, and the 50-megawatt Garissa solar farm, providing two percent of the country's energy. These developments are necessary for sustainability, but the immediate environmental and cultural implications are being overlooked, not least the displacement of the entire village of Sarima in favor of a single windmill. The treatment of the countryside as a tabula rasa for development ignores the fact that there are vital ecosystems for communities and wildlife in these apparently blank spaces.

LNG Yes, Turkana and Garissa are ambitious projects that inch us closer to the Kenyan government's goal for 100 percent renewable energy. It's a very welcome agenda as we all grapple with runaway climate change and the need for cleaner sources of energy. But such projects, located in extremely remote regions of Kenya, have implications for the countryside. There is already a spike in tourism (both local and international) to these regions, attracted by the megaprojects, and the prospect of more reliable and constant power supply in the area. These megaprojects could even see the beginnings of more permanent forms of settlement, in regions which are home to nomadic pastoralists who practice seasonal movement with their herds across communally owned land. Our *Ocha* is changing at such an alarming rate, influenced by a confluence of so many forces beyond our control.

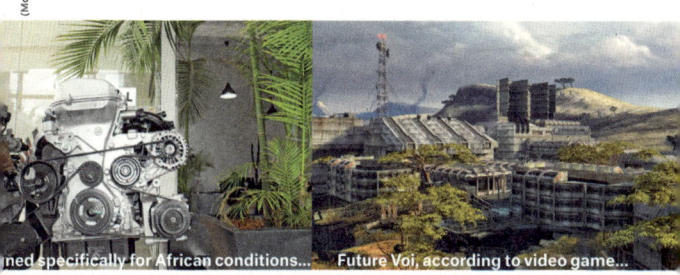

...ned specifically for African conditions... Future Voi, according to video game...

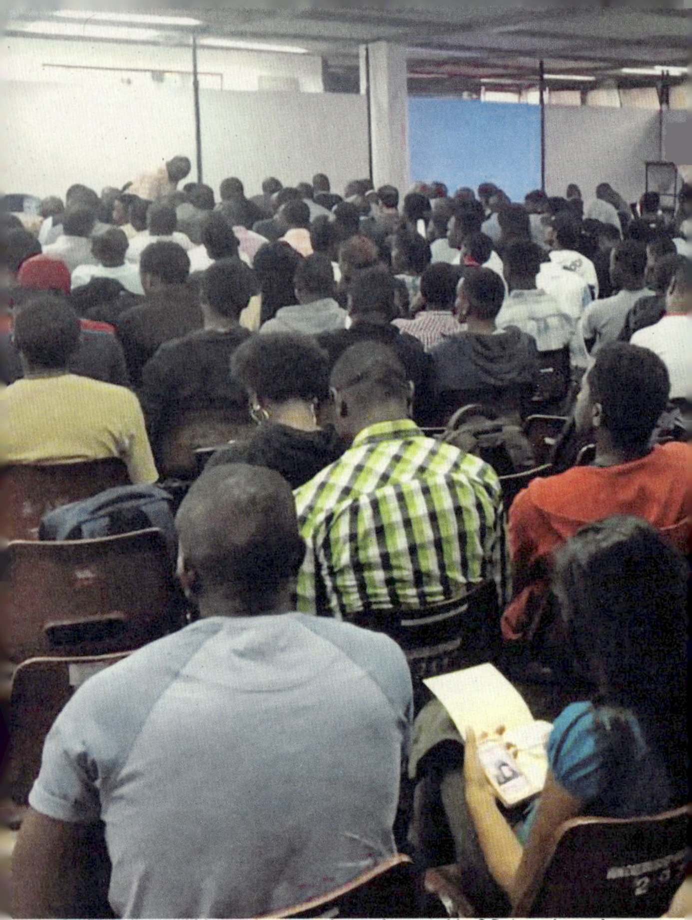

Could Africa avoid becoming a continent of mega cities? By creating a dense...

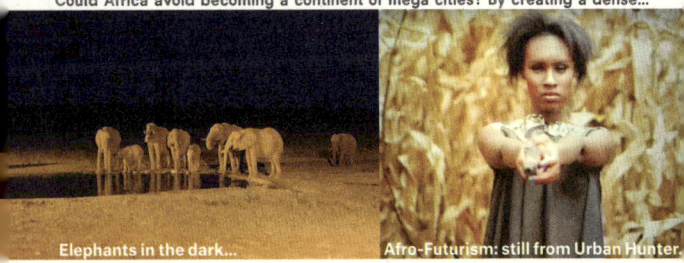

Elephants in the dark...

Afro-Futurism: still from Urban Hunter.

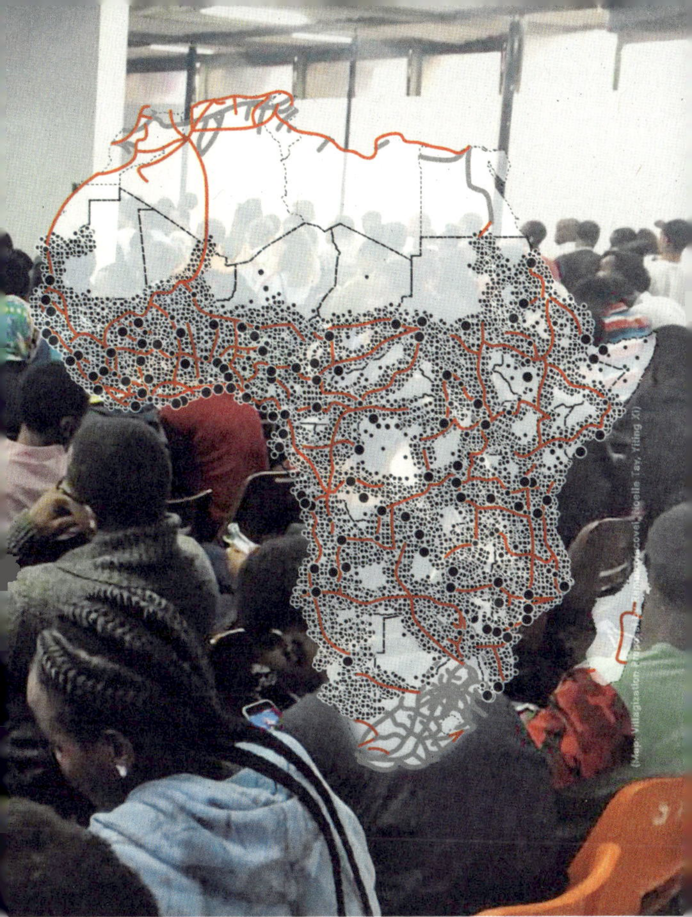

...countryside where traditional and contemporary lives coexist.

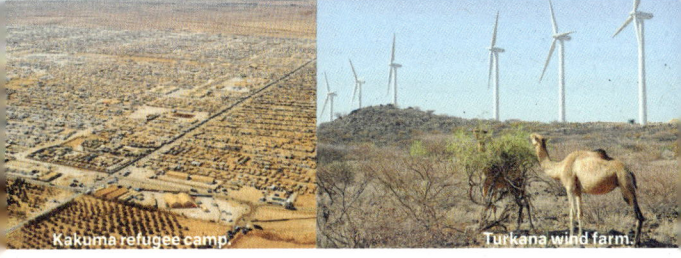

Kakuma refugee camp.

Turkana wind farm.

Botscape
Keigo Kobayashi

Since the triple meltdown in 2011, robots have been employed to infiltrate the reactor at Fukushima Daiichi, since no human can enter there and survive. The robots' mission: investigate the reactor, measure radioactivity, decontaminate, and, most importantly, locate, surveil, and retrieve the fuel debris. More than 40 robot varieties have attempted the mission; many of them "died" along the way, due to radiation frying their circuitry or debris proving insurmountable. Some now lie abandoned inside the reactor. The following robot story takes place in Fukushima—and it's no coincidence that it does —but it's not *that* story. It's even more unexpected; a response to the triple-threat facing Japan: natural disasters, an aging and shrinking population, and crumbling infrastructure.

Japan is already deep into its infamous demographic crisis, the double whammy of depopulation and aging. By 2100, the population will roughly halve, shrinking to early 19th-century levels, and the proportion of elderly to working population will be about 1:1. Every worker will essentially gain a statistical grandparent they have to support, on top of their own family.

Depopulation will hit the Japanese countryside hardest. Eighty percent of Japan is mountainous, largely uninhabitable and unworkable. Modern infrastructure connects metropolitan areas, bridging and tunneling through the rugged terrain in between. Much of this infrastructure was built in a frenzy of reconstruction between the end of the Second World War and the run-up to the 1960 Tokyo Olympics, Japan's redemptive reentry onto the world stage. Like the same generation of infrastructure in the United States, Japan's roads, bridges, and tunnels are coming to the end of their natural life. Repairs and rebuilding will be needed en masse in the coming decades. But who will do the work, if everybody is gone, too old, or overburdened? Hundreds of towns and villages in Japan's countryside are facing extinction in the 21st century. A combination of depopulation and the associated decline in tax revenue means there will be no money and no local governance to sustain these areas or protect them from natural disasters. Inhabitants may be forced to move to cities, or live like nomads across lawless

areas, or—in a dream scenario—become self-organizing with highly devolved forms of community power.
Will the triple threat facing Japan trigger grand plans like those birthed after the war, but this time with a shrinking rather than a booming population? When we went to the Ministry of Economy, Trade and Industry to ask about their Robot Revolution plans as a means of handling shrinkage and the imminent collapse of the nation's infrastructure, they told us: "Well, did you know that we're constructing a robot testing field in Fukushima?"

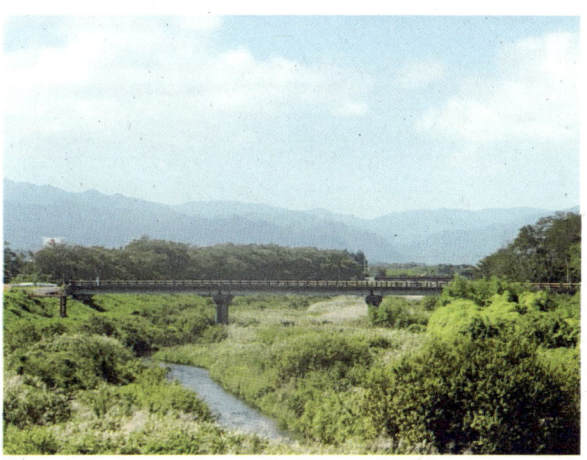

So we hit the road, myself, RK and PB. We drove north from Tokyo, through green and rolling countryside, with an element or two of infrastructure embedded...

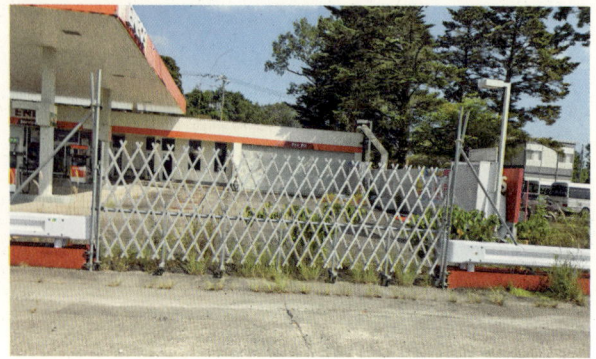

Three hours and 155 miles later, the Joban Expressway threads through the ghost town of Okuma where we begin seeing metal concertina fences in front of nearly every premises, vegetation overgrowing in gardens. The town looks intact, but it's completely empty—except for a steady stream of heavy-duty trucks (more on those later).

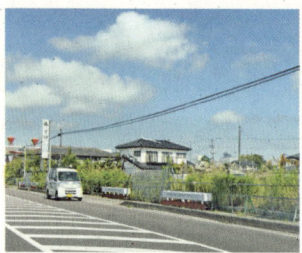 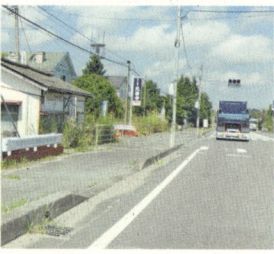

Fifty thousand people are still unable to return to their homes across the entire Fukushima Daiichi evacuation zone. Original estimates for the cost and duration of the cleanup were $50 billion and 40 years; now, it's $188 billion and the time frame is even more uncertain.

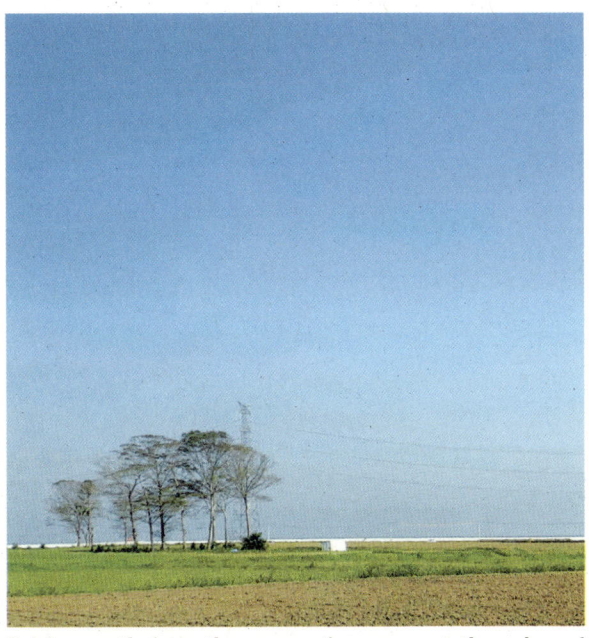

Driving north from the evacuation zone, at the edge of huge expanses that used to be agriculture (the soil ruined by saltwater from the tsunami), we see a thin white line hugging the Pacific coast. This is the new sea wall, built after the tsunami inundated the area in 2011. Despite the radioactivity and enforced emptiness around here, mitigation and regeneration projects like this are widespread. The Fukushima Innovation Coast initiative is trying to lure industries lost since 2011, in the fields of agriculture, forestry, fisheries, energy, and recycling... and robotics.

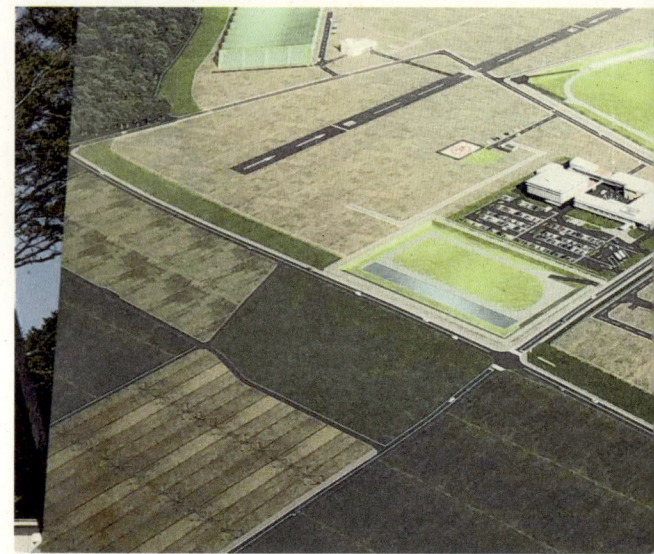

Twenty miles (30 km) north of Fukushima Daiichi, near Minamisoma City, we finally arrive at our destination: the Fukushima Robot Test Field, built on a perfectly flat 125-acre tabula rasa created after farmlands and houses were washed away by the 2011 tsunami. It is the first facility of its kind in the world. Parts are still under construction; we can only look through the fences. Inside what looks like a military compound or small airport is in fact a simulation of a city / exurban condition, meant for testing the robots that can—or must—respond to natural disasters in Japan and take responsibility for the maintenance of infrastructure when there aren't enough people left to do it.

The facility includes, at 1:1 scale,

- the Development Platform Area for preparing and analysing robot performance, and indoor testing with controlled areas of wind, rain, fog, water, temperature, humidity, vibration, and radio waves;
- the Urban Field residential zone, which can be flooded to test aquatic reconnaissance and recovery robots;

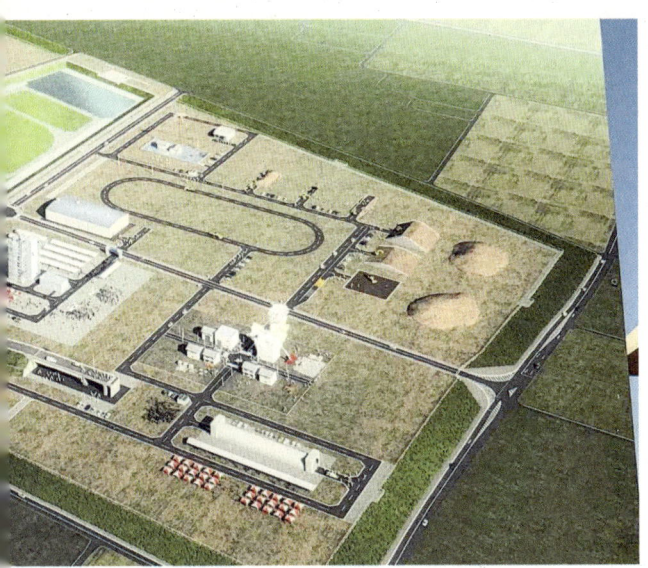

- an unfinished segment of an elevated highway for testing robotic repair of infrastructure damaged by time or disaster;
- the Test Plant, a skeleton of a residential tower for testing rescue and repair capabilities after earthquakes or fire;
- a segment of a tunnel, another vital piece of infrastructure that will be left in the hands of robots.

It would be tempting to call this an uncanny dreamscape of disaster preparation if everything in it—the structures, the scenarios, the robots that will inhabit it—weren't so realistic and pragmatic. There is nothing sci-fi about this place. You can already test robots here for around $250 for a half day session. But there are none in sight the day we visit.

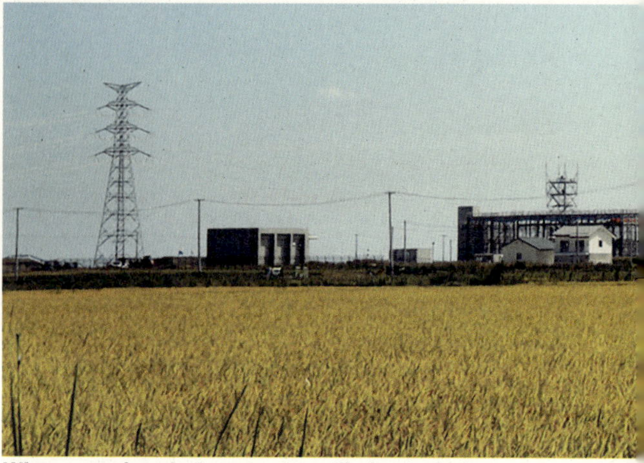

When completed, the test site will also include:

- Debris and Landslide Field
- runway for unmanned fixed wing drones (and, according to the website: "It can also be used as a test facility in the early stages of flying car development");
- wind tunnel;
- unmanned vehicle test track, where a solar car was recently tested by the Fukushima Techno Academy;
- drone testing field, covered by a large net, where drones and pilots can be trained in collision avoidance, emergency landing, and "falling." One drone test carried out here involving the transport of blood over a distance of six miles, and dropping it for emergency transfusions. It was conducted by Tokyo Metropolitan Bokuto Hospital, Toho University School of Medicine, and Keio University SFC Takeda Keiji Laboratory.

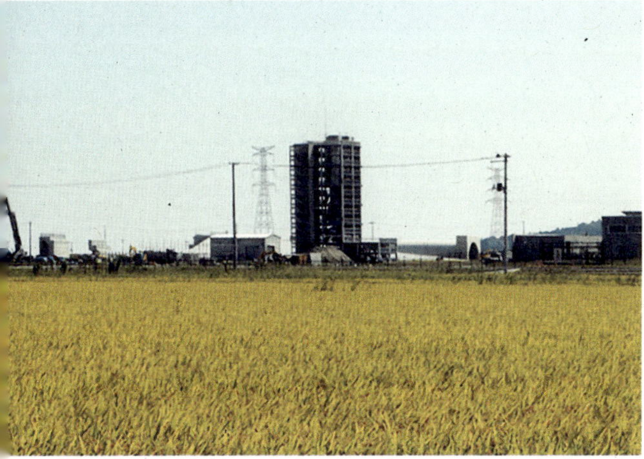

The Urban Field contains four houses, two nondescript buildings, intersections with traffic lights; a 164 x 62-foot part of it can be flooded at will. Robots will practice obstacle removal and conduct search and rescue training.

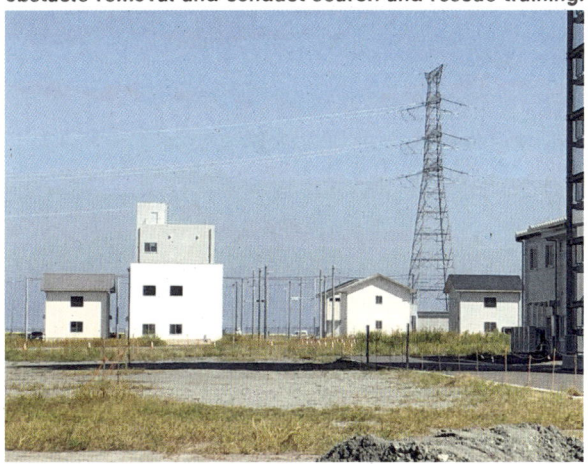

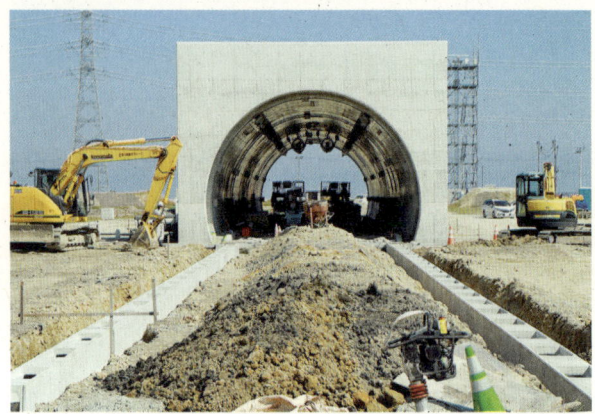
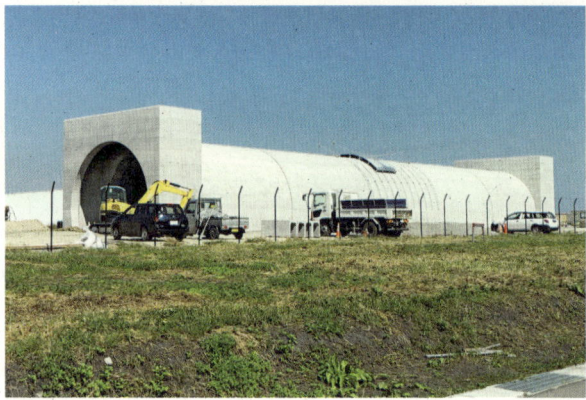

The 164-foot-long test tunnel—which will be featured at the World Robot Summit in August 2020—will stage traffic accidents, collapses, and the effects of aging. Japan has 11,000 tunnels connecting its mountainous and remote countryside areas. Forty percent of the tunnels will be more than 50 years old by 2033 and in desperate need of maintenance.

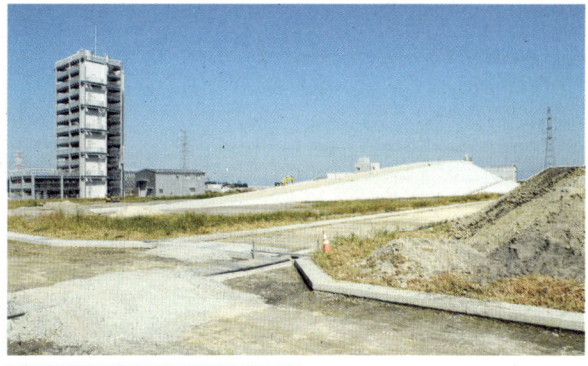

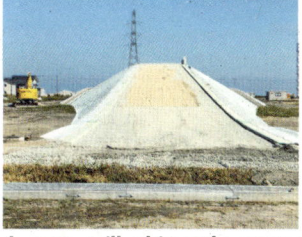

A ramp will ultimately connect to a highway bridge still under construction. According to the government's 2014 "Final Warning" assessment, 700,000 bridges across Japan are already too aged or possibly too decayed to be left unrepaired.

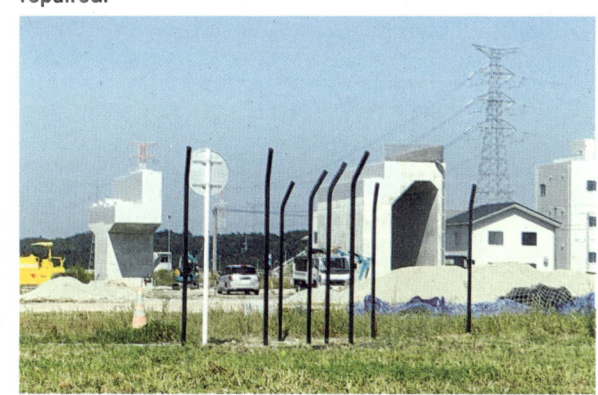

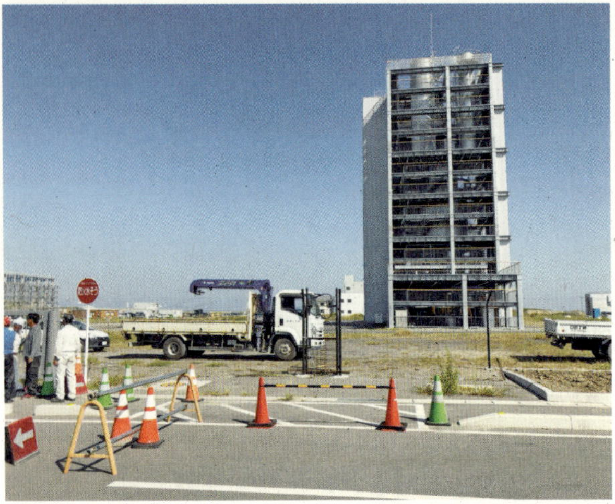

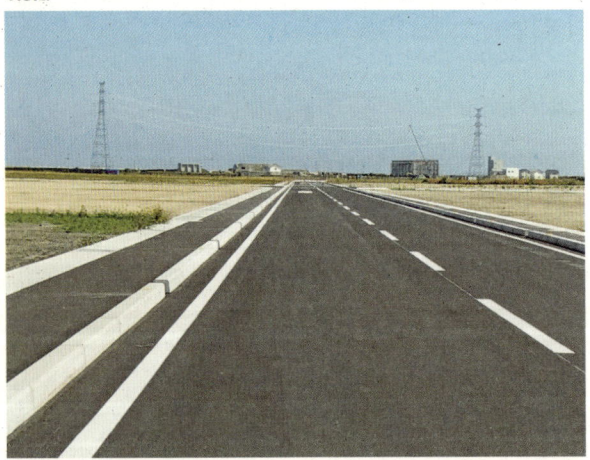

The Test Plant "building" is crammed with ducts, stairs, ladders, and catwalks in which robotic maintenance in various disaster and deterioration scenarios can be tested. Close by are the only humans we saw during the whole visit.

A freshly minted road connects Minamisoma City with the Reconstruction Industrial Park, built post-2011.

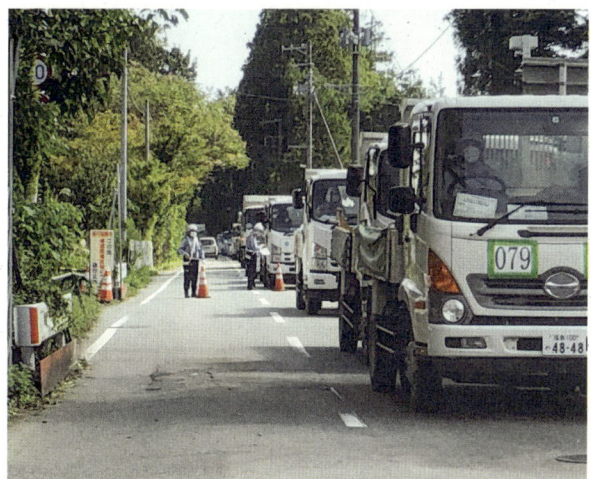

Heading back south, into the evacuation zone, we see a chain of trucks and workmen wearing white masks. the trucks are transporting radioactive soil to sites near the nuclear power plant for "temporary" storage. So far, 17.4 million cubic yards of contaminated soil has been stored in Fukushima Prefecture.

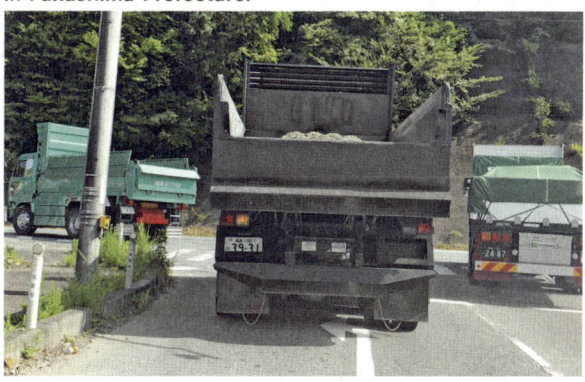

Disasters—sudden, gradual, inexorable—demand unthinkable amounts of labor and time. Seeing the incessant work and traffic of so many machines and people here, the robot rationale becomes understandable.

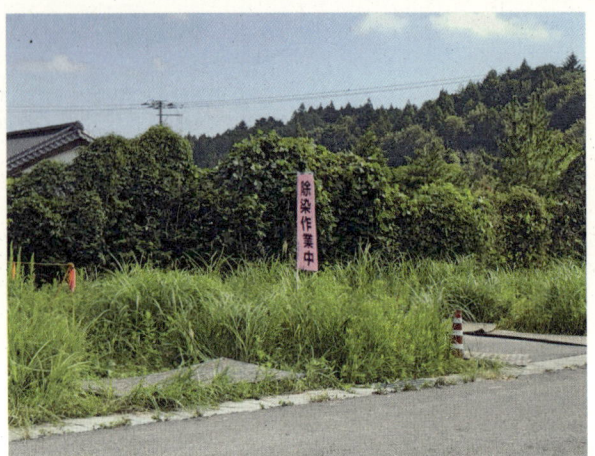

"Decontamination in progress."

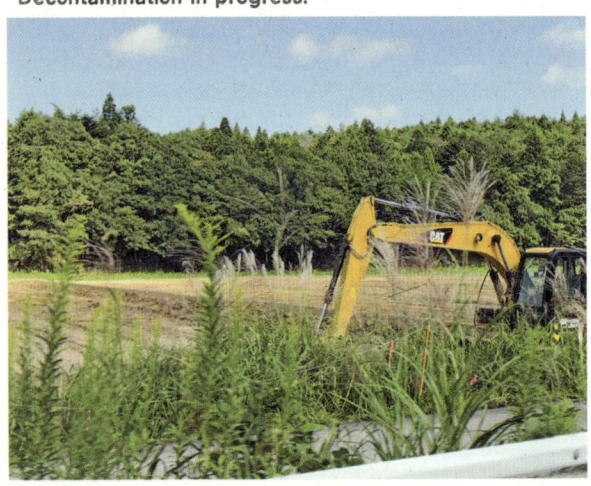

A contaminated former agricultural field is stripped of its topsoil...

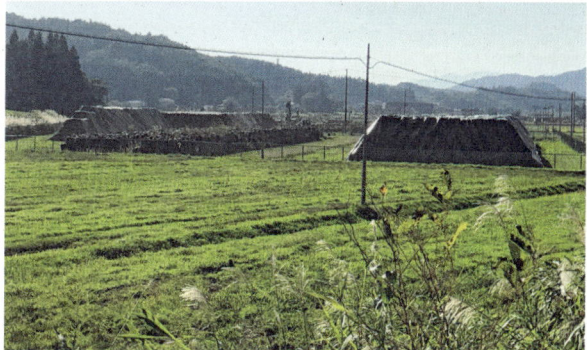

Its resting place: a ziggurat entombed in thick plastic.

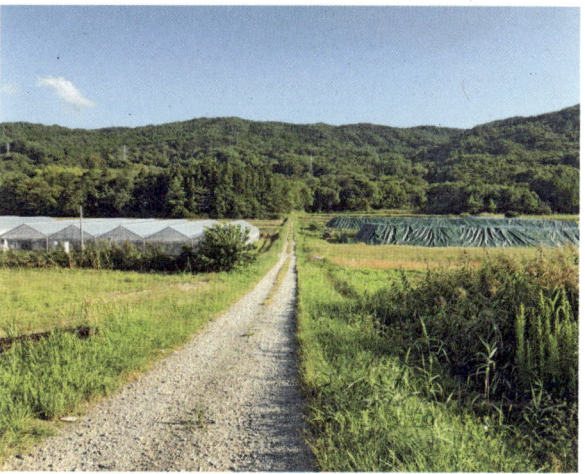

In Iidate village, we encounter a before and after: greenhouses for strawberries on the left, heaps of contaminated soil on the right. A temporary and inevitable cohabitation of the controllable and the uncontrollable.

A few weeks after our visit, Typhoon No. 19, aka Hagibis, damaged and submerged parts of the Fukushima Robot Test Field.

(Photos: Petra Blaisse, Keigo Kobayashi, RK)

Sea Lovers
Ingo Niermann

Large parts of the sea are used in a similar fashion as the countryside: Fish and algae are cultivated in farms, the seabed is mined for oil and other natural resources, wind and tidal farms deliver renewable energy, cruise ships and yachts serve as nomadic recreational resorts and diving as undersea hiking. Pioneers move offshore. The sea is the new countryside. Still, its liquidity and enormous size sustain substantial differences. It's not feasible to claim ownership of the oceans' main constituent — water. The oceans slip away from national and personal ownership just as they slip away from national and personal liability. Our particularly exploitive treatment of the sea —overfishing, mining, and polluting—corresponds to our difficulty in creating an affective relationship with its inhabitants. We usually don't see them, we don't hear them, and when we dive down to them, it's harmful, if not impossible, to touch them. Sea creatures are too prickly, poisonous, anxious, or delicate. The Sea Lovers, a subdivision of the Army of Love, train for a more intimate relation with the ocean. Nourished by the knowledge of indigenous sea nomads, ocean scientists, and passionate divers, they learn to enjoy not just the cute and the intelligent but also the gloomy and the uncanny. Together they envision a *mare amoris*—a sea of love— where all creatures help and celebrate each other.

AMPHIBIOUS SEA PARK

During the Industrial Revolution, amusement parks played a major role in accustoming the masses to its auspicious and frightening implications. In the first years of the 20th century, Coney Island introduced millions of people of all classes to seminal inventions and speculations like electric lighting, skydiving, space travel, modern warfare, electrocution, infant incubation, rapid acceleration, and public lewdness. What would a Luna Park look like that keeps up with our amphibious future? In contemporary sea parks, visitors stay fully dressed and watch well-behaved marine mammals from a safe distance as they perform acrobatic tricks in crystal-clear water. Sea parks are aquatic circuses plus water rides.

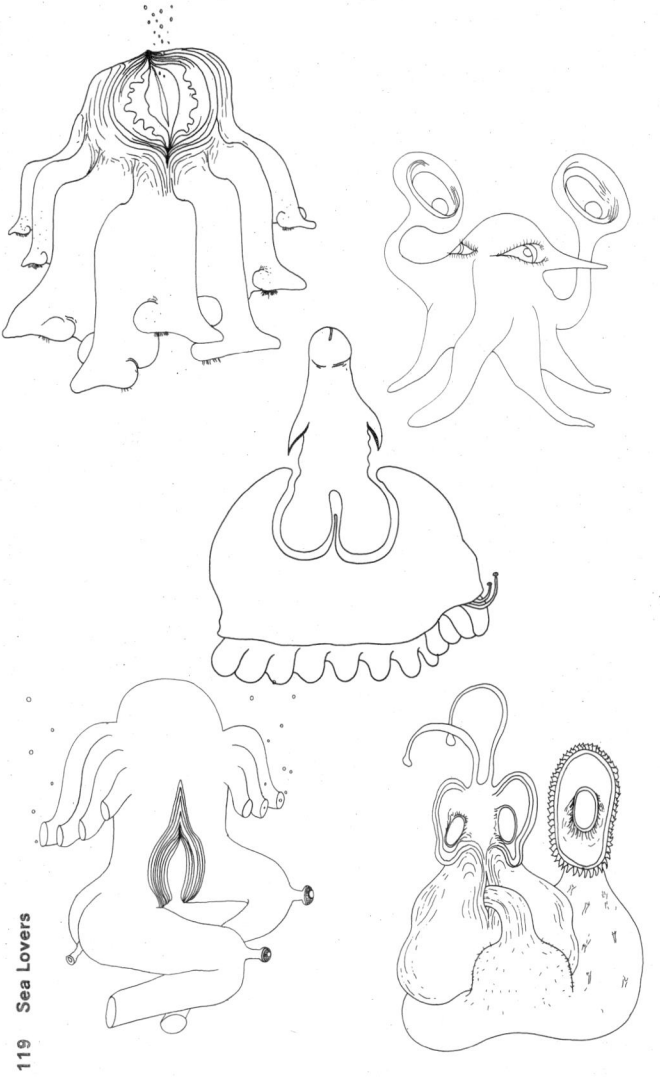

Ingo Niermann, Eduardo Navarro & Esther Hunziker
"Wet Gods," HD, 2020. Commissioned by TBA21–Academy.

An amphibious sea park, in contrast, engages us personally with the sea. It invites us to communicate with sea animals through movement and machine translation. It invites us to imitate or dress up and interact as fantastic creatures of the sea. It doesn't shy away from thrilling us with the ugly, the slimy, and the dangerous. It speculates and experiments on how to make the ocean more joyful and less gruesome.

SEA PETS

What sea creature could love us unconditionally and make us love unconditionally like a dog? Tease and seduce us like a cat? The first bet is dolphins. They speak, they regularly have to go up for air, and always look like they are smiling. But dolphins need a lot of food and a large pool to swim. They are desperate for the company of their own kind and can easily turn violent in captivity. The octopus could be a more convenient sea pet. It continues to fascinate us as a strikingly accomplished yet completely different life-form: It has three hearts and blue blood, squeezes through tiny holes and slits, and each of its eight arms operates autonomously and is covered with individually grasping suckers. The octopus as the great other has inspired legends about gigantic monsters like the kraken. But in recent years, octopuses have rapidly gained in popularity for their decentralized brain, their enormous flexibility, and their unique ability to camouflage their surface and form. Octopuses are able to differentiate humans, to like or dislike them, to develop trust or resentment.
What makes octopuses most unique as pets is how they feel to the touch: the slimy wetness; the soft head; the tentative sucking; the speed at which several arms entwine your arm, grip it, and suck it; knowing that they taste and see with their skin. Octopuses are quiet, you don't have to walk them, and they are available in sizes from an arm span of one inch to 13 feet. Unfortunately they are messy eaters, need live food (at least while growing), spend most of the day hiding, and don't get older than a few years. But our mutual domestication has not yet begun. How intelligent and wise could octopuses become if they didn't die so young? Will future octopuses be able to stay outside the water or will they get us to live in the water? With their multitasking and shape-shifting skills, octopuses will teach if not replace us.

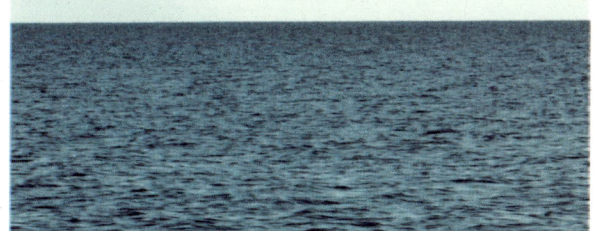

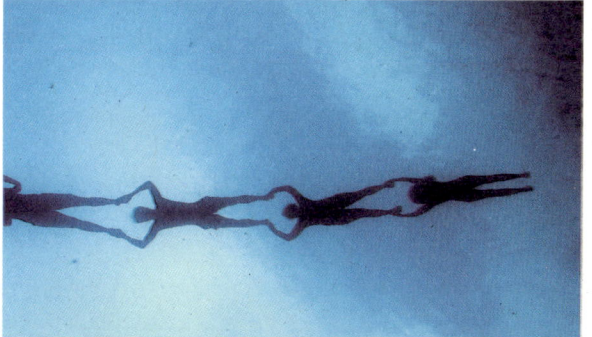

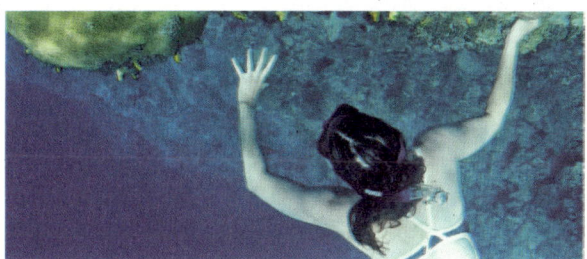

Wet Gods populate a future sea of love.

Sea Lovers

Ingo Niermann with Ana Maria Millán, Roman Bayarri,
Ville Haimala, Franziska Aigner & Dan Bodan
"Sea Lovers", HD, 2020. Commissioned by TBA21–Academy.

LIQUID PRIVACY

We have to feel safe to let others in. We have to secure our privacy to avoid resentment and xenophobia. That's why the next trillion dollar enterprise won't be about connecting but about keeping one's distance. While social media allows us to get into contact without any effort, wherever we are, this endeavor will allow us to be by ourselves without any effort, wherever we are.
On the sea, there is no place to hide beyond the outlines of one's vessel. Here it's even more urgent to establish a new mode of privacy than on land. And in fact, it's easier. On a level field without any fixed obstacles where all objects follow a rather straight course at a steady speed, there isn't too much computation needed to keep them all at a proper distance by smoothly altering their speed and direction. On international waters, most vessels are already on autopilot, monitored via an automat.
 This liquid privacy can also be applied to keep boats away from sensitive sea animals or to keep predators and their prey at a distance. Both receive signals to shy away from each other. Instead, the predators are lured to artificial prey and the prey to birth control. The sea becomes a place where Jainism is not just a personal practice but a general disposition. The ocean turns truly common—and not just for humankind.

SEA HUG

The sea lifts us, pushes us, and glides away to be seamlessly replaced by its kind. Nobody hugs more evenly, more expansively, more patiently than the sea. All we have to do is comply with this hug and not fear it. When a wave is breaking, we have to roll ourselves into its enormous hug. When the water is calm and caresses us in the smoothest way, we just have to stay still, except for some occasional, thankful little strokes. When we jump into the water, it encloses us in no time. To hug a tree is a unilateral, paternalistic gesture. The tree can't initiate, return, refuse, or escape the encounter. Is it intrigued or repelled by our microbes, touch, and smell? We have no idea. When we let the sea hug us, we take the receptive, enduring position that we used to assign to the sea. We can experience this hug on our own, together with friends, or in groups of hundreds and thousands. We can hug other humans while being hugged

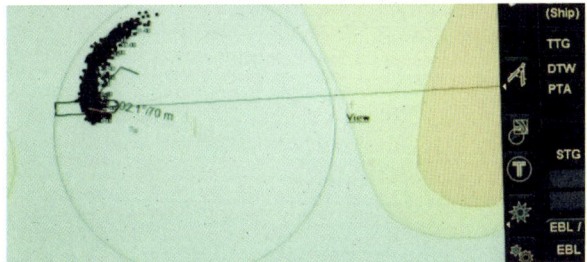

by the sea. Several of us can cling, hum, and sweat together as one fluent, gurgling, seeping mass. We can reconfigure as a floating chain that can stop certain ships from entering a harbor. The chain manifests in collective humming, singing, and swinging. Or we build circles and gently bump into unknown parts of others' bodies—trusting each other just as the sea.

AQUATIC LOVE ROBOT

As we move in water or have water moving around us, it touches us all over our bodies. By moving water we can touch others in a mediated, softened, and extended way. Even if we touch each other directly, the lack of gravity and the resistance of the water will soften our movements. Even if a wave or someone presses us down (not for too long), we will come up again easily. As soon as we get close to a lake or the sea, sensing its breeze and its vastness, we relax and open up to undress, to touch and to love. In addition, the aquatic love robot allows us to breathe like fish. It lets us look not just through it, at others; it also shines in response to our movements and moods. The same applies to sounds and smells. The aquatic love robot grips, caresses, kisses, and penetrates us with varying densities of water and allows us to respond in the same way. Whatever we feel like, the aquatic love robot exposes or shields us accordingly.

It's the sea that created us. We are not limited to mystical ("oceanic") contemplation, we can actually enter the sea and celebrate our origins in amphibious devotion. To give something back we could turn the sea into the greatest intelligence and benevolence ever—*mare amoris*, the Sea of Love. © Ingo Niermann

Villages with Chinese Characteristics
Stephan Petermann

"不管黑猫白猫，能捉老鼠的就是好猫"
"It doesn't matter if the cat is black or white, as long as it catches mice."—Deng Xiaoping, Communist Youth League conference on July 7, 1962

China celebrates its specific economic system by adding "...with Chinese characteristics" to it. There might also be a countryside "with Chinese characteristics." In parallel to decades of urbanization, the Chinese government has—with much less fanfare and global attention—been dramatically redefining its countryside. With a long-standing political foundation in the countryside—the 1949 revolution was largely a victory of the countryside over the city, and the nation's subsequent leaders have all had strong rural ties—and with investments in infrastructure and poverty alleviation unmatched by Western counterparts, China's stage-setting for urban-rural connections in the 21st century might be equally unanticipated. The UN's World Population Prospects suggest the Chinese countryside, together with the rural population in Africa, is facing the strongest demographic transition in the world. They predict 300 million people will be moving from the countryside to the city in the coming decades. But seeing the current difficulties in urban areas, with large cities like Shanghai and Beijing struggling and even shrinking, will this actually happen? Migration from the countryside to large production plants in the southeast of China has largely come to a halt and shifted to more localized migration to smaller cities close by. There's a growing desire for community-based living both in off- and online communities. A new generation might be giving a totally new direction to what China will look like.

The latest installment of the Five-Year Plan announced a new era for the countryside as a national priority. The following are reports from China's countryside "villages"—often full of skyscrapers—gathered from over two years of visits with architecture students from the Central Academy of Fine Arts (CAFA), in Beijing. The following are on-the-ground observations from prototypical communities embracing digital growth, finding new modes of leisure, new ways to accelerate food production, and even radical new ways to stay—or appear—the same as they have always been. Taobao village, Dong Feng, February 22, 2017 Dong Feng in Jiangsu province, a four-hour train ride at 190 mph from Beijing, is one of the first and most successful prototypes of more than 4,000 so-called Taobao villages centered around e-commerce. The development of Dong Feng presented, at least in theory, a first step towards a new mode of urbanism, with organization, production, storage, and distribution all done from the countryside—and the traditional position of the city as a hub up for drastic reconsideration.

Dong Feng used to be a village based on pig breeding and the waste recycling industry. But after a visit to IKEA Shanghai in 2005, three young villagers decided to set up an online store combining IKEA's flat-packing efficiency with cheaper, Chinese-inspired furniture designs. They sell their flat-packs through Taobao.com. Launched in 2003 as part of Alibaba (China's ingenious mash-up of eBay and Amazon), Taobao is a platform for local producers to create e-shops and sell the products they make directly to customers across China, from electronics to furniture and local produce. After initial success in cities, Taobao sales began accelerating in the countryside. In recognition of this growth, rural areas with a certain concentration of online shops and a collective 10 million renminbi ($1.4 million) turnover qualify as a Taobao village. This entitles the village to government subsidies for training, marketing, and expanding infrastructure connected to the platform. The number of Taobao shops in Dong Feng has increased from three in the beginning to nearly 16,000 when we visit. More than 35,000 jobs are connected to Taobao commerce. The previous "Singles' Day" (the largest offline and online shopping day in the world) the village had a turnover of 493 million renminbi ($69 million). Dong Feng's best seller is a bunk bed, also known as "The Bed," of which 433,000 copies were sold in 2017. Upon arrival we are welcomed by the snarling sound of power tools cutting and sanding wood and cheerful ting-tong smartphone sounds. The success of Taobao is fueled by the Aliwangwang messenger app, which allows consumers and producers to talk directly and customize their orders. With every message, you hear the ting-tong sound. We meet Mr. Sun, one of the first Taobao traders in the village, at his four-story office along Taobao Road. with the messy appeal of a Silicon Valley startup. The ting-tong sounds form a cloud

around young workers processing orders, texting clients, and refilling inkjet printers churning out IKEA-like instruction manuals. We are greeted by Sun himself. According to Song Yu, our Chinese collaborator at CAFA, the handsome Sun is clearly media trained. But the picture he presents to us, after a decade or more of unmitigated growth, is not entirely rosy. "The situation is delicate," he says. "The competition is very strong and the emphasis on cost reduction is making it difficult for everyone to make profits." Sun takes us on a tour. After striding through the ground-floor workshops where middle-aged men and women cut, sand, and treat the wood that will become Taobao furniture, we stop at the design department. Design is practiced in an eclectic fin-de-siècle way with around ten people mixing existing templates and molding collages together in 3ds Max, reshaping the online shop almost in real time and for individual customers. Sun's shop seems to be doing what 3D printers were supposed to be doing by now: customized design for the masses. Sun drives us down the road to the Party Secretary building in his new but dusty BMW 7 Series for a meeting with the deputy secretary of the village. We hope to resolve the lack of accurate sources for documenting the spatial development of the village for our research studio. Dong Feng's furniture production industry began as a home-based enterprise, with the first factories emerging within the traditional courtyard houses. The explosion of Taobao triggered the construction of multistory factories attached to the houses. Most of the factories, like Sun's, sprung up along Taobao Road. They function as factory-IKEA-fulfillment center all in one, where fabrication, sales, and distribution all happen in the same spaces, without the physical presence of the customer. Small- and medium-sized factories continuously consume large heaps of wood and spit out cardboard flatpacks awaiting delivery. Along the road we pass young people smoking cigarettes and spray-painting table parts. The average age seems to deviate from the cliché of "dying" villages. Dong Feng skews young, with a considerable amount of people having come from nearby villages. The village is plastered with slogans like:
"A pleasant wealth miracle, easy like a trifling matter," "To be rich, e-commerce leads the way Put down the hoe, pick up the mouse."
Other slogans promote equal rights and are gender sensitive, like "Women are powerful, busy with Business."

Compared with Facebook's "Move fast and break things" or Amazon's "Invent and simplify," Taobao's propaganda seems more socially considerate, inclusive, and optimistic.

At the secretary office, the deputy secretary enthusiastically greets us. He admits that Dong Feng is like a mini-Dubai during its most intense phase of construction: growing too fast to record. He corrects our maps by hand, expanding the village's footprint in the relatively indistinct flat delta area. Our final stop in Dong Feng is the rural e-commerce HQ, a large multistory building to showcase the village's success. A young woman wearing a hoodie guides us through the 21,500 square foot (2,000 m2) showroom. The central item in the exhibition is The Bed. Graphs on the walls show logarithmic growth. In the back of the exhibition room there's a huge model of Dong Feng's newly planned expansion, which both private and public parties are feverishly building. It is a strict modern plan where all aspects of the new Taobao economy are separated into distinct clusters for logistics, production, research and investment, and living. Where Taobao initially broke with Fordist production, combining designing, making and selling in single spaces, the new Dong Feng is reverting to a Fordist model of production. The new town avoids all of the ad-hoc qualities of the existing fabric that led to Dong Feng's success in the first place.

There's something else: with signs saying "do not photograph" posted everywhere, the village feels at points like a classified military zone. Secrecy thrives. Sun hinted to this, that the success of some has made neighbors envious and fueled a fierce competition to cut costs, degrading not only the quality of production but also the environment. Like other internet customer-to-customer (c2c) platforms like Uber, Dong Feng is suffering from a race to the bottom. Social cohesion in the village is under pressure. Successful products are immediately copied by others, which leads to the same product being offered in different versions by dozens, if not hundreds of different Taobao shops. Affluent Chinese are increasingly avoiding buying products on Taobao because of their high chance of being "fake" or simply of poor quality. Instead of selling what is unique, Taobao shops sell what is popular, and by saving on costs, they undermine themselves. The freedom that the platform was supposed to generate for these vendors, paradoxically might have to be better controlled if their businesses and villages are to keep on thriving. Energy–Beijing, March 2, 2017 In Beijing, in a hall packed with students, Prof. Wen Tiejun announces that things will have to radically change in the Chinese countryside. Wen Tiejun is professor at Renmin University, board member of the China Agricultural Bank, and has the ear of the president for agricultural policy. He presents a collection of crises, first and foremost the trade surplus, which he sees impacting countryside production facilities. Another crisis is China's reliance on Western farming methods, which will have to change due to the resulting soil, water, and climate degradation. China will need to revert back to its 40 centuries of experience of regenerative farming and permaculture. Senior members of the Communist Party vehemently agree and present different development models and proposals for the countryside, like reorganizing the complex land use rights systems. When the session ends, the students—unaccustomed to political visits at the school—stay and continue the discussions. The absence of the pessimism that usually attends rural discussions is compelling: it's the most ambitious countryside meeting I have ever witnessed. Greenhouse bonanza–Shouguang, April 20, 2017 A month later I am on the 14th floor of a skyscraper in Shouguang in Shandong province, overlooking an endless landscape of greenhouses encircling the city with one of the students and a farming couple. It feels Houellebecqian. Earlier that day we reached Shouguang in another brand new high-speed train from Beijing. The last 15 minutes of the journey were spent slicing through a landscape of endless greenhouses. Shouguang is almost twice the size of Europe's largest greenhouse area, around Almera in Spain, and about 30 times the size of Manhattan. What I see around me is at least as impressive as the rise of the Chinese megacities. When we arrived at one of the towers on the city's perimeter, we rang a doorbell randomly. The occupants, Zhou Mingan and Zhang Chunhua—who unsurprisingly turned out to be greenhouse farmers—invited us to come up to their apartment. It's the early afternoon and they invite us to join them at lunch. We get apples. They kindly show us their apartment, which is roughly the same size as their previous house in a village that was torn down. The place is clean and bright, the floors are tiled, and dirty shoes—shoes still get dirty in a greenhouse—are left neatly at the door. After lunch, Mingan and Chunhua invite us to their greenhouse. We emerge from the tower's underground parking, and drive through the urban fabric around the towers until the surroundings start to shift from urban to Shouguang's version of rural, with building blocks interspersed with more and more greenhouses. There is hardly any signage. We wouldn't have a chance of finding the right greenhouse without our guides. Small trucks and minivans drive around the maze, laden with boxes of vegetables and supplies.

Space has become an issue in Shouguang. Only seven percent of China's landmass is suitable for farming. But by employing greenhouses, Shouguang uses 0.0002 percent of China's landmass and produces five percent of China's vegetables. Since the late 70s, when most of the land around Shouguang was still occupied by field crops and small villages, the area has managed to increase its production of vegetables tenfold. The rise of greenhouse production firstly swallowed the crop production, and more recently also some of the villages, which were demolished or concentrated. The shortage of space is now forcing the "village" to grow upwards. We park along the concrete road and walk up to their greenhouse. It's a so-called "fifth generation" greenhouse, built on top of an older village in 2016 (the same year the tower they live in was built). You enter the greenhouse through a little house, followed by a narrow cave-like passage. It's hot inside, at least 10 degrees hotter and more humid than outside. On one side there is a massive dike-like wall, around eight meters high. On the other side, slender pre-cast concrete columns support a lightweight aluminum structure covered by a transparent plastic membrane. Rows upon row of lush plants grow their way upwards on strings. Mingan explains the logic of the greenhouse. The hefty walls are made of soil excavated from the ground. They collect solar heat during the day and release it during the cold night. The walls also protect the plants from prevailing cold winds coming from inland. Chunhua looks at the flowers of the plants and grabs a small paintbrush, which he uses to pollinate the flowers—a surprisingly delicate and small-scale action. They are farming eggplant this year. A gamble, but it's paying off for now. His wife is putting the big eggplants in large Styrofoam boxes. The waste goes to a bio-gas station nearby, built from what was leftover from the government subsidies they received when they were instructed to move. Mingan and Chunhua explain how they are currently leasing two farms. You can't fully own the greenhouses as all land in China is public. The lease of the greenhouses are distributed according to families registered in the area and their size. (Some families choose to outsource their rights to a plot of land.) The couple's other farm is managed by migrant laborers from Hainan province. Like in the West, farming is increasingly the terrain of the poor. At sunset we climb the earth wall of the solar farm. On top there are thick sheets of polyester. We use them to cover the plastic greenhouse roof, tucking the greenhouse into bed, and drive back to Shouguang. We park the car in the underground parking and go one floor up, where several farmers are practicing line dancing. On another floor there is a gym, pool table, and lecture space. Tonight there will be a lecture on calligraphy, but they also show popular movies. On the 14th floor it's dark now with the cityscape illuminating the greenhouses beyond. The Big Beige Books–Beijing, October 17, 2017 The CAFA students are ecstatic. In Xi Jinping's speech announcing the next Five-Year Plan, he declared that the countryside is now the nation's absolute priority. Many Chinese leaders have stressed the importance of the countryside, but Xi's words open the door for new development models, experimental plans, and funding. The students see good business ahead. Work is getting thinner for architects in urban areas and there are signs of a slowdown in the economy. Xi's speech coincided with me finishing reading two volumes of his collected writings. It seemed bizarre that I could hardly find reviews of his work, which seems clearly important. When I mention it to the students, they look puzzled. They always have a hard time understanding what Xi means when he speaks. I give them the English translation and they tell me it's less poetic, more concrete. It is a tough read. The book is impressive, superficial, and deep at the same time. Superficial due to the repetitive axioms on justice, honesty, and innovation—not unlike international political and corporate speech. Deep as you see how it shapes the country. China's concentration of power leads to every phrase becoming a slogan. If Xi would reveal detailed proposals it would lead to a mad rush of Party members trying to please and up their ranks. But this also appears strange since guidebooks are immensely popular in China. The publication department of the National Library specializes in wonderful books ranging from manuals for fixing high-speed trains, to instructions for making a rocket engine, to a guide to experimental surgery. Shortly after his speech, CAFA receives a letter from Xi congratulating the school on its 100-year anniversary, praising its achievements, and putting it forward as an example to the nation. Over lunch we ask the school leadership what the letter means. The school leadership says they studied the letter carefully for several days with the management, but do not reveal what they concluded.

Lucid waters and lush mountains–Yubulu and Banwang, June 16, 2018 "Lucid waters and lush mountains are invaluable assets. China must pursue the vision of innovative, coordinated, green and open development that is for everyone, accelerate forming spatial patterns, industrial structures, production and living modes that are resource-saving and environmentally-friendly, and provide time and space for the natural ecology to rehabilitate."—Xi Jinping

In 2014, the government of Guizhou in the southwest commissioned the dean of CAFA's architecture department Lv Pinying to redevelop two small hamlets as part of a project to rejuvenate the countryside. Pinying's passion as an architect lies in the countryside, focusing on the preservation of vernacular crafts and intangible heritage. Yubulu, one of the hamlets Pinying worked on, is a tiny village with 200 inhabitants in the Shangri-la-like soft hills of China's southwest. The area has long been the recipient of China's poverty alleviation program. This governmental program, active since the 70s, has brought 800 million people out of poverty. Each year the program tears down and rebuilds hundreds of villages like Yubulu. We have been puzzling about this seemingly crude practice. Only when presented with severe conditions and local dilemmas in the countryside can you see what the instigators were trying to achieve. But Yubulu was not destroyed, it was preserved. The plan is to face economic, social, and cultural challenges by catering to urbanites' growing desires for relaxing experiences in the "real" countryside. And Yubulu comes close to this mythic ideal.

From Xingyi Airport, we drive on a brand new, remarkably flat highway, as if we are still driving through Holland. But the landscape underneath us is hilly. And some of the overpasses float a hundred meters above existing villages. We pass several large coal power plants before passing through an impressive gate where the road is clad in stone rather than tarmac. It feels like driving into a paradisal garden. The surroundings are stunningly green, full of animal life (the coal plant now just out of view). The renovations designed by Pinying look subtle. In the "before" pictures shared by Pinying, the village had generic concrete flat-roofed houses. Decades of opening up have resulted in the majority of construction in the countryside in China being made of concrete. Pinying's project added pitched roofs to the flat structures, generating in some cases new spaces for tourists. Some facades are now clad with natural stone and some more authentic reconstruction efforts use traditional woodcraft.

We are visiting just after a public holiday that brought a lot of tourists to the village. The students are setting up a village shop selling books and design items. One of the students worked on the design of the houses, and later in the day we meet more locals to talk about upgrading their houses too so they can receive tourists. The tourist economy is largely generated by Chinese Airbnb-like platforms that facilitate the booming interest in spending time in the countryside. More radical perhaps than the physical interventions, the government's plans include courses for the farmers on dealing with guest expectations, and providing touristic services. In the fields where there used to be rice paddies, now more expensive plants used in traditional Chinese medicine are grown. A piece of land art in the shape of a sinkhole, made by V studio, is an Instagrammable / WeChatable highlight. Just a quick hike away is a large nature reserve with dramatic waterfalls and several newly built lookout points and trails. A bit further on, a section of a mountain has been covered by solar panels—also part of a governmental anti-poverty plan.   Upon arrival in the hamlet of Banwang, a smartphone filming exchange erupts in which locals film us, and we film them. Banwang is home to 800 villagers belonging to the Miao people, one of 55 minority groups in China. Before traveling to the village someone told me there are issues with alcoholism and after 45 minutes and five cups of local *baiju* I get the point. I visit the public toilet—a covered platform hanging over a cliff with holes in the floor—where next to me a villager is playing a game on the just released iPhone XR. Pinying's key projects in Banwang are a large new school built with a classical timber frame, and the reconstruction of rammed-earth houses. They include new spaces for a restaurant and traditional cloth production. They both look like they're flourishing, but there's a problem with the school. Just after competition, the local government decided to centralize the schooling system, so it seems likely the school will not be used. The kids will leave the village and go into boarding schools, despite the strong opposition of the villagers and Pinying. In the evening we are treated to a theater performance by locals, followed by a clever young singer we met earlier called Moshe. He was successful on *China's Got Talent* and has a passion for reinventing traditional Chinese instruments. As minority culture preserved by good governmental intentions meets with a famous figure of 21st century China who in turn builds his career on Chinese tradition, we leave Banwang unable to make up our mind on what is happening in the village.   Dong Feng, October 3, 2018 We return to the Taobao village for the Taobao Summit and to see what happened with Dong Feng's ambitious plans for expansion. As part of a large group of guests and experts we are escorted through the recently finished village additions. It's nothing like the original businesses of the previous visit. The ting-tong sound is gone, the saws quieter. It's clean, with brand new woodworking equipment still in its packaging. In the workshop we encounter a small shrine to Mr. Sun, who apparently is now celebrated like a local deity. The exhibition area we visited before has received a dramatic upgrade. An enlarged model has replaced last year's plans for the village. New tower clusters have appeared. In the background, a wall of screens shows Dong Feng's trade in real time, with maps and gauges indicating the current flow of goods. The megaphone-equipped guide calls us to get back on the bus to see the next Taobao village, which explores a hybrid of production and tourism.   The next day in the hotel we bump into Mr. Sun at the breakfast buffet. We have a meeting with Aaron Chen, research director at AliResearch. By training an urban planner, he admits that the Ali group had to "learn" the countryside just like us. The platform has a rural development arm with 10 billion renminbi ($1.4 billion) in funding. Part of their mission is extending education and marketing into rural areas, making the relationship between the urban and rural more reciprocal. He points out that their data is showing remarkable migration patterns: a return to the countryside for sure, but also returnees again moving from the countryside to smaller cities when a certain economic threshold is met. Initially, the so-called rural service stations—small e-commerce centers—increased online spending in rural areas. A governmental push moved Ali to help locals start shops as well. A case in point is an

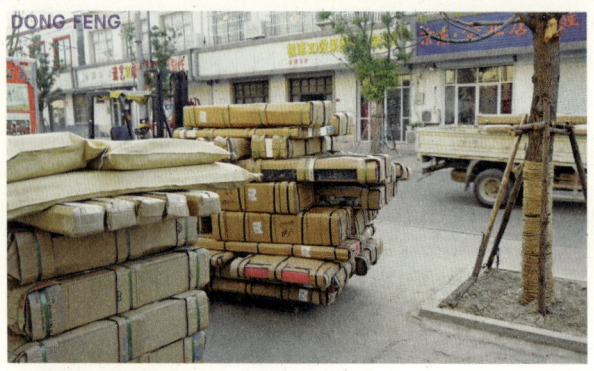

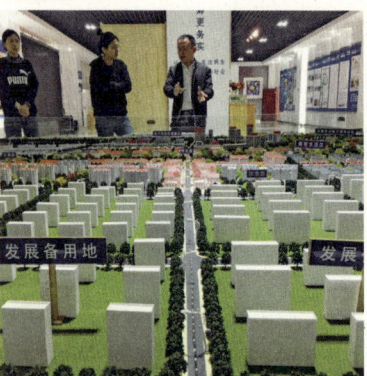

Above: Taobao Road, Dong Feng: village as fulfillment center.

Left and below: Between our visit in 2017 and our second a year later, the model for the expansion of the village quadrupled in size, and shifted from home-based start-ups to Fordist production and Modernist planning.

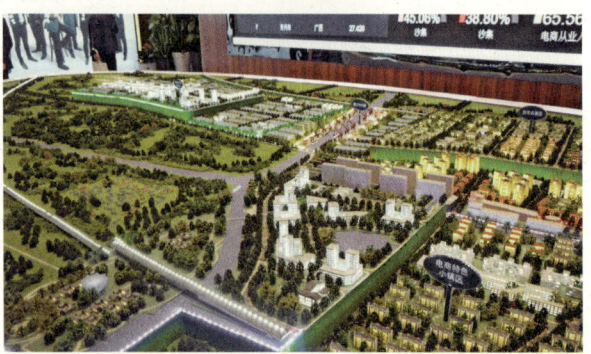

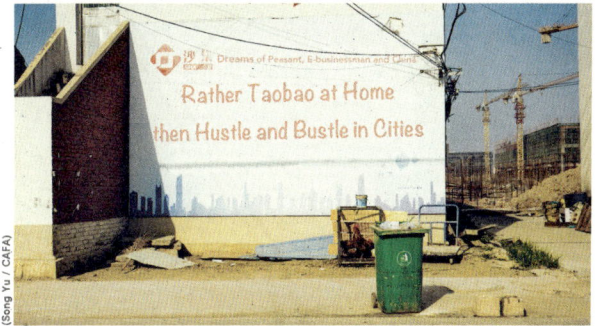

Above: Slogans also promote equal rights and are gender sensitive: "Women are powerful, busy with Business." Compared with Facebook's "Move fast and break things," Taobao's propaganda seems more inclusive and optimistic.

Left: Designers merge existing furniture templates and molding collages in 3ds Max, reshaping the online furniture shop almost in realtime for individual customers.

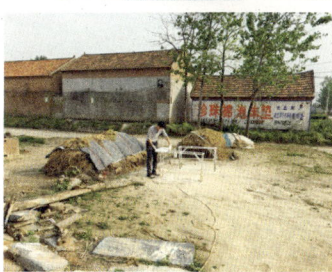

Left: Dong Feng's furniture industry began as a homebased enterprise, with factories emerging inside traditional courtyard houses; new factories are in dedicated buildings. Both function as factory-IKEA-fulfillment center all in one, where construction, sales, and distribution all happen in the same spaces, without the physical presence of the customer.

Left: "The Bed" is Dong Feng's most popular item with sales of more than 400,000. The now-iconic design can be adapted by individual customers through the Aliwangwang app.

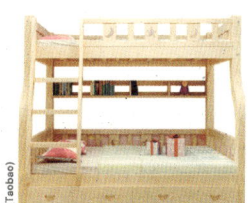

(Stephan Petermann, unless otherwise credited.)

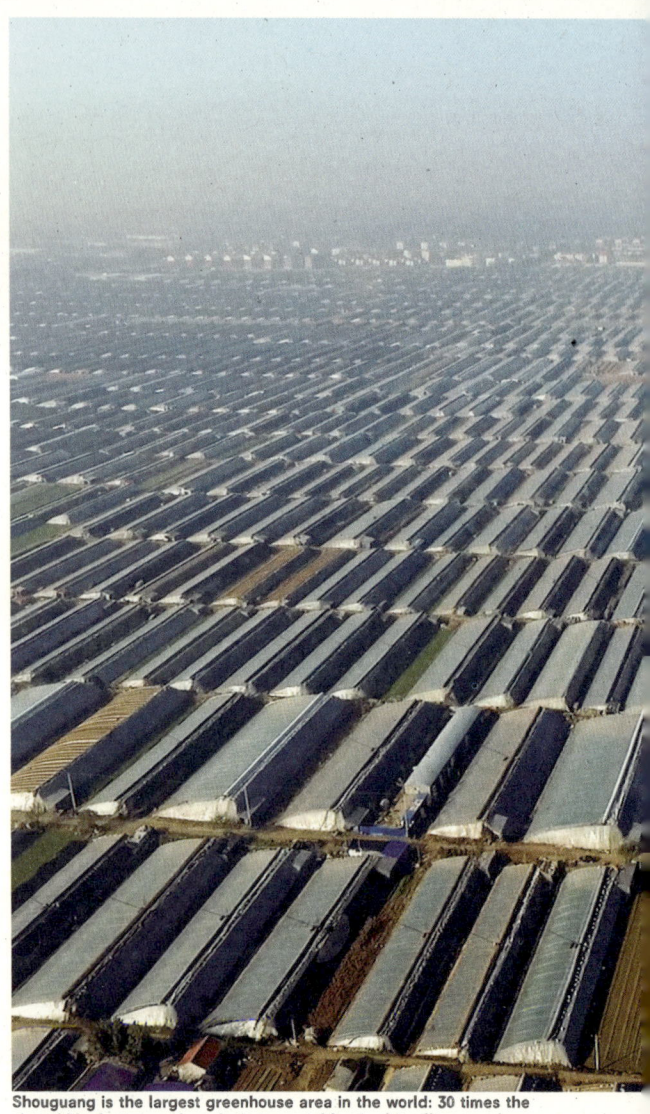

Shouguang is the largest greenhouse area in the world: 30 times the size of Manhattan, and producing vegetables for 60 million people.

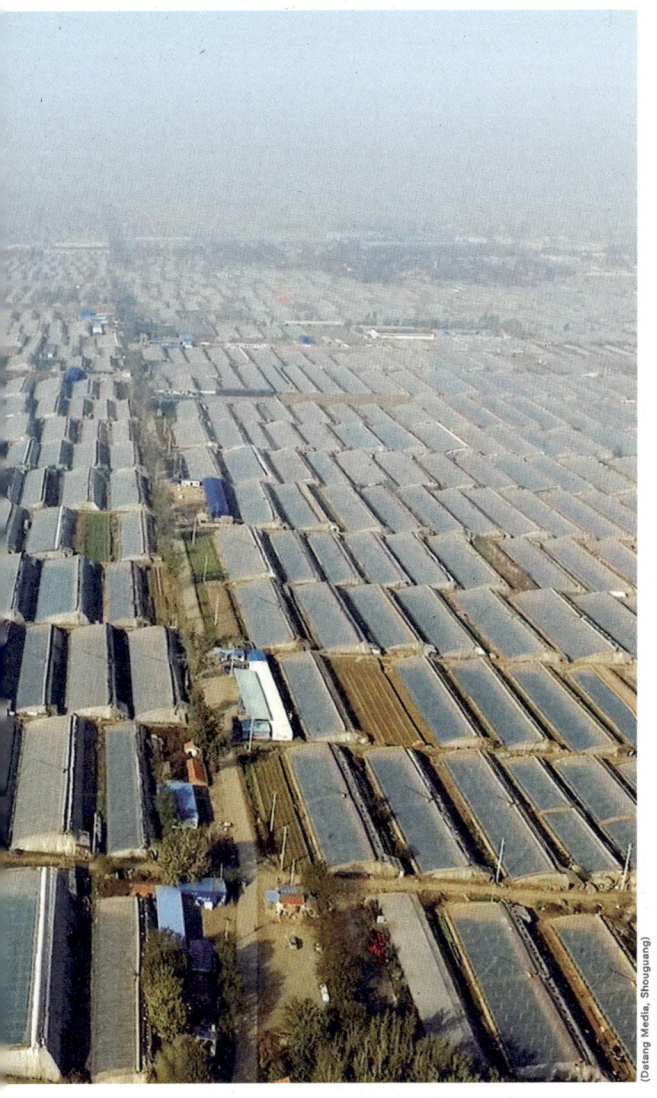

SHOUGUANG

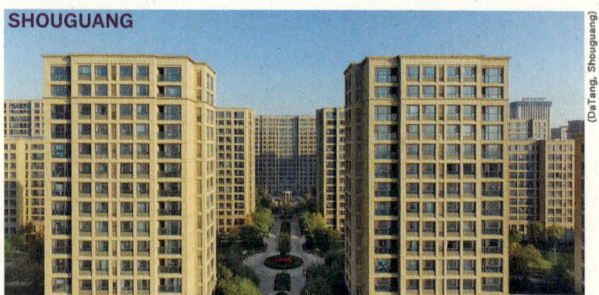
Tun Tien Towers, Shouguang (population: 1.2 million), where communities of farmers live their urban lifestyles at night.

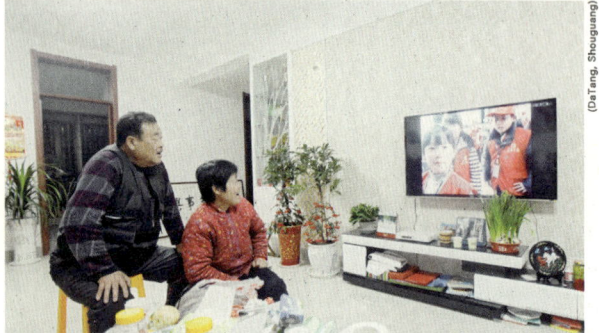
Greenhouse farmers Zhang Chunhua and husband Zhuo Mingan, Tun Tien towers, 15th floor.

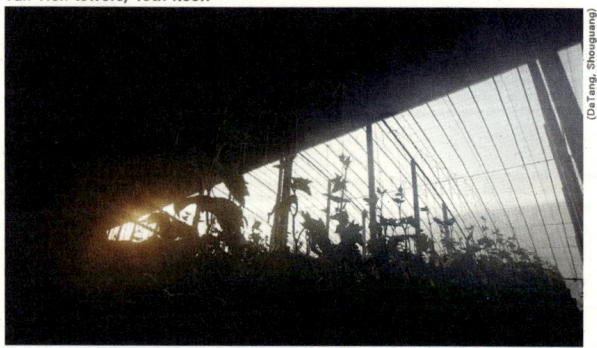
Zhuo at sunrise, opening up the farm: the greenhouses are covered with blankets to keep heat inside during the night.

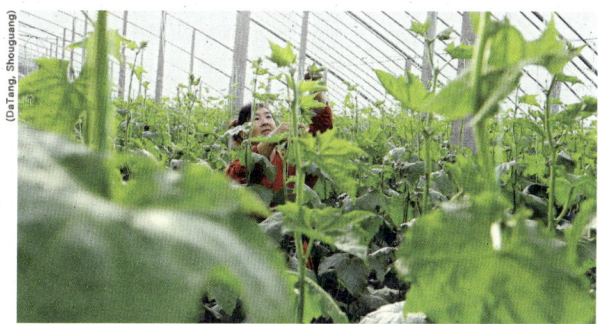

Zhang looking after luffa plants, carefully trimming each plant by hand to make sure they grow at a working-level height.

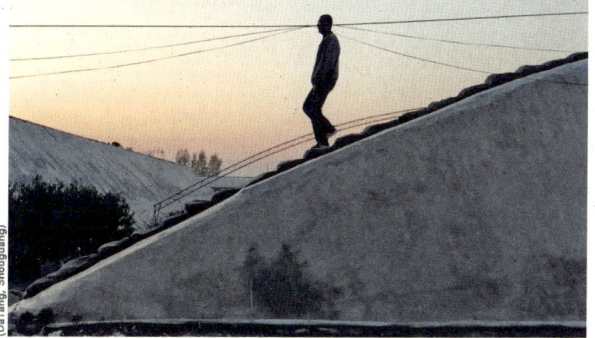

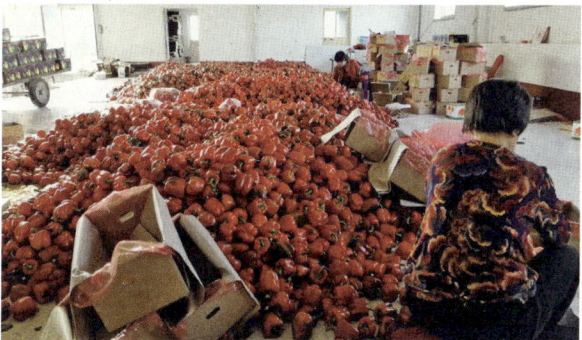

Sorting station close to Zhang and Zhou's farm where peppers are packed, to be loaded on a large truck bound for Russia.

YUBULU

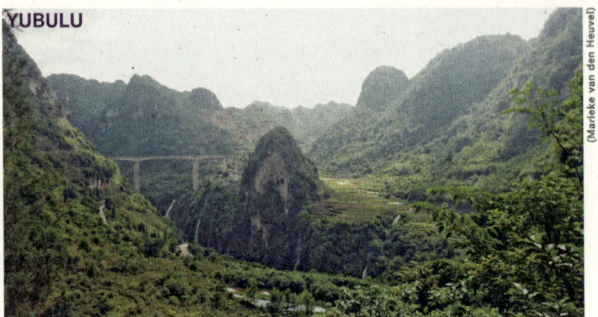

Yubulu overlooks the hilly terrain of the southwestern region of Guizhou, on occasions pierced with new elevated highways and high-speed train tracks.

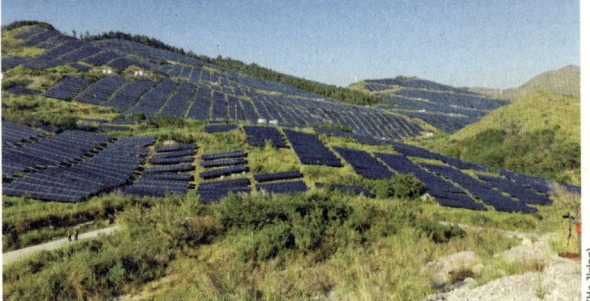

Within a mile of Yubulu, three large development projects are just out of view: an immense solar farm adapting to the curvature of the hills, a fish farm, and three massive coal power plants.

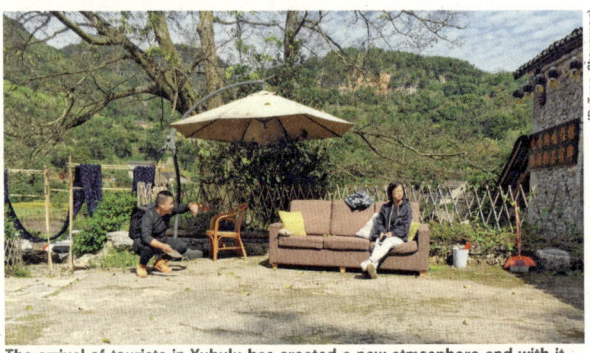

The arrival of tourists in Yubulu has created a new atmosphere and with it new objects: the luxury umbrella hanging over the outdoor couch, ripe for social media posts.

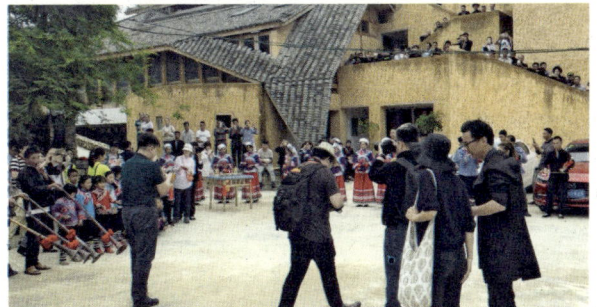

The tiny hamlet of Banwang is home to 800 villagers belonging to the Miao people, one of 55 minority groups in China.

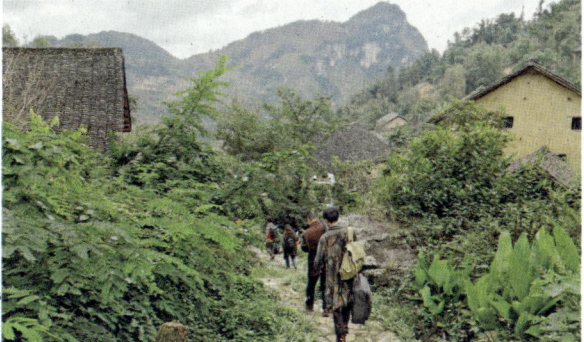

Banwang village: modern reconstructions of traditional rammed-earth houses are part of government anti-poverty plans for the Miao minority, preserving village life and adding tourism.

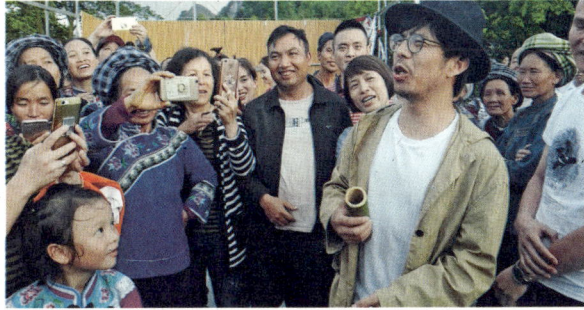

Beijing-based singer Moshe, a modest celebrity after participating in *China's Got Talent*, is establishing a library of traditional musical instruments from the countryside.

LIUZHUANG

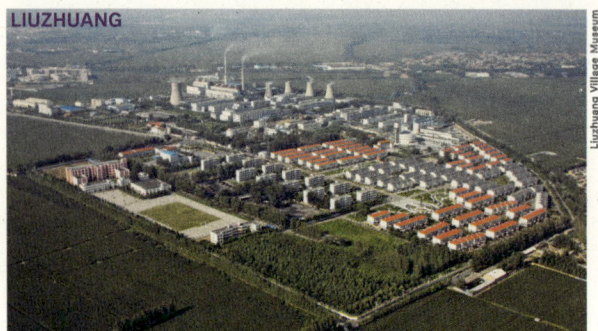

The workers commune of Liuzhuang, in Henan province. Liuzhuang is the longest surviving Maoist commune in the world, still functioning on the premise of absolute social equality.

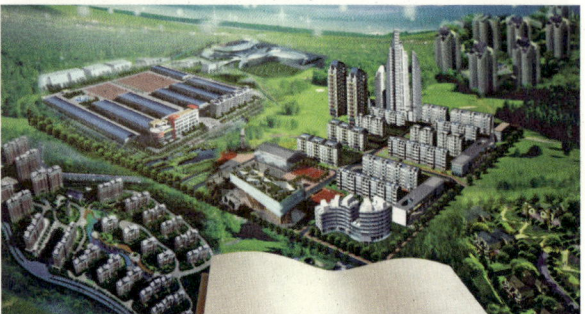

The future village, with parts resembling holiday resorts and a downtown of skyscrapers.

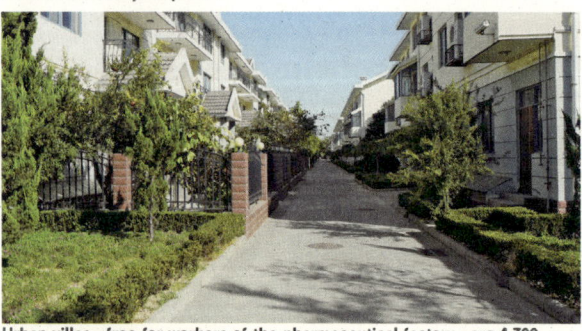

Urban villas—free for workers of the pharmaceutical factory—are 4,300 square feet (400 m²) per family, with a/c, large kitchen, several bathrooms, and a small garden.

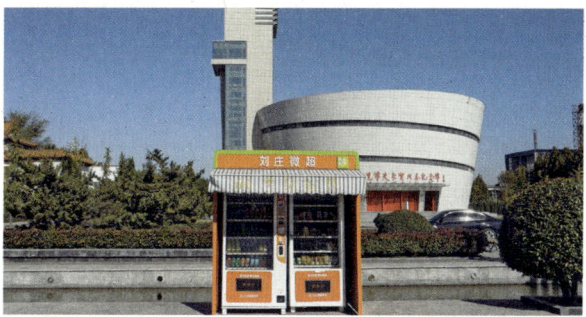
The village has a large museum, designed by government architects from Beijing, loosely based on Frank Lloyd Wright's Guggenheim Museum in New York.

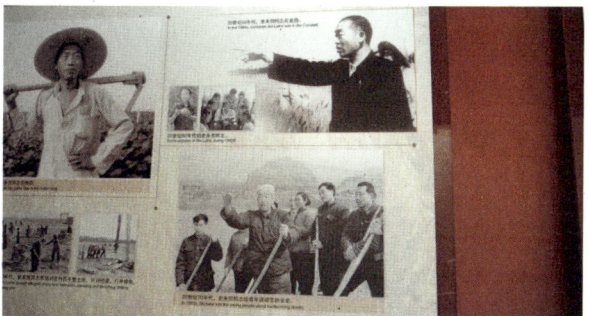
Skillfully composed photos of the village's first leader, Shi Laihe, inspecting the fields.

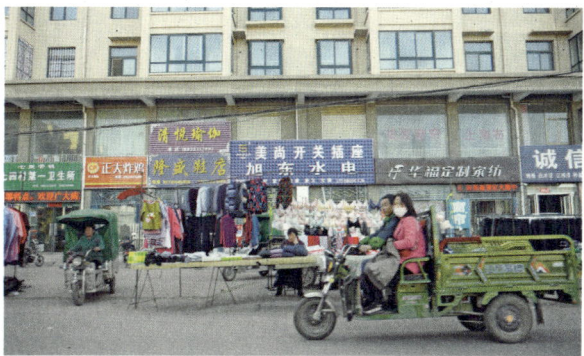
Outside Liuzhuang's gates, China explodes again with its frantic and messy reality.

experiment where ecologically produced honey is prioritized in the search algorithm. A few months later the scandal of Amazon prioritizing products that are more profitable reminds me of Chen's words.

The last real commune—Liuzhuang, February 2019

Where most of China feverishly embraced the country's form of a market economy, Liuzhuang remained faithful to the origins of Mao's commune life. It is the longest-lasting communist experiment in the world. At a moment when every global city is working on its versions of inclusivity and universal basic income, Liuzhuang is a 60-year experiment in equality. The slowdown of the economy is destined to trigger a renewed debate on the communist origins that make Liuzhuang so interesting.

After a five-hour train ride from Beijing, the taxi we took to reach the village stops at a gate on the middle of the road. The gate opens after a minute and we enter the village. It's absolutely unChinese quiet in Liuzhuang. Not because there are no people. They flow by without making sound on e-bikes and on an electric marriage between a pick-up truck and a scooter. Now and again a child passes on a bike. The villagers speak softly, seemingly concentrated and relaxed.

It's noon and a new shift has just started at Liuzhuang's medicine factory. They make antacids and antibiotics. Men and women in blue overalls head from the large rusting chemical plant to their urban villas. With 4,300 square feet (400 m2) per family, air-conditioning, a large kitchen, several bathrooms, and a small garden, it's not too shabby. The streets in Liuzhuang are well-maintained and the village park looks bright and fresh. In the square there are daily line dancing classes. In the center of the square is an obelisk-like monument with a large plaque containing classical communist phrases: *Fourteen families, hand in hand, heart to heart, unity is strength, harmoniously upward, keeping in pace with the times, creating brilliance; Hold the hope of tomorrow, construct the beautiful homeland.*

Everybody in this village is equal. "OK, almost," says village vice-secretary Ms. Liu. "The engineers get a little premium. But not much!" She holds her thumb close to her index finger, to emphasize that the difference is minimal. "But apart from that everybody gets the same. A large modern house. Every five days one pound of meat per head of the family. Every time something different. As many vegetables and fruit as you like. Education is free, just like healthcare, a large TV and fast internet. And every year we travel abroad for holidays. This year, 370 villagers are going to Thailand!" It immediately feels like fun. Apart from the above each villager receives the equivalent of $500 a month. The "catch" is that they all have to work for the medicine factory.   The widely held assumption that communism leads to a lack of incentive to perform isn't borne out in Liuzhuang. The village is situated on the banks of the Yellow River, which, with its frequent flooding, has left a hefty layer of river clay in the village. In the early 20th century the village was extremely poor, its people suffering from disease and hunger. But the village was able to raise itself from absolute poverty to relative wealth in a few years by cleverly investing in modern infrastructure and agriculture, and was heralded as one of the model villages to follow in the nation. Ever since, almost every Chinese political leader has visited the village to pay tribute.   Liuzhuang feels a bit like a holiday resort. Life is very simple. The only store in the village is a small vending machine. It makes sense: why would you need a store if everything is catered for? It's against village regulations to start your own store. There is no advertising. On closer inspection the urban villas of the villagers appear to be too large. Where the average residential area per inhabitant in China is around 420 square feet (39 m2), Liuzhuang is easily double or even triple that amount. It seems most top floors are hardly used. The village has a large, impressive museum loosely based on Frank Lloyd Wright's Guggenheim Museum, dreamed up by government designers in Beijing. The museum is dedicated to the village and more evidently its historic leader who is responsible for its prosperous condition: Shi Laihe. As you enter he is sitting in front of you in the center of the rotunda: a double life-size marble figure with a charismatic grin on his face, wearing slippers. The spiraling ramp revolves around him.   Ms. Liu has poured the tea for nearly all the high-level Party figures visiting the village over the years. She starts to shine when she speaks about the visit of Jiang Zemin in 1991, shortly before he became president. "He couldn't stop shaking his [Shi Laihe's] hand. He kept on patting him on his shoulder." Photos in the museum show China's previous president Hu Jintao highly concentrated, making notes in conversation with Shi Laihe. Xi Jinping visited in 2006 and can be seen chatting with locals sitting on a large sofa. That Jiang Zemin was so happy with Liuzhuang can be explained. He was the first leader who, after Deng Xiaoping's reforms, had to give shape to the experimental / alchemic mix of market forces and communism. Liuzhuang had done this quite cleverly. From the 1970s onwards the responsibility of the economy was shifted from work units back to families under the so-called household responsibility system. Liuzhuang had reneged by deciding that the village remained a collective but it would use this power to work for the market. The entire village became wealthy, quite fast – exactly what the government in Beijing was aiming for. It remains hard to substantiate why Liuzhuang was so successful and other villages weren't. Their position in governmental circles might have helped, but if you look through the propaganda in the museum, you might conclude that Shi Laihe was just very talented. He realized in the early 1960s that mechanized agriculture wouldn't be profitable enough for the village to grow and moved to industrial production of car horns and ice cream. He also noted a decade later that industrial production wouldn't cut it either and shifted to pharmaceuticals, which remains the largest source of income for the village. Within the political climate under and after Mao he managed to stick to the party line, using the right words at the right moments without giving up his own vision of the village. In 2003, Shi Laihe died. His son took his place after his death. The actual decay of the village had started earlier. Competition in the production of medicine in China has increased, and the economic health of the factory is poor it seems. There is a shortage of workers in the village. Although the village managed to retain far more inhabitants than in most villages in China, mostly young women are leaving.

The future village presented at the end of the exhibition is a large messy collage with parts that resemble holiday resorts and parts skyscrapers. In front of it is a solid white book with no content. Ms. Liu: "Some people in the village think tourism is the future for Liuzhuang. Now people visit the museum, they have lunch at the hotel, but then they leave." We ask about the possibilities of the digital economy. Before coming to Liuzhuang we attended a conference which boasted the Chinese digital economy as the undoubted future of the nation, urban and rural. Ms. Liu shows her smartphone and explains she also shops on Taobao. But for the village, she doesn't know where they would start. Life in Liuzhuang largely surpasses the national goals that the

Communist Party has set for becoming a moderately prosperous society by 2020—something you read a lot about in the texts of the president combined with his notion of The Chinese Dream. The village achieved this. The problem however seems that prosperity outside of the village is even larger. The nearby town with new luxury hotels, cars and shops is more wealthy. From Liuzhuang it is observed with contempt.   We bump into a young father in the village park. With his one-year-old daughter he lives in the village but is one of the few who works outside, for China Telecom. "In principle the premiums of the village are not available for those who don't work in the village, but I make sure the village gets a good deal for its phone and internet connections, so that makes it OK." He's happy with his life there, but doesn't see a bright future ahead. We ask him what's wrong. "Everything is so fixed. No fundamental renewal. For example it's not allowed to have a Taobao shop." We ask what keeps him from addressing this. Earlier the party secretary explained the democratic setup of the village decision-making with a Swiss-like referendum system and smaller subcommittees spreading power over the community. "In practice the power is mainly in the hand of a few families," he says. He suggests that higher positions are reserved for villagers who are members of the Communist Party. And to get into the Party you have to pass several tough exams. With easier money to be made in the city, studying to climb the ranks of the cadres isn't alluring. "There are a few guys who have secret Taobao shops selling honest, organic produce from the land. That's something I'd really like to do." For a moment you feel the energy of Shi Laihe re-emerging. We leave the village via the gate. Outside, China explodes again with its frantic and messy reality—we are stuck in traffic, along a busy shopping street with a lady using a megaphone to help sell bras.

The 2017–19 CAFA-AMO Research and design studios at CAFA were led by Lv Pinying, RK, Stephan Petermann, Li Shao Jun, Shi Yang, and Vivian Song with support from Karl-Otto Ellefsen, Jiang Jun and Dongmei Yao.

Thaw
Janna Bystrykh

Yakutsk is a city of 300,000 inhabitants, built largely on permafrost, on the left (western) bank of the river Lena in central Siberia. It's a night flight east from Moscow, but closer to Seoul, which is only four hours south and in the same time zone. It's mid-February when I arrive. Sidewalks are full of people. The temperature is below −22°F, which is considered a "friendly" cold. Beyond −40°F is when people migrate inside. Almost no one has their phone out—the cold drains the battery. The grills of cars (many right-hand drive, imported from Japan) are covered in insulation to protect the engine while driving. The fish market has no smell: frozen solid, the catch from the Lena is displayed like baguettes in baskets, and in small piles like logs. The sun shines brightly, as it typically does in this dry, near-Arctic climate—until the temperature drops further and the city is wrapped in ice fog.

Talking about the cold is an easy way to start up a conversation here. People reminisce about the periods of extreme cold (−58°F), which are getting noticeably shorter and rarer. In summer, temperatures climb into the upper 80s and 90s. The average temperature in Yakutsk has risen by 5.4°F since the 1970s.[1] Temperatures across the circum-polar region are rising faster than anywhere else; this was anticipated in climate models, but not at the current rate: Some areas have already warmed by 9°F.

The abrupt warming, together with the resulting increase in precipitation, is causing rapid thaw and destabilization of the permafrost—the perennially frozen ground—beneath Yakutsk. Permafrost is a rendering of the Russian *vechnaya merzlota*, meaning "eternal frost."[2] A more commonly used scientific term today is *mnogoletnyaya merzlota*, or "multiyear frost." Permafrost is defined as any ground that remains frozen for more than two consecutive years, but much of it has been frozen for thousands. It covers nearly a quarter of the land area of the northern hemisphere: 50 percent of Canada, 60 percent of Russia, and 85 percent of Alaska.

Some of the most extreme land disturbances due to thaw are occurring in this region. I'm in Yakutsk to learn about the impact, and to hear about the science and emergency plans emerging in response. Yakutsk is the unofficial historic and cultural capital of permafrost research and home to the Melnikov Permafrost Institute. Pavel Melnikov, a pioneer in the field who helped launch an international exchange on permafrost starting in the 1950s, creating the foundation for the international permafrost collaboration today. His institute hosted the International Conference on Permafrost (ICOP) in 1973, attended by some 400 participants from 16 countries.[3] This was one of a series of international scientific and state events during the 1960s and 70s, a collaboration at the height of the Cold War driven largely by personal friendships, in which experts regularly visited each other's deep hinterlands, with conferences and state visits hosted in Siberia, Alaska, northern Canada, and other remote areas. Despite drastic political differences, leaders were open to the importance of scientific progress. Today the scientific collaboration is stronger than ever, but the political vision is missing.

Looking from my hotel room on the seventh floor, the city ends abruptly, the vast taiga landscape taking over. Yakutsk is the capital of Sakha Republic, unofficially also known as Yakutia. The region is five times the size of France with less than one million inhabitants, home to multiple native cultures and languages—Sakha, Evenki, Even and others. They can all be heard on the street in passing along with Russian as the shared language. Today, Sakha is the largest ethnic group in the region, making up 50 percent of the population.

YEDOMA

Across the region, permafrost can reach down to 5,000 feet, some of the deepest permafrost in the world. Yedoma is a specific permafrost type common here, rich in organic matter and underground ice, and particularly susceptible to rapid thawing. The simplicity of the term—thawing—hides the complexity of the invasive process spreading beneath the surface, devastating the topography above. The scientific term for the often shocking patterns and landforms from the thawing of ice-rich permafrost is somehow more evocative: *thermokarst*.[4] The ground in this region is collapsing, sinking, sliding, slumping, cratering, "hillocking"; vast areas are being inundated with water. These phenomena are damaging soil, agriculture, vegetation, ecosystems, buildings, and infrastructure, making vast areas inaccessible, unworkable, and uninhabitable. In February 2019, a meeting between permafrost scientists and the Supreme Council of Elders of the Sakha Republic announced drastic proposals to relocate sections of Yakutsk, riverfront communities, and Arctic coastal communities to more solid, rockier ground.

By 2050, loss of ground stability will impact four million people—three-quarters of the population—living in the northern hemisphere's permafrost zone, and nearly three-quarters of its infrastructure.[5] There is no technical solution to halt large-scale thaw. By the end of this century, large parts of this landscape will become wetlands; other regions will be covered by the sea, a new emerging coastline. Relocation or evacuation of settlements seems unavoidable in the short- to medium-term future.

CARBON

While the IPCC's 2019 "Climate Change and Land" paper described how land use and land degradation are one of the biggest drivers of climate change, in the permafrost zone today the script flips—one of the biggest impacts of climate change on *land* is playing out here. But permafrost has been under the radar of our collective consciousness. Located in some of the most isolated tracts of the planet, and impossible to detect by satellite and remote sensing until recently, for decades permafrost came in fourth in priority when discussing climate, after ice, snow, and glacier cover—all of which could be seen and measured from above. Any conception of current conditions—the apocalypse playing out right now on the ground in Yakutia and elsewhere—has been overshadowed by the alarm over methane release and the catastrophic climate feedback loops it will likely trigger. As with so many other calamities, concern over the (mostly) future climate trumps current ecological devastation. But the international permafrost science community is trying hard to redress the balance. Still, the concern over the carbon stored in the permafrost is more than warranted, and the starkness of the situation is—like the permafrost region itself—pushed to the corners of our imagination. Permafrost across the Arctic and boreal region contains between 1.46 and 1.6 trillion tons of organic carbon—almost twice the amount present in the atmosphere today.[6] The term "carbon" here designates ancient pockets of methane, plus "new" methane and carbon dioxide released by microbial activity in long-frozen organic matter awakened as permafrost thaws. A "baseline" projection for methane release, modeled according to a progressive—meaning slow and steady—thawing of permafrost was published in 2018,[7] but did not take into account the erratic and rapid changes that are now common. Vladimir Romanovsky, one of the leading permafrost scientists and thinkers, at the University of Alaska told me in January 2018 over Skype that it will probably take another four to five years to develop a detailed model and map of the carbon content of permafrost and the process of its release.

All of this release will, or is already, creating a climate feedback loop: more warming, more carbon released from permafrost; more carbon released from permafrost, more warming. But this feedback loop was ignored in the Paris 2015 targets, despite warnings over thawing and additional carbon release having been featured in IPCC reports since the very first one, in 1990. Modeling the rates of thawing, quantities of carbon, the rates of release, and the compound impact on global climate is extremely difficult. But it's not controversial to suggest that permafrost carbon release will send the climate *far* beyond any "safe" limits. Meanwhile, the geopolitics of the Arctic region remain fixated on sovereignty, military strength, and economic "opportunities" released by warming, like another human-made feedback loop: northern sea routes, mining, the extraction of minerals and more fossil fuels.

INDUSTRIAL AGRICULTURE

I drive through Yakutsk to meet with Professor Alexander Fedorov, adjunct director at the Melnikov Permafrost Institute. It's a yellow-painted classical three-story building on the south side of Yakutsk, with a woolly mammoth sculpture in front. Inside, the institute is forested with potted plants, and an underground tunnel serves as a laboratory for studying the permafrost in situ. I meet Fedorov in his small sunlit office, the walls crowded with maps he's worked on over the years of Yakutia's permafrost—a never-ending task. Fedorov calmly and patiently takes me through his archive of shocking images of arable fields, pasture, rural settlements, buildings, infrastructure, and wilderness impacted by thermokarst, going back more than ten years across Central Yakutia. With his colleagues, Fedorov recently published a paper on the use of remote sensing and drone technology to detect and analyze such thermokarst disturbances,[8] as well as producing an updated map of Yakutia's permafrost. Together with the young researcher and drone pilot Nikolai Basharin, Fedorov conducts annual field research in the agricultural areas of Central Yakutia during the summer months. They're currently in the midst of another remote sensing project to estimate the percentage of agricultural land that can no longer be used. Fedorov's team works with a small budget but massive determination: there is no technical solution to stop thawing, but they can work to understand it, predict its impacts, develop adaptive measures where possible, and even legislation. Central Yakutia is the only permafrost region in the world where industrial agriculture is practiced, introduced in the 1960s. Today, the compacting and thinning out of the organic matter in the top layer of the soil (due to intensive cultivation) makes agricultural areas particularly susceptible to rapid thermokarst. One of the main culprits are hillocks—fields full of them, which gradually transform into ever-growing lakes. Individual hillocks can be 50 feet in diameter, with depressions of seven feet between them. Agricultural landscape afflicted by hillocking is inaccessible to machinery and often must be abandoned. There are efforts in active agricultural land to prevent or slow down hillocking through applying new topsoil as a thermal buffer. This sometimes delays the degradation by a few seasons, but cannot arrest it. Much thermokarst terminology originates from the Sakha language: *alas*, a large depression produced by the thawing of thick and exceedingly ice-rich permafrost;[9] *byllary*, the hillock landscape. For many people, identity is still strongly linked to landscapes, traditions, territories, and indigenous communities far beyond the city. Many people still partake in the daily ritual of greeting the essence of the forest, animals, and their spirits. Yakut verse legends—*Olonkho*—are recognized by UNESCO as global "intangible heritage." This cocktail of strong traditions and the advanced scientific practice here hints at why people are so intimately connected to the effects of warming on the landscape. Fedorov is deeply concerned about the quality of life in Yakutia's agricultural settlements, searching for means to postpone relocation. He recommends the introduction of drainage systems in settlements to remove "new" water from the thawing ground before it refreezes on the surface during winter, causing upheavals and depressions in the ground. Fedorov also advocates reforestation, as much as possible —in now-unusable arable fields and pasture, in areas destroyed by forest fires, in open spaces in and around settlements— to create a thermal buffer above permafrost that's still intact. But this technique comes with the risk of depleting the limited nutrients in the soil, and even mature forests often cannot prevent thermokarst. Another entry in the catalogue of bizarre thawing effects is the "drunken forest," with trees sagging and lurching in different directions as the ground they're rooted in begins collapsing. Beyond faint hopes of mitigation lie programs of deep adaptation,[10] which essentially mean the drawing down of human civilization in Yakutia and other permafrost regions. Fedorov drove regional legislation passed in May 2018 to protect permafrost landscape for as long as possible. This means rezoning will begin, red-lining areas where new construction, agriculture, settlement, or other intense human land use should be avoided altogether, since developing land accelerates the thermokarst process that's already being supercharged by warming. The legislation heralds a new period of deindustrialization and another kind of inhabitation in this fragile (near) Arctic landscape. The legislation is a major global precedent, but still cannot keep up with the rapid pace of thermokarst in progress, and does not offer support for communities and landscapes that have already been damaged. People whose homes are no longer inhabitable often relocate within the same area, sometimes just a few meters from new fields of hillocks.

The scale of the degradation seen up close in Yakutia demolishes the early 20th-century fantasies of vast swathes of post-permafrost land becoming available for agriculture. Yet a techno-optimistic and political dream still lingers today, projecting a new territory for feeding the world that will seamlessly replace other latitudes made useless for farming by warming. Much of the land will simply be inaccessible or underwater. Even if areas disfigured by thermokarst could be suitable for farming in terms of temperature, it would take decades for the soil to recover and become productive again. And efforts to cultivate the ground would probably result in release of even more deep-lying carbon.

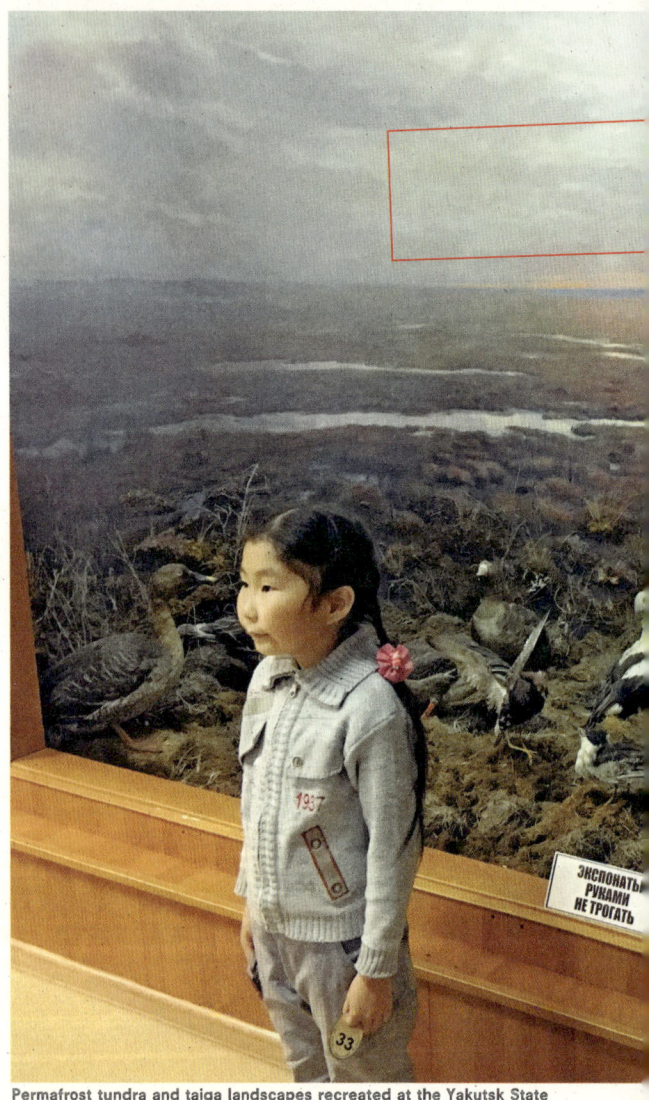

Permafrost tundra and taiga landscapes recreated at the Yakutsk State Museum of History and Culture of the People of the North.

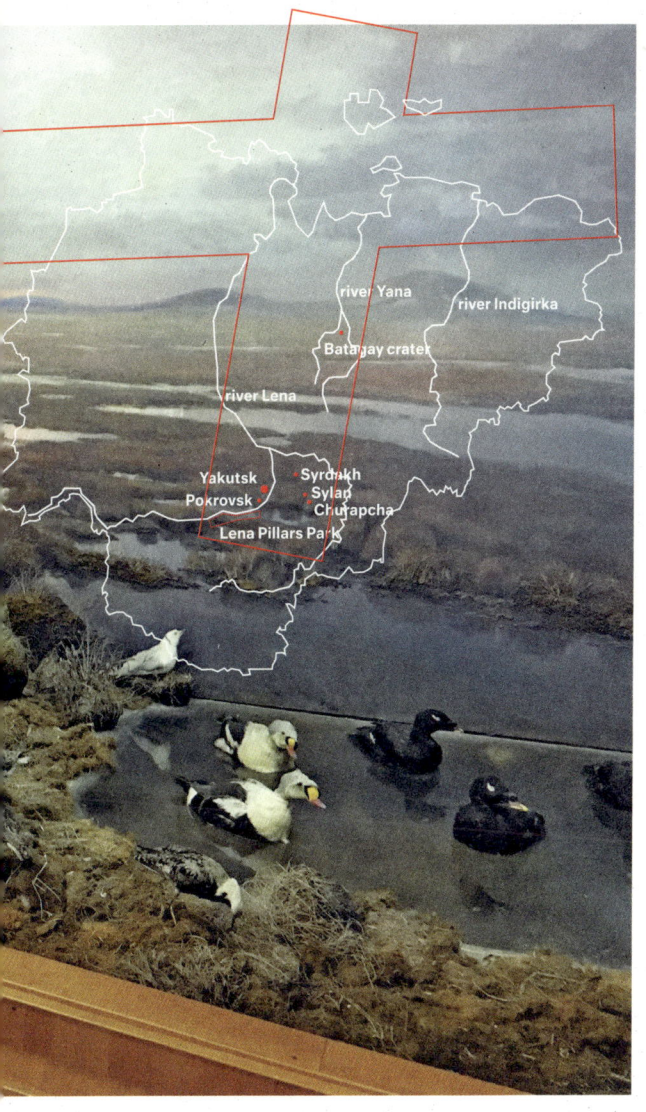

(All images by Janna Bystrykh, unless otherwise credited.)

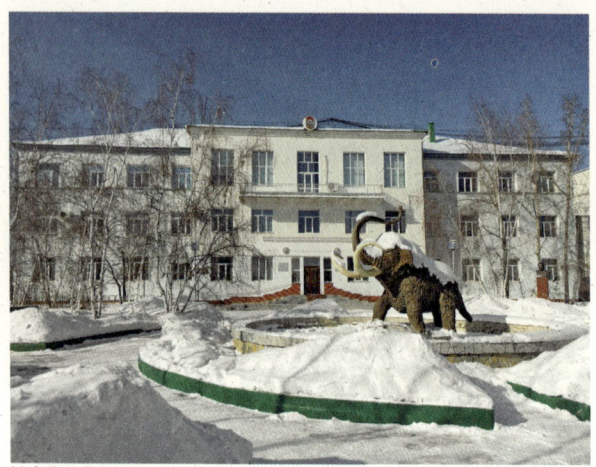

Melnikov Permafrost Institute, Yakutsk: cultural and historic landmark of international permafrost research.

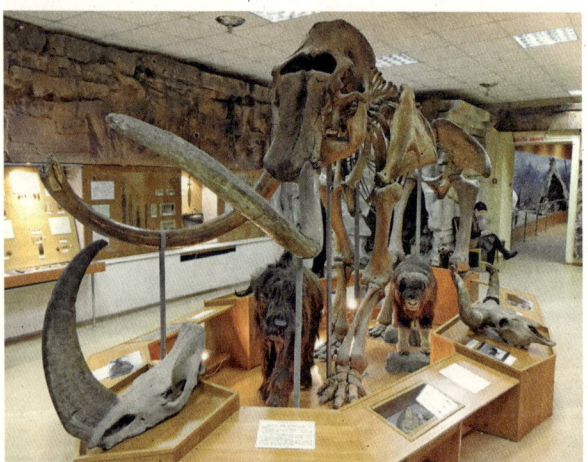

Male mammoth skeleton, found by a hunter in 1970 along the river Tirekhtyakh, a tributary of the Indigirka.

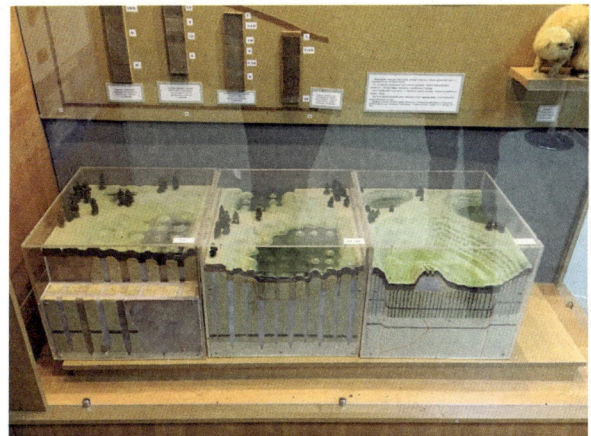

Models of the formation of thermokarst—"the process by which characteristic landforms result from the thawing of ice-rich permafrost or the melting of massive ice, common in Sakha Republic" (Multi-Language Glossary of Permafrost, 2005). Beginning at the end of the last ice age, thermokast is accelerating rapidly with global warming.

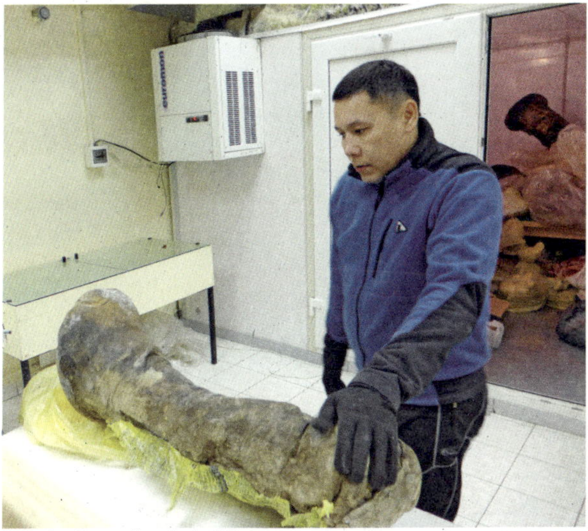

With thawing, archaeological findings are becoming more frequent, brought in from the field each summer into the various research centers and laboratories in Yakutsk.

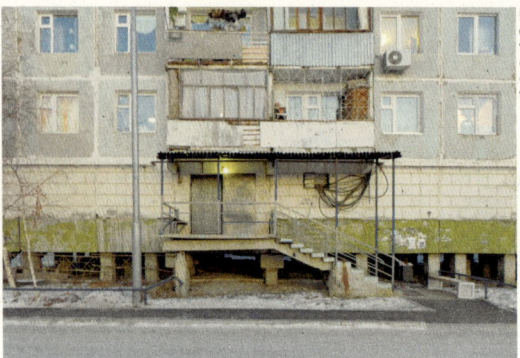

Buildings raised on concrete piles to prevent heat escaping into, and destabilizing, the frozen ground.

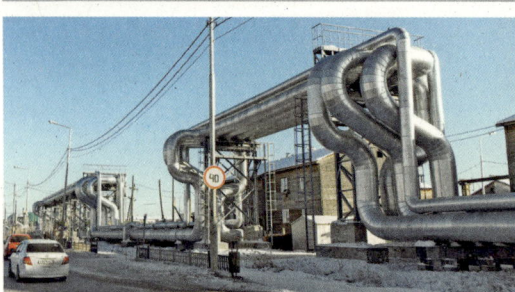

Utility lines raised above ground to protect permafrost from heat leakage.

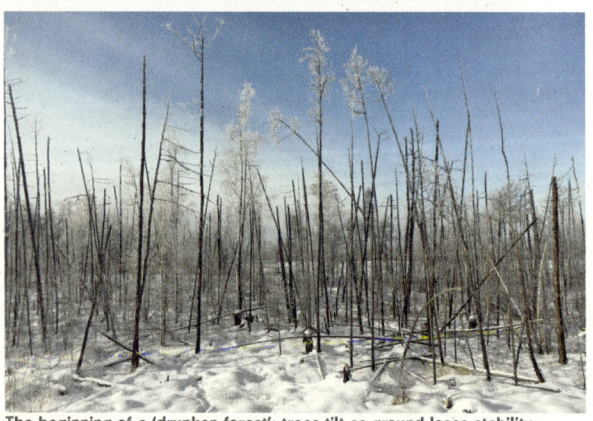

The beginning of a 'drunken forest': trees tilt as ground loses stability due to thawing.

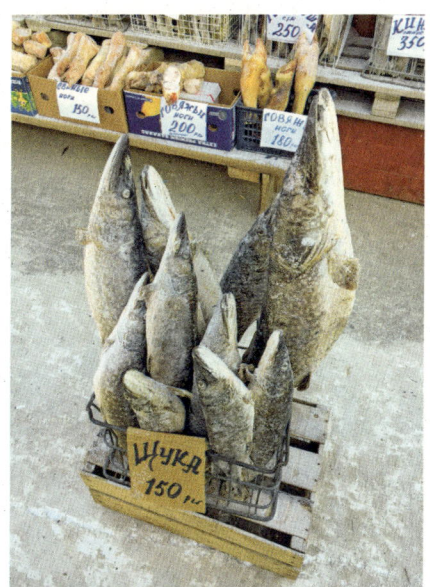
Yakutsk's central market: fish have no smell, frozen solid.

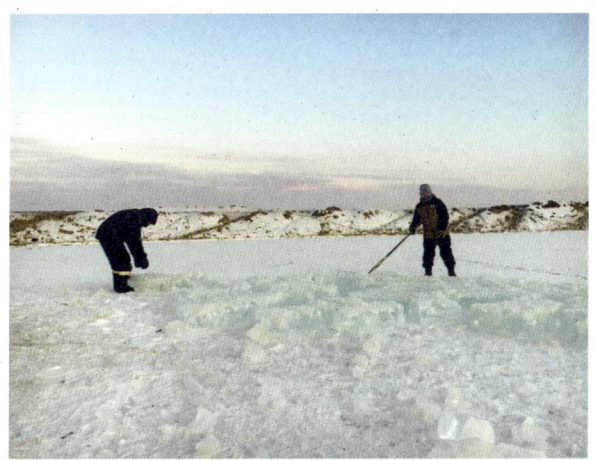
Ice harvesting, used for drinking water near Pokrovsk; in some areas a necessity, for many a treasured winter tradition.

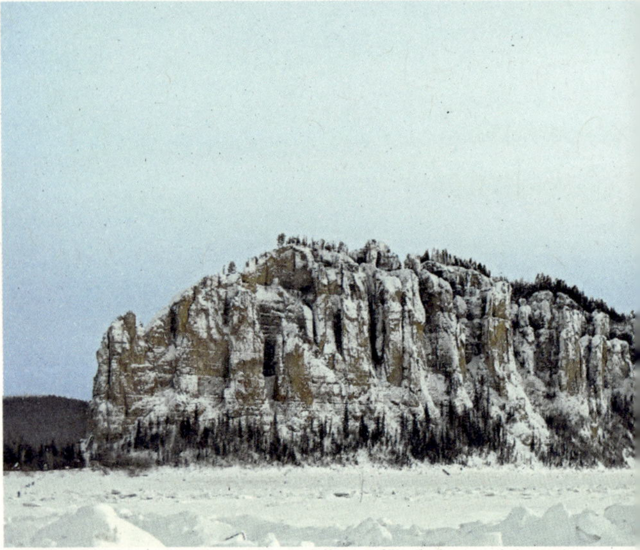

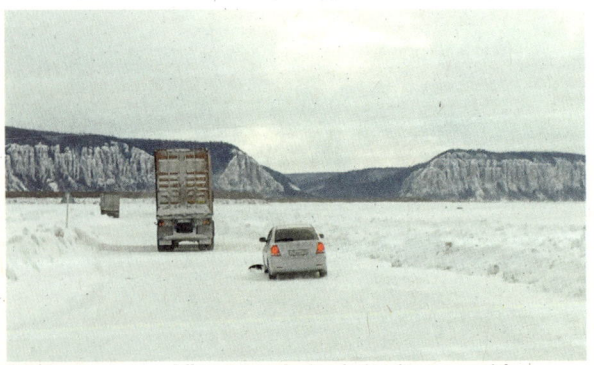

UNESCO World Heritiage Site, the Lena Pillars, a 25-mile long rock formation of towers and spindles, formed 400,000 years ago.

Driving towards Lena Pillars across the frozen river Lena, a crucial wintertime connection between towns and settlements on either side. Winters are warmer, and the period during which the river functions as a road is becoming shorter.

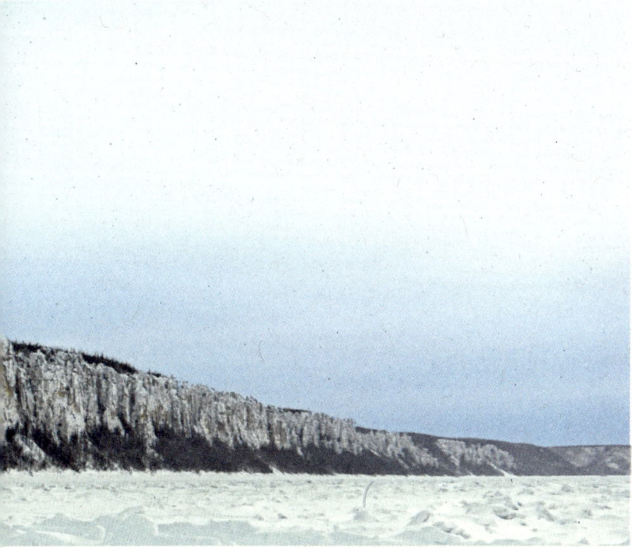

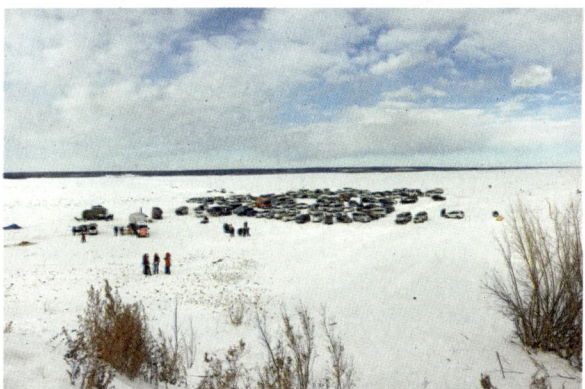

Tourists and vendors park on the frozen river at the foot of the Lena Pillars park entrance.

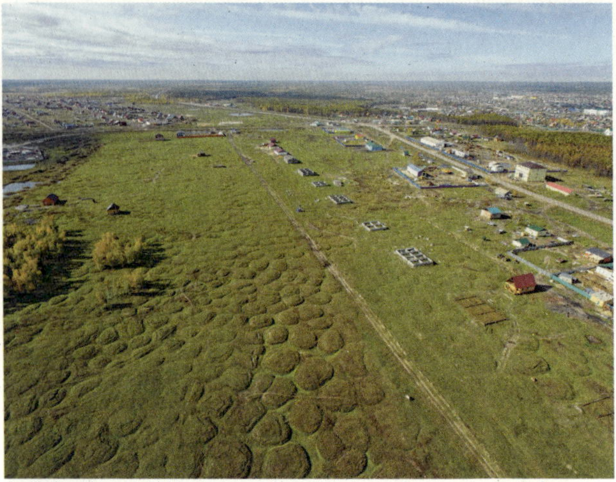

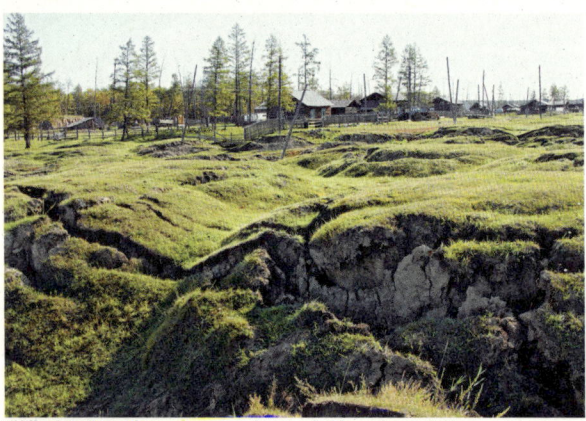

Agricultural and inhabited areas affected by forest fires are particularly susceptible to rapid thermokarst. "Hillocks" are spreading around Churapcha in Central Yakutia; adjacent, new homes are constructed regardless.
(Nikolai Basharin, 2017)

"Hillocking" up close: the ground can subside up to six feet (Sylan, Central Yakutia, 2009). (Alexander Fedorov)

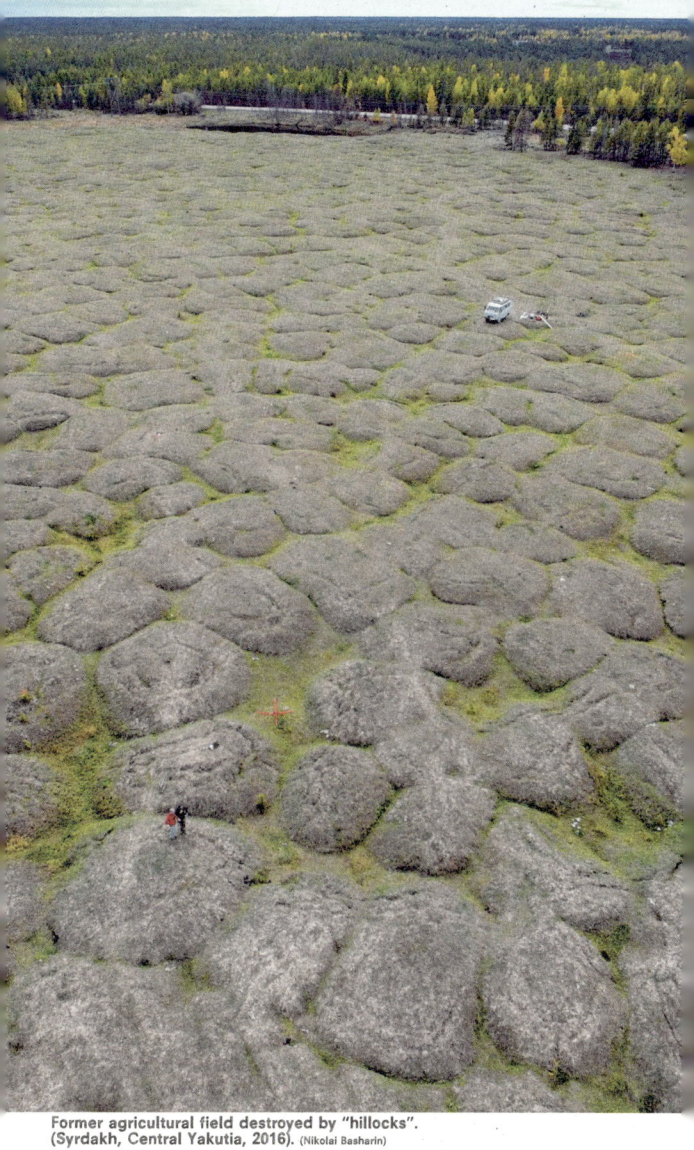
Former agricultural field destroyed by "hillocks". (Syrdakh, Central Yakutia, 2016). (Nikolai Basharin)

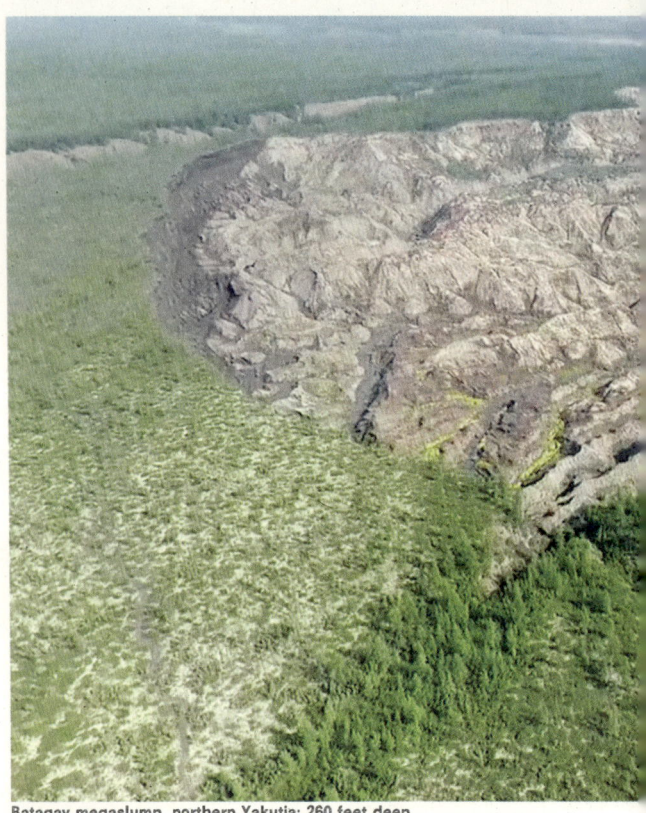

Batagay megaslump, northern Yakutia: 260 feet deep and 0.6-mile-wide, the crater grows each summer as exposed permafrost in its walls thaws and subsides (2017).
(Mammoth Museum of North-East Federal University, Russia)

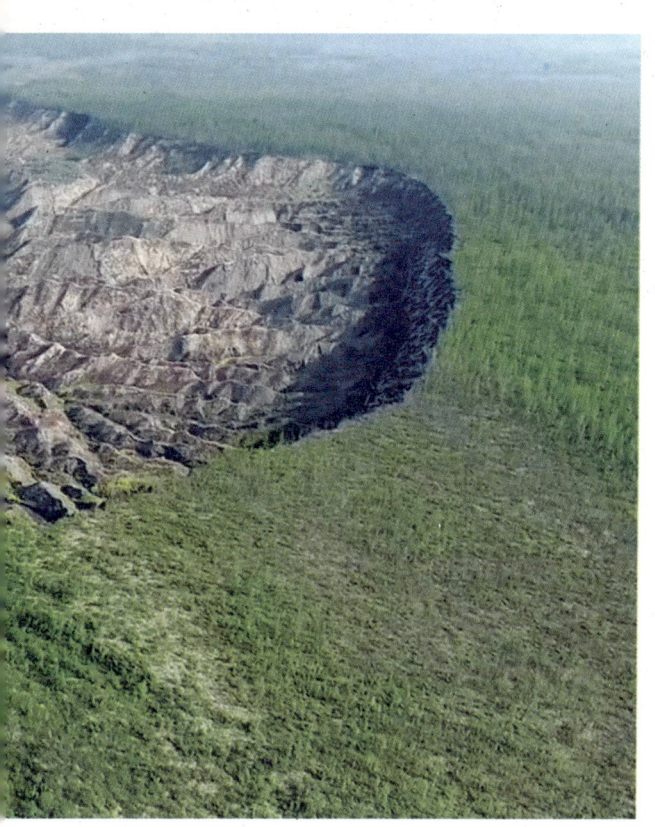

MEGASLUMP

The mammoth, extinct for more than 4,000 years, is still part of daily life here—an icon and a totem in museums, children's literature, toys, and public art. A five-minute drive from the Melnikov Permafrost Institute is the Lazarev Mammoth Museum Laboratory, part of the northeastern Federal University. The shelves of the laboratory at the Lazarev Museum are packed with the remains of paleolithic creatures—woolly mammoths, mammoth calves, woolly rhinoceroses. Smaller species like birds are sorted in containers, almost lunch boxes. It's a boom time for findings: As the warming ground breaks up and subsides, remains are exposed. Remains with soft tissue intact are stored in the large cool cell, wrapped in bags. The smell of age—of deep time unearthed, or bacteria awakened—is intense.   I meet the museum's paleontology team in their office on the third floor of the Natural Science building. One of their key research sites is the Batagay megaslump, one of the most extreme single examples of thermokarst in the world. Seven hundred kilometers north of Yakutsk, close to the settlement of Batagay (population: 4,000), the megaslump is a 260-foot-deep, 0.6-mile-wide crater, growing constantly, and dragging the surrounding forest down into its vortex. This summer, they will guide several international documentary film crews and researchers into this remote location, in parallel with conducting their own research. At the bottom of the crater, near the walls, the team tells me they can hear the thawing ice cracking in the summer. The megaslump probably started to form after deforestation in the 1970s—another example of human intervention triggering or accelerating thermokarst—but it grew exponentially as thawing intensified in the 2000s. For now, the Batagay megaslump is unique, but more such craters are anticipated in this taiga landscape.

PASSIVE PRINCIPLE

Compared to other Siberian cities and regional capitals, which were a focus of development in the Soviet era, Yakutsk is relatively small. It's made up of pockets of low-rise wooden housing, Soviet-era mid-rise neighborhoods, with sporadic flashy new developments—hotels, malls, offices, apartments, including two new riverfront neighborhoods in progress, built on alluvial sand, which is more stable than permafrost; the technique could be part of long term technical solution. Its parking lot is wrapped with a massive insulating blanket. The permafrost beneath Yakutsk is continuous, ranging from zero to 820 feet in depth. Most modern buildings are raised up one or two meters above the ground on concrete piles. This is the "passive principle" of foundation-making, conceived by engineer Mikhael Kim in 1956 specifically for building on permafrost. Kim's techniques facilitated the urbanization of areas of the Russian Arctic.[11] The priority is not so much to keep the cold *out* of the building, but to stop its warmth leaking *into* the permafrost below. If a building sits squarely on the ground, it can trigger a hyper-local mini-thaw underneath, causing the ground to lose stability, and the building to eventually collapse. In one new residential project here, foundations with active cooling are being tested, to try to keep the ground immediately under the building frozen. But this method, dependent on continuous maintenance and attention, is extremely fragile in the long term. Thanks to the passive principle, damage to buildings in Yakutsk due to thermokarst has so far been relatively minimal. But scientific models predict that continued warming will reach a critical point for Yakutsk in just 20 years' time. Radically different building and engineering techniques will be needed together with realistic plans for relocation.

A WAY TO STAY

The streets of Yakutsk are filled with movie ads and billboards—none are from Hollywood. A booming film industry has grown here since the 1990s, with films conceived, shot and produced locally, and often in the Sakha language, translated into Russian and English. The international film festivals are taking notice, with more awards given to films from Yakutia every year. With long winters, vast unexplored wilderness bordering isolated cities and settlements, a rapidly warming climate, monstrous transformations of landscape portending doom, and vigorous traditions of legends and storytelling, Sakha Republic certainly lends itself to filmmaking. The industry is potentially becoming an important cultural and economic substitute for the decline of agriculture, fishing, and other industries here. Film might be a raison d'être, a way to stay as life gets even harder. The vast landscape here typically plays a crucial role in these films, a character in itself, which gives added expression to every genre here: ancient legends, domestic dramas, virus apocalypse, zombie apocalypse, love stories. Budgets are small; non-actors are stars. Sakhafilm, one of the biggest film companies, strives to support the growing network of independent filmmakers, lending out equipment and theatre space for screenings. The culture of communication between filmmakers, audience, and critics is being rewritten here as well. I attend a screening of *Bonfire* at Sakhafilm with invited critics and journalists. Set in remote Yakutia, the film tells the intricate story of a bereaved father and his newly adopted son. After the movie, the audience speculates about possible alternative endings.

LENA PILLARS

It's ice harvesting season. People are out on the frozen tributaries of the Lena cutting ice bricks and pulling them out with heavy picks. The bricks are stacked in front of homes to provide drinking water over winter—many rural areas lack running water; in others, drinking harvested ice water remains a tradition. Most buildings in rural areas sit on a framework of logs as a thermal barrier between the warmth of the home and the frozen ground—the older method of protecting permafrost, pre-passive principle. But this traditional practice is in many cases no longer enough to provide stability on warming and subsiding ground. There are few roads out of Yakutsk, and no railways—there are however plans to construct a major rail connection into the northern corner of Far Eastern Russia, but this would pass on the other side of the river. The federal highway passes on the other side of the Lena as well, and there is no bridge. In winter, the river itself functions as a road, frozen solid. All sizes of cars and trucks take the ice road across to the agricultural towns and fields on the other side. The Lena is around 10km wide near Yakutsk, and is filled with slowly forming sand islands, which are used for cattle grazing. We pass by a permanently inhabited island, a small rural community, in a way like many others, but set on some of the more stable ground in the area, as there is no permafrost in the middle of the river. Electricity in this village is seasonal, in winter only, drawn across the ice on mobile wooden posts that stand on the ice. Wild horses roam the vast expanse, on the river banks and the islands. There are no fences. Cows wander in massive open fields.

Leaving the smooth asphalt of the city and driving along the bumpy rural roads and the endless flatness of frozen river, it takes nearly four hours to travel the 75 miles to the Lena Pillars, a UNESCO World Heritage Site, and a popular day trip from Yakutsk. An overwhelming number of cars are parked neatly on the ice at the park's border. Vendors have set up stalls selling hot tea and grilled meat sandwiches, exposed to the harsh winds on the river. The Lena Pillars formed around 400,000 years ago through another kind of karst process, breaking up the Cambrian limestone plateau into a 25-mile chain of thousands of pillars, spindly towers reaching up to 25-mile tall—a relic from deep history of unimaginably powerful landscape transformation. It's a hike through dense forest, past signs warning of the bear population, to the top of the cliff, where views open up to the fragile permafrost-taiga stretching out in all directions, seemingly endless, but no longer "eternal." The landscape as it's been known here for thousands of years, and the means of living in this vast wilderness is disappearing. As people struggle to remain, and civilization prepares to retreat, new-ancient forces are being released, together with the carbon, a resurgence of myth and storytelling...

1 A.N. Gorokhov and A.N. Fedorov, "Current Trends in Climate Change in Yakutia," *Geography and Natural Resources*, 39 (2), 2018.
2 First used by a Russian-born American scientist, Siemon Muller.
3 Jerry Brown and H. Jesse Walker, "Report from the International Permafrost Association: A brief history of the international permafrost conferences (1963–2003)," *Permafrost and Periglacial Processes*, 18 (4), 2007.
4 Robert O. van Everdingen, *Multi-language glossary of permafrost and related ground-ice terms: in Chinese, English, French, German, Icelandic, Italian, Norwegian, Polish, Romanian, Russian, Spanish, and Swedish* (Calgary: Arctic Institute of North America, 1998).
5 Hjort J, O Karjalainen, J. Aalto, S. Westermann, V.E. Romanovsky, F.E. Nelson, B. Etzelmüller, and M. Luoto, "Degrading permafrost puts Arctic infrastructure at risk by mid-century," *Nature Communications*, 9 (1), 2018.
6 Intergovernmental Panel on Climate Change, *Special report on the ocean and cryosphere in a changing climate*, 2019.
7 McGuire, A. David, David M. Lawrence, Charles Koven, Joy S. Clein, Eleanor Burke, Guangsheng Chen, Elchin Jafarov, et al., "Dependence of the evolution of carbon dynamics in the northern permafrost region on the trajectory of climate change," *Proceedings of the National Academy of Sciences* 115 (15), 2018.
8 Hitoshi Saito, Yoshihiro Iijima, Nikolay Basharin, Alexander Fedorov, and Viktor Kunitsk, "Thermokarst Development Detected from High-Definition Topographic Data in Central Yakutia," *Remote Sensing*, 10 (10), 2018.
9 Van Everdingen, 1998.
10 Term coined by Jem Bendell in: "Deep Adaptation," IFLAS Occasional Paper 2, July 27, 2018.
11 Dmitry Streletskiy and Nikolay Shiklomanov, *Arctic Cities through the Prism of Permafrost* (2016).

Gorilla Politics

An interview with Johannes Refisch, head of the Great Apes Survival Partnership (GRASP), an alliance of member nations, research institutions, conservation organizations, United Nations agencies, and private supporters based at the UN headquarters in Nairobi, Kenya. Not so long ago, mountain gorillas had a strong natural fear of humans. Now, they have changed: After decades of primatologists getting gorillas used to human presence, it is now possible even for tourists to spend time in close proximity to the Great Apes. Are we domesticating one of the last wildernesses—or are we helping it to survive?

I remember that discussion very well—in the early 90s, specifically in the mountain gorilla world, there were two camps. One said, "You're taking a high risk because if these individuals contract diseases from humans, you might lose the whole gorilla population." The other was saying, "Yes, it's a risk but the other risk is that we're losing the habitat because we have a growing human population, they need income, they need to feed their children." Retrospectively, it was the right decision. Both parks in Rwanda and Uganda have almost no poaching issues, no habitat loss. True. And mountain gorillas are the only great ape sub-species increasing in numbers: they almost doubled, to over 1,000 in total. Every other great ape species and sub-species is losing dramatically. We're having an orangutan crisis, a bonobo crisis, a chimpanzee crisis—so with the mountain gorillas, we're in a unique situation. Yet, they are still endangered by other threats—even climate change. We have indications that changes in the climate have an impact on the availability of food, and gorillas might be obliged to shift their diets. But in most cases the indirect impacts are stronger: Climate change has a massive impact on local communities, with longer dry spells, and more erratic rainfall resulting in mudslides and floods. People enter the park for drinking water during the dry season and this leads to additional disturbance. In some areas of the park the gorilla densities might be close to carrying capacity. So we might end up in a situation where fertility goes down or leads to more conflict, and population numbers go down because there is more stress. The Rwandan government has the vision to expand the park, but this is a complex process as there are many people living in close

proximity. Is it getting more difficult to protect nature without harming humans? The Virunga National Park in the DR Congo was created in 1924. At that time there were very few people. Now, the human population density is high. For me, the question is: How do I reconcile development and conservation? One of the answers for us is cross-sectoral land use planning. And is that something only the UN can negotiate? Why do we need the UN, if there are so many NGOs? We don't duplicate what NGOs do. Many conservation NGOs like WWF or WCS do a great job and we work very closely, but often, since we deal with major development projects, they're hitting a ceiling. We use the convening power of the UN and provide a platform for dialogue and cooperation. We try to help them with a cross-sectoral stakeholder dialogue, sometimes even with trans-boundary collaboration. Sometimes other governments can do this, but they never have the neutrality or the convening power of the UN. It's amazing. Often NGOs talk with the Ministry of Environment, but we have to include other ministries in the dialogue too, and the UN can facilitate this process.
Are you able to encourage alternative models of generating income, like hydroelectric dams, instead of oil drilling in Parks like the Virunga? The Virunga National Park has implemented a number of micro-hydropower plants, which provide "green energy." Also, there's a discussion about building a mega-dam for the Congo, which would be two times larger than the biggest in the world, the Three Gorges Dam in China. But do you have a chance to defend gorilla interests against oil companies who want to drill in the parks? You are referring to the case of Soco, an oil and gas exploration company based in the UK. Five years ago, they were doing test drills in the Virungas, the oldest national park in Africa, a world heritage site, home to gorillas, chimpanzees, elephants... It is said that the plan was to reduce the park's size by 20 percent, and that Soco was intimidating people who stood up against their project. Soco's endeavor was unjustifiable, and because it's a British company under British law, we took it to the British parliament—with the WWF in the lead, and the whole consortium of NGOs behind them. There was a parliamentary investigation, shareholders were approached; finally, under massive public pressure, the company gave up its plans.
Interview by RK & Niklas Maak, Nairobi, September 24, 2018

Gorilla Theory: In the Buffer Zone
Niklas Maak

THE KYAGURILO CASE

On a stormy April night in 2015, a group of mountain gorillas nested on top of one of the highest hills in the Bwindi Rain Forests, in Uganda. Rukina, a silverback and at this point the leader of a group of 21 gorillas, had built his nest next to a tall tree. Some rumors had it that he climbed that tree when the storm arrived, then drummed his chest when the lightning and thunder came closer, like a mythological Greek hero revolting against the gods; and that he was struck by lightning and fell off the tree. But that was pure speculation; maybe he just sat peacefully under that tree when, during the tempest, lightning hit the tree and passed into him. Rukina presumably died on the spot. In the morning after the storm, rangers discovered the group gathering around the silverback's dead body. Then the group moved on, but, as researchers observed, later they came back. The young ones touched him for the last time. Mountain gorillas are only found in two small habitats—in the Virunga Massif, straddling the boundaries between Rwanda, Uganda and the Democratic Republic of Congo, and in the 128-square-mile Bwindi Impenetrable National Park, a rainforest designated a nature reserve in 1991 in southwestern Uganda, not far from the borders of Rwanda and the Democratic Republic of Congo, on the edge of the Albertine Rift.

The two habitats are situated only about 20 miles apart, but both are surrounded by some of the highest densities of human population living in a rural setting, with 775 to 1,550 people per square mile, reliant mostly on subsistence farming; the wilderness had almost automatically become a park. Getting killed by lightning was the most unlikely death for a gorilla. What happened after Rukina's unlikely demise was even more unlikely: the group's decisions shook up popular theories about gorilla behavior.

When Rukina died, his group was the largest size it had ever been, with 21 members, among them two other silverbacks: Rukara and 15-year-old Mukiza. They fought once; Mukiza suffered a severe bite wound to his jaw, but survived; Rukara obtained alpha status. Gorilla groups always contain one or more silverbacks; adult females are never found on their own, presumably because they need a silverback to protect them and their offspring against other males—silverbacks are effectively hired guns. As a result of the presence of the two silverbacks, the group stayed together—for a while. But almost a year after the lightning strike, in 2016, the Kyagurilo group fissioned into two groups. Researchers observed an unusual phenomenon: Rukara retained ten individuals, among them just three adult females. More females went with the subordinate one, Mukiza. He also got ten members, including four adult females and one sub-adult female. Primatologist Martha Robbins told us, when we visited her at the Max Planck Institute for Evolutionary Anthropology in Leipzig: "Presumably, Mukiza and Rukara wanted to go to different areas and females followed whichever silverback they preferred." But why did more females go with the subordinate one, if among primates it's all about "male dominance" and strength? Or was that just a false assumption, a projection of (certain) human values onto the lives of gorillas?

"Fissioning in gorilla groups is not a common occurrence and only occurs in groups that contain more than one silverback," Robbins explains. "Fissioning is an example of female choice. Each female chose which silverback to stay with." But why did the silverbacks not fight, as popular theories suggest, to retain or attain the alpha status? "Maybe they were too closely matched in size and strength, resulting in a stalemate. Gorillas are one of the few mammal species in which adult females move between social groups, choosing which male to reside with. There's evidence that bigger males—with larger crests on their heads and wider shoulders—have more females in their groups, but it's difficult to disentangle the 'power' of males due to their size and strength and the 'power' of females to choose a male." Martha Robbins started her career in the early 1990s at the Karisoke Research Center in Rwanda, where she did her PhD on the mountain gorillas initially habituated in the late 1960s by the famous primatologist Dian Fossey. Fossey established the foundations of modern gorilla conservation in a moment when the species was at the brink of extinction: the Virunga population and the Bwindi population were estimated to have dropped as low as 250 each in the mid-1980s. In late 1985, Fossey was found murdered in her remote cabin, probably killed by poachers. She and Robbins never met. In

1998, Robbins embarked on long-term research in Uganda's Bwindi Impenetrable National Park. In hardly any other field have theories about animal behavior been so saturated with the ideologies of their time as in the study of gorillas.¹ In 1902, the German explorer Friedrich Robert von Beringe shot two mountain gorillas in the volcanic Virunga Mountains in Rwanda. This moment was framed, in the Western world, as the "discovery" of a species that of course was well known by the local population, but was still named *Gorilla beringei beringei*, after the German explorer who "discovered" them in a very colonial German way, by lethal immobilization. Ever since, the gorilla has been a highly ideologized construct in Western science and popular culture, reflecting preoccupations with nature, race, power, sexuality, and identity. The descriptions of gorillas by mostly male explorers and artists read like a mixture of job advertisements for mercenary armies and classic chauvinist fantasies about assertive force and alpha-male behavior (think of the French sculptor Frémiet's violent *Gorilla Carrying off a Negress*²). Gorilla theory traditionally emphasizes the concept of male dominance. The strongest silverback gets it all, among other means through "courtship aggression" towards females.

Depicted as a ferocious beast by the colonialists, the image shifted to "gentle giant" in the age of the hippies: in 1967, a year before the film *Planet of the Apes* presented a scenario where mutated apes took over man's role, holding humans in slavery, Fossey arrived in Africa and almost single-handedly changed the image of the ape.

After Fossey, female scientists became leaders in the field. While early male explorers zeroed in on a lustful-anxious identification with the silverbacks, by the 1980s the focus expanded to females and relationships among them; Pascale Sicotte did groundbreaking work on "female choice" in the late 1980s, at Karisoke. In a way, the history of recent primatology also reflects paradigmatic changes in discussions of gender and race, feminism, and postcolonial theory. After reading Donna Haraway's groundbreaking *Primate Visions*, Jacques Derrida's *The Animal That Therefore I Am*, or, more recently, Frans De Waal's *Are We Smart Enough to Know How Smart Animals Are?* and Georgina M. Montgomery's *Primates* in the *Real World: Escaping Primate Folklore and Creating Primate Science*, the jungle all of a sudden looks different.

Did male researchers overemphasize the importance of the—still-relevant—concept of male dominance and marginalize the role of female choice? Or did circumstances change, and with them the apes? Do we have to remove the ideological language that has hampered our ability to analyze or even to observe the behavior of the animals? What happened in the Kyagurilo group? Was Mukiza, the subordinate silverback, more interesting to the younger females? Did three of the four older females join Rukara because they had all known Mukiza since he was an infant? If they chose to go with him though he was maybe less skilled as a fighter, what else influenced their decision? Was the weaker, subordinate gorilla maybe a better groomer? Grooming is a cultural technique passed from one generation to another. There are groomer groups and groups that groom less. It's a mixture of hygiene and caressing. Is grooming, in a carefully supervised and curated wilderness, the new strong? Robbins was cautious when it came to such speculations. She is a scientist. "Mukiza does groom his females quite a bit," Robbins said. "But you can't really understand without analyzing the data. Some silverbacks groom frequently and others not at all. Similarly, some adult females groom others. How much a gorilla grooms others can also change over time," Robbins explained. "It would be interesting to see if male behavior is passed on to their sons. But this work has not been done."

What we do know is that, as with human primates, it seems to be of great importance for the immature gorilla's education, and character, that they play and interact with other kids, and have strong social bonds with the mother. It's hard to imagine that it plays no role whether the silverback is a groomer or aloof, authoritarian and strict, or permissive and playful. What if the focus on male dominance was an ideologically conditioned framing that cannot represent a much more complex reality?[3] Following terminology established by colonial explorers from the West, do we only see a blurry caricature of Western preoccupations when we look at gorillas?

RADICAL CONSERVATION AND HABITUATION

In the 1980s, less than 250 mountain gorillas remained in the Virungas, endangered by habitat destruction, poaching, disease, and from 1990 on, also by civil conflict. But due to massive conservation efforts, by 2018, the population of the Virungas more than doubled to 600 gorillas. In total, the entire subspecies surpassed 1,000 gorillas. A recent

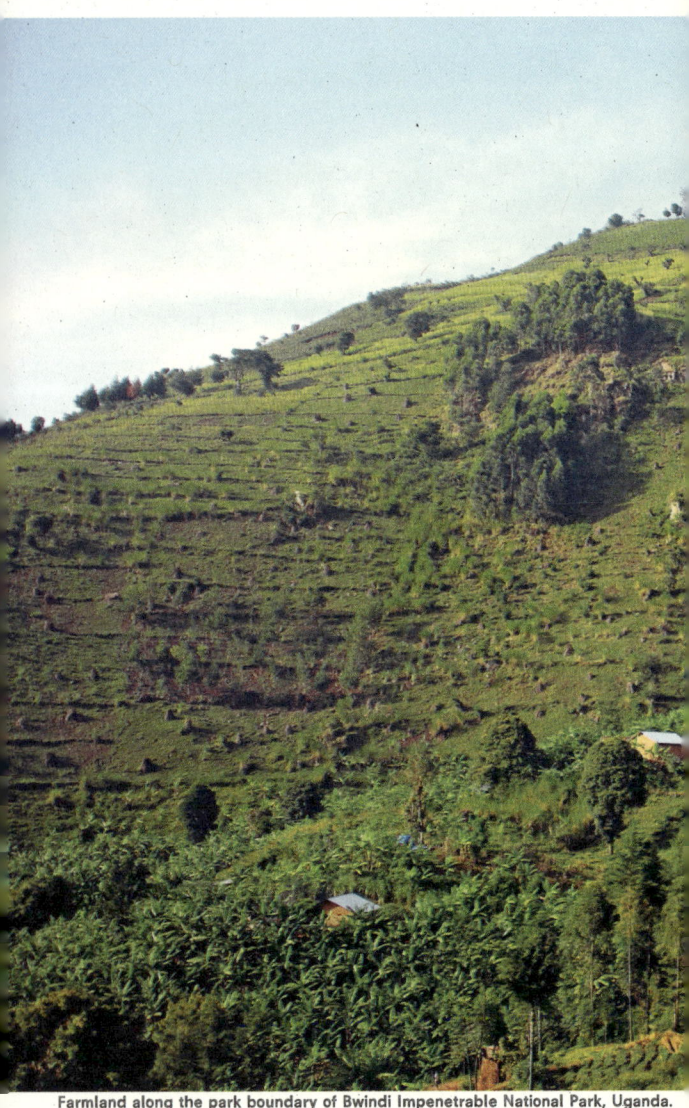
Farmland along the park boundary of Bwindi Impenetrable National Park, Uganda.

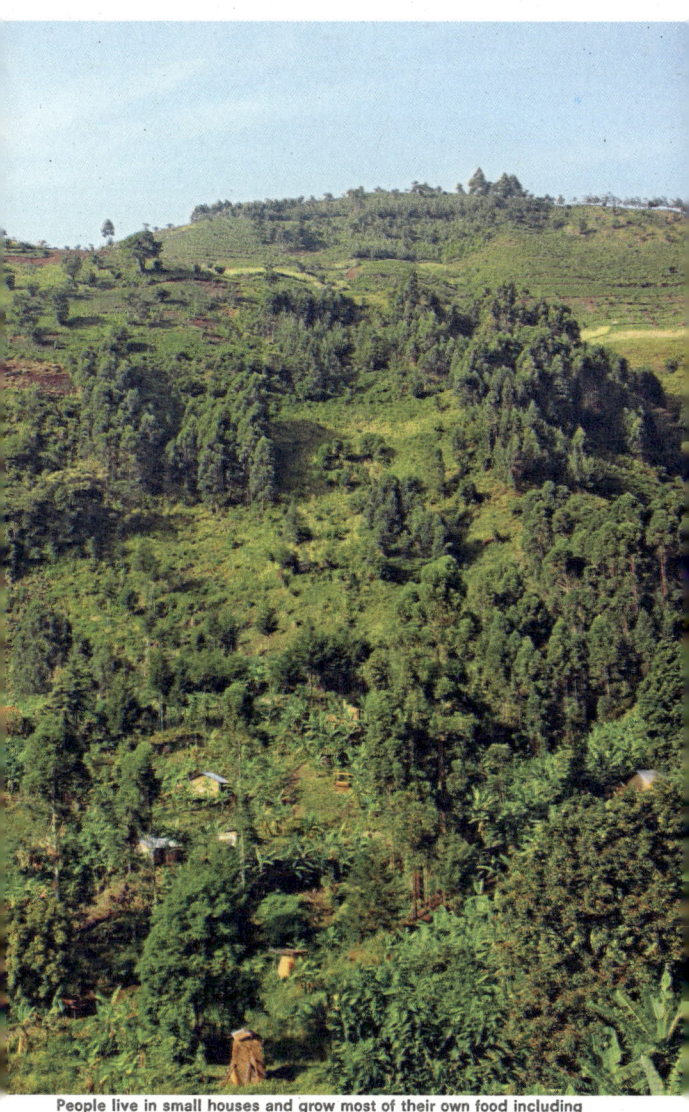
People live in small houses and grow most of their own food including potatoes, beans, corn, sorghum, and bananas. (Martha M. Robbins/MPI-EVAN)

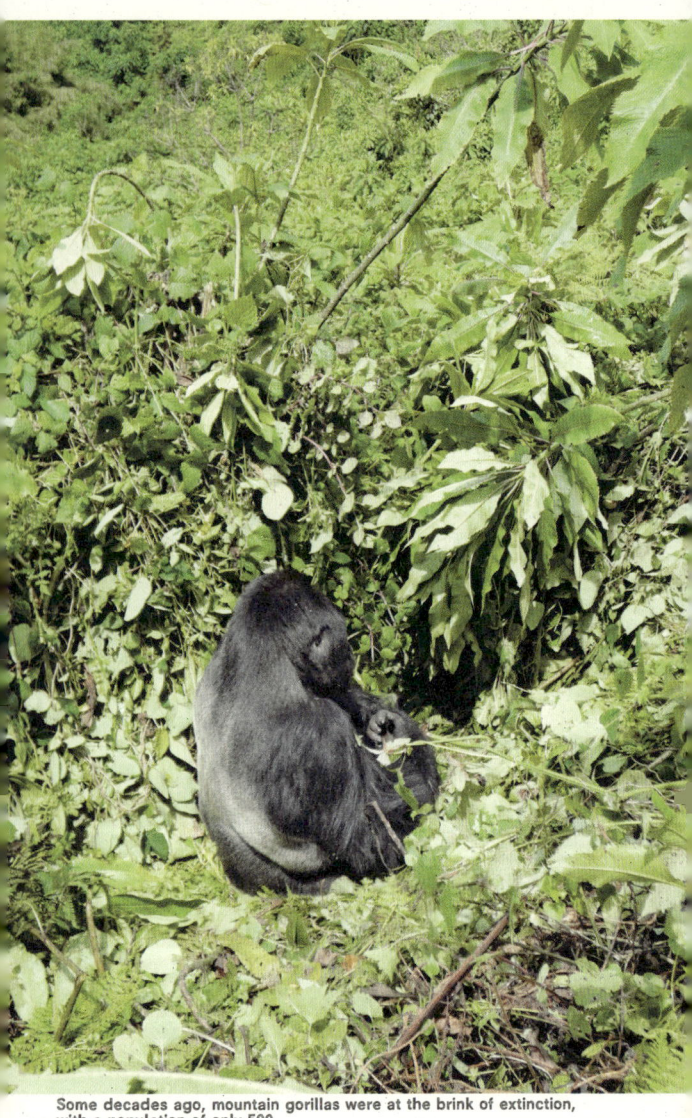
Some decades ago, mountain gorillas were at the brink of extinction, with a population of only 500.

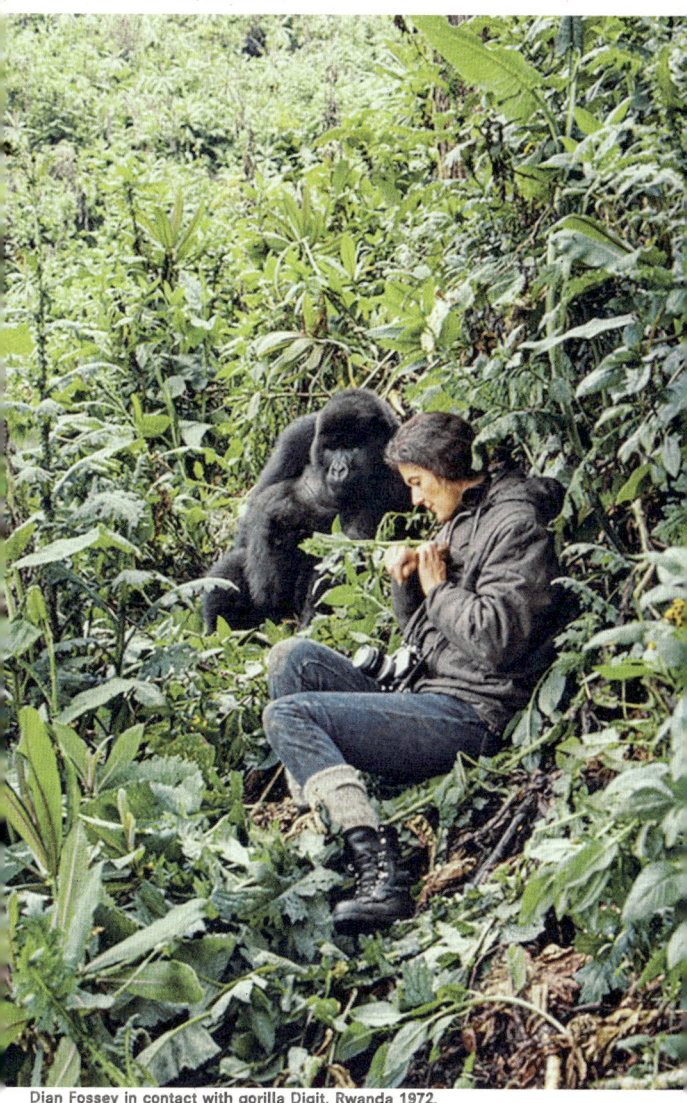

Dian Fossey in contact with gorilla Digit, Rwanda 1972.
(Bob Campbell Papers, Special and Area Studies Collections, George A. Smathers Libraries, University of Florida, Gainesville, Florida.)

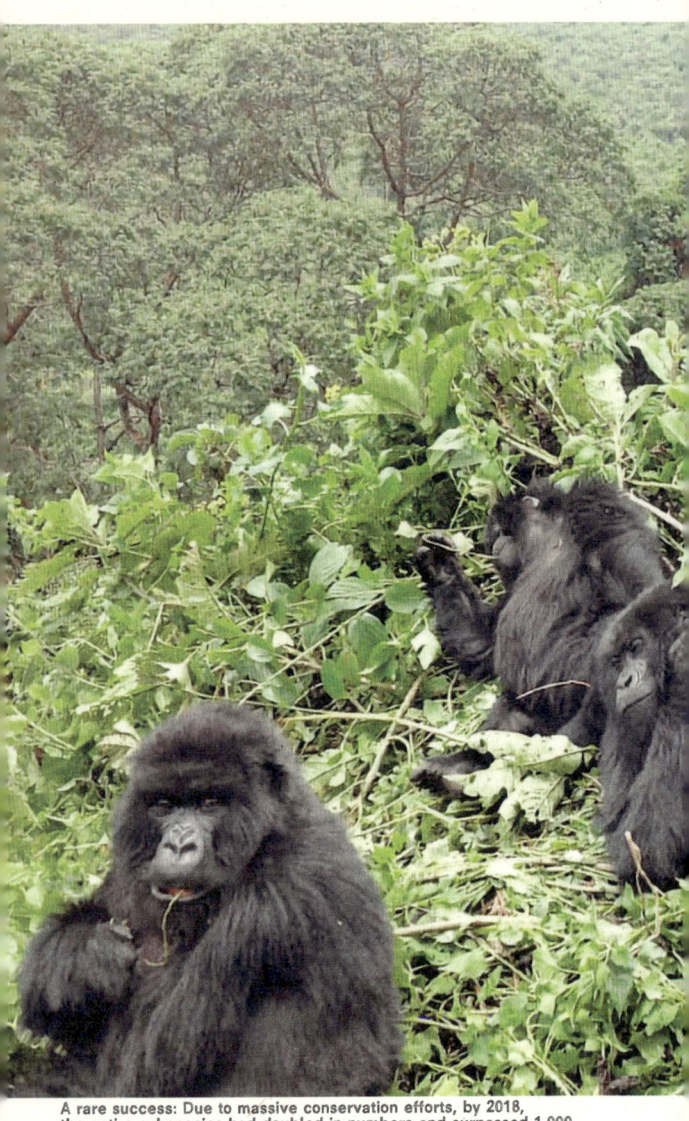

A rare success: Due to massive conservation efforts, by 2018, the entire subspecies had doubled in numbers and surpassed 1,000.

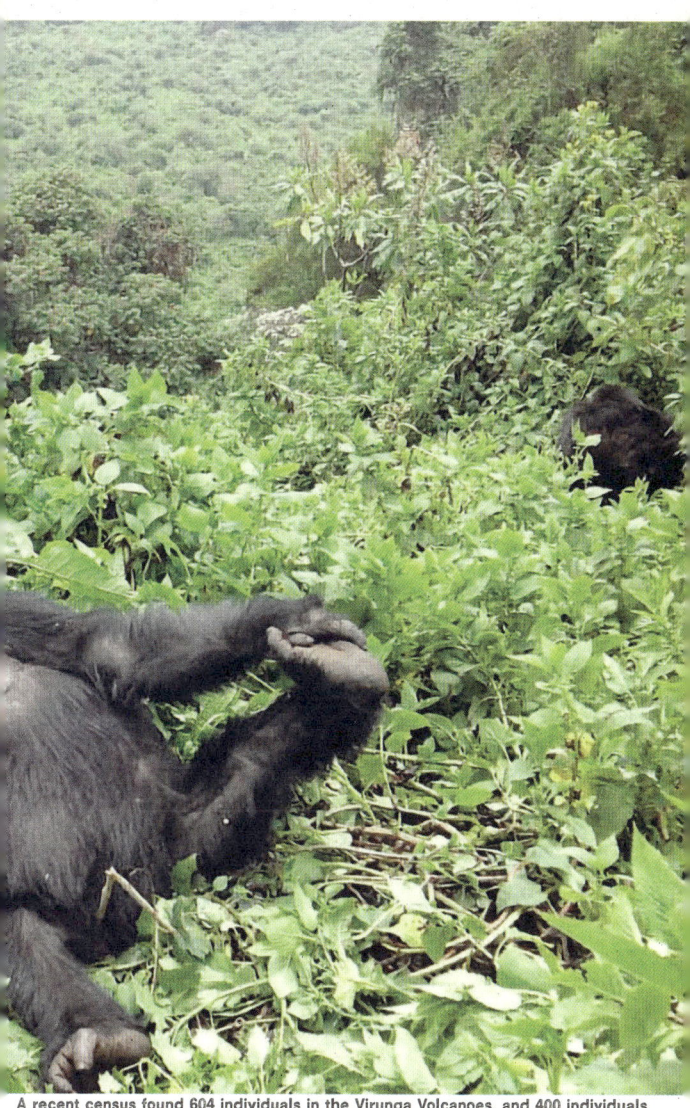
A recent census found 604 individuals in the Virunga Volcanoes, and 400 individuals living in the only other population, in Bwindi. Yet the risk of extinction remains.

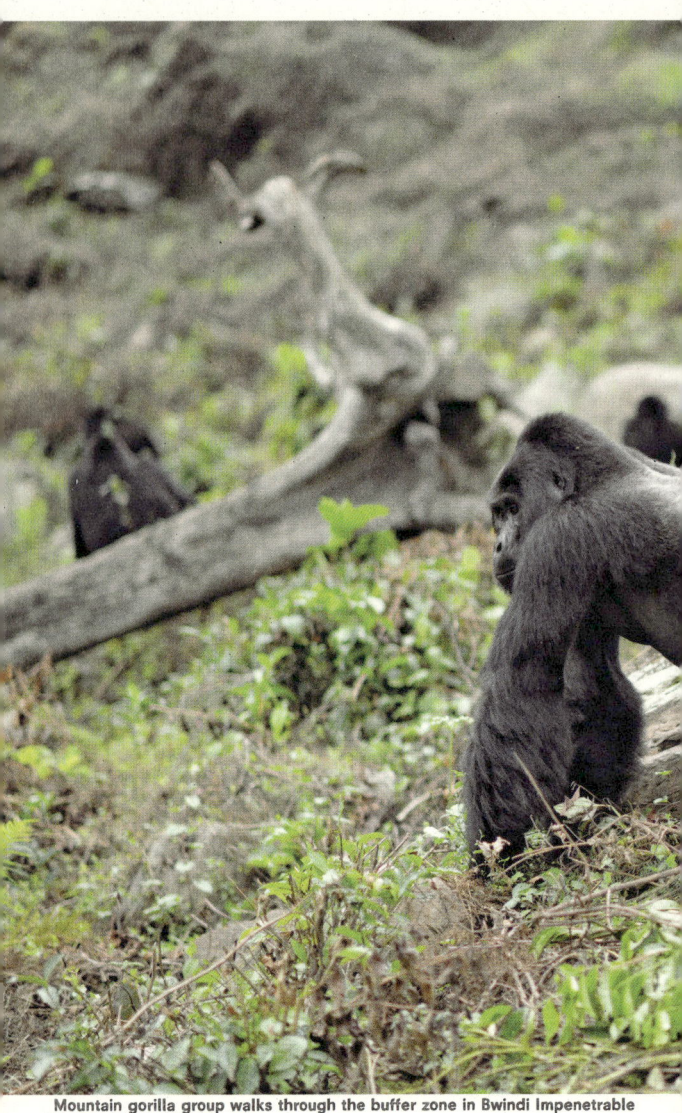

Mountain gorilla group walks through the buffer zone in Bwindi Impenetrable National Park, Uganda.

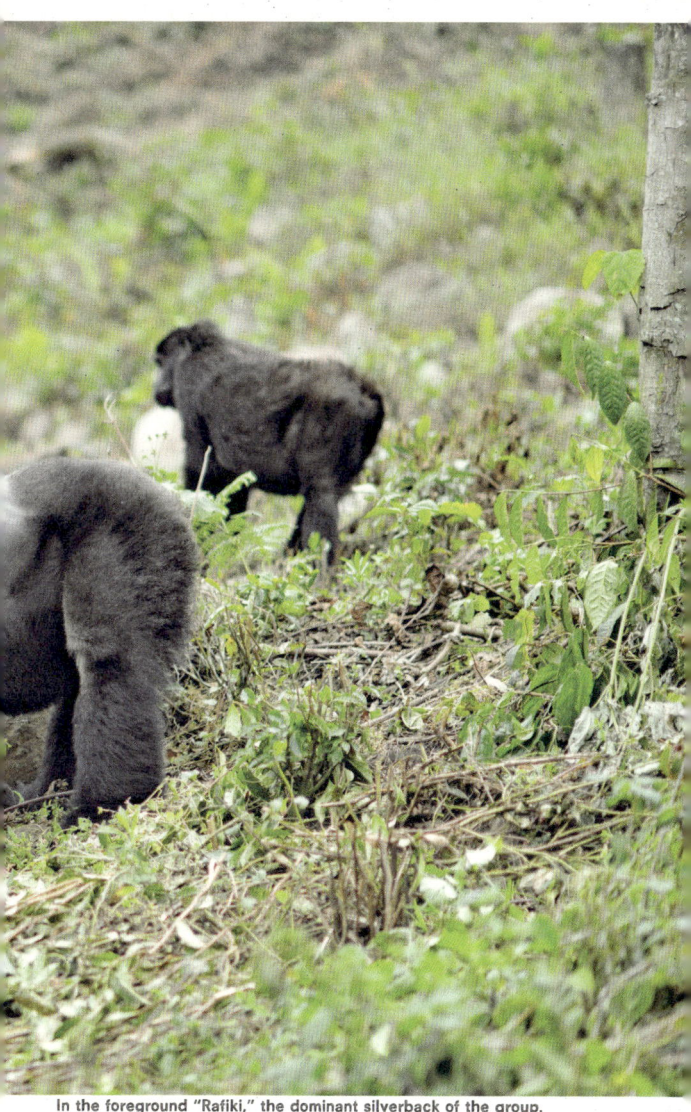
In the foreground "Rafiki," the dominant silverback of the group.
(Jack Richardson/ MPI-EVAN)

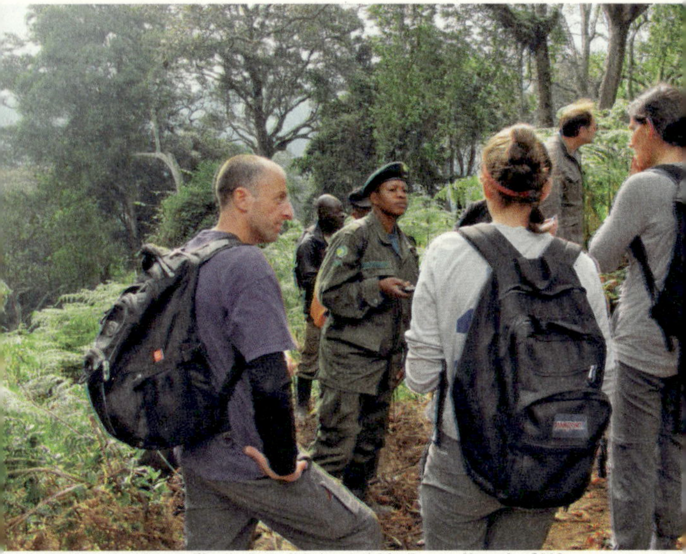

Looking for the gorillas in Bwindi impenetrable Forest, Uganda, 2018.
Bwindi impenetrable Forest, Uganda, 2018. (Stefan Sauter)

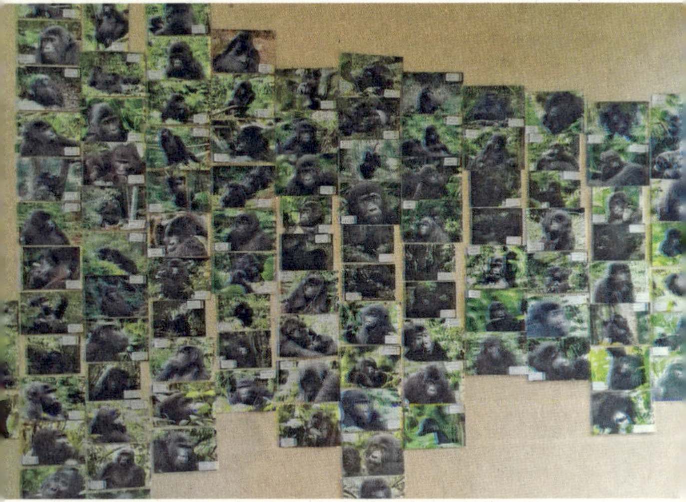

"Gorilla Wall" in primatologist Martha Robbins' house, in Uganda.

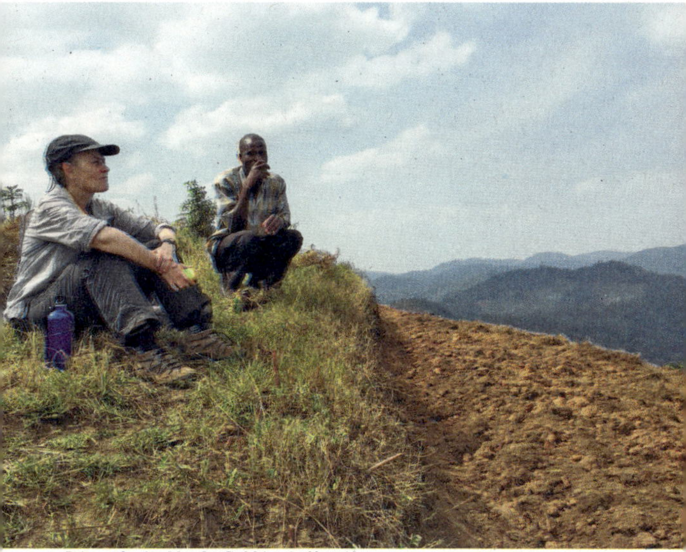

Primatologist Martha Robbins in Uganda.

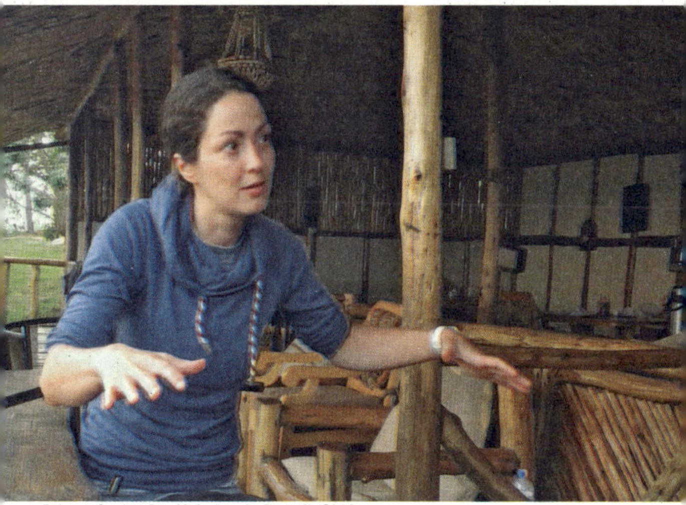

Primatologist Cat Hobaiter in Bwindi, 2018.
(Stefan Sauter)

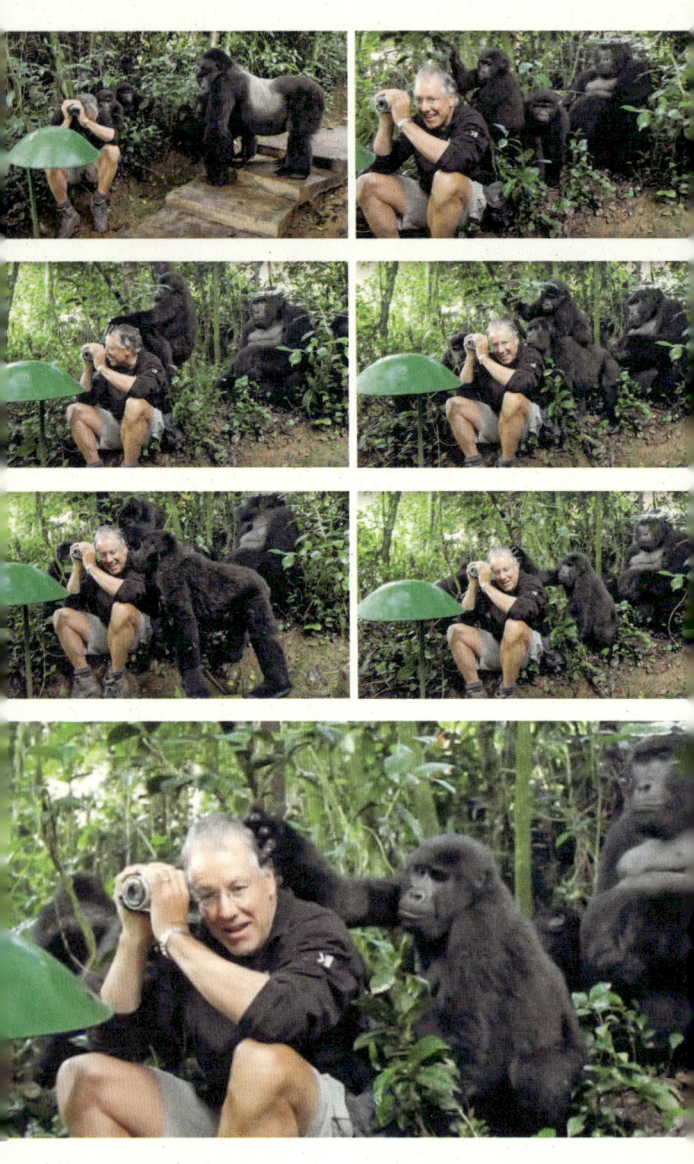

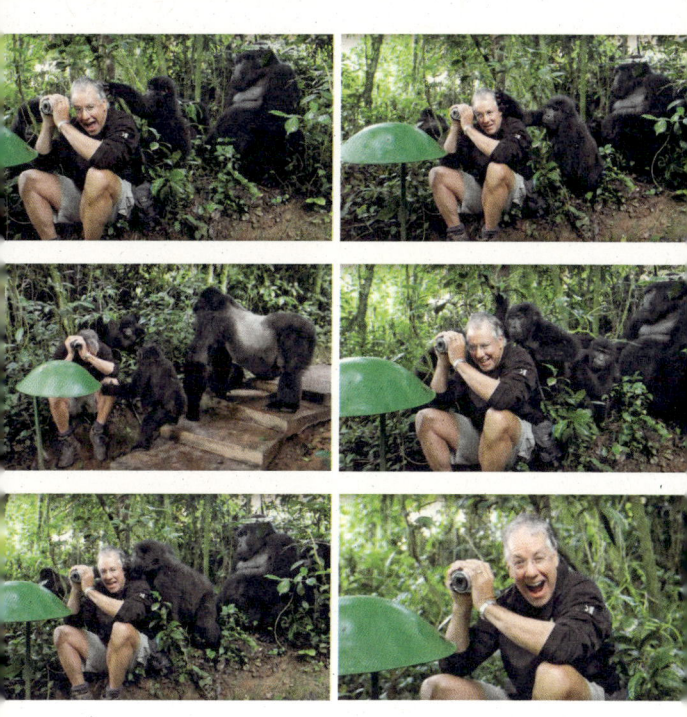

Apparently, habituated gorillas can identify humans as some kind of hairless, yet groomable ape, as this incident near the Gorilla safari lodge, at the western border of the Bwindi Park, shows.

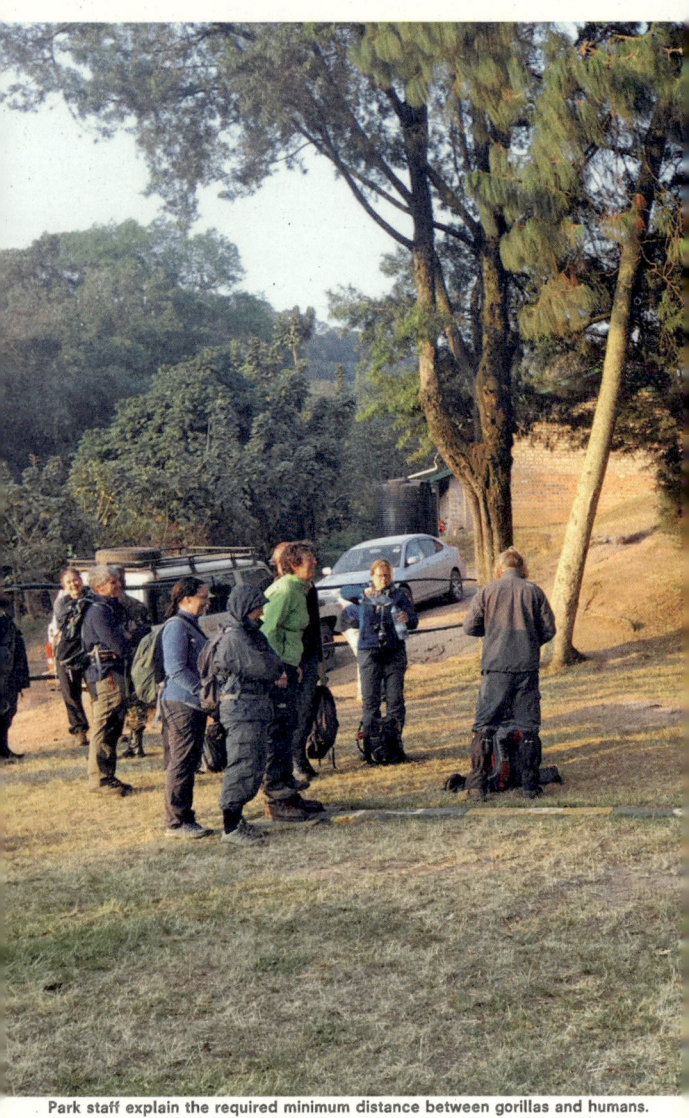
Park staff explain the required minimum distance between gorillas and humans.

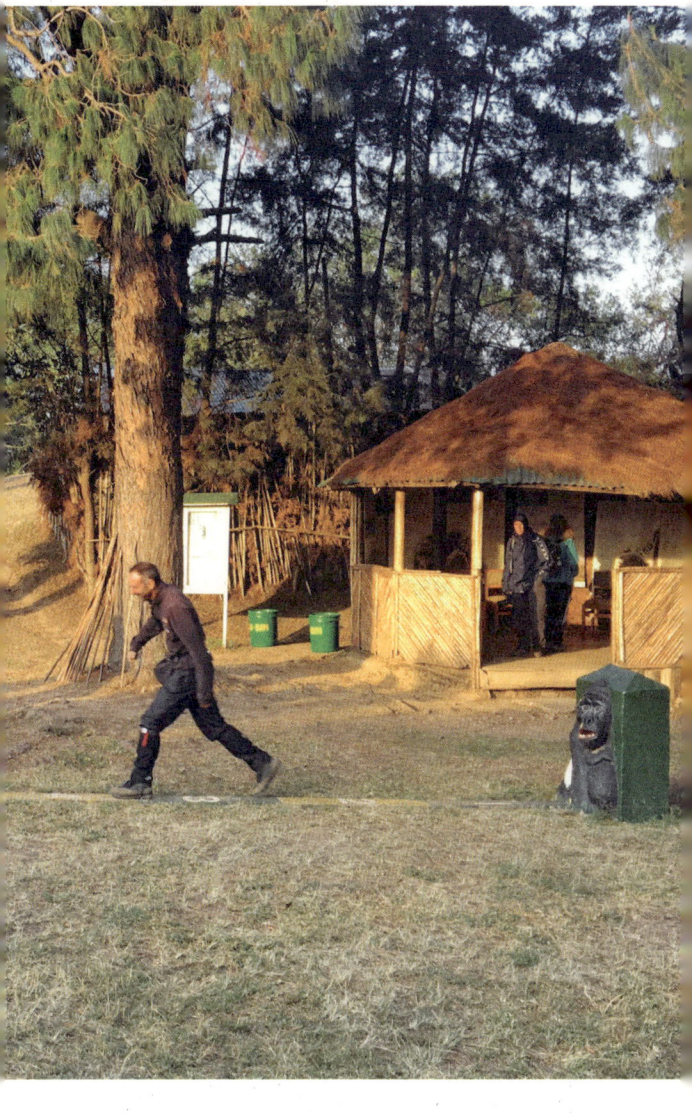

census, Martha Robbins said, found 604 individuals in the Virunga Mountains, and 400 individuals living in the only other population, in Bwindi. This increase led to them being a rare case of downlisting on the IUCN Red List from critically endangered to endangered status in late 2018. Despite the downlisting, the risk of extinction remains.

Fossey famously cuddled with gorillas to show how human they are—not ferocious beasts, but close relatives. "Today," Robbins said, "we don't want the gorillas touching us, nor should we touch them, however tempting it is. We try to stay at least eight yards away. One of the biggest concerns is disease transmission from humans to the gorillas. A common cold or flu for us can turn into something life-threatening for wild gorillas. There are these old photographs of Fossey cuddling with gorillas. But I highly discourage that. I want the gorillas to behave as gorillas. I want to see a window into their world without me being an influence on it." Robbins tries to keep them as "wild" as possible. Which is not so easy. Because one of the reasons for this unusual success story in animal conservation is what primatologists call the process of habituation. Wild gorillas are afraid of humans; they will flee or charge if people get close to them. The aim of habituation is to get the gorillas used to viewing humans as neutral beings in their environment. In the past four decades, gorilla groups in Bwindi and the Virungas have experienced almost daily proximity with researchers and primatologists, and the animals have lost their strong natural fear of humans. Robbins actively helped to habituate (without breaching the seven-meter rule) numerous groups, making up almost half of Bwindi's gorillas. Seventy-five percent of the mountain gorillas in the Virunga Mountains are habituated. "Without habituation, we can't observe gorillas up close and learn about their social lives," Robbins said. Habituated gorillas can be treated by veterinarians – and almost as a side effect, the habituated gorillas also accept a certain number of tourists in their habitat. Tourism thus has become a significant source of revenue, with visiting fees of up to $1,500 per person. Critics hold that the local population should profit more from the distribution of the benefits, and that not only does the danger of disease transmission rise with habituation, but also the character of the wild animal is noticeably changed. It is evident that the gorilla's response to humans has changed. Yet some primatologists confidently claim that habituation does not change gorilla–gorilla behavior. That is a rather apodictic claim, and maybe wishful thinking.

FIRST ENCOUNTER

The first time I traveled to see gorillas, in 2010, I went to Rwanda. We drove up from Kigali Airport towards the volcanoes, past bars, tea plantations, and some supermarkets. We saw hills and more hills—and constant rain. Then, further up the mountains, it was eucalyptus country, the stems of the trees red, since they soak up the red earth with the water. Around 10:00 p.m., we checked into our bungalows. At midnight, the rain stopped, and the tips of the Virunga volcanoes emerged as gray silhouettes in the moonlight. It was cold. A man came by and silently lit a fire. There were more stars than anywhere else in the world.

In the morning, the grass was damp; fog hung over the mountain meadows and in the tops of the eucalyptus trees. The trackers stood by their jeeps, their fingers playing languidly with their AK-47s. François, the guide, stood in front of a map and went through the rules of conduct and answered questions.

- What if, said one of the tourists with a trembling voice, a gorilla attacks me?
- They don't do that, François said. What would you do if one approached you?
- Not run away.
- Very good.
- Raise arms and make a noise to drive him away, another tourist added.
- Bad idea. You can do that with hyenas in the savannah, but not with gorillas.
- So what do we do?
- When a gorilla approaches you, you slowly move as far away as possible. Be calm. Don't look him in the eyes. Pretend to eat a leaf. That calms them down. They're like us. If you have a picnic on a meadow, you'll be more comfortable with someone also picnicking than with someone who gets in your way and stares at you.

John, our tracker, walked a few yards ahead of us. He wore boots and an AK-47 on his back. *Juste au cas où*, he said. Just in case.

- What kind of case?
- In case we meet buffaloes. The buffaloes are dangerous. If they are aggressive, we'll fire a warning shot.

We kept going. The trackers used their machetes to cut an elegant swathe into the undergrowth of the ever-damp cloud forest of the volcanoes, moving their arms as if they were directing an adagio. In a clearing, we found an abandoned nightly nest site of the gorillas. On their search for food, they travel 550 yards a day. As dusk falls, they make a nest for the night. The home range of a group is eight to ten square miles. They were not far now. They were maybe 10 yards away. Even before you saw the animals, before you saw their soft fur in the sun, before their smell pervaded the bushes, you could hear them. That is: you actually only heard a peculiar cracking, as if some children ripped open a bag of chips and were devouring them. *crackcrackcrack.* François assumed a gorilla-like posture and pushed his jaw forward to make as gorillaish sound that was supposed to announce our presence to the gorillas, as gorillas don't hear that well and don't like surprises. The gorillas sat there, in a clearing on a slope, leaning back into the undergrowth, looking at the valley (at least that's what it looked like), feeding on wild celery with devotion, and a comforting growl. They looked very beautiful. They had long, shiny black fur; from a distance, if they walked on all fours, they rather resembled a strangely oversized Newfoundland dog. They did not look like ferocious beasts or King Kong, but peaceful and almost philosophical. They held the celery sticks a bit like cigars. There is no mafia film in which the actor manages to lean so elegantly casual against a tree, look into the distance and then put a stem into his mouth. They get up as the sun rises, around 6:00 a.m., then feed for some hours, then rest, and feed again. Gorillas are vegetarians. They primarily eat leaves, stems and pith of herbaceous vegetation. Adult males digest up to 25 kilos of vegetation each day. In the Virungas, their diet consists of only four species of plants: wild celery, bedstraw, nettles, and thistles whose stem contains as much water as a bottle of Evian. In Bwindi, gorillas have a more varied diet. A young gorilla rocked on an absurdly thin branch until it bent, whereupon the animal rolled down the thickly vegetated, steep slope. She apparently enjoyed it. You would have liked to imitate this, if you were not worried about your bones and the whims of the gorillas. You must not slip—which is not so easy on the steep, humid slopes—as they don't like violent cracks and noises. That's why the trackers make strange grunts, believing that these sounds sound like what the gorillas do when they're in a good mood, but maybe the gorillas are only too happy to realize that when the humans approach them, they always reliably repeat the same noise, like a truck that beeps when reversing.

The silverback looked relaxed. That's not always the case, said François, who used to work as a porter for Dian Fossey. Sometimes they come at you when you're standing in their way—and you never know if you are, because there are no marked trails in the jungle – and then they might even push you aside with a serious look and a hearty grasp. But these gorillas did not do that. They ate their celery. They plucked a thistle stem and chewed it (gorillas do not drink, so they have to suck the water from the thistle and other stems). The silverback was permissive, allowing the boy to climb on top of him. One gorilla looked at me. We were only two yards away from each other.

You can't sit like this with a group of lions. You should not do it with any wild animal of a certain size and teeth like this. A gorilla could potentially kill you, but will not just do it. There seems to be a deep generosity in these animals letting a bunch of hairless apes in ugly functional clothing into their world. Sitting with gorillas has been described as an "archaic" experience, a descent into man's origins. But it's rather an ascent, and it feels more like a visit to an advanced, peaceful, admirably relaxed future civilization. I sat down where a gorilla had just left. In the distance, the volcanoes emerged from the morning haze. There are a total of eight, the highest at 14,787 feet, being the Karisimbi; they belong to the East African Rift Valley, which begins in the highlands of Ethiopia. In the valley, the new tin roofs of the huts reflected the sun. Two gorillas sat a few yards away and seemed to look in the same direction. Further back, a tourist group appeared. The international guidelines are that each habituated group of gorillas can be visited by one group with a maximum of eight tourists for only one hour per day. Every day a strictly controlled number of people are allowed to go up to the gorillas in the mountains, which is only possible because they've been habituated—otherwise they would run away. Over the decades, they've gotten used to seeing strange, hairless apes in their world; the young gorillas do not even care about guests anymore.

In fact, habituated gorillas do not only have higher population growth rates; they are also changing their behavior. They are curious. As a film of an incident outside a park shows, young habituated gorillas even groom humans. One morning in late 2011, the photographer John King watched a group of gorillas coming to his lodge in Western Bwindi National Park. They walked

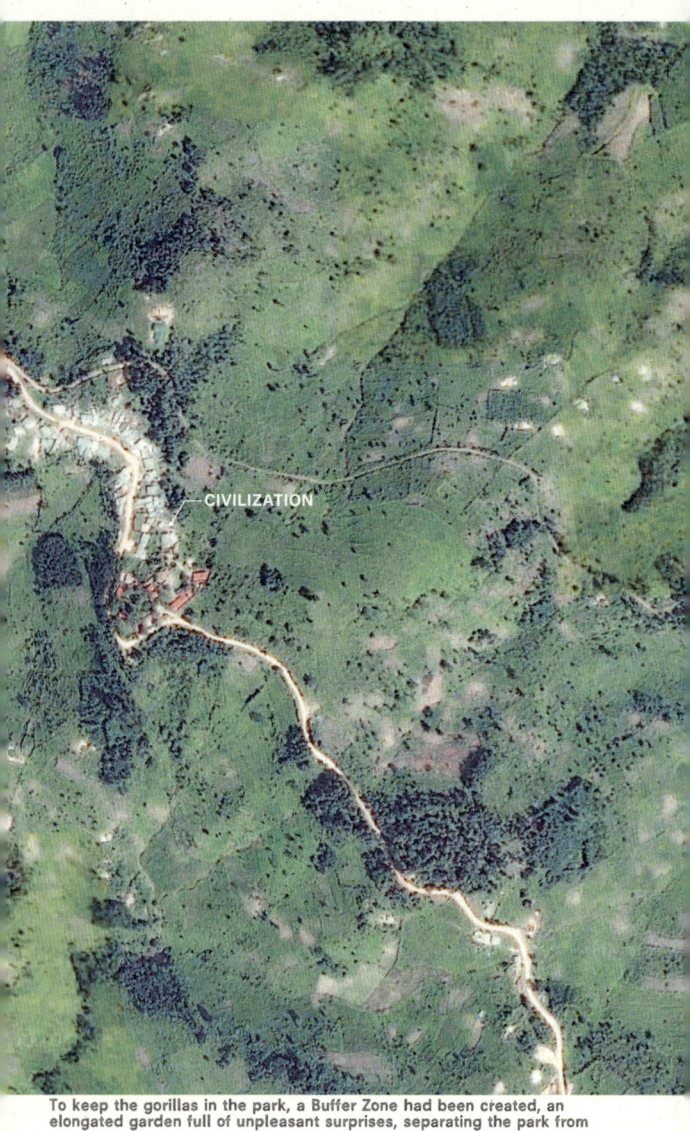

To keep the gorillas in the park, a Buffer Zone had been created, an elongated garden full of unpleasant surprises, separating the park from

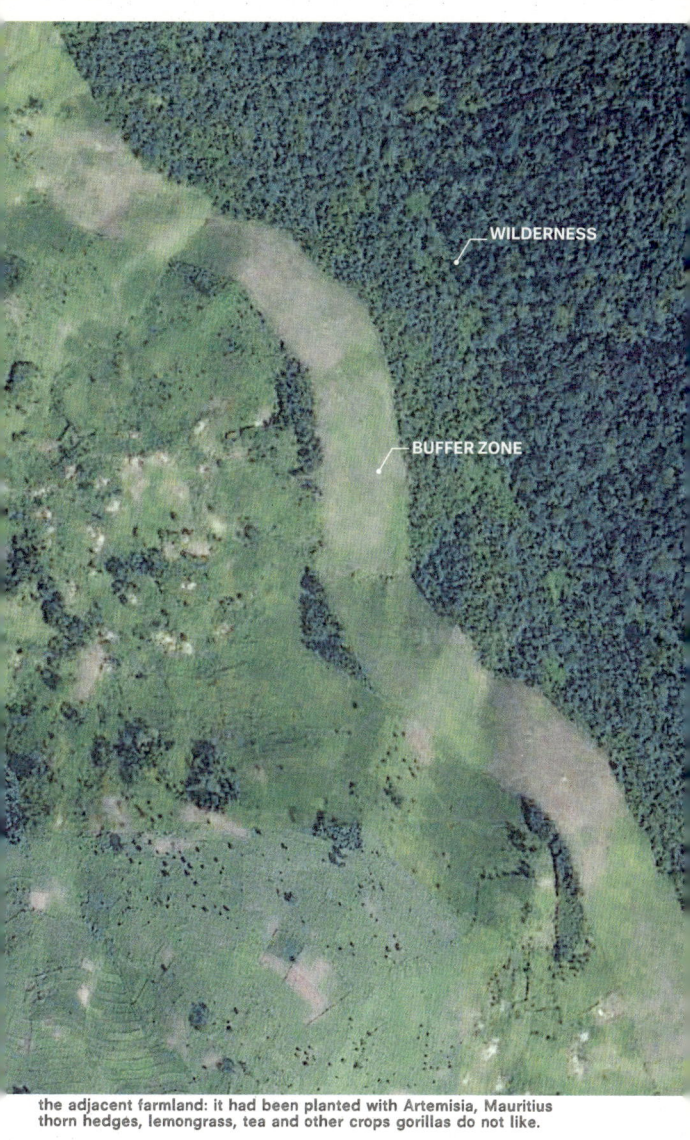

the adjacent farmland: it had been planted with Artemisia, Mauritius thorn hedges, lemongrass, tea and other crops gorillas do not like.

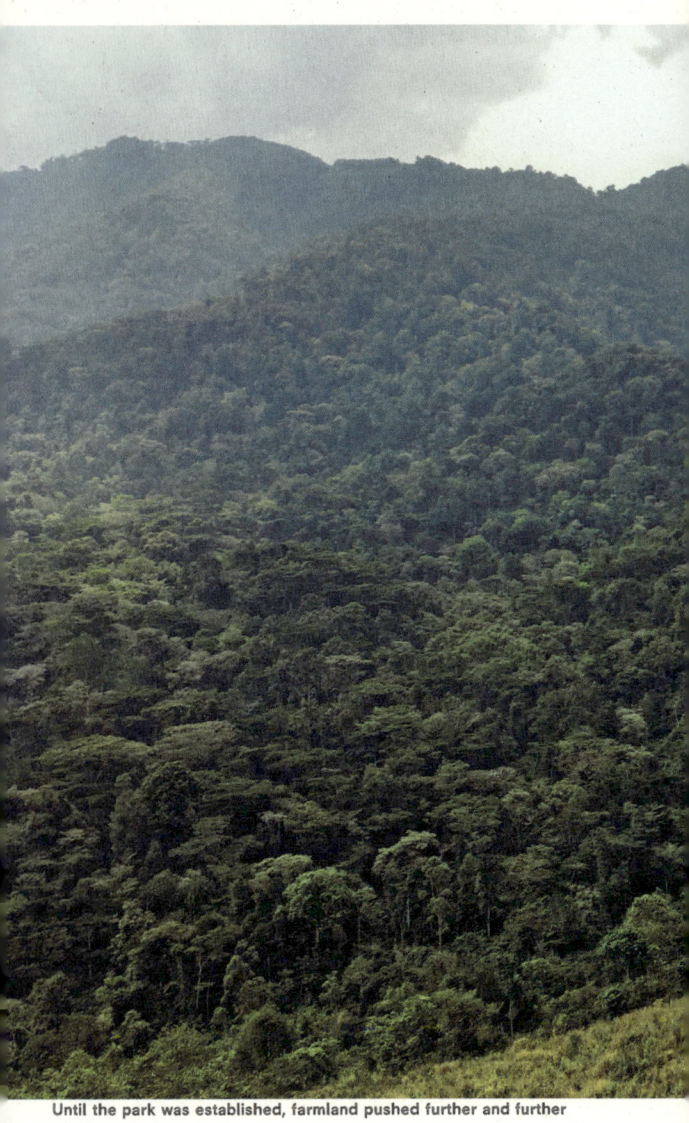
Until the park was established, farmland pushed further and further

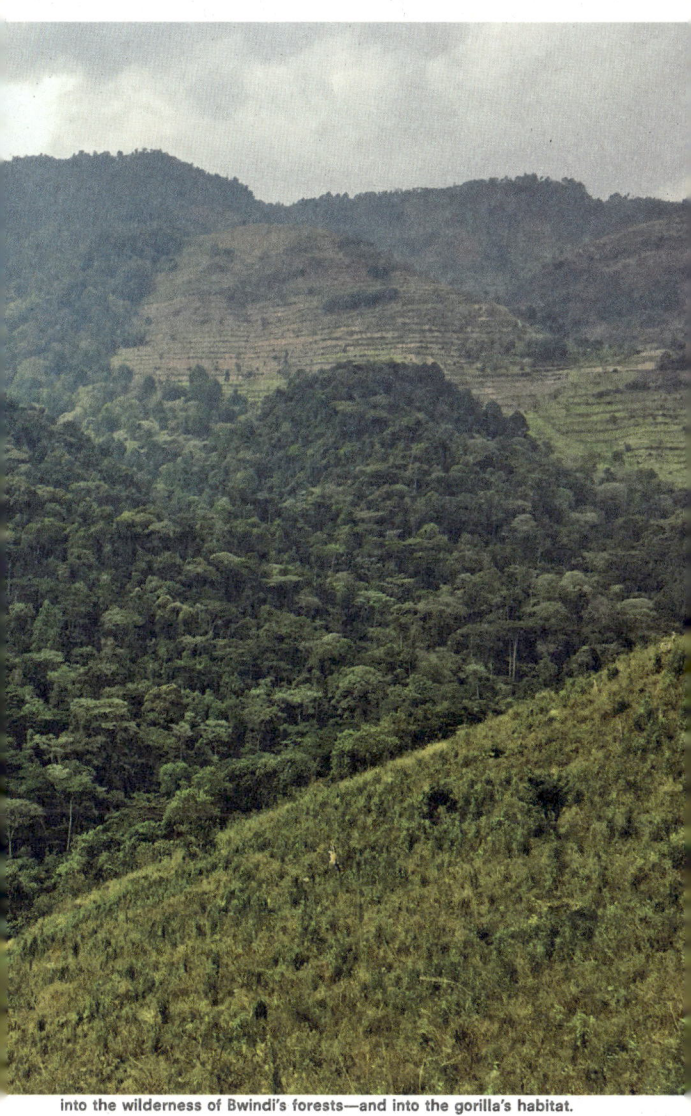
into the wilderness of Bwindi's forests—and into the gorilla's habitat.

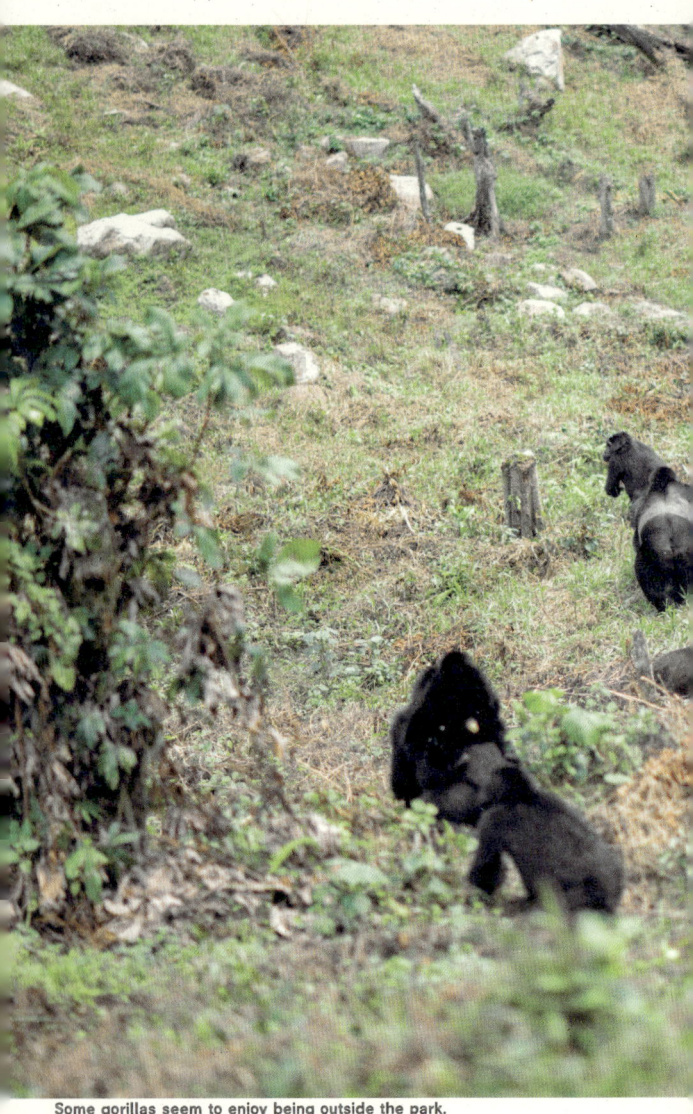
Some gorillas seem to enjoy being outside the park. They find new food sources, like Eucalyptus trees.

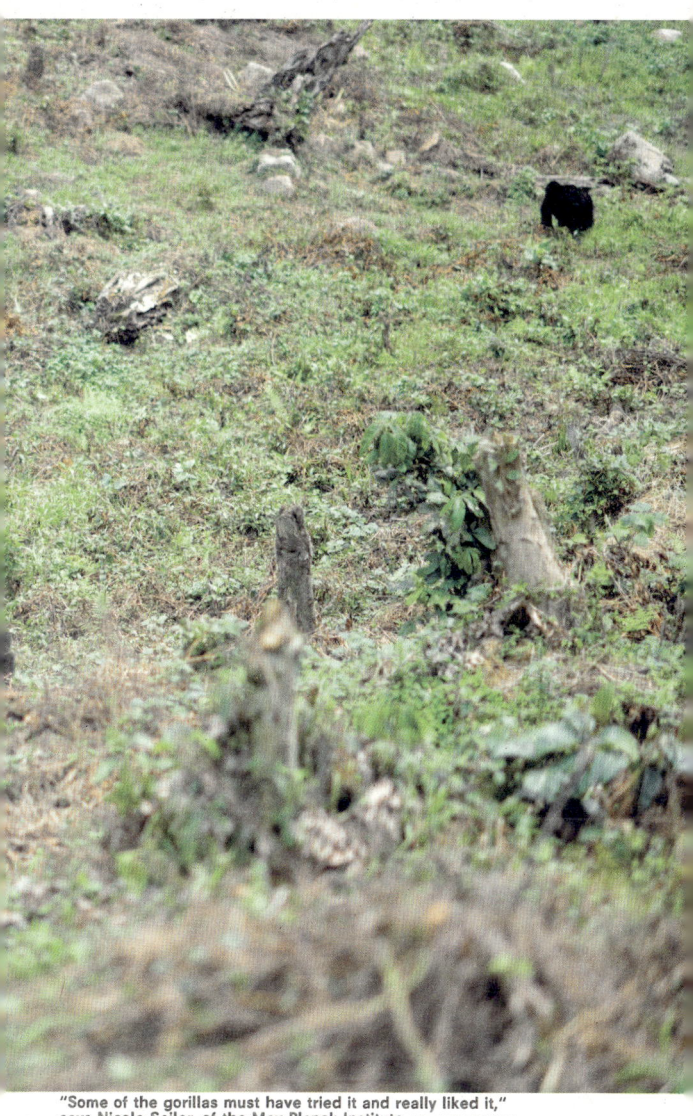
"Some of the gorillas must have tried it and really liked it," says Nicole Seiler, of the Max Planck Institute. (Dr. Martha Robbins)

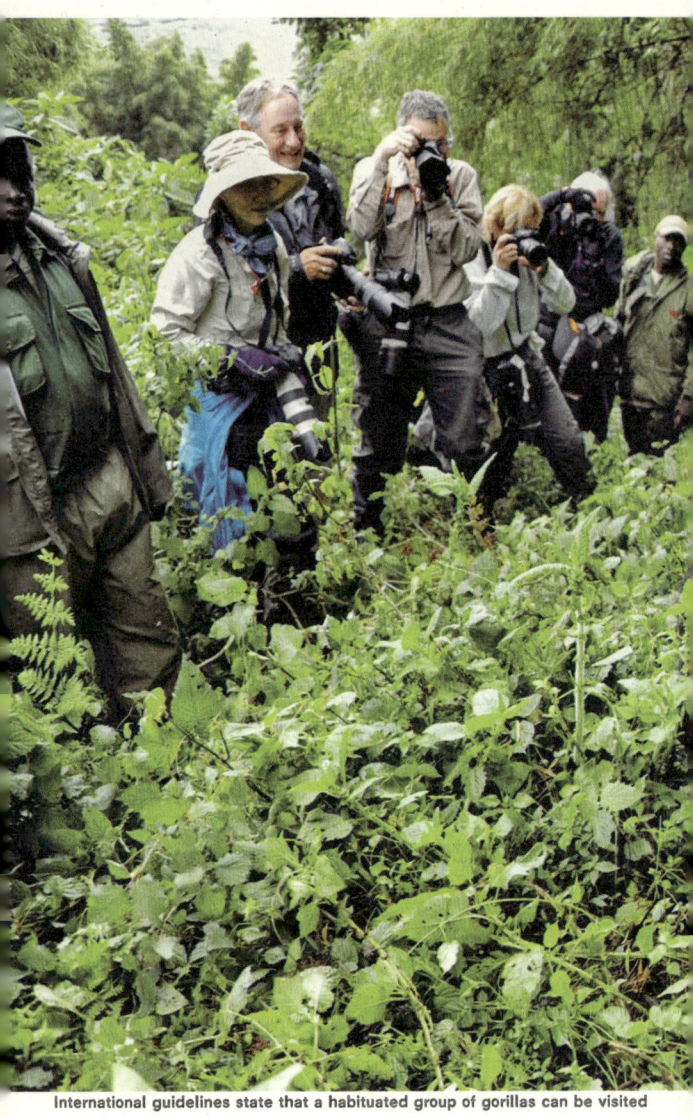

International guidelines state that a habituated group of gorillas can be visited

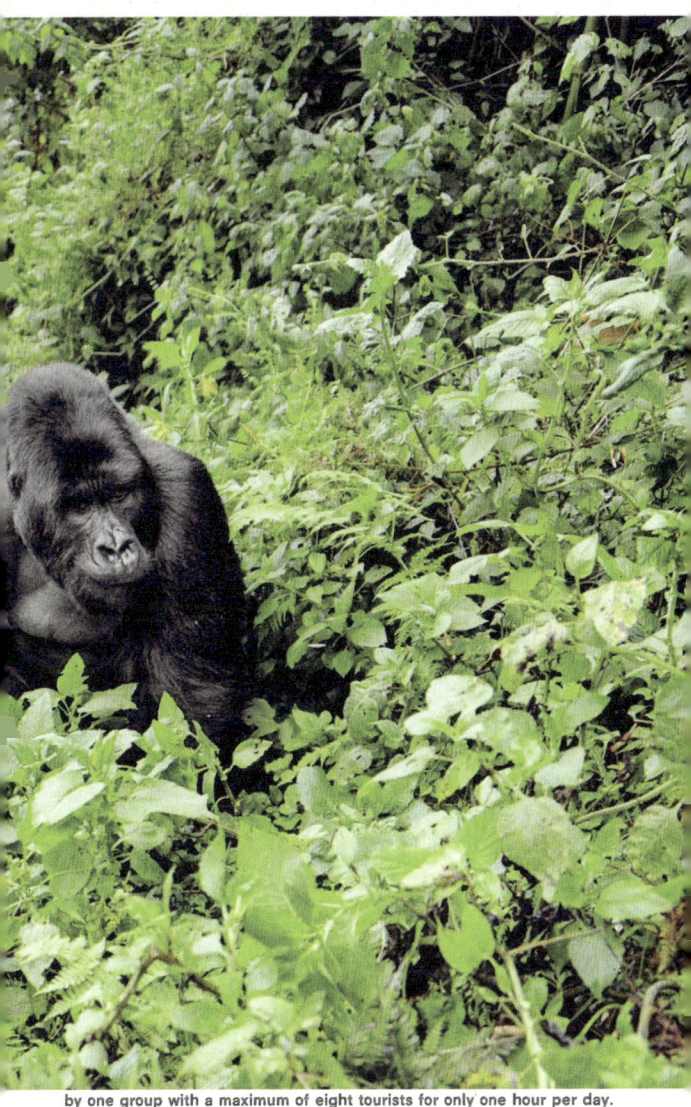
by one group with a maximum of eight tourists for only one hour per day.
(Agape Travels)

up and down the concrete stairs; finally, a young gorilla sat behind him and started to groom his hair (as he could not find any fur on his back). Apparently, the habituated gorilla can identify humans as some kind of hairless, yet groomable ape. "They were 50 yards away, I wanted to sit and watch them," the King told me when we talked about the incident. "All of a sudden they came closer. A young male stopped and grabbed my leg." The young gorilla sat behind him and started to look at his back. What did he look for? What did he see? A deplorable furless primate? We are smart enough to understand that gorillas are close relatives to us; but are we smart enough, to paraphrase Frans de Waal, to know that the gorilla is clearly also able to identify *us* as her close relative? "After some moments," John said, "the young gorilla started to groom my hair. His touch was extremely gentle." Primatologists are not happy about this behavior; it is an unintended byproduct of habituation.

It seems that one of "man's closest relatives" is getting even closer, at a much faster pace than expected: Radical conservation paradoxically leads to the emergence of radical mutations, at least in the behavior of the species.

CONSERVATION PARADOXES

Might habituated gorillas become a form of hybrid animal, neither tame nor wild? In the attempt to preserve an authentic, original condition, that condition itself is inevitably altered; habituation inevitably means that the habituated animal's behavior towards humans changes. "One could view the habituated gorillas as a little less wild than gorillas that are unhabituated," Robbins explained in Leipzig. "But they're still wild. They're not like pets, they are not zoo animals, they do not rely on humans for food, but yes, a bit of that wildness has been taken away."

Will habituated gorillas influence, or even educate unhabituated gorillas with their new insights and experiences? If an unhabituated gorilla joins a habituated group, she is initially afraid of humans, as all unhabituated gorillas are, but when she sees that the other habituated gorillas are not reacting with fear to humans, she becomes habituated much faster. "One could say this is a form of social learning," Robbins said. "Essentially, the unhabituated gorilla sees people and goes 'oh my goodness, we should run,'" Robbins said. "But they take cues from the habituated gorillas. And then they're like, 'Well, everybody else in the group thinks these people are OK,' so they join the club." The habituated gorilla might still be considered "more wild than tame" by primatologists. But with boundaries between human and nonhuman primates becoming ever more elusive, concepts like "absolute wilderness" are called more into question, while at the same time, the only chance to help them survive will be to insist on preserving their natural habitat.

BWINDI

After our first encounter with gorillas in Rwanda, we decided to meet Martha Robbins again in Bwindi, where a buffer zone had just been erected, to keep the gorillas in the forest. We stayed a night at the Serena Hotel on Lake Kivu, in the border town of Gisenyi. From the hotel pool, we saw the volcanoes disappearing in the mist; only the Nyiragongo volcano stood dark against the sky. I read a book I bought at a Toronto antiquarian, entitled *Gorilla: Tracking and Capturing the Ape-Man of Africa*, by the Jacksonville real-estate man, hunter, and filmmaker Ben Burbridge, who, in 1925, ventured into the Belgian Congo with guides, guns and a camera, shooting several gorillas and a film that was produced by Joseph P. Kennedy, father of John, Bobby and Ted. In his book, Burbridge admitted that the animals were beautiful, almost human, but that he shot them when they charged at him in an attempt to rescue their young. He named one of the captives Miss Congo and brought it to Jacksonville, where the animal lived in his vast garden; newspaper articles told how she "prefers automobile riding to any other sport." Today, the book reads like a confession to an all-pervading pathological delight in extreme forms of violence, an obituary to Western humanism. On the other side of the border, a Russian airplane landed. At the hotel's conference room, businessmen negotiated with a delegation of Chinese entrepreneurs. In 2016, Rwanda accounted for half of the global tantalum production; tantalum from coltan is used to build capacitors needed in smartphones, laptops, cameras and cars. Often, uncontrolled mining takes place in the DRC's natural parks, threatening the eastern mountain gorilla population there. According to local reports, miners even hunt gorillas; the gorilla population in the DRC fell from 17,000 to 5,000 in the last decade. Miners in and around Kahuzi-Biéga National Park are producing cassiterite, gold, coltan, and wolframite. In a way, the gorillas are sitting on the foundation of the digital age; the future is mined under a crust that accommodates some of homo sapiens' ancestry. The next morning, we drove to the Ugandan border. Our driver was not allowed to cross the frontier, so we walked for 10 minutes past trucks and billboards with ads for Chinese mobile phones. A Ugandan driver picked us up in a dented Nissan. We started up the red dusty road into Uganda. After several hours, we arrived at a village near the Bwindi Forest. We drove by a corner bar where a team of melancholic Austrians drank enormous amounts of elephant beer and dropped our luggage in a beautiful lodge with views of the forest, encountering an aghast tourist who'd been told he'd only have electricity for an hour per day and no phone connection. Finally, we went over to Martha Robbins's house. Night was falling. Her Land Cruiser, covered in red mud, was parked in front of the house. A fire was burning in the fireplace. On the wall, like a family album, were photos of different gorillas. "During his 11-year tenure as the dominant silverback, Rukina attracted four females into his group from neighboring groups," Robbins said. What was so appealing about him? "He was a large, attractive male. He spent two years challenging the previous silverback for alpha status. And he was very tolerant and permissive," Robbins added. "He spent a lot of time with the adult females as well as his many infants. In October 2012, he even let Rukara, a young silverback from the neighboring Bitukura group, immigrate into the Kyagurilo Group. It was the first documented immigration of a mature silverback into an established gorilla group."

Later at our lodge, we met Cat Hobaiter, a young field primatologist working for the School of Psychology and Neuroscience at the University of St. Andrews, who'd come to Uganda to study communication and cognition in wild apes. She talked about a new interest in forms of female choice among gorilla groups. "A week ago," she said, "I saw a dominant silverback mate with one of the females. And straight away, another female who was socially bonded to the silverback came and lay in front of him, and he just groomed her for half an hour. That's a sign that he's investing in their relationship and that she can demand that. There's a balance there. That's not about him copulating, taking what he wants, and to hell with the rest of it." Gorilla exploration has turned from a male occupation (where the object of interest was often killed as a first step to understand it) to a science with a majority of female researchers; simultaneously the image of gorillas changed from genetically determined bio-machine to an animal whose behavior is massively impacted by environmental factors and individual character. But did the apes change or just our vision of them? "Even when they're incredibly well habituated and they ignore you, you're in their group, you're in their social dynamic," Hobaiter concluded. "No matter how neutral you try to be, we are potentially creating a new culture in terms of their behavior."

BUFFER ZONE

As conservation efforts and tourism have brought humans and gorillas into increasingly closer proximity, more frequent encounters have begun to reshape the behavior of the gorilla. Having lost their fear of humans, habituated gorillas leave the forest, roaming further and further afield, entering nearby villages and raiding crops. Some habituated groups of gorillas spend more than half their time outside the park. The Nkuringo group ranged deep in the Bwindi Impenetrable National Park; after habituation, they started coming to the edge of the forest. Blurring the boundaries set by humans to distinguish wildlife from culture and wilderness from farmland, the gorillas were spending 60 percent of their time on community land outside the park, and making short forays into the farmland, Geoffrey Twinomuhangi of Uganda Wildlife Authority said. Volunteers from HuGo (Human Gorilla Conflict Resolution team) program had to chase the gorillas back to the park. Among other confusing impacts, this development threatens tourism: Tourists don't want to see gorillas crop-raiding near villages, they would rather maintain the illusion of total impenetrability in the forest.

In an attempt to avoid conflicts between local farmers and gorillas, and to re-establish the boundaries between the "impenetrable forest" and farmland, Western NGOs and conservation groups like WWF joined together to buy up a swathe of land lying between the park and the communities next to it. This buffer zone is a demarcation line drawn by Western institutions. Its purpose is to separate two formerly distinguishable concepts: wilderness and the countryside.   The next day, we took our car to the western part of the park. We drove for hours, past a lake, and then the road climbed through endless serpentines and up steep hills and more hills; at 2:00 p.m., we reached the buffer zone.   Habituation made it possible to visit the gorilla in his habitat, but changed his behavior in such a way that he started to reciprocate the human interest in his world by visiting humans in their habitat. This was a surprise to humans. They responded by fabricating a mischievous anti-park, an elongated garden full of unpleasant surprises: It had an outer and an inner zone planted with Artemisia, Mauritius thorn hedges, lemongrass, tea, and other nonpalatable crops that gorillas do not like. The curious primate is meant to learn that outside the world assigned to him, there is nothing of interest: The nearly 20-mile-long, 360-yard-wide buffer zone is therefore a mise-en-scène of supposed total boredom for animals.

Standing on the hill, looking down into the buffer zone, the first impression was that of an incredible, almost frivolous luxury: In one of the most densely populated areas of Africa, a space is created that is neither farmland nor part of the equally scarce impenetrable jungle, but a carefully manicured strip of homogenous green, a mixture of an ambitious land art project and a depressed French garden that has been forced by British landscape architects to fold over a bucolically sinuous terrain. Typologically, it felt like an almost surreal insertion of Western strategies of problem-solving through the implementation of voids and partitions (the Berlin Wall; the Hungarian border with its defenses against refugees coming from the south; the sandy paths in forests, cleared to avoid the spread of fires). It was a decisively modern urbanistic gesture, a Cartesian *tabula rasa* created to install order between two seemingly chaotic, uncontrollable realms. But this example of malignant gardening was not *rasa* enough; it looked from the first moment like an overgrown ruin of a too-ambitious highway project. And in fact, it was a ruin.

Quickly, the wind had carried seeds that gorillas *do* like into this garden of boredom and unpleasant surprises. Delicious plants grew among the unpalatable hedges. The buffer zone turned into a kind of Garden of Eden. "Eucalyptus trees are found in the inner buffer zone. Some of the gorillas must have tried it and really liked it," said Nicole Seiler, of the Max Planck Institute. Eucalyptus bark is very high in sodium. Farmers also began incursions into the buffer zone, using the outer buffer as an extension of their fields. Some gorillas even ventured beyond the buffer zone. What was conceived as a partition became a space of adaptation, overlay, and complex encounters. The buffer zone, which wants to be neither countryside nor park, but a dividing void, was almost a perfect spatial equivalent of the new status of habituated gorillas as "neither wild nor tame." Designed to differentiate one from the other, it became a space for inter-species negotiation, the paradoxical monument of a sometimes longed-for, sometimes unwanted rapprochement, an unintentional model for a possible future of both wilderness and countryside, human and non-human cohabitation.

Gorilla conservation rhetorics used to emphasize property rights and claims to the ground; a territory is either attributed to one species or the other. The gorillas let us into their world, conservationists used to say, but it is considered unacceptable that they leave "their" territory to enter "our" world to raid the crops and touch surprised humans. In the buffer zone, gorillas appear like tourists, and rangers are chasing them back into the jungle; in some cases, they have even been shot with a tranq gun and carried, in an almost ceremonial procession, back into the realm of carefully curated impenetrability. Given its unintentional attraction and sojourn quality for gorillas, the buffer was a success and a failure at the same time, with gorillas apparently being able to adapt more quickly to changing circumstances than Westerners and NGOs.

The buffer zone could become a third territory beyond the either-or divide, beyond a belligerent framing of the animal's or human's behavior as "ingression"— an almost utopian, nonhierarchical space of hospitality that belongs to no one and will be, from time to time, occupied by either human or nonhuman primates, who will meet as strangers on neutral terrain, in a surplus zone, and negotiate their needs, plant or roam, raid or harvest.

This is only possible if habituation and tourism do not expand at the expense of those subsistence farmers who live close to the park and already suffer from droughts and other climate change-related problems, and now also from the changing behavior of curious habituated gorillas. That said, it must also be mentioned that the assumed conflict between a growing gorilla population and a growing human population is, in its seeming inevitability, a cynical Western construct. Many farmers and villagers don't stay in the area and in extreme poverty because they love their homeland so much, but because they are not given other possibilities, education, or health care; many miners in DRC would prefer sending their children to school in Goma or elsewhere, instead of being forced into drilling illegal mines into protected parkland, under unbearable conditions, and into living from precarious subsistence farming. If politicians and corporations treated humans more humanely, gorilla protection would benefit too.

A FUTURE HABITAT

Conservation success in the Virungas and Bwindi leads to new challenges. The carrying capacity of the parks might soon be reached. An extension of the park is unlikely to happen, as not only the number of gorillas grows, but also the number of humans surrounding the park. In parallel, the effects of climate change might require changes in diet and less exuberant resources; droughts and storms will threaten food security for both humans and animals.

Should conservationists accept an eventual decline in fertility due to growing social stress and a fight for food resources, leading to stagnation or even a decline in gorilla population? "We tend to think in terms of business models," Robbins said, "where increasing growth can be the only sign of success, but in limited habitat, conservationists will need to think more in terms of a stable population size." Should gorilla families be moved out to similar habitats with similar food, disturbing the existing ecosystem, or could artificial forest habitats be created, a new typology between a park and a zoo? Conservation becomes an increasingly dynamic process, depending on whole landscapes, including surrounding agricultural areas and a carefully curated "wilderness," with new conditions and new pressures emerging, along with new forms of behavior.

AGAINST INTERPRETATION

What is on the gorilla's mind when he leaves the park and grooms deplorably hairless primates carrying cameras and wearing sweaters? Who knows. Negotiating territories between humans and animals also means surrendering to inexplicability: A new language would be needed to relate adequately to a surprisingly innovative animal intelligence.

In railway language, a buffer is just a clunky metal part to reduce damage in case of a shock; in IT language, it's the part of a computer's memory that stores information before exchanging it with an external drive. This definition of the buffer as an *Aufhebung* (in the sense of preservation) within an *Aufhebung* (in the sense of removal and dissolution) might lead beyond its reduction to a static defense line widely ignored by those it is supposed to defend. The buffer is not a line, a fence or a wall; it's a zone, a 360-yard wide space. In Western thought, this spatiality is an aggravation of the dividing character of a line (like the large, dead empty strip of sand in front of the Berlin Wall); but once overgrown, it could also be seen as a labyrinth that more gently prevents its intruders from crossing, not through emptiness, but exuberance, inhabitability instead of inhibition. Already today, the buffer zone is not a homogenous partition. It offers a panorama of scenarios. The desire to protect the status quo paradoxically turns the buffer into a zone of experimentation and massive instability—a model for inter-species encounter and coexistence, a more amalgamated future.

1 Since antiquity, reports about gorillas have spurred the imagination of western audiences. The ancient voyager Hanno described, in the 5th century BC, a wild and ferocious animal called gorilla. Ever since, descriptions and illustrations of the animals became a fantastic genre, revealing more about the desires and fears of those who described them than about the gorilla itself. Descartes insisted on man's superiority to presumably souless "brutes": "there are no men so dull and stupid, not even idiots, to be incapable of joining together different words" – a statement that was angrily contradicted by Carl von Linné, who stated in 1735 that surely, Descartes never saw an ape. Actually, for a very long time, no one in the western world saw a gorilla: they remained scientifically unknown until 1847, when the American missionary Thomas Staughton Savage acquired an unusually large primate skull. In the 1920s, the taxidermist, conservationist, and alleged inventor of sprayed concrete, Carl Akeley, anthromorphized the male gorilla, labeling him father of a nuclear family, while Akeley's travel companion, the writer Mary Hastings Bradley, exploited the popular image of the hypersexual, polygamous ape. In a colonial discourse, the gorilla was the incarnation of a dangerous, menacing, but extremely energetic continent in need of domestication. See, for the cultural history of the gorilla, *Ape Culture*, edited by Anselm Franke and Hila Peleg (Spector books, 2016).
2 In the 19th century, tales of "ferocious" gorillas became part of larger narrative to justify brutal colonialist ingressions in Africa. In 1859, the year Darwin published Origin of the Species, the sculptor Emmanuel Frémiet submitted at the Paris Salon a larger than life-size plaster composition, entitled "Gorilla carrying off a Negress," which later served as a blueprint for various King Kong tales. "Since the young woman in question was a Negress, I thought my górilla might pass," Frémiet says later, revealing the racist and misogynist logics of its time, but "this was not to be. The jury's condemnation was unanimous. My work was declared to be seriously offensive to public morality, and it was banished pitilessly from the Salon." (Frémiet, interviewed in Thiébault-Sisson, 'Au jour le jour, une vie d'artiste. Emmanuel Frémiet', Le Temps, January 3, 1896; see also Ted Gott, "Stowed Away: Emmanuel Frémiet's Gorilla carrying off a woman," Art Journal, May 23, 2014). Still seen as too violent and offending in 1859, it is telling that in 1887, Fremiet won a Medal of Honor at the Salon with another version of his sculpture: time was ripe for celebrating rape and racism; the gorilla incorporated the enemy, but, as an emblem of extreme energies and forces in need of taming, also a role model for western explorers.

Off-(Jefferson's)Grid
Anne M. Schneider

We're trying to get off-grid, but we need the grid to get us there. We start out from San Diego, the bottom-left of the United States, the absolute termination point: Mexico visible a few miles south, the ocean to the west. Manifest Destiny's end of the line. The drop into the desert on Interstate 8 feels like a space landing, an abrupt winding descent through dense forest that makes a clean break at the Borrego Desert as we hit the straightaway—the infinity line of Jefferson's grid. The AC goes on and stays on for the rest of the trip.

The grid is America's creation myth: starting in the late 18th century, the survey system began parceling "savage wilderness" into six-mile square townships made up of 36 plots, 640 square acres each, populated by self-reliant, virtuous homesteaders—unfurling westwards it created a country. Jefferson's grid covered 75 percent of the continental United States; a flexible matrix equally suited to developers and speculation as it was to yeoman farmers and the dream of agrarian democracy. But the fill-in-the-blank spaces of the grid coupled with the remoteness of the American countryside meant there were holes large enough for utopias to slip through, room at the margins for dissidents and outsiders. As the government and its grid outlined a nation their progress was paralleled, and occasionally exceeded, by small deviations, accidents, loopholes, and alternative societies.

We move in the L-shaped path of a knight on a chessboard, sliding along the X and Y axes of America's back of house, where things that are too big, too ugly and too distasteful happen; where the sausage gets made. The South West, the most inhospitable swathe of desert, is where the grid's true nature is revealed. Land the US government was still giving away to homesteaders in the 1970s is now an industrialized infrastructure of solar farms, feedlots, monoculture, dams, irrigation, and highways. Everything is on its way somewhere else, the water, the energy, the food, the long haul truckers. Threaded through the extra-large organizational framework of the nation—the survey grid that divided the west before we'd even seen it—are places and people that, to this day, resist cultivation, organization, and the grid's imperative of productivity. The Imperial Valley is a complex ecosystem; a swirling Cartesian vortex of big-box retail, feedlots, solar farms, ICE Border Control checkpoints, drainage ditches, and train tracks. The map is populated with names like Mirage, Siberia, and Bagdad, a nod to both the remoteness and the climate. Out of the Sonoran desert, in the sunniest place in the United States, miraculously, there are fields of bleached alfalfa unrolling as far as the eye can see. An improbable muddy trickle of the hyper-controlled Colorado river cuts through the desert via 1,600 miles of all-American canals; choking the mighty river off at the border from Mexico.[1]

The Salton Sea, the largest body of water in California, is an accident of liquid prometheanism—in the desert, you steal water not fire. An aerial view of the Imperial Valley will give you a mistaken impression of causality, but farms *created* the Salton Sea, not the other way around. A climb over the berm reveals the inland lake—I'd been expecting a smell, but there is only a cloying humidity, thick and stickily distasteful, and the powdered sugar softness of silt not sand underfoot.

Before irrigation, this stretch of desert was an afterthought, the survey grid of 1852 was scratched in hastily, a speculative gesture from a distance, off by as much as two miles, and left to return to the sand.[2] In 1903, the desert bloomed almost overnight thanks to canals dug by private developers, they brought the river to the desert and created a boomtown. The Salton Sink, more than 233' below sea level, became the Imperial Valley—just add water. Saltworks were built, thousands of acres of agricultural land cultivated, train lines laid, and towns built.

In 1905 the canals that created the Imperial Valley almost destroyed it. Hastily dug and poorly managed, the canals filled with silt. After heavy rains, they burst their banks and hemorrhaged the Colorado River into the Salton Sink, creating the Sea. It reads like an Old Testament plague—a wall of water ten miles wide washed away towns, train tracks, farmland.

Snakes fled the waters into surrounding settlements, in a reversal of St. Patrick's legend. Thousands of fish carried into the Salton Sink, killed by the salinating water, putrefying in the desert sun, could be smelled for miles around.[3] For two years, the deluge menaced cities, farms, and waterworks upstream and down. When they finally put the river back, the Sea remained. Despite the heat and average rainfall of less than three inches a year, the lake never evaporated: it was fed by a continual supply of agricultural runoff. Today, the Salton Sea is almost 40 miles long and 15 miles wide, the Colorado River's final resting place. Underlying it all is a subterranean unease; the Salton Sea is volcanically active, gurgling and hissing, it sits on top of the San Andreas fault line, California's ticking time bomb. Water in the desert, no matter how toxic, is irresistible. Many have tried to make something of the Sea. Would-be fisherman and hoteliers stocked it with dozens of species of fish, none of which survived, and imported sea lions that disappeared without a trace. It was a short-lived naval base and a speedboat time trial site. Test wells for geothermal energy were dug and abandoned. In the 1950s, leisure resorts, yacht clubs, and golf courses sprang up around the 'California Riviera.' Ringed by improbably named beaches—the North Shore, Mecca, and Bombay Beach— it became, for a time, a desert mirage vacation destination attracting the likes of Frank Sinatra, the Beach Boys, the Marx Brothers, and Jerry Lewis.[4] Festering in the sun, getting saltier and more toxic by the day, the few surviving fish, stewing in agricultural run-off, are nothing short of miraculous. Born of obsessive productivity and shameless speculation, all the ingredients of the grid gone horribly awry, the Salton Sea is an extra-large accident that refuses to evaporate.

SALVATION MOUNTAIN

We get hung up on Salvation Mountain, out of the scrubby baldness of the desert, it's a half-slumped mirage, a cartoonist's idea of an LSD trip. Driven by messianic visions to build with whatever materials he had on hand, artist outsider Leonard Knight built out of the desert:

adobe, straw, driftwood, plus 500,000 gallons of latex paint applied directly to the canvas of the desert. Began in 1984—and rebuilt after the first version collapsed—Salvation Mountain is covered in technicolor patterns and ecstatic verse, some biblical, some original. "Jesus I'm a sinner, please come upon my body and into my heart," Knight pleads; "God is Love" he declares in three-meter high letters. It's the St. Peters of the Mojave, a roadside curio so far from the nearest road that it's not a pit stop but a pilgrimage; no one comes here by accident. It's 9:00 am, 100 degrees, and we're alone for thirty minutes before another pair of tourists arrive.

SLAB CITY

Salvation Mountain is the gateway to Slab City, a two-minute drive down a soft dirt road that google hasn't streetviewed. Shirtless and dreadlocked, he approaches with a bouncing gait and a friendly smile in a setting where any life seems improbable, in a heat so intense no one sane would be outside. Our first reaction is fear. "First time on the Slabs?" he asks. Our not-as-white-as-it-was-when-we-left Prius answers for us. He tells us to check out East Jesus. East Jesus, middle of nowhere, all you have to do is turn right. 640 acres of homestead land nobody wanted, Slab City is home to the homeless (including, until he died in 2014, Leonard Knight himself). Wealthy retirees, poor retirees, recluses, off-griders, aged hippies, army veterans, Christian fundamentalists, burners, and drop-outs park their mobile homes on concrete slabs, which are all that remains of Camp Dunlap, a WWII military base, where rumor has it General Patton drilled and the Enola Gay dropped practice H Bombs.

Officially, Slab City doesn't exist. Like its residents, it has fallen through the cracks. There is no running water, no mail, no electricity, no garbage collection, no municipal services of any kind. There are also no laws, no taxes, and no foreclosures. Residents call it "the last free place." Jefferson spliced this aberration into the DNA of the land ordinance: section 36, Slab City's lucky number, is designated for public education. This section 36 happens to be a square in the desert that no one wants, intended for a school that was never built, owned by a state that can't manage it, to benefit a teacher's retirement fund that can't sell it, and under the jurisdiction of a sheriff's department that rarely patrols it. Federal, state, and local authorities all turn a blind eye to one of the longest-lived squats in American history. Slab City has existed for almost 70 years and it has everything you would expect from a town: a church, a library, a (pet) cemetery, a main street, and "good" and "bad" parts of town. The population of the slabs fluctuates with the seasons—from less than one hundred during the sweltering summer months to over a thousand at its peak. We are the only thing moving for miles and it feels like we're trespassing; the whole place has an air of abandonment.

The sand has erased the edges and softened the slabs, their boundaries are reinforced with fences, tin cans, shards of metal that broadcast "keep out." Slab City's nearest neighbors are a naval gunnery range, desert, and solar farms; it is a landscape of scraped subsistence and neglect. "It's illegal," the woman from the planning department informs me, "to park an RV for more than two weeks. Nobody's counting," she adds, "but you can tell." Many of the mobile homes in Slab City haven't moved in two years or two decades. Most aren't capable of movement at all. Here at the end of July, I am seeing only the permanent residents, everyone who could leave has already left. In winter, the population swells with snowbirds and retirees in $300,000 shiny Coachmen and Ramblers parked in orderly rows. Every Saturday night there is a well-attended talent show and open mic night. Every night there are dinner dances and board games in the clubhouse trailer and a neighborhood watch patrol. Slab City has been advertised in *Trailer Life* magazine targeted towards budget-conscious retirees as a free place to park.[5] It may be the last free place to park your RV *anywhere*, and maybe the last free place, period. It's an unintentional community held together by a legal loophole and neglect, there's no cohering ideology or faith or belief. It's an enduring accident created by the grid itself. In the words of WW Robinson, every American is a squatter at heart.[6]

ARCOSANTI

The vast American countryside has always siphoned off the most ambitious, radical, truculent, and anti-social elements from the cities. Since the 18th century, off-grid groups put into practice free childcare, education, healthcare, racial and gender equality: social policies that wouldn't be out of place on the new left agenda of a freshman Democrat. Communal efforts collapsed, disbanded, flooded, burned down, broke up, or moved on but many other utopian visions retired with vested joint-stock options. The Oneida Perfectionists (1848–1880), who were scandalizing their neighbors with free love 100 years before the hippies, are today one of the largest producers of stainless steel and silver-plated cutlery in the world. The Amanas (1843–1932), a group of German Christian-Mystics who followed divine inspiration west, still produce refrigerators, ovens, fabrics, and furniture. "Very good refrigerators," my grandmother assured me. Our next stop is a more recent utopia, a survivor of the 1970s counter-culture movement, we leave Slab City and head east towards Arcosanti, Arizona. We move along a checkerboard of federal, state, and private land, the distinctions indistinguishable in the 112-degree 10:00 am heat. Gridded rows of date palms emerge as we edge past Coachella and Palm Springs, twinkles of escapist leisure and flower crowns on the periphery of a landscape where the US government simulated desert warfare. We cut north on Box Canyon Road. It's so empty, I spend the drive thinking about what would happen if the car broke down, how long we would last. Glints on the horizon aren't water but more solar farms. A sign warns us not to pick up hitchhikers as we pass Ironwood State Prison, another sign warns us that poisonous snakes and insects inhabit the area, another sign alerts us "Brush Fire Level: HIGH."

Six hours after leaving the Salton Sea, the nightmare gyre of the Phoenix ring roads finally release us and we begin the climb into the high desert. Arcosanti has its own exit off the 17 North, a vector through scrubland, paralleled by the electrical tendrils of massive power lines. The crunch of gravel is auditory confirmation we're off the road, off the grid. It's monsoon season and we roll in to camp at the same time as a flash flood on the night of a super blood moon. On the lip of the Sonoran Desert, Arcosanti sits atop a rich vein of desert gold—an aquifer, the subterranean Colorado River. The high desert is a landscape of extremes: boiling summers and freezing winters. So our room has a fan and a space heater, extra wool blankets, and no screens on the door.

We confront the question, is a cross breeze worth the mosquito bites? It's after 10:00 pm and still well over 80 degrees, we bare sacrificial limbs and hope the mosquitoes will spare our faces. Arcosanti is a techno-primitivist moonscape of arches and cyprus spires manned by self-described Arconauts. Founded in 1970, just as the spaceship earth theory gained momentum and the back-to-the-land movement flourished, Arcosanti was one of 3,000 communes that sprang into existence during the late 60s and early 70s.[7] The counterculture's run-for-the-hills moment, fueled by social, sexual, and pharmaceutical freedom, cast a haloed glow on Arcosanti. But Hippies gravitated there because of the timing, not Arcosanti's particular ideology. Unlike many of its counterculture contemporaries, communalism was a by-product, not the focus, of Arcosanti. A building experiment and pedagogical exercise, Arcosanti was and is a working laboratory, a demonstration of "Arcology" (architecture + ecology)—high density and low impact. Built by communal labor, it was fundamentally anti-egalitarian, the vision of a single man, Paolo Soleri. Many off-grid communities don't survive the death of their founder—it's the final test to see if ideology, not personality, can cohere a group of people. At Arcosanti it was a one-two punch, #MeToo clocked them so hard it has a link on the website. Daniela Soleri, Paolo Soleri's daughter, published an open letter revealing years of abuse, sexual molestation, and attempted rape by her father. When I visit, the revelations are still fresh. How do you deal with a legacy of predation, exploitation, and narcissism, incubated alongside arcology in this remote piece of desert? Answers range from "Fuck that guy" to the board of directors' party line, that we must "distinguish the work from the man." But the man is still present: his designs, his words, and his name. Another response strips Arcosanti of Soleri completely, "He didn't build it, thousands of volunteers and students built it." And they still are. Six-week long, $2,000 workshops put students to work, a continually replenished source of labor doing everything from roofing to 3D modeling to casting bronze bells in the foundry and learning silt casting in the ceramics studio. An empty folding chair implies a site supervisor who has just gone on break; there are orange hazard cones and a concrete mixer. I walk to dinner that night past a prop-like crane and the set pieces of unfinished buildings, bedraggled Greeks in togas and eyeliner smoke cigarettes on the path in front of me. Arcosanti is a performance and I've wandered backstage. Tonight it's a student performance of *Hecuba*, a story of female survival and visceral revenge—a fallen queen putting out the eyes of her enemy and murdering his sons.

The day-to-day reality of running a utopian community is messy. Hand-lettered signage is ubiquitous, with messages like "close this door, skunks get in." The communal whiteboard lists "beer delivery," "baby goats for sale," "resident satisfaction survey," "Conviviality Monday 7:00 pm Vaults," "Thanks Grant for Mosquito Control," "found sunglasses." Away from the amphitheater and the gift shop, the for-sale spectacle of Soleri's Arcology, there are communal programs: a gym, a store, the laundry room, a library. I spot *Walden 2*, a science-fiction novel from the 1930s and the founding document of another long-lived experiment, Twin Oaks, Virginia. It sits askew on the shelf, like someone has picked it up, thumbed through it, and put it back in favor of a different manifesto.

I meet photographers, former MMA fighters, mechanics, and career Arconauts that dropped out, left careers and cities, chased by a vague, or sometimes very specific, sense of dissatisfaction. There's a small-town vibe: everyone I pass says hello or even stops to chat. I ask about the metal sphere I'd seen in the main vault. "It's for Burning Man," I'm told, in the tone of someone who has heard *ad nauseum* the story of "getting lost on the Playa but finding yourself." I thought Burning Man was a week-long release valve, a temporal off-grid retreat—head into the desert to do drugs, live in community, experiment socially and artistically... weren't we already there? The eye-roll is almost audible, there's a certain kind of disaffection that comes from overexposure to utopian visions. It's my first clue that I'm not as off-the-grid as I thought I was. The gift shop is the next clue, the rooms on Airbnb the third, the chlorinated blue pool and beer is straight out of a So-Cal Frat party. In conversation, I mention AMO and an architecture student (wearing all black in 90-degree heat) hangs his head over a second-floor balcony to talk shop. A relic of radicality with a canceled founding father, Arcosanti is a utopian vision getting thick in the middle. Permanent residents are thinning out and ex-Arconauts, already called alumni, graduate and move on. Its planned greenhouses have been turned into guest rooms and the next project on the books is a conference center. Arcosanti seems destined to become half spa, half sleek educational campus. Unable to sustain itself on gift shop bell sales, it's in the process of becoming just another good the countryside produces and the city consumes. If Arcosanti was ever off-grid, it isn't anymore.

OUTSIDE VEGAS

The terrain changes as we head north towards Nevada, the sage green brush fades into sand and the American flag becomes omnipresent; along the side of the road, in gas stations, on bumper stickers. We cross the Colorado River twice, doubling back to the Hoover Dam. We're hundreds of miles upstream but cause and effect aren't linear—the Salton Sea, an accident of in-the-grid ambition, forced the Federal government to take over the management of waterways, a self-calibration of the infrastructural grid that created the Hoover Dam and the largest reservoir in the United States—drained to near-emergency levels after a 19-year drought.

The Dam, thronged with tourists in the July heat, is a hinge; to the south, everything we've just seen; north, it's an eight-hour drive to the Tahoe-Reno Industrial Complex; an hour more and we'd be at the site of Burning Man—relatively small distances on the scale of the west. It's an hour to Vegas, that sparkling perturbance of grid-sanctioned excess, and two hours to the Nevada Test Site (NTS), a pocked and cratered stretch of desert the size of Rhode Island—the site of over 1,000 atmospheric and subterranean nuclear detonations. Decades before Silicon Valley claimed it as a staging area—as the first RV parked at Slab City and Bombay Beach was hosting luaus on the Salton Sea—the US government was nuking Nevada. In view of the Strip are military outposts, closed villages, sometimes just clusters of buildings, named Mercury, Chloride City, Sugar Bunker. Next-door, in the shadow of last century's doomsday scenario is the Bundy Ranch, the epicenter of a confrontational, occasionally violent, off-grid divestment; armed separatists and sovereign citizens, preaching end-of-days, are facing off with the US government (in court and with guns) and winning. In a state that is 81 percent federally owned, ranchers, the long shadows of the wild west's cowboys, violently reject federal authority and the confines of the grid. We don't stop to visit. Both are, in a way, active security sites—fortified and secure. There's a two-year waiting list to visit the NTS, background check required, and we're not welcome / we don't have the extremist bona fides to visit the Bundy Ranch. The desert's isolation paradoxically holds the promise of survival—the land around the NTS is peppered with extremists, and modern-day millenarianists of the billionaire variety. Hard Luck Mine Castle, a doomsday prepper's dreamhouse, listed for $1.2 million this year; in Las Vegas itself, the famed Underground House was listed for $18 million.

We're as far as we can get from the grid's East Coast origin point but the urban creep of infrastructural countryside is almost impossible to escape. Running for the hills is a choice between dusty utopian communes or isolated survivalist "communities"—bronze bells or bunkers and bug out bags. When we need it most, it's getting harder to go off-grid.

1 Imperial Irrigation District, "All-American Canal," accessed November 21, 2019. https://www.iid.com/water/water-transportation-system/colorado-river-facilities/all-american-canal.
2 Hailey, Charlie, and Donovan Wylie, *Slab City: Dispatches from the Last Free Place*. (MIT, 2018).
3 Pat Laflin, *The Salton Sea: California's Overlooked Treasure*, p. 30.
4 Laflin, p. 41.
5 Sanjiv Bhattacharya, "Land of the Free," Guardian, March 22, 2003.
6 Travis Du Bry, "Slab City: Squatter's Paradise?" in *On the Border: Society and Culture between the United States and Mexico*, edited by Andrew Grant Wood. (SR Books, 2004).
7 Liselotte & O.M. Ungers, *Communes in the New World*, 1972.

(All images by Anne M. Schneider, unless otherwise credited.)

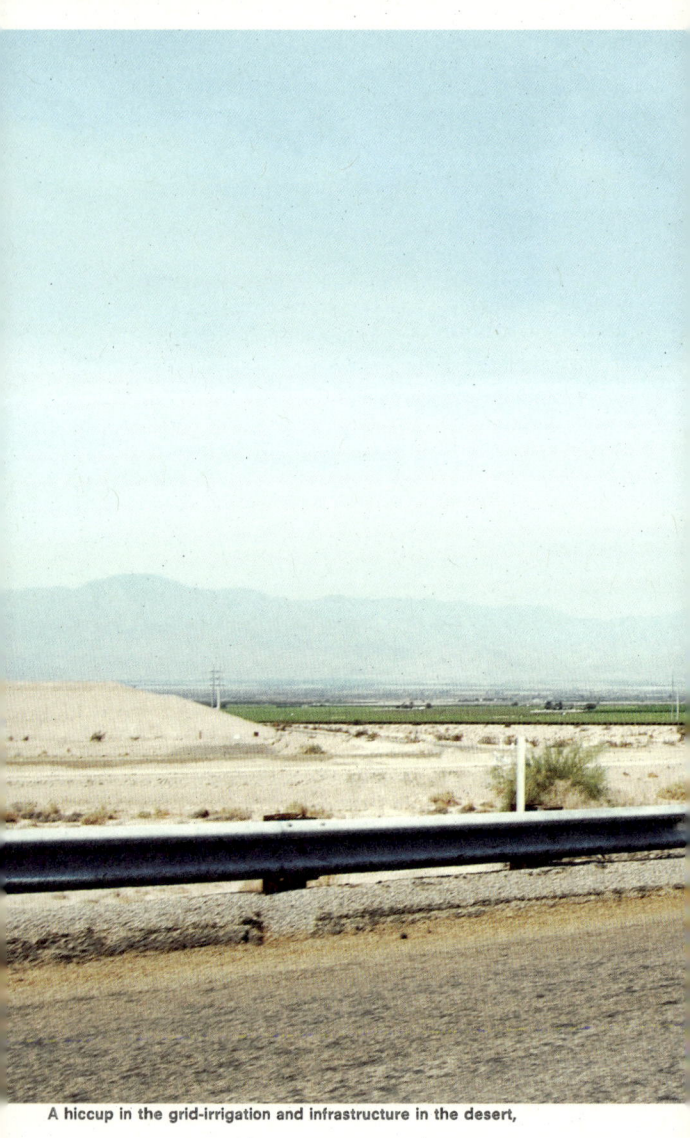
A hiccup in the grid-irrigation and infrastructure in the desert,

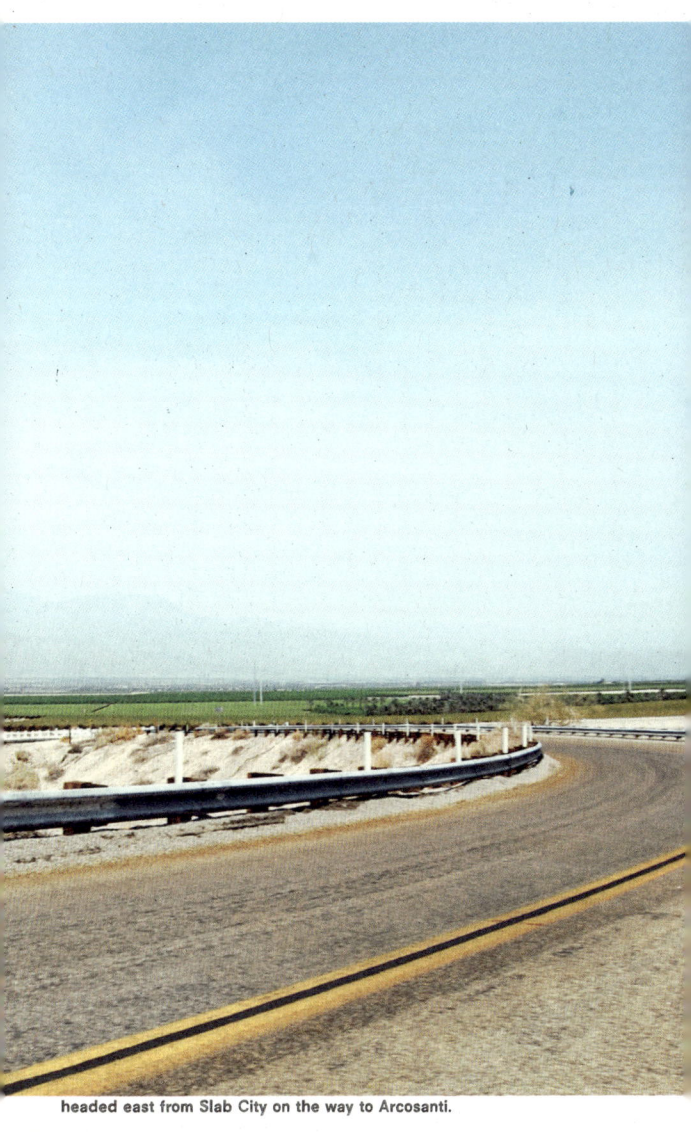
headed east from Slab City on the way to Arcosanti.

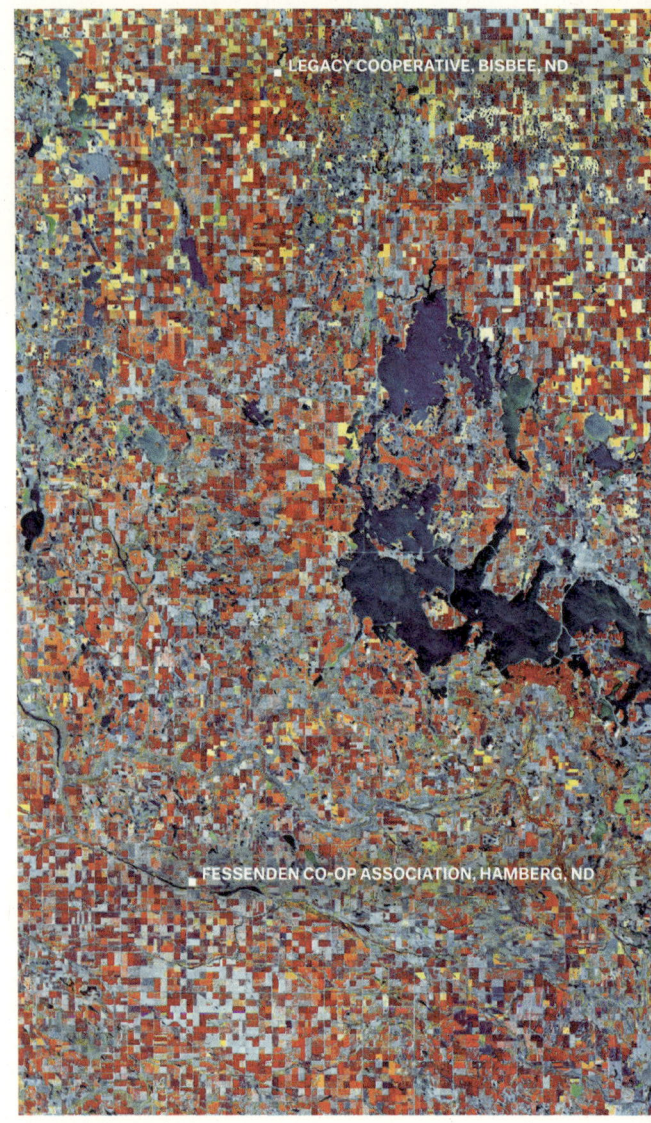

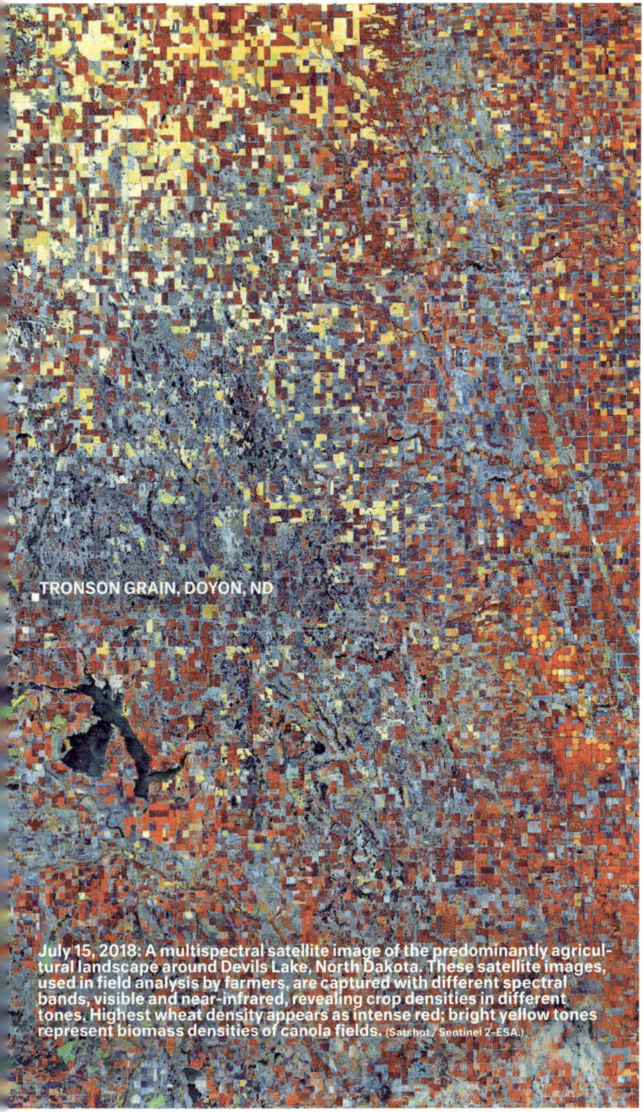

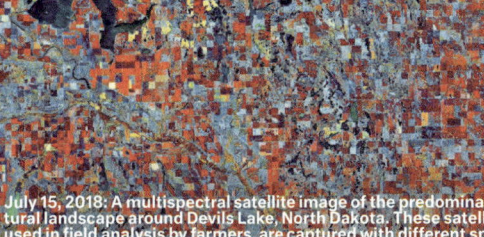

TRONSON GRAIN, DOYON, ND

July 15, 2018: A multispectral satellite image of the predominantly agricultural landscape around Devils Lake, North Dakota. These satellite images, used in field analysis by farmers, are captured with different spectral bands, visible and near-infrared, revealing crop densities in different tones. Highest wheat density appears as intense red; bright yellow tones represent biomass densities of canola fields. (Satshot/Sentinel 2-ESA.)

Industrial Farming Blues
Janna Bystrykh

GREAT PLA(I)NS

The following is a condensed composite of more than 15 hours of conversations with farmers of all stripes, from the industrial-scale to the regenerative, in rural North Dakota and Minnesota. Lanny Faleide, a farmer who created Satshot—one of the first satellite analysis companies for agriculture—together with his wife Lisa Swanson Faleide, a writer, were the connection and collaborators in this conversation marathon. Faleide's introduction of remote sensing and satellite analysis in the 1990s helped launch "precision farming," which now dominates industrial agriculture in the United States, Canada, Brazil, and elsewhere. From nearly live satellite data and drone imagery to weather forecasts for specific fields, sensor readings of soil, seed, and crop conditions, automated and customized application of seeds, fertilizer, pesticides, and herbicides, precision farming is designed for optimization and maximal yields. Its methods can also be applied to regenerative farming. Precision farming has accelerated the growth of industrial farming, a systemic imperative locked into American farming at least since the Freedom to Farm Act, 1996, which scrapped supply management. When prices are high, farmers plant more; when prices are low, farmers *have* to plant more.
The relentless growth has yielded a new industrial farming typology in North Dakota: A massive rail loop connecting grain elevators, bean storage and processing plants, fertilizer plants, gas pumps, and office buildings—an agricultural business park with a distinctive footprint on Google Earth, overwhelming in scale when viewed on the ground. The loop connects with the mainline, loading grain into the American market, which, by all accounts, is already "full." Emotions were high: trade tensions with China were escalating. Confronted with unstable prices, some farmers will go even bigger in the race to survive. Others are choosing new directions: Smaller, smarter, regenerative; scripting and automating to improve soil health, biodiversity, crop diversity, and water quality.

PARTICIPANTS
MARK WATNE President, North Dakota Farmers Union, Jamestown, ND
MARK HOVLAND General Manager Fessenden Co-op Association, Hamberg, ND
PAUL OVERBY Regenerative agriculture, consultant, educator; Lee Farms, Wolford, ND
GARY WAGNER Programmer, educator, early precision farming adopter; A.W.G. Farms Inc., Crookston, MN
LANNY FALEIDE Founder and President of Satshot, Fargo, ND
LISA SWANSON FALEIDE Writer, theologian, Fargo, ND JB Editor
Conversations took place in August 2019.

SIGNED BY MY GREAT-GREAT GRANDMOTHER

LISA SWANSON FALEIDE One of the topics we want to talk about is cooperatives, which are very strong here in the Upper Midwest. Mark, could you say something about where we started and where we are now?

MARK WATNE North Dakota in the grand scheme of things is a really young state. I still have the homestead document signed by my great-great grandmother. Next to her quarter, my grandfather homesteaded 160 acres. When he married, my grandparents together had two quarter sections of land. That was around 1903—not that long ago. North Dakota was built with the theory that rural areas were going to be populated with a lot of people. The initial infrastructure was set up to deal with that, but it didn't happen. In fact we barely got through the Great Depression.

Nobody anticipated the full impact of automation. It allowed us to farm substantially differently: You couldn't make a lot of money farming, so you found efficiencies by growing in size. That's a double-edged sword in a system where you have farmers trying to sell into a full marketplace, with very few buyers. This started a process of farmers organizing themselves. The Capper-Volstead Act[1] allowed us to form cooperative businesses. The cooperative structure was trying to make everyone honest. At the beginning, the farmers unions, their central exchanges, the oil companies, and grain terminal associations were owned by these little companies out here. Eventually they grew into CENEX and Harvest States, which then came together, changing their name to CHS. They're still a cooperative, but they were a Fortune 100 company at one point.

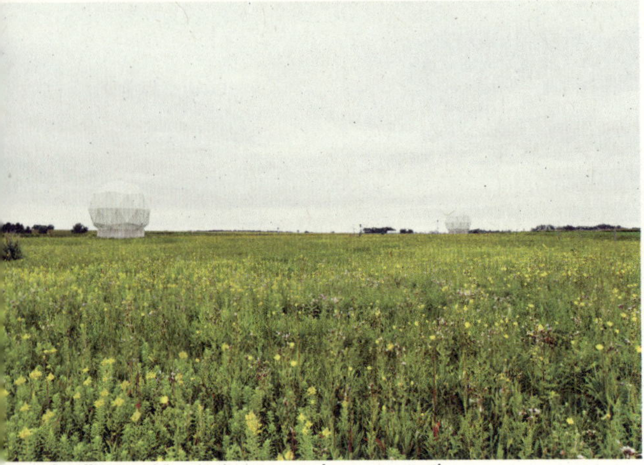

Satellite receiving stations on a carbon sequestration field, Faleide farm, Maddock, ND.

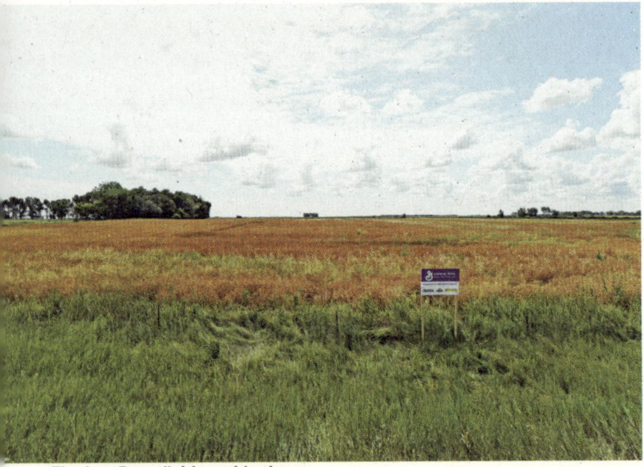

The Lee Farm field used in the General Mills sustainability project.

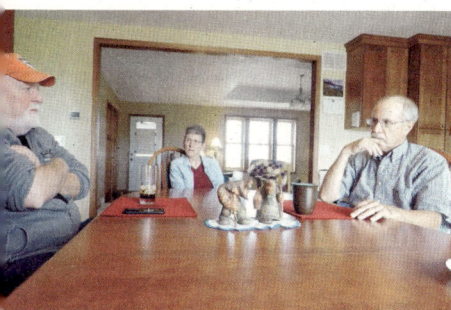

Precision farming pioneer Lanny Faleide, in conversation with regenerative farmer Paul Overby and Diane Overby at Lee Farm, Wolford, ND.

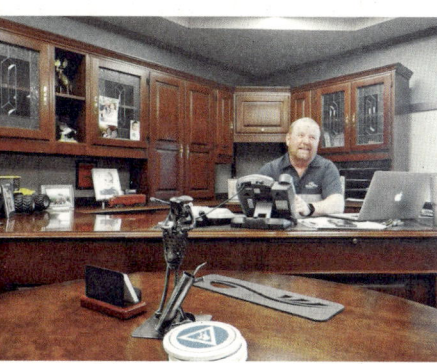

Mark Watne: president, North Dakota Farmers Union, in his office, Jamestown, ND.

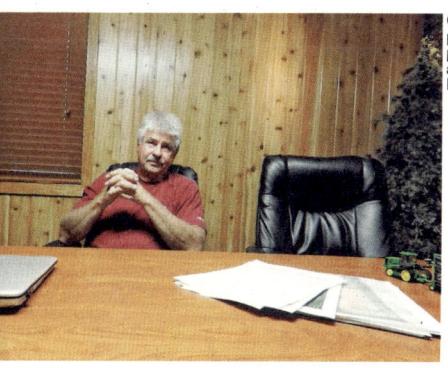

Gary Wagner: farmer, programmer, early precision farming adopter; A.W.G. Farms Inc., Crookston, MN.

JANNA BYSTRYKH What has been the biggest shift in American agriculture in the last few decades?

MW In the US we went away from supply management systems—like acreage control or conservation reserves—and instead challenged our farmers to produce more and do it for less.[2] By the late 1990s, it destroyed the market, and took commodity prices down to nothing. We had four out of five years of economic bailouts. And while input costs continue to creep up, as a farmer you only have one choice: You have to maximize your production, even if it means prices continue to fall. Because if you decide not to plant, someone else will. This puts us in a vicious circle because in the US we have too much supply, and we put it into a "full market" that has insufficient demand and prices that are too low. The endgame is sadly "one farm" worldwide, meaning as few farms as necessary to actually organize and drive the world price.

JB Who benefits from this system?

MW The good news is that from a consumer perspective, with the capacity we have in the US, we can maintain what is called an inexpensive food system. But the American consumer does not truly understand the cost of food. This creates a lot of challenges. First of all we have depleted the number of farmers out here, because efficiency forces us to spread capital cost over more acres. At the same time there's an interest in having a diverse number of family farms across the land. Having that diversity is good for overall national stability and adequate food supply. These large companies are trying to have more influence over the whole process rather than just being a mass purchaser of product. We are not winning this fight as much as we would like. We are slowing down the growth of mega farms. But when you draw a graph of farmers' profitability, since 2013 we have been sliding back some 50 percent.

JB What are some of the specificities of North Dakota's agricultural landscape?

MW It's really important to understand we live in a commodity state. We are unique in North Dakota because there are very few products out here that go directly to the consumer, without going through a processing channel.[3] That makes any movement to specialized production harder. Consumers like directly sourced products. If you're growing fresh, tasty, maybe organic spinach, or perfectly red ripe tomatoes, you will get a premium. With grain it's more difficult. We battle a lot with other farm states. If you are from a farm state that has a huge urban center, you have a market. We have just 700,000 people in the whole state.[4]

THE RAILROAD WANTED IT

JB With cooperatives to protect the farmers' interests, what are the pressures from suppliers and purchasers?

MW Concentration is a big issue. It has become acceptable in the US to allow monopolistic practices. We don't value our anti-trust laws as highly as we should. They generally do not stop mergers, even if they impact the consumer or the farmer. There are only three companies left in the whole world that produce seed: Bayer-Monsanto, Dow Chemical Company-Dupont, and Syngenta-ChemChina. To me that's tremendously scary. Seed has shifted from being our lowest cost item to almost our highest cost item. Another example of concentration is in meat processing. For beef, 85 percent of the facilities are owned by four companies; for pork, 74 percent is owned by four companies, and one of them, Smithfield Foods, is owned by a Chinese company; in poultry it's 54 percent owned by four companies. Then there's rail: We only have four major rail lines that ship 96 percent of all commodities in the US, and their territories almost don't overlap. They are literally telling us the direction in which we will ship our grain.

LANNY FALEIDE Are you saying that the future of agriculture here, and the construction of these new grain complexes in Hamberg, Doyon, and Bisbee, with their own rail loop, is basically being dictated by the rail companies?

MW Definitely. The railway is saying if you want better rates, you have to be able to load a 110-car train in 24 hours, and you have to be on this track next to the main line. The farmer co-ops or ag companies have to finance and build these rail loops themselves, in the hope they'll save money in lower freight rates.

PAUL OVERBY That circle track in Hamberg is there for one reason only: The railroad wanted it. Ironically, it's the same reason Hamberg had to move a century ago to where it is now, next to the main line. Because the railroad wanted it there. I was on the Agate Farmers Union Oil Co-operative board when the co-ops were starting to get pressured by the rail companies to put in these 110-car loops. We saw that happen at the Bisbee Legacy Cooperative too. So the rail companies dictate the movement of grain. And when we've financed and built the rail loops, then we need to build grain elevators big enough to fill those massive trains.

JB Mark, could you talk about the growth of your co-op's infrastructure at Hamberg? What were the triggers?

MH Our expansion efforts started in 2005, as corn and beans entered the market. We needed more storage, and we were struggling to access all the markets. With our new rail loop at Hamberg, we're now on the BNSF Railway, which is just a better connection and service. And we can now load a train in less than seven hours, which we could never do before. The other benefit is we get to use the rail company's locomotives. You can only do that on a loop track.

LF Fessenden Co-op has been a success story, consistently able to keep its margins positive.

MH It's getting kind of bloody out there. We're holding our own, and it's mainly because of diversity: We have seven locations, and we have agronomy, fertilizer, seed, chemicals, and then we have the grain and edible beans. And we do some service: Spreading, spraying, and trucking. So we're generating income on different things, and it helps us utilize our people and assets more efficiently between the work at the grain elevator, fertilizer plant, bean processing plant, and the office. With us there's always something going on as long as you have a crop.

JB And the gas pumps up front?

MH They're well used. It's not a high dollar margin for us—it was more a convenience thing. These complexes are a true convenience store, even if there's no store.

FREEDOM TO FARM

JB It seems there was a period in the 20th century when the

economic and spatial development of agriculture in the US was steered by government initiatives and programs—farm bills and agricultural acts, soil conservation programs. But by this point the market has gained nearly full control. Is a spatial and economic design intent now missing?

MW Absolutely. It started in the mid-90s with the Freedom to Farm Act,[5] and they ended up dismantling any supply management, the farmers were going to grow and feed the world. The notion was "Get the government off your back, plant whatever you want, plant for the market, and we'll sell it." It was the worst program ever. It introduced decoupled payment, which simply meant they were going to send you money whether you needed it or not. It was too little when the prices were low, it was not friendly to the taxpayer, and there were people who cheated the system, receiving massive payments unwarranted. I was with the Farmers Union, not yet president, and we were eager to convince the government that this system had to be rewritten. We now have a farm program that has base yields, but it still has no supply management component. We're still overplanting.

PO Moving away from direct payments is the worst thing we could have ever done. Back then I would receive, let's say, $15 an acre, and I could concentrate on doing what I needed to do for quality purposes and it did not matter how much yield I had. We're now in this yield mode, even the market adjustment payment[6] is counting yields. The industry wants more, because the more throughput you have, the more you supply, the more products you use, and the more your equipment wears out.

WE CAN BECOME THE INDUSTRIAL SPECIALTY SUPPLIERS

JB Mark, you mentioned a "full market." Could you say what's meant by that?

MW On every crop, we have the capacity to produce more than we can consume and export. The American market is full of product. So without a major weather scare, or failure in another country, or part of our country, there's not enough demand to swallow the supply.

PO When prices go up you raise more crops because you make more money. But when prices go down you also have

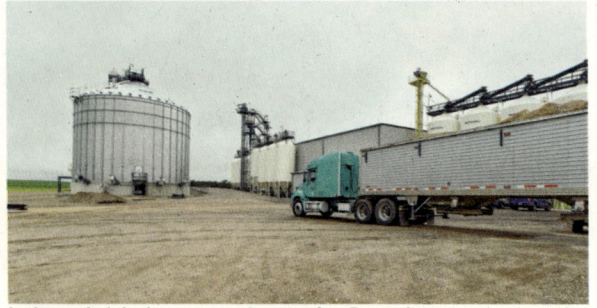
In the yard of the bean processing complex, Fessenden Co-op Association.

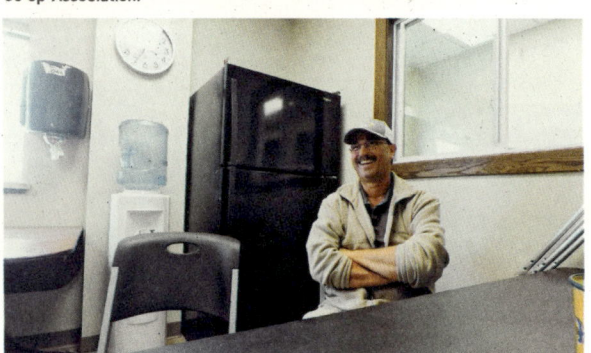
Mark Hovland, general manager at Hamberg, in the coffee room of the bean processing plant.

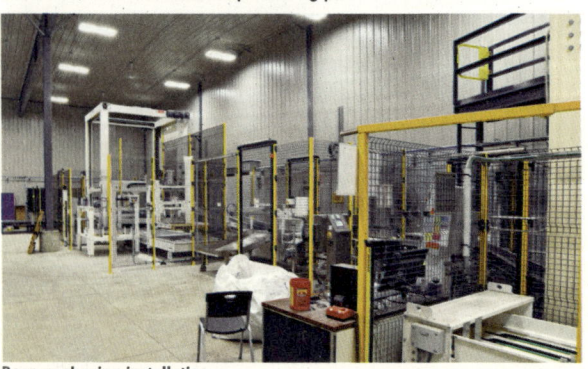
Bean packaging installation.

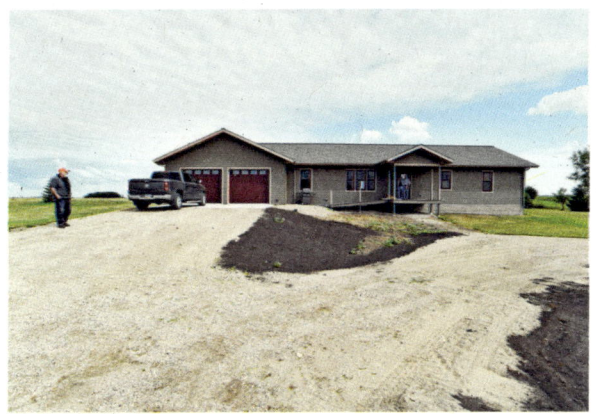

The Overby family home.

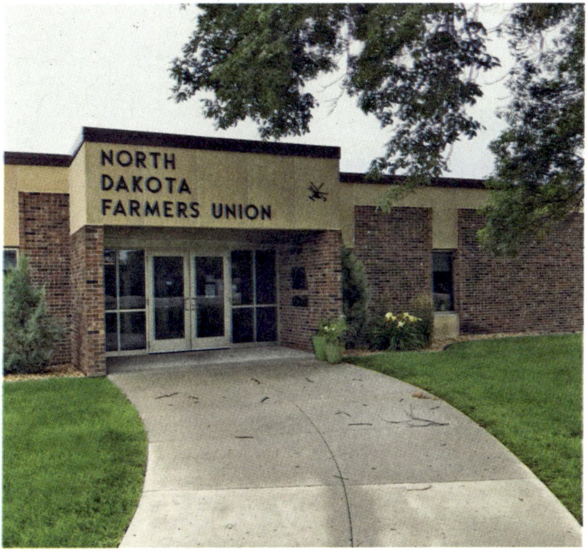

Jamestown, ND.

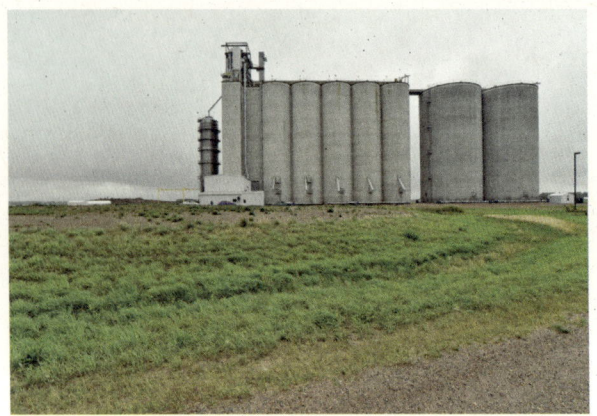

Grain elevator bins of Fessenden Co-Op Association, as seen on Mark Pederson's screen.

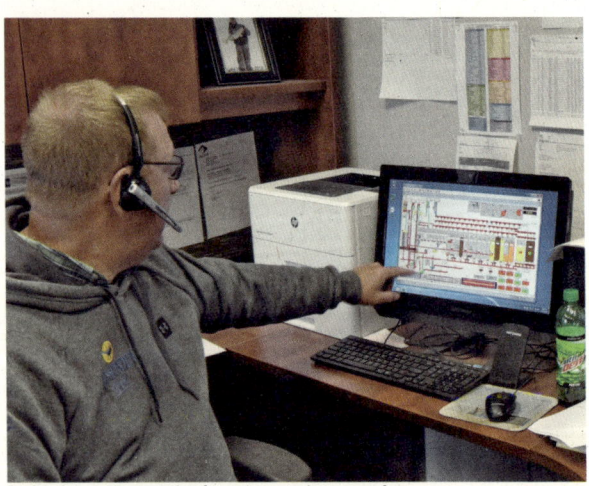

Pederson monitors grain elevator capacity remotely from the office building.

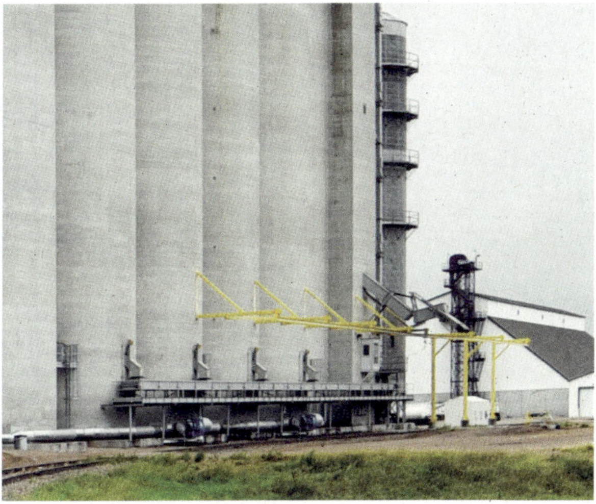

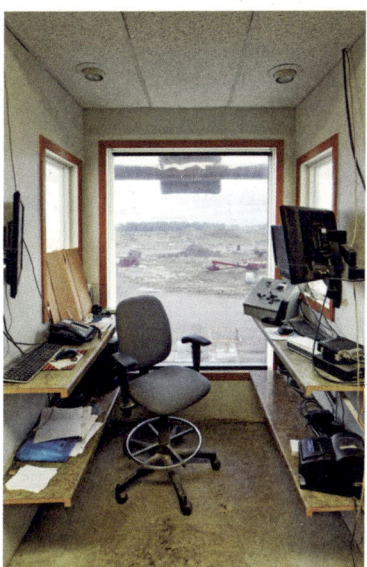

Office for loading the train, propped in-between the elevator's grain cylinders.

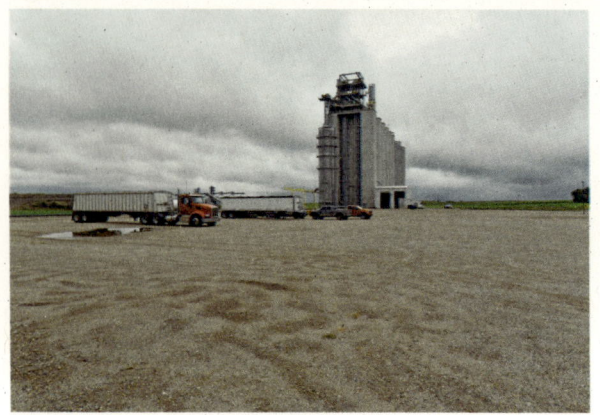

Fessenden Co-op Association, Hamberg, ND.

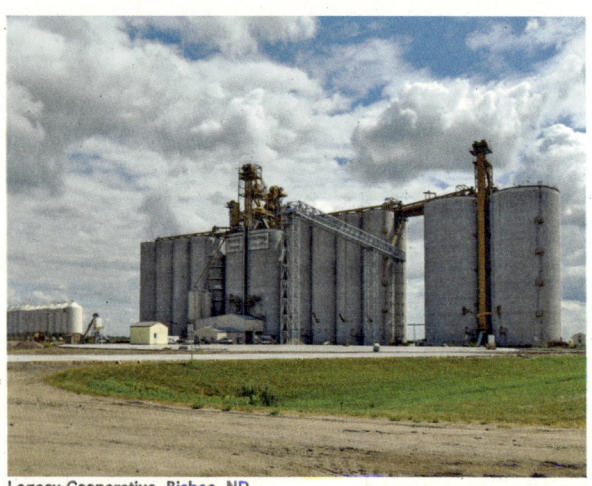

Legacy Cooperative, Bisbee, ND.

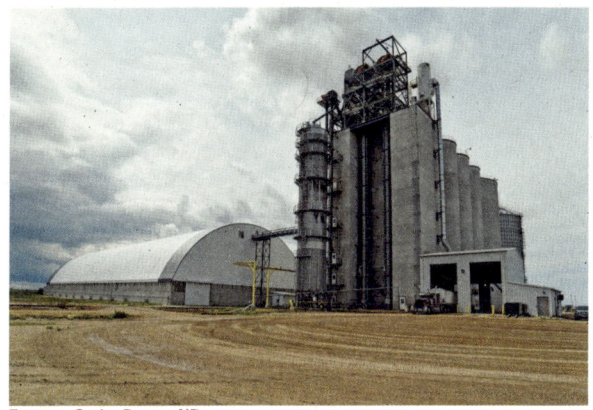
Tronson Grain, Doyon, ND.

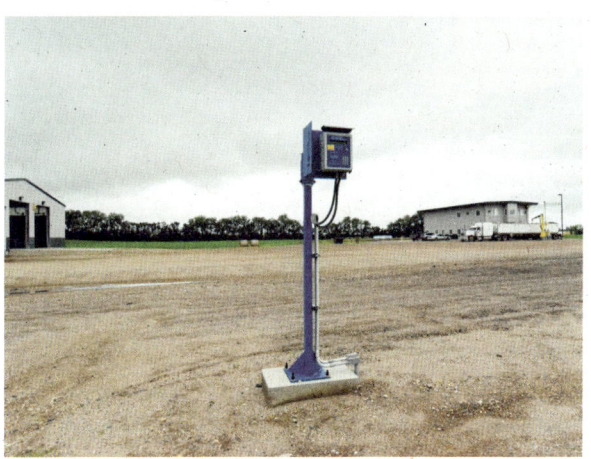
Self check-in point for grain truck drivers, bringing grain to the elevators.

to raise more, just to survive. So the pressure is always to produce more. That's true whether you're raising wheat or mining copper. You've got countries like Russia now coming on full tilt producing wheat, soybeans. They sent their first trainload of soybeans to China. They're doing all the things we were doing 40 years ago, building up their industry. They're buying Concord air drills and other equipment from Fargo and shipping it. They're going to become the low cost producers, the new global commodity growers. If we're trying to compete with those farms, we need 100,000-acre farms, because that's what they have. And if we're going to continue on this treadmill trying to be the low-cost producer, without massive government subsidies paying the salaries, like they have in Europe, the mega farm is the model. As long as everybody understands that. At the same time in Russia they don't yet have the technology or the infrastructure to segment their production into specialty products. So, while Europe continues subsidized agriculture, we can become the industrial specialty suppliers— we have the technology and the capacity. The question is: Do we have the will to do it? We can raise different types of wheat for different types of bread, and build that market. Instead what we're doing is blending different varieties of wheat to meet different protein specs. So we get this homogenized type of flour that works great in a factory with a row of 50 robotic mixers producing bread that all tastes the same.

DILEMMAS OF REGENERATIVE FARMING

JB Paul, from a farmer and co-op perspective, what do you see as the next step in this progression in the scale of grain elevators, processing, and transportation?

PO There are a couple of different paths. One is to keep doing more with less, but that means increasingly smaller margins. The industry looks big but there's not a lot of room for error. The path we've been gearing our regenerative farm down is less. I want to use less fertilizer, I want to use less chemicals, less tillage.

LF Could you talk about the dilemmas of regenerative farming, where you aim to save your soil by going into no-till agriculture[7] but still need a substance like Roundup to control the weeds?

PO The no-tillers finally had an opportunity to go fully no-till when Roundup came out in the 1990s. It changed the game. We finally had full-spectrum weed control, without having to till. It was expensive. When it first came out, Roundup was about $80 per gallon. Last year, I think I bought ours for $14 per gallon. So we are down from $18 per acre to $3 or $4 for our pre-plant burndown pass. That part of the technology has been good, but if we want to maintain the technology of any herbicide you have to minimize its use. One of my fears was that farmers would overuse Roundup, just like they do in Iowa and Missouri, and now they have weed resistances. Part of it was improper marketing. When the marketers were out here at our farm meetings telling us how to use it, they promoted it as a one-pass system.[8] But at the same time, they said: "If you have some weeds you missed the first time, just come back with Roundup a second time and it'll get them."

JB What's the interaction between GMO, Roundup, and no-till?

PO There was an attempt in North Dakota to create a Roundup-ready wheat. I was adamantly opposed to that. We stayed away from GMO crops by and large, but not entirely, because I wanted to protect the ability to use glyphosate[9] for our burndown program, so we wouldn't overload the system. But even with cautious application, we're getting some glyphosate-resistant weeds on our farm and in the area. We're going to have to deal with this, because it's spreading. For me as a no-till farmer, it's very concerning.

ELECTROCUTE THE WEED

JB What are the alternatives to chemical full-spectrum weed control? Is the industry doing enough to create alternative methods?

PO A lot of research got cut because Roundup was so dominant. At this point all the alternatives to glyphosate are more toxic. In the US, one of the choices is Paraquat, sold under a variety of trade names. Unlike glyphosate, Paraquat can only be applied by certified operators because it has toxicity in its fumes as well as from extended skin contact. Most farmers go through training every few years to be certified to use these chemicals.
But for non-chemical choices, cover crops can be really successful at controlling weeds, particularly

rye planted in the fall. Rye is allelopathic to a number of plants, so it prohibits their germination in the spring. And it's vigorous so it can smother out other plants. Soybeans are often planted directly into the cover crop, which is then terminated with glyphosate. But many farmers are now experimenting with "crimpers," or heavy rollers with serrations on them, to crush the weed's stem and effectively kill it before the soybeans emerge. Another technique is using a high current electrical wire to electrocute the weed when it makes contact. Then we get into an interesting synergy of precision and regenerative ag: There are some optic sensors being developed to see individual weeds. John Deere and Trimble both have optic systems coupled with conventional sprayers which are activated when a weed is detected. Another company is researching using those same optics to fire a blast of grit at the weed instead of chemicals.

A LOT OF THE PEOPLE AROUND HERE DON'T SOIL TEST

JB When did farmers here start becoming concerned about soil health?

PO A number of people, primarily in the USDA's Natural Resources Conservation Service, Ag Research Centers, and some not-for-profits started raising the issue of soil health in the mid-2000s. This research didn't find a ready audience for a while because the late 2000s and early 2010s were boom years and farmers were doing well with existing management practices. Unfortunately farmers also began to take land out of the Conservation Reserve Program and started breaking up pasture that should never have been farmed. The collapse of commodity prices by 2014 and 2015 changed the calculus. Farmers now seem to be more open to hearing what they previously had ignored. I'm cautiously optimistic that we are starting to see a growing awareness of the need to farm differently.

JB What practices do you incorporate to maintain soil health, and what are the benefits?

PO I'm out there in the field, pulling out soil cores to do my own tests. But that's not part of most farming operations. A lot of the people around here don't soil test. One of my neighbors is a good farmer—gets his stuff done, good yields. We started farming this little 30-acre strip that he used to farm. First year I went out there and soil tested, it showed there could have been 90 pounds of residual nitrogen in the soil. How much has leached away through the years, I have no idea. At about 45 cents per pound, it was $45 an acre of free money for me. Multiply that by 2,000 acres, that's $90,000 of fertilizer that could be sitting in his field today that he didn't know about. He would have used a removal rate calculation: I harvested 50 bushels of wheat, multiplied by 2.5 that's 125 pounds of nitrogen removed, so we'll put down 125 pounds of fertilizer for the next crop. He just kept applying.

TILLAGE IS TO SOIL WHAT A TORNADO IS TO A CITY

JB So how did you transition into regenerative farming?

PO There was an organization called Manitoba North Dakota Zero Tillage Farmers Association, and my dad went to their meetings in the 1980s, when it was so dry. People were trying to figure out how to conserve moisture, but they didn't have the equipment to do it. They were using conventional drills that weren't designed to seed into stubble. Finally in the 90s, the tech started coming around. Monsanto had their "Fields of Tomorrow" program, which was a push for no-till farming facilitated by the use of Roundup. Around 2000, I started going to USDA programs, to the zero-till meetings. In the beginning I couldn't afford a new drill to plant seeds without tilling, so we were still doing what we had to do to get the crop planted. Finally in 2005 we found some good used equipment, and we've been working with it ever since. By that point I had done about five years of homework, and I was pretty convinced that it would work, so we transitioned the whole farm in one fell swoop into no-till.

JB Are there particular crops that could ease the transition into no-till farming?

PO In the fall when you're done harvesting soy beans there's hardly any residue—any stubble—leftover. So if there's a perfect candidate to leave alone, it's soy beans. But there are still farmers who take a chisel plough and work up their soy ground to get it "ready" for wheat the next year, even if they have a no-till drill. Some of them have realized over the years that it's not necessary. But many farmers can't help it: They've got to till, it's kind of in their DNA. But at least if they use a coulter it's less invasive. With a chisel plow, you're destroying the whole soil structure, but with a coulter you're only messing up the top inch or two, and so the microbiology can recover a lot faster. I like the soil health analogy: Tillage is to soil what a tornado is to a city. It destroys everything. Vertical tillage, done correctly, is more like a wind blowing over the city, knocking off branches of a few trees.

JB Do you have an impression of how many farmers today are practicing no-till farming in North Dakota?

PO In western North Dakota, from Rugby on west, you're probably looking at more than 60 percent. From Rugby this way it's probably down to 30 percent.

LF What's your classification of no-till based on?

PO I don't agree with the absolute no-till purists. I would include farmers if what they're doing causes very little disturbance—so no chisel plowing and no full field tillage. They might have one pass, they might harrow the stubble, and then seed directly. I would also include someone who does strip till—tilling eight inches and leaving 22 inches untilled. We're starting to understand how even with no-till, soil stratification can still occur, particularly with phosphorus. Depending on the microbial action, it might not be getting down into the soil. So rain or melt water picks up that organic phosphorus in the top stratified layer and moves it into our waterways. Some soil turnover, but minimizing it with an air-seeder like ours, working in a narrow seedbed, a strip till, or by injecting underneath—that may not be a bad thing. So this purist approach of trying to only do a single disk opening, a slot—from a soil health point of view they are finding that that's not critical.

JB What about cover crops?

PO We also work with cover crops, growing this nice green cover into the winter, which dies and then lays there on top of the soil. We've seen on our fields that microbial activity actually warms up the soil earlier. So when that snow melts or the second rain comes, the water can get down into the soil, as opposed to running off. Which also means if we have a nice snow cover, I can take a shovel out to our fields in January and stick it in the ground, and I guarantee you could not do that in a black till field.

I COULD SEND MY 15-YEAR-OLD GRANDSON OUT THERE

JB Gary, could you talk a bit about the reach of precision agriculture practice?

GW Farmers in this region didn't take to this occupation to sit behind a computer. They want to work with their hands. But precision agriculture brings technology and computer work. All our tractors now have computers in them, and we have to understand how to program them to a limited extent. I have gotten to a point where I can document what we did last year out in the fields, how we set particular equipment up, what we applied and how.

JB What are the daily advantages of this technology?

GW The idea is that, once the tech is set up properly, I could send my 15-year-old grandson out there and he would be just as productive as guys who have been out there for 30 years. He could make the proper turns at the end of the field, and all he'd have to do is monitor and, if something goes wrong, hit the stop button and call someone.

JB What are some of the most recent precision farming technologies you've adopted?

GW We started flying a quadcopter over our fields this year to calculate plant population. I'm like a kid in a candy store. We planted 35,000 seeds across a field but we have anywhere between 27,000 and 33,000 plants. That's up to 8,000 seeds that never made it out of the ground. And we're using variable rate application for seeds, chemicals and fertilizer based on geolocation, crop type, soil, weather, and other data. We have a sprayer and three types of fertilizer, and that's delivered by tubes that spread it on the ground. Each tank is controlled by our computer and a seed meter, so we can put different quantities in different parts of the field. Same thing with the anhydrous.[10] We use elevation data—

LF Could you talk a bit about that? This is one of the flattest areas in the world here, and yet you're doing elevation analysis. Why is it important?

GW Drainage is the most important thing we do on our farm. Once the snow melts there's only a very short period of time to get rid of the excess water in the fields before we need to start planting. So the quicker we can get that water to exit the field, the quicker it will dry up. We run the elevation data through specialized GIS software for watershed monitoring, just like it's done for large rivers, but we do it for a field, to determine where the water would naturally want to run. Then we use GPS-controlled equipment to create drainage pathways in the field.

I BOUGHT MY FIRST COMPUTER IN 1978

LF One farmer I spoke to recently said: "I don't want to build these variable rate maps[11] myself, I want someone else to do it for me." Where does your desire to do this yourself come from?

GW Lanny and I met at a trade show in 95/96, and he got me interested in remote sensing. I had a bunch of yield data with me and we tried out his Satshot software before it was on sale. Lanny had never been on my farm and yet he was telling me what was happening in my field, and it was true. We slowly increased our use of variable rates, a few new fields every year, and learned from each step. Then we started to apply precision methods to the whole farm. Today, when people want to do precision ag, they get overwhelmed and give up. They think they have to do it all at once, on all their fields.

JB Could you talk about the steps you've taken over the years to adopt this technology?

GW I've always been fascinated with computers. The biggest thing that happened on this farm operation is that when I was 22 years old, my father passed away. So with my brother, who's two years older, we had control of the farm from that point on, without a father figure saying: "You can't spend money on a computer, you can't spend money doing these kinds of things." We had to control our own future. I bought my first computer in 1978, and realized that with computers you can't do anything unless you learn how to program, so I started to teach myself. Some people work with wood or go fishing. My relaxation is sitting behind a computer and being creative.

JB What's next for you in terms of technology?

GW I've developed an in-house software package that we use on our phones and iPads that collects real-time data from the field. We have a server in the other room. Farmers used to sit down and write everything in notebooks—what was applied, what variety. Now, we're collecting all this data electronically, and it gets updated immediately so everyone has access to it. We call it small data—what rate did you plant this time last year, how effective was it, what was the temperature, what was the wind speed?

NOT BIGGER-BIGGER, BUT SMALLER-SMARTER

JB What about the cost of your equipment?

GW It's a big problem. An extremely large tractor or combine may cost me half a million dollars each. The life span for that tractor on this farm would probably be five years. At the end of those five years, who's going to be able to buy it? There's a class of farmers with 1,000 to 3,000 acres, and another class of 20,000 to 25,000 acres. A small farm will never need that kind of extremely large machine, and could never afford it even secondhand. So we have to look not only at the technology but also the resale value of this equipment, because the prices we are paying are astronomical. John Deere told us some time ago that they try to develop not bigger-bigger, but smaller-smarter—this includes the partially autonomous combines, a so-called leader-follower system, where one combine is working behind another. So the day you want to sell that machine, a farmer with smaller acreage would be able to buy it, and it would be worth something.

JB Are there other models of buying equipment?

GW At one point you could buy the license for the product, now they want to sell you a subscription service. For these companies to keep improving their technology they have to have a steady revenue stream, but there's only so many subscriptions we can afford. So either there has to be some real technological breakthroughs, or I am going to say at a point that what I already have is good enough. There has to be a definite payback for the cost of tech. I think this is one of the reasons a lot of the farmers still haven't really adopted precision farming.

LF What are your thoughts on full automation? Some are saying five years, others say we're still 50 years out from it.

GW I don't see a lot of that partial autonomy yet, but you are starting to see a movement away from bigger machines, with drones being used for spot spraying. We're still worlds away from sitting behind a computer and letting robots do all the work. I don't know if we farmers can afford the equipment yet. The technology is there, but there always has to be someone in the driving seat of that combine because there are too many lawyers in the world.

JB How could technology help improve the state of the soil?

PO Instead of me having to do all that soil testing, which is rather tedious, it could be done by an autonomous machine, and I could be making decisions based on that. Right now I do my weed scouting, and then I drive the sprayer. With sensors in the fields it's possible to time the fungicide application better, without paying a field scout. What happens if, in 25 years, the sprayer is driving itself, and all I have to do is stay one field ahead, scouting the field and getting everything ready? There's potential for better control and to use less products. But everything in our system is geared towards using more.

MARRY PRECISION AGRICULTURE AND REGENERATIVE AGRICULTURE

JB So precision farming can aid soil health through the targeted use of pesticides and fertilizers?

PO For many years, I've been trying to marry precision agriculture and regenerative agriculture into one package. Are there going to be enough smaller farmers who have the soil health mindset, and are the regenerative farmers going to be willing to adopt semiautonomous technology, and give up some of their hands-on experience? Because if I'm putting down the exactly correct amount of fertilizer in just the area of my field that needs it, there are so many environmental benefits. There's less transportation, I don't have excess amounts that leach away or convert to gas and escape into the atmosphere. And I save money. All in one fell swoop. I challenge the small farmers, the Jodis and the Abbeys[12] of the world, to bring precision farming into their discussion.

LF So how do you convince people of the benefit of understanding the soil as a living organism, versus letting the economics drive the decisions?

PO The food companies. Consumers are putting pressure on the food companies, raising moral and ethical questions. So food companies come back to us farmers and suppliers and say "This is the way we want our crops raised." We're part of the General Mills Regenerative Agriculture program, which is kind of a neat group of experts and farmers. PepsiCo is doing the same thing. The companies are working with farmers who are willing to try things, to raise products in a soil-friendly way. The problem is that the industry learning curve is long, and these companies are in danger of overpromising to the consumer in terms of what they can deliver. Right now I have one field in this scheme—40 acres out of 1,400 crop acres, that's all. General Mills has a goal of one million regenerative acres, which sounds like a lot, but there are 30 million acres of cropland in North Dakota alone.

GW We're also involved with a General Mills project. They want to prove to their customers that they're trying to reduce the carbon footprint in farming. They measure how many miles we have to haul our trucks, how many trucks, how much fertilizer we put on.

PO The technology they tested on our farm is kind of cool. A group from Denmark was here with an optical sensor to measure insect biodiversity, which is an indicator of soil health. Jonathan Lundgren from Blue Dasher Farm set up three transects in the field that had nectar cups and feeding traps to measure the bugs. General Mills is testing technology to measure biodiversity, rather than have someone come out here and do a big study. They're also doing carbon testing and soil testing. Those are the technologies needed for regenerative agriculture to take hold.

HOW DO WE BACK OUT OF THIS SYSTEM?

JB What do you think will be the long-term impact of tariffs on agriculture?

PO The price of soybeans is being hammered because of the tariffs, and people are starting to look at alternatives.

One of the crops we attempted to raise is faba beans. We're seeing a push by the fake meat and alternative protein market, but the tariffs have driven the prices down.

JB What other crops provide these alternative proteins?

PO The ingredient market is gaining traction. Soybean protein is part of it, but it's not going to be used much in meat substitutes because it has a distinct flavor. Pea protein is in high demand because it has a neutral flavor. Which brings us back to the question of the large agricultural complexes like Hamberg with this huge 110-car train loading capacity. Their challenge is going to be: Where do they drop 110 cars that have eight different grains in it? And that's our challenge today too: Pushed into it by the rail companies and not because farmers wanted it, we built an infrastructure for raising commodities and shipping big amounts of homogenized products, and yet the market is moving towards segmented, differentiated products. How do we back out of this system?

JB Is the next generation of farmers going to achieve it?

PO Well, if the reality is that the low-cost producer is the winner because the system is structured that way, will there be any opportunity for the smaller producer to get into the game? Some of these younger people who are interested in alternative ways of doing things are really struggling. There's nobody in North Dakota asking who's going to replace me and my neighbors, who are all in our 60s. And now this tariff fight may obliterate so many small farms that there's no coming back.

MW In North Dakota, only family corporations of less than 15 members can exist here. We had to fight for that. But if every other state passes laws expanding corporate farming, it will be hard for us to keep this anti-corporate farming law on the books.

JB Do you think a shift from commodity growers to specialty farmers is theoretically possible in North Dakota?

MW We've been developing "value-added agriculture." That means integrating the farmer up the food chain, so we can extract more profit by being more in touch with the customer. We've tried pasta plants, spring wheat baking plants, but we weren't going up in the marketplace until we launched the Founding Farmers restaurants, a chain owned by the Union and roughly 200 farmers. The restaurants and the model have been a success.

JB Farmers make up less than two percent of the population in the US. How low can that figure go?

GW We don't have the big families we used to. If you're not born into a farm operation, the chances of you buying in, and generating enough revenue, is very small. What's going to happen to the rural population? In Crookston, Minnesota, when I graduated from high school in 1972, I had 250 classmates. In the same area, my grandson in his ninth grade class has 85 students. I think the family farm is going to disappear. But can the big farm be more productive than they already are? I don't think so.

JB Is moving from commodities to value-added agriculture, segmented, and diverse products the way forward?

MW I think it's the only solution, unless we go into government-mandated supply management. But it all depends on what you want agriculture to look like. If you want enough farmers and people on the land, farming and maintaining the local infrastructure and communities, either you turn to supply management, or you find alternate dividend sources through segmentation and value-added products. The current model of large-scale farming is only able to promote ever-larger farms and more production. The question becomes: Can they continue to maintain this efficiency? What I always tell somebody who's growing larger is: Think about how you're going to have roads, how you're going to get your products, where are you going to shop? Are you adding these hidden costs into your farm operation? It's easy to put a farm budget together, not easy to make it work at true cost.

RAIL LOOPS AT...

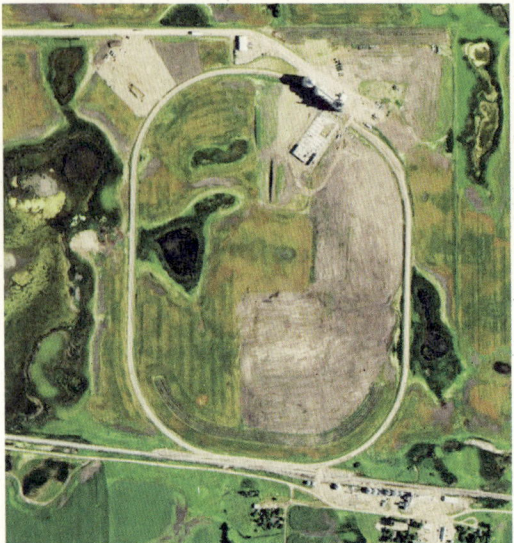

...Tronson Grain, Doyon, ND.

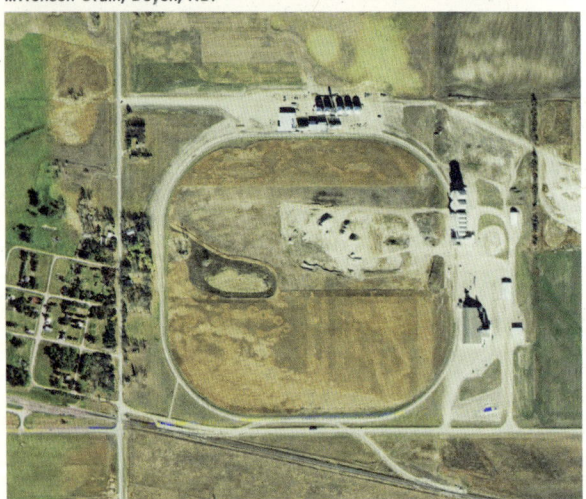

...Fessenden Co-op Association, Hamberg, ND.

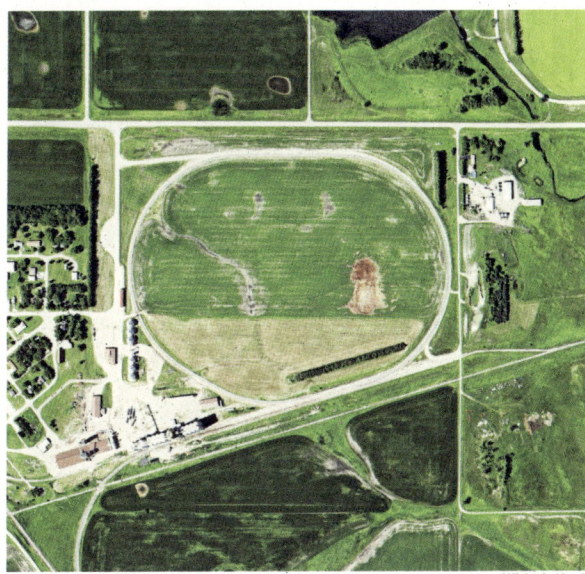

...Legacy Cooperative, Bisbee, ND. (All Apple Maps)

1 The Capper-Volstead Act (1922) allowed farmers to market products collectively (which formerly could lead to prosecution); the act also instituted legal remedies if monopolistic practices unduly inflated prices.
2 The Federal Agriculture Improvement and Reform Act (1996) replaced price support and supply control with direct payments based on historical production. Guaranteed a subsidy now, regardless of what they planted and how it impacted the market, farmers could plant any crop in any quantity.
3 Seventy-five percent of agricultural products sold in North Dakota are grains, oilseeds, dry beans and dry peas; cattle and calves are 16 percent; other crops and hay is four percent (USDA, 2017).
4 For comparison: North Dakota, with 700,000 inhabitants, is twice the area of Portugal, which has a population of more than 10 million.
5 Or the Federal Agriculture Improvement and Reform Act, 1996.
6 Brought in by the USDA in 2019, the Market Facilitation Program subsidizers farmers whose products—especially soy—are now too expensive to sell on the international market, the result of the Trump administration's trade war with China.
7 No-till agriculture plants seeds in unplowed ground, recognizing that tilling damages the soil's ecosystem and increases erosion and runoff. No-till agriculture improves soil health, water and air quality, retains more nitrogen, increases carbon sequestration, and reduces costs of farm operation. Conventional no-till farming relies on herbicides to manage weeds; alternatives include cover crops, crop rotation, and tractor implements such as heavy rollers to crush weeds. In the Northern Great Plains, which includes North Dakota, 49 percent of farms practice no-till and strip-till, higher than the national average (USDA, 2016, USDA Agricultural Research Management Survey 2010-11).
8 A 'one pass' system means applying herbicide only once per crop cycle.
9 E.g. Roundup.
10 Anhydrous ammonia (NH3), one of the most widely used nitrogen fertilizers for corn and wheat.
11 This would involve using satellite images of the relevant field in the app, and running it through a variable rate function before uploading the processed map to the tractor or its mounted equipment.
12 Jodi DeJong Hughes and Abbey Wick, researchers and educators in soil health in the northern Great Plains.

Buying = Saving: Doug Tompkins's Chile Campaign
Federico Martelli, Cookies

2020 NATURE'S BOUNTY The current annual value of the world's ecosystem services is estimated at $115–$123 trillion.[1] However, over the past several decades, the goods and services they provide have been significantly degraded, severely endangering life and civilization as we know it.

OCTOBER 2019 RIOT Building on a protest in Santiago against a price hike on metro tickets, citizens take to the streets across Chile demanding social reform on pensions, health, and education. Riots spread throughout the country. President Sebastián Piñera, the billionaire former owner of the national airline and several TV stations, who made his fortune introducing credit cards to Chile in the early 1980s, is under pressure to resign for misjudging the depth of social discontent. There are calls for the constitution to be rewritten through an assembly that includes citizens and lawmakers from all parties. Ratified in 1980, during Pinochet's dictatorship, the present constitution was designed to encourage economic development via the protection of property; inadvertently, the lack of regulation for ownership also allows a new type of large-scale land-ownership for the purpose of preservation.

MAY 2019 FINAL WARNING The IPBES (Intergovernmental Science-Policy Platform on Biodiversity and Ecosystem Services) publishes the Global Assessment Report on biodiversity. One million species are threatened with extinction and the current global response is insufficient: "Ecosystems, species, wild populations, local varieties and breeds of domesticated plants and animals are shrinking, deteriorating or vanishing. The essential, interconnected web of life on Earth is getting smaller and increasingly frayed. This loss is a direct result of human activity and constitutes a direct threat to human well-being in all regions of the world," Prof. Josef Settele (co-chair, IPBES).

UNEQUAL PROTECTION In Chile, the areas with highest endemism are also the areas with the most productive soils, leading to the introduction of destructive non-native species like avocado, grapevines, pines, and eucalyptus. Furthermore, "Not all biomes are equally protected ... only 0.3 percent of the total area with tropical dry forest is under some category of protection in Mesoamerica. ... In the southern temperate forest ecoregion, extensive protected areas are owned by private individuals, NGOs, and governments (Soutullo and Gudynas 2006; Rozzi et al., 2012). For example, 57.3 percent of the Magallanes Region in southernmost Chile is under government protection (SIB Magallanes, 2017)."[2]

2018 PRIVATE-PUBLIC LAND TRANSFER The Conservation Land Trust—created by the American Douglas Tompkins, founder of The North Face and Esprit, and his wife Kristine McDivitt Tompkins—transfers 1,550 square miles to the Chilean state. It is the biggest ever donation of land from a private entity to a nation-state. After buying and stewarding huge swathes of Chile since 1991, the CLT now trusts the Chilean state to be the guardian of its land. The Pumalín Douglas Tompkins National Park is one of five new national parks enshrined by the Chilean government. Named for the pumas that roam there, the park consists of dense southern temperate rainforests, including endangered stands of alerce trees, climbing from fjords by the Pacific to snow-capped volcanoes in the high Andes. Most of the land is so steep it's nearly impossible to access, so the ecosystem has been kept largely intact. The once-private park is now administered by the Chilean national forest commission following strict quality standards established by the CLT. The deal is part of the largest-ever expansion of Chile's national parks, in which 15,500 square miles of public and formerly-private land is granted protected status, more than doubling the previous area.

2017 DAM BUSTED ENEL, the Italian energy giant, together with Colbun, owned by the Matte family, the third richest in Chile, announce the cancellation, after more than a decade of opposition, of the HidroAysén dam megaproject in the Baker and Pascua Rivers. ENEL and Colburn also return their water rights to the Chilean state. The campaign against the project was financed in part by Tompkins's foundation.

CHILE'S PARKS Nicole Mintz, part of the group of environmentalists that brought Tompkins to Chile in the 1990s, recalls in an interview with the author: "Doug used to say: 'You know, I don't care if they don't understand. This is going to be done.' Well, everybody else did care. Everything I was doing in conservation had to stop, because it was all about Doug Tompkins, it was no longer about conservation in Chile. We spent many years feeling like this was Doug Tompkins's park. It took him a full 25 years, with the help of Kris, to realize that this was something that Chileans have to feel like belongs to them."

2015 DEATH OF A NATURALIST Douglas Tompkins, 72, dies of acute hypothermia after 40 mph winds and eight-foot swells capsize his kayak in the 40°F waters of Lake General Carrera, southern Chile. Tompkins was kayaking with five friends, including Yvon Chouinard, 77, founder of the Patagonia clothing brand, with whom he first traveled to Chile in the late 1960s. Lake General Carrera is located near Patagonia Park and Jeiniemeni Reserve, two of Tompkin's largest conservation efforts; the lake is the source of the Baker River, which ENEL and Colburn are, at the time, planning to dam. Of the 3,500 square miles held by Tompkins's foundations, 775 square miles had been converted into five national parks. In his final interview, Tompkins said: "National parks are the best expression of social equity that there is. It's like paying our rent for living on the planet."

GESTALT Tompkins, obsessed with design and beauty, was also a "designer" of nature: Each park under his foundation's ownership has a different aesthetic for its visitor facilities, right down to the bathrooms. At the time of his death, Tompkins was trying to create the Patagonia National Park, a 300-square-mile former sheep ranch in between two existing reserves in the Chacabuco Valley in the Aysén Region, northern Patagonia. Handover proposals include the creation of "two campgrounds, a six-bedroom lodge, a restaurant, a visitor's center, and employee housing ... 38 miles of hiking trails, white water paddling on the nearby Baker River, the opportunity to see an elusive puma, and a restaurant that serves organic meals like asado grilled lamb and greens straight from the organic garden out back." A key part of Tompkins's conservation philosophy was to "establish an architectural style in each park" and "stick with it religiously and comprehensively so that it comes out as a gestalt."[3]

2012 GOOD DESIGN Tompkins and his wife Kristine write: "Good design and architecture have been integral to the conservation area and farm projects in Chile. Emphasis is placed on function, energy efficiency, and always crafting infrastructure that is consistent with the regional, vernacular architectural style. Care is taken that finishing standards are within the traditional techniques of local craftsmen and builders. Aesthetic considerations guide all design decisions under the maxim that *if it does not look good, it is not good* ... Buying land for conservation, with the objective to own that land for a relatively short period of time, restore it where necessary, and then repatriate it from the private sector to the public sector is, in our minds, one of the most noble efforts anyone can make."

INTRINSIC VALUE "[W]e believe that wilderness areas and wildlife have intrinsic value – that wild places and the creatures at home in them have a right to exist for their own sake. Every human being should care about the diversity of life, the myriad species that are our fellow members of the land community, and be willing to take action, at whatever level necessary, to see that there is enough secure habitat for all species to flourish. Protecting additional conservation land is an ecological imperative."[4]

MAY 2011 FIVE DAMS President Sebastián Piñera, in his first term in power, approves HidroAysén, a plan for the construction of five dams, two in the Baker River and three in the Pascua River. His decision comes despite the huge *Patagonia Sin Represas* ("Patagonia Without Dams") campaign, backed by the Tompkins Foundation and the CLT, which produced detailed technical comments in response to the project's environmental impact assessments, delaying the project and forcing a re-examination; and despite a huge media campaign from dam opponents, with hundreds of billboards throughout Chile, full-page ads in local and national newspapers, radio and TV spots, and social media to generate support.

2010 UN-ZEN In the documentary *180 Degrees South*, Yvon Chouinard describes Tompkins: "He's more bothered, probably, about the end of society and mankind and stuff than I am because he wants to do something about it. And I'm just kind of a laid-back Zen Buddhist, and just say, well, I'll do what I can and so be it." Tompkins replies: "Well, you better tell my buddy Yvon, the good Buddhist,

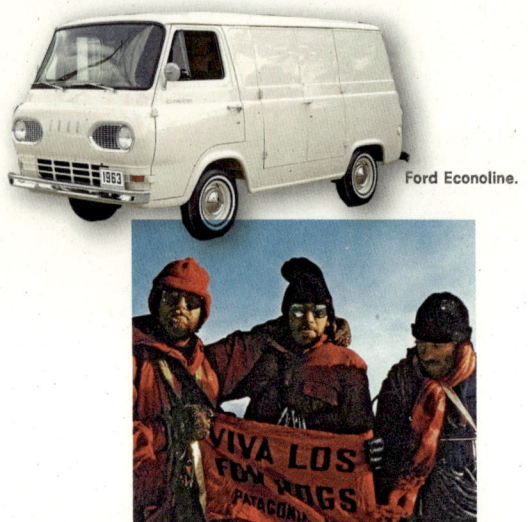

Ford Econoline.

1968 Tompkins travels with four friends from California to Patagonia where they put up the first ascent of Cerro Fitz Roy's Southwest Buttress and make the documentary Mountain of Storms.

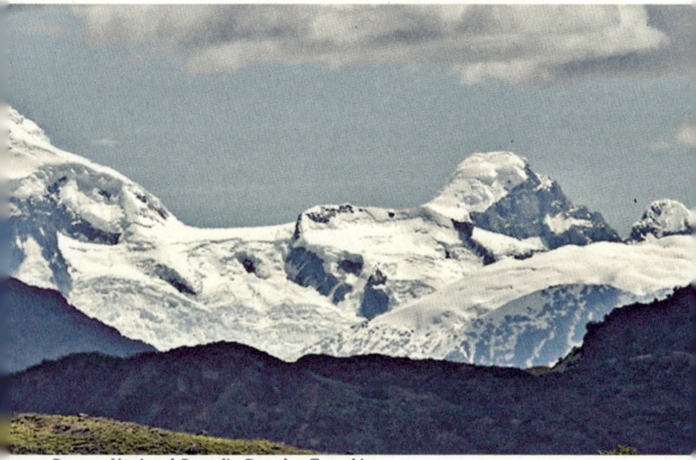

Parque Nacional Pumalin Douglas Tompkins.

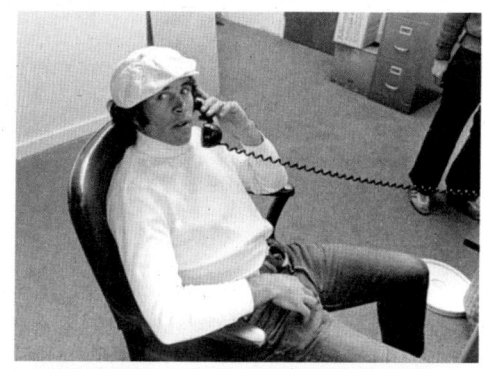

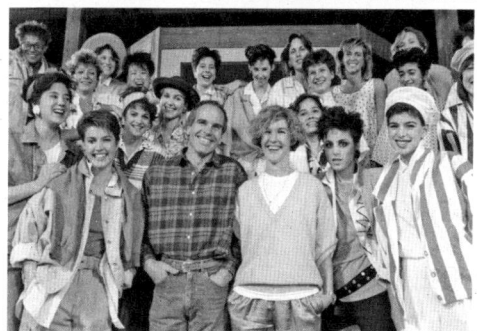

Tompkins tries out the role of retail mogul.

In 1999, Tompkins's Foundation for Deep Ecology buys a series of full-page ads in the *New York Times*.

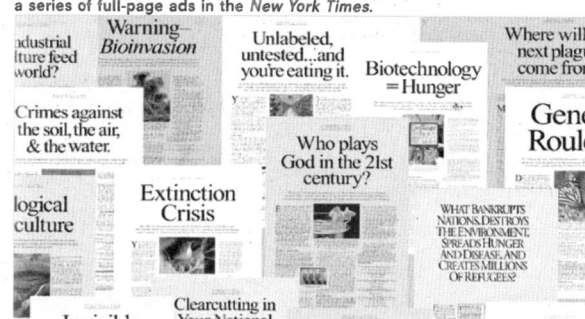

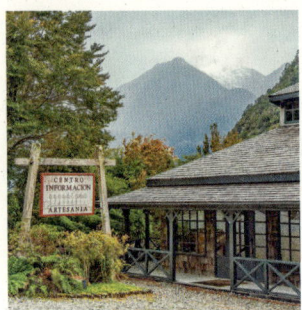

Visitor center at Parque Pumalin, designed under Tompkins' ethic "if it does not look good, it is not good."

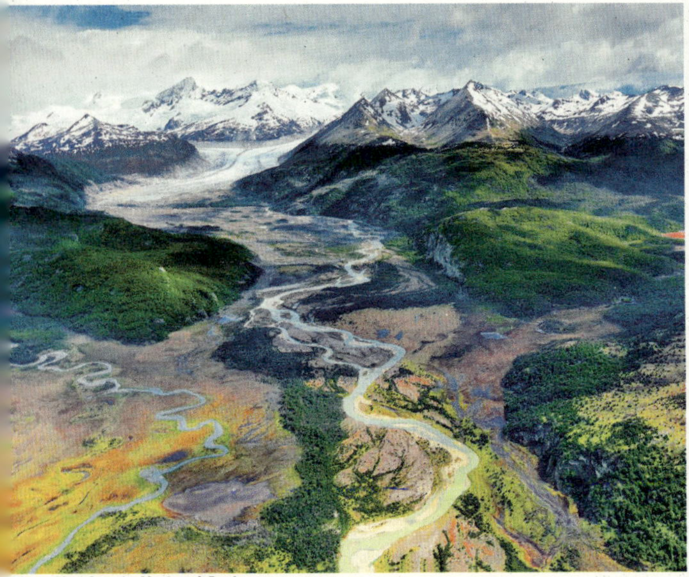

Yendagaia National Park.
(Tompkins Conservation)

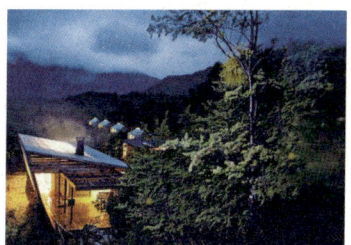

Valle California Membership lodges.
Available for rent for $300 per night
(Patagonia Sur).

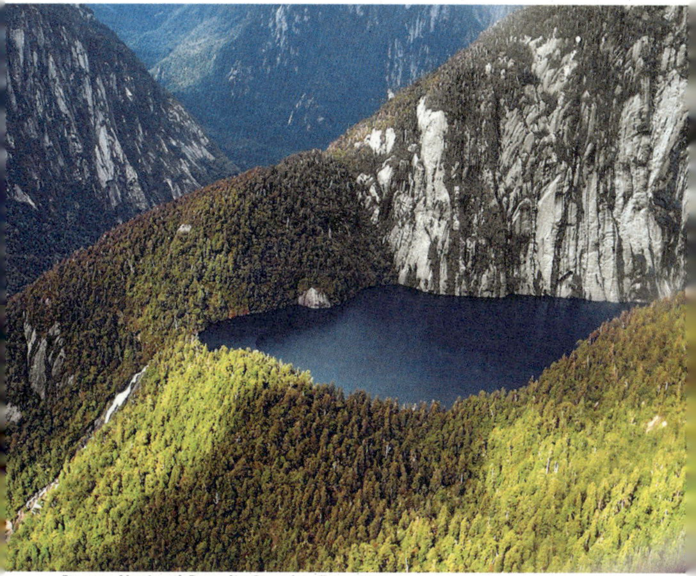

Parque Nacional Pumalin Douglas Tompkins.
(Tompkins Conservation)

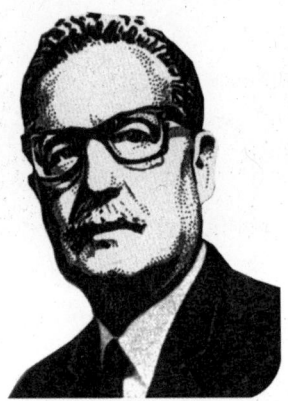

Salvador Allende, president of Chile 1970–1973: the first and only Marxist democratically elected. During his mandate he redistributes land from wealthy landowners to farmers.

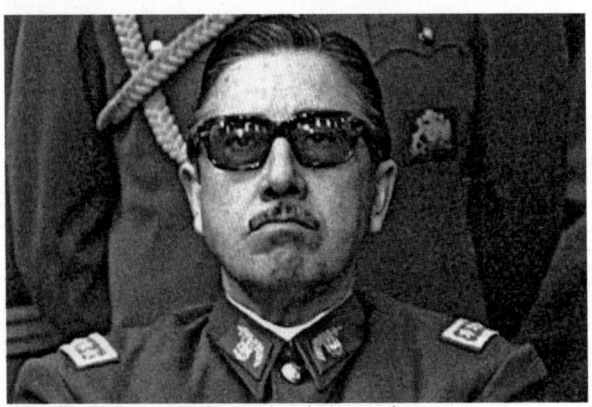

Following politic and social unrest largely triggered by US-backed economic warfare, Augusto Pinochet, general of the army, leads a coup d'etat to overthrow Salvador Allende in 1973. Pinochet stays in power for the following 17 years.

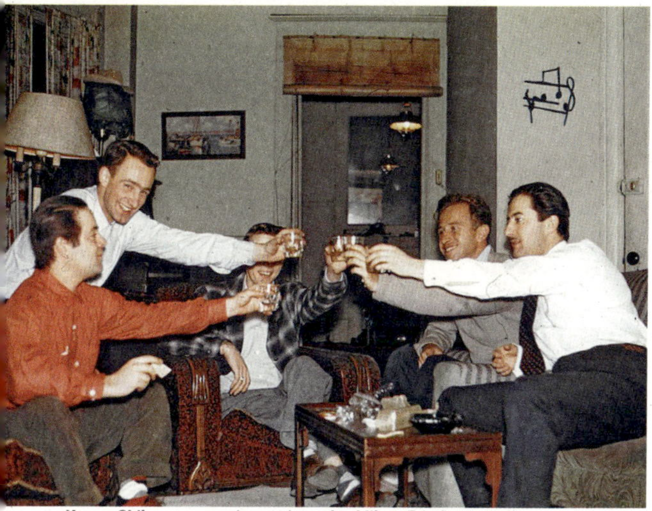

Young Chilean economists train under Milton Friedman at the University of Chicago, bringing neoliberalism back with them.

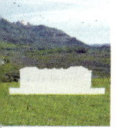

EL MORRO:
23 hectares
400 buildable
sq.ft

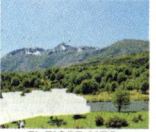

EL TIGRE ALTO:
42 hectares
31,200 buildable
sq.ft

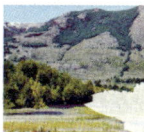

LAS LAGUNAS:
17 hectares
15,300 buildable
sq.ft

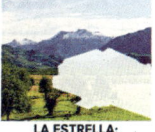

LA ESTRELLA:
102 hectares
46,650 buildable
sq.ft

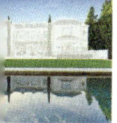

0 N ALTA DR.
ly Hills, CA 90210
$29,000,000
8,087 sqft

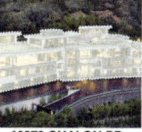

10979 CHALON RD
Los Angeles, CA 90077
$90,000,000
31,000 sq.ft

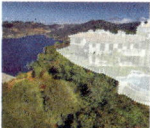

1940 BEL AIR RD.
Los Angeles, CA 90077
$28,500,000
17,297 sq.ft

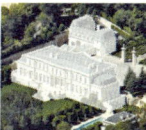

FLEUR DE LYS
Los Angeles, CA 90077
$102,000,000
50,000 sq.ft.

Patagonia Sur, founded in 2006 is a for-profit real estate company that sells parcels of land in Patagonia as investments, but also to ensure their longevity and protection. From the website: "Patagonia Sur has created an innovative model of world-class real estate development focused on conservation."

(American-style mansions collaged onto wilderness by Andrew Bako.)

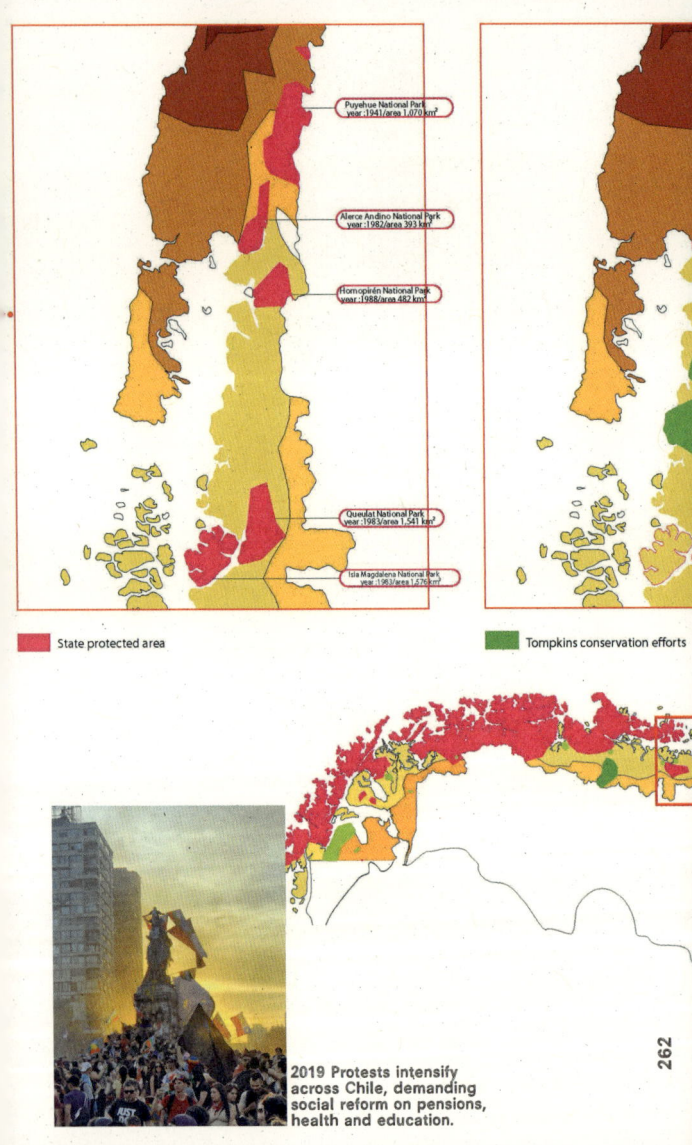

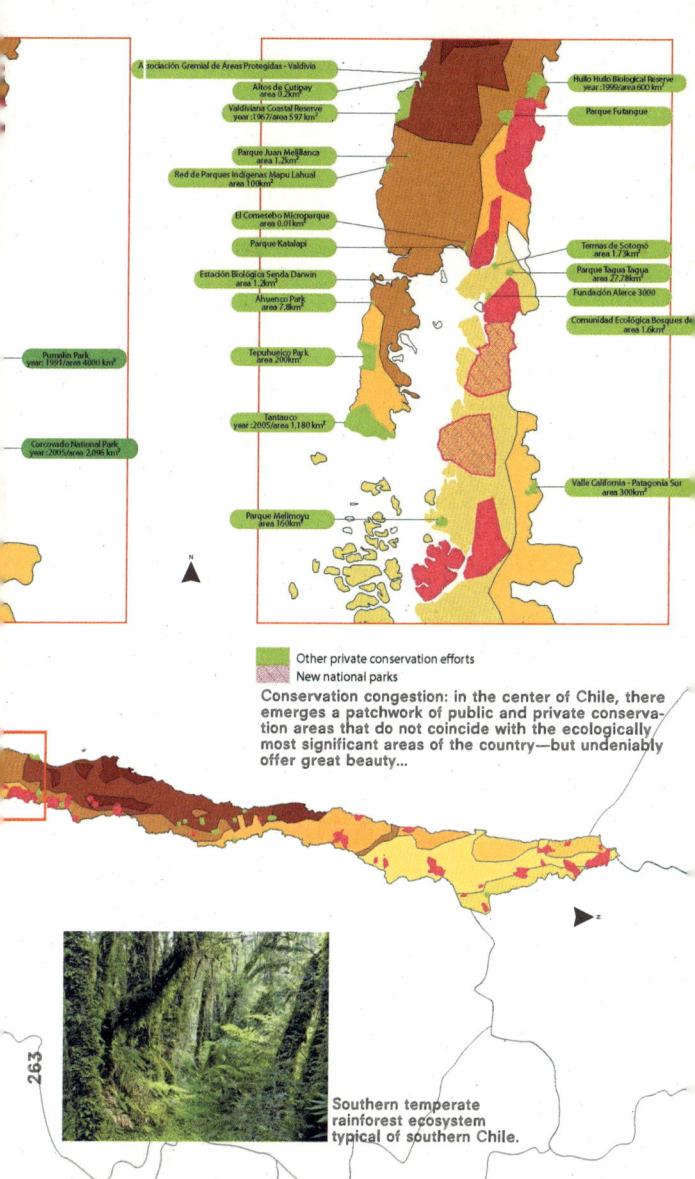

- Asociación Gremial de Áreas Protegidas - Valdivia
- Altos de Cutipay area 0.2km²
- Valdiviana Coastal Reserve year:1967/area 597 km²
- Parque Juan Melillanca area 1.2km²
- Red de Parques Indígenas Mapu Lahual area 100km²
- El Cornesebo Microparque area 0.01km²
- Parque Katalapi
- Estación Biológica Senda Darwin area 1.2km²
- Ahuenco Park area 7.8km²
- Tepuhueico Park area 200km²
- Tantauco year:2005/area 1,180 km²
- Parque Melimoyu area 160km²
- Huilo Huilo Biological Reserve year:1999/area 600 km²
- Parque Futangue
- Termas de Sotogrú area 1.73km²
- Parque Tagua Tagua area 27.78km²
- Fundación Alerce 3000
- Comunidad Ecológica Bosques de area 1.6km²
- Valle California - Patagonia Sur area 300km²
- Pumalín Park year:1991/area 4000 km²
- Corcovado National Park year:2005/area 2,096 km²

Other private conservation efforts
New national parks

Conservation congestion: in the center of Chile, there emerges a patchwork of public and private conservation areas that do not coincide with the ecologically most significant areas of the country—but undeniably offer great beauty...

Southern temperate rainforest ecosystem typical of southern Chile.

he has to take his bodhisattva vows, which means that before self-enlightenment, one has to end the suffering in the world."

2009 MITIGATION Goldman Sachs donates land on the Chilean portion of the Isla Grande de Tierra del Fuego—purchased from Trillium, a distressed Chilean logging company—to the Wildlife Conservation Society (WCS). The Karukinka Natural Park is born.

2007 THIS LAND IS YOUR LAND Facing opposition over his land purchases in Argentina, Tompkins recounts: "We said to the ministries and to [the] president ... 'Hey look guys. We are taking land from the private sector—sometimes buying it from foreigners—and giving it back to the state.' That has a tendency to quell a lot of waters." In another interview, Tompkins says: "[Y]ou never know if you're doing the right thing. But the way I see it, with land conservation of this type, the risk of something negative coming from this seems to be rather small compared with taking an exploitative approach."

2005 BILLIONAIRE'S PARK Piñera—still businessman, not yet politician—creates Tantauco Park, a 450-square-mile private natural reserve on the south end of Chiloé Island. ENEL/Colbun presents the HidroAysén project for environmental impact assessment to the National Commission for the Environment. The project is only possible because it takes advantage of the water rights that ENEL inherited from its precursor ENDESA, enabled by Pinochet's constitution.

NO MORE BUYING Tompkins announces he will not buy any more land in Chile; his work on establishing parks and protecting land he already owns, and preparing its transfer to the Chilean government is "going to take the rest of our lives to finish."

COLONIALIST Antonio Horvath, a conservative Chilean senator, tells the *New York Times*: "If I were to go to the United States and buy a big area of Florida as an environmental preserve and tell people they can't go here or there, I think the US would kick me right out of there. Every nation wants some degree of protection of its territory, and Chile is no different."

LITTLE APPRECIATED Carlos Weber, director of Chile's National Forestry Corporation says: "[T]hough the local authorities still have in their heads a model based on settler colonies that raze the forest to plant potatoes and raise animals, what Tompkins is doing offers the best opportunity for sustainable development in that region. He is little appreciated, understood or welcomed in Chile today, but I predict that 30 years from now, after people's thinking has matured and they see results, no one will be against him."[5]

1999 PUBLIC SERVICE ANNOUNCEMENT Tompkins's Foundation for Deep Ecology buys a series of full-page ads in the *New York Times*, to self-publish warnings on the extinction crisis, industrial agriculture, globalization, and genetic engineering. An ad titled "Invisible Government," published on November 29, 1999 helps trigger the anti-WTO protests in Seattle. "The central idea of the WTO," Tompkins's ad says, "is that free trade—actually the values and interests of global corporations—should supersede all other values. Any obstacles to global trade are viewed with suspicion. In practice, these 'obstacles' are the laws of nation-states that protect the environment, small businesses, human rights, consumers, labor as well as national sovereignty and democracy."

OFFER REJECTED Tompkins attempts to buy the 125-square-mile parcel of land separating the north and south sections of Pumalín Park; the Christian Democratic government blocks him, and the Roman Catholic university that owns the land sells it to a Spanish-controlled energy company instead, even though Tompkins is offering a better price.

1997 CARBON MARKETPLACE The Kyoto Protocol attempts to establish a marketplace of carbon credits. After the introduction of a carbon quota, nations would trade their surpluses or deficits, harnessing market forces to "naturally" discourage emissions. The southern temperate rainforests, including those in Chile, because they are mature, already sequester a huge amount of carbon. But their maturity also means they remain neutral in their atmospheric carbon intake: they are in equilibrium between the degradation and production of organic matter. This is problematic for Chile because, initially, carbon credits are awarded only to projects that would help the additional capture of atmospheric carbon. An unintended effect of the system is, therefore, the incentivization of deforestation, creating land for new fast-growing trees that would absorb more carbon, thus generating revenue from the carbon credit system.

1997 A PRICE ON NATURE Ecological economist Robert Costanza leads an attempted valuation of the global ecosystem ("The value of the world's ecosystem services and natural capital," *Nature*, May 1997): $33 trillion, with a range from $16 trillion to $54 trillion (in 1997, total global GDP is $27 trillion). Ecological economics is envisioned as transdisciplinary, developing valuation techniques based on the interaction of built, human, social, and natural capital. Costanza writes: "Because ecosystem services are not fully 'captured' in commercial markets or adequately quantified in terms comparable with economic services and manufactured capital, they are often given too little weight in policy decisions. This neglect may ultimately compromise the sustainability of humans in the biosphere. The economies of the Earth would grind to a halt without the services of ecological life-support systems, so in one sense their total value to the economy is infinite. However, it can be instructive to estimate the 'incremental' or 'marginal' value of ecosystem services (the estimated rate of change of value compared with changes in ecosystem services from their current levels). ... We must begin to give the natural capital stock that produces these services adequate weight in the decision-making process, otherwise current and continued future human welfare may drastically suffer."

1995 RESISTANCE Chile's congress debates Douglas Tompkins's increasingly large purchases of land in the south of Chile. National security concerns are paramount, since the land borders Argentina; there are also rumors that Tompkins is building either a new Jewish or neo-Nazi state, and that he is colluding with the Rockefeller family to control water resources. Tompkins decides to speak directly in congress to the commission scrutinizing his large-scale land purchasing.

CONGRESS "Will the Foundation facilitate the introduction of Israeli settlers with the objective of creating a new republic called Andin?"

TOMPKINS "Neither Bosque Pumalín Foundation nor EDUCEC Foundation have or have had any contact with any ethnic groups who wish to move to this area and populate the areas in or around Pumalín Park. We are not aware of the meaning of Republica Andin or of any documents that could have generated this question. In any case, we would like to make clear, that by the way the question has been formulated, it could refer to antisemitic content. Both Mr. Tompkins and the Foundation categorically deny any type of discrimination based on race, gender or religion."

CONGRESSWOMAN MARIA ANGELICA CRISTI "On a recent visit to Chaitén, I could see that there is a kind of collective psychosis because of the purchase of almost 300,000 hectares [740,000 acres] by this American citizen. One of the concerns of the settlers is that the acquisition of land in order to build an ecological park could impede the tourist development of the region."

CONGRESSMAN ELGUETA "Thanks to the Constitution of 1980, in Chile we have absolute private property... It cannot be said that an American citizen, who is making use of the right established in the 1980 Constitution for absolute ownership of private property, is committing a series of abuses, without these being specified."

1991 STRIP PRESERVATION Tompkins and his second wife, Kristine McDivitt Tompkins (former CEO of Patagonia, Inc.) purchase 1,040 square miles of land, for $25 million, to create Pumalín Park on land stretching from the Argentinian border to the fjords in the Pacific, forming a strip of preservation that essentially splits Chile in two. Both the Chilean and Argentinian governments oppose the purchase but cannot stop it; it is part of a larger purchase of 3,500 square miles of land in both countries. Pumalín is the only privately-owned park open for public access and tourism.

1990 DEEP CHANGES Pinochet's dictatorship formally ends after 17 years; democracy returns to Chile. Tompkins creates the Foundation for Deep Ecology, inspired by Norwegian philosopher Arne Næss. Deep ecology posits an ethical obligation, for those who recognize humanity's interconnection with the living world, to protect it. Living beings are intrinsically valuable regardless of the "ecosystem services" they provide to human civilization.

1989 FIRST PRIVATE RESERVE El Cani Sanctuary is formed when Ancient Forest International asks a group of philanthropists, including Tompkins and Yvon Chouinard, founder of Patagonia, to join Chilean conservationists Nicole Mintz, Adriana Hoffmann, Manfred Max Neef, and Sergio Vergara, in purchasing a tranche of southern temperate rainforest threatened by a logging company.

1989 ECOLOGICAL EPIPHANY Tompkins sells his stake in Esprit for $150 million, struggling with the contradiction of producing and selling fashion while trying to convince people to reuse and recycle; industrial civilization, Tompkins writes, is fundamentally incompatible with maintaining biodiversity. He leaves his San Francisco estate to live in Chile, immersing himself in the literature of conservation.

1988 HIGH-TECH RETAIL With over $1 billion in annual sales, Tompkins's Esprit retail empire hires Norman Foster to design the flagship store in Sloane Square, London.

1985 EIGHTIES AESTHETIC Susie Tompkins, Esprit's creative director, and Doug Tompkins, image director, commission Ettore Sottssas and the Memphis Group to design the interior of Esprit stores, pioneering the colorful aesthetics that characterize the 1980s.

1981 NEW CONSTITUTION Pinochet enacts the new Chilean constitution, liberalizing and privatizing resources and redefining water rights as property rights, which can be assigned in perpetuity. Water itself is now considered an asset independently from the land where it is located. International mining and electricity companies start investing heavily in Chile. Land redistributed to small farmers under the socialist government of the early 70s is given back to large landowners.

1976 MOBILE STORE Upon returning to San Francisco from Patagonia after making adventure documentary films, Tompkins founds Esprit with his then-wife Susie Tompkins, selling clothing out the back of their VW bus.

1975 CHICAGO BOYS Young Chilean economists trained at the University of Chicago by Milton Friedman arrive back in Chile and help develop Pinochet's economic program, liberalizing the economy, enshrining private property, and encouraging foreign investment. They are called "The Chicago Boys."

1973 COUP Following political and social unrest, largely triggered by U.S.-backed economic warfare against the socialist government, the Chilean military leads a violent coup d'etat to overthrow Salvador Allende's Popular Unity government. The military establishes a junta that suspends all political activity and represses communist and socialist parties. Large landowners, mostly descendants from colonialist families, celebrate the coup with the hope that their expropriated lands would be returned.

1970 LAND REDISTRIBUTION Salvador Allende becomes the first Marxist to be democratically elected. He begins nationalizing industries, healthcare, and education, and redistributing land from large-scale owners to farmers and peasants. Under the slogan "The land belongs to those who work it," the aim is to increase agricultural efficiency and production.

1969 DROPPING OUT Tompkins sells his ownership in The North Face for $50,000.

1968 *MOUNTAIN OF STORMS* Tompkins makes a film about his travels with four friends, including Yvon Chouinard, who pile into a van in California and surf, ski and climb their way south toward Patagonia, where they put up the first ascent of Cerro Fitz Roy's Southwest Buttress, the so-called "California Route." The film is about a new breed of explorer who leaves behind the comfort of life on the West Coast to immerse themselves in the undeveloped lands of Latin America.

1964 BEGINNINGS Tompkins launches The North Face with his first wife, Susan, after dropping out of high-school and spending several years climbing and skiing from Colorado to Chile.

1 Kubiszewski et al., "The future value of ecosystem services: Global scenarios and national implications," *Ecosystem Services*, 2017.
2 IPBES, *The Regional Assessment Report on Biodiversity and Ecosystem Services for the Americas*, 2019.
3 Stephanie Pearson, "The 21st Century Teddy Roosevelt," *Outside*, November 4, 2015.
4 Kristine and Douglas Tompkins, *Land: A Personal Ethic* (2012).
5 Larry Rohter, "An American in Chile Finds Conservation a Hard Slog," *New York Times*, August 7, 2005.

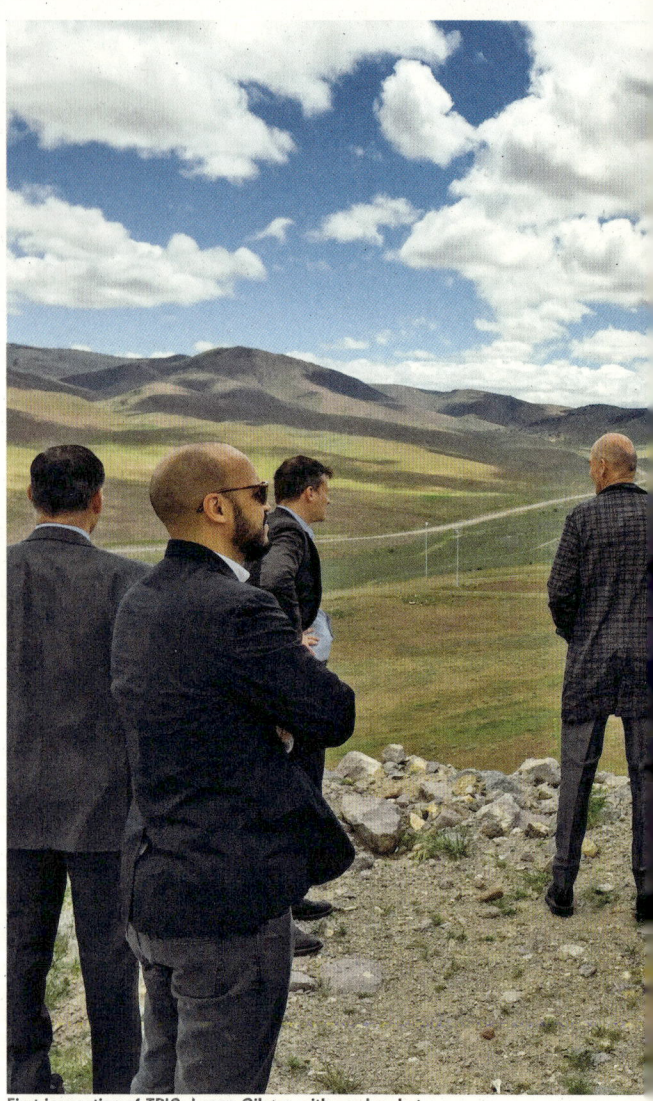

First inspection of TRIC; Lance Gilman with cowboy hat.

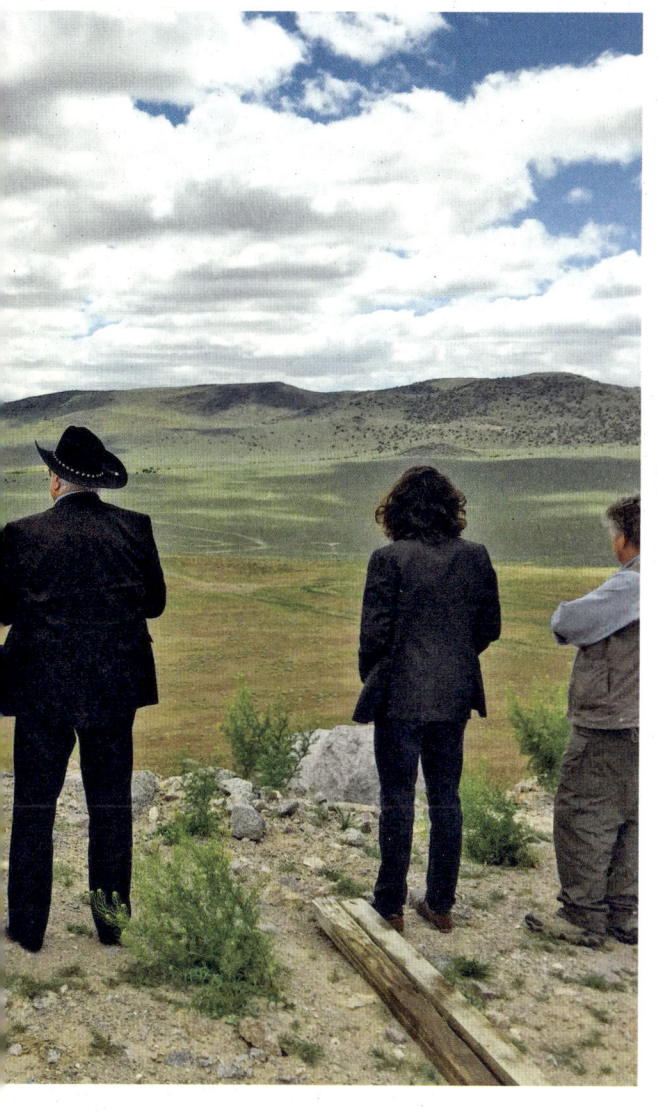

TRIC: Post-human Architecture
RK

Nature, unmolested. Rolling hills covered in light green vegetation, wild horses run in the distance. Tahoe Reno Industrial Center, bigger than Reno itself. Lance Gilman, who still owns the notorious Mustang Ranch, creates a corporate utopia of instant permits here that enable a brave new architecture to be realized in record time, without bureaucratic interference. His HQ is a white container.
There is no planning; brisk millennials under thirty-two create the (always rectangular) buildings without the "help" of architects. The clients represent a *Who's Who* of unicorns; large sections of the territory have apparently been bought by Google. There are rumors of a secret track where self-driving "cars" can roam in relative privacy. It is a repository for buildings so big they don't fit in any city. They "coexist" at TRIC in seemingly random arrangement, without connections or shared aim. Most are surrounded by colossal loading bays, but parking lots—America's earlier contribution to the sublime—are of a timid size. They can be small, there are no workers. Some structures have invested in aggressive, highly visible deterrence, others offer neutral accessibility. Barely one percent of the white metallic surfaces—vertical or horizontal—is transparent, facades and roofs are vast, uniform planes. With a shock, you sense that "degree zero" has not been achieved before... this is the real thing.

We are programmed to think that any "next" architecture can only be the outcome of a struggle. Modernism was born in a relentless campaign of stripping: of ornament, bourgeois values, frivolity. Because it takes place in the countryside, this is a stealth revolution... TRIC: a rare virgin birth ? The buildings here are not for humans but for things and machines. Thousands of years of architectural and cultural history are ditched. Debates, predictions, ideologies ignored, literally. It is post-human.
There has been no Architecture of a similar vigor in the last 100 years. It is based strictly on codes, algorithms, technologies, engineering, and performance, not intention. Its boredom is hypnotic, its banality breathtaking. Inside, because there is no daylight, the effect of multiple light sources, vibrating machines, is mesmerizing. "Degree zero"

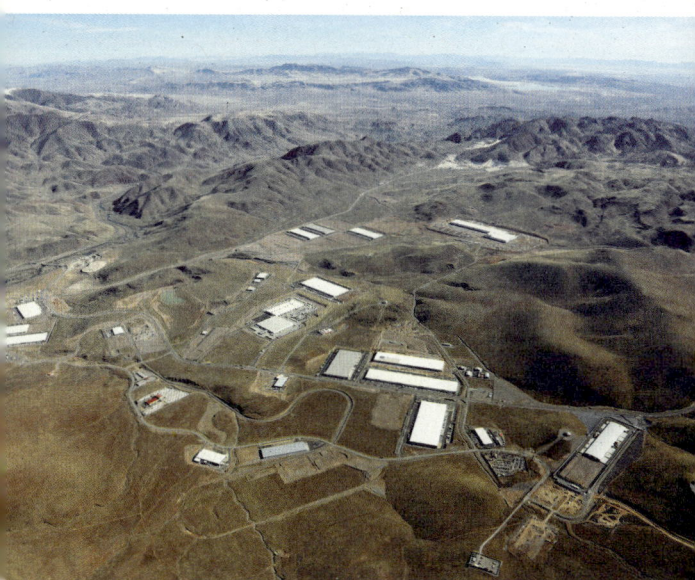

Drone over TRIC.

is attractive.　　　　　　　A new architecture is born beyond our attention, without any symptoms of humanism. We can get rid of handicapped access. There is no reason to articulate anything. There is no entrance, there are no users... robots don't need beige. There is no tradition. Not to sabotage process is the only ambition. There is no context. There is no expectation. There is nothing. But the implication is exhilarating.　　　　　　　We have seen their predecessors from the air, surrounding cities with gray batteries of boxes, but now the boxes have matured. In terms of scale, TRIC is a metropolis; in terms of its inhabitants, a tiny village. This coexistence needs new words. Things? Space? Things in space?

Descartes Was Here
Clemens Driessen

IN SEARCH OF THE ORIGIN OF CARTESIAN SPACE

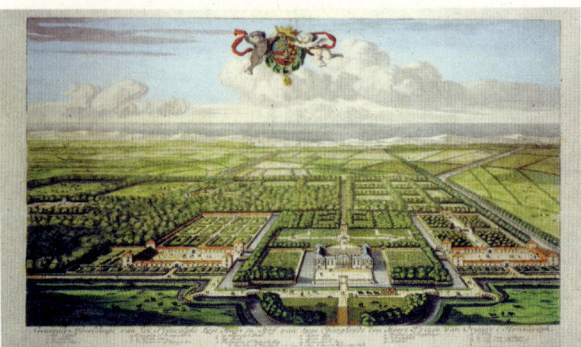

Honselersdijk Palace, Westland, drawn in 1683.

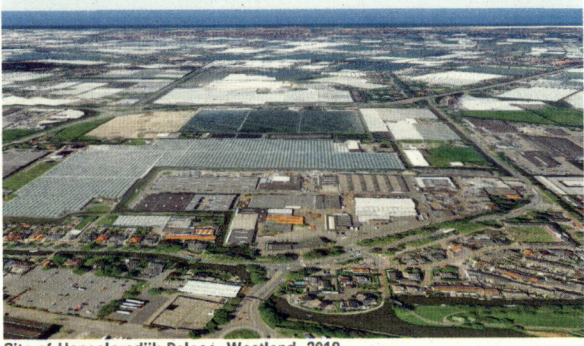

Site of Honselersdijk Palace, Westland, 2019.

the origin of Cartesian space? The very point of Cartesian space is that it is placeless. The mathematics underlying all space is independent of any particular site, and has only a random origin. The x/y coordinate system assigns no meaning to its "center," other than offering a point zero from which to develop algebraic formulas to describe shape or movement in space. Because the resulting grid essentially erased the very idea of an origin, it is hard to think of Cartesian space somehow bearing traces of the place where it was first imagined, from which mathematical space was then rolled out over the globe.

but surely this invention must have started somewhere, in an actual place? Tracing the origin of Cartesian space could help provincialize modernity (*no bad thing?*) by identifying the particular time and place where the cosmology we now labor under—the dominant mode of abstract thought and transforming space—actually began.
so could we retrieve some original, pre-Cartesian world? At least we might see a ground zero of our modern metaphysics, where Descartes started erasing meaning, myth, and purpose from the world...
or could we, by finding its point of origin, construct a richer Cartesian program, with less destructive forms of reductionism? And through it, maybe we could think of more lively patterns of spatial complexity.

WAGENINGEN / WESTLAND / CARTESIANISM

– I'm a cultural geographer at Wageningen University, a global hub of agricultural and associated (life) sciences (ecology, farm technology, plant breeding, soil science, rural sociology, etc.), located in the middle of the Netherlands. This is where possible futures for agriculture are thought out. The first time Rem and his AMO team came to Wageningen, in 2016, they were already using the label "Cartesian" for their hunch about where the countryside as a space of production is going, or already is. Cartesian clearly meant regularity, order, grid-like spaces that allow for calculating and maximizing use: spaces for efficiency, easily worked by large machines, automated systems, or humans who appreciate clarity and repetition. Artificiality, imposed onto space and life.
– the countryside everywhere is made more productive through being rendered Cartesian. From the United States and its Jeffersonian grid, to the globally emerging "plantationocene," to what we started to see as perhaps the most Cartesian of all: Westland. A greenhouse megapolis just a few miles west of AMO's Rotterdam head office. A central node in the global production and logistics of vegetables and flowers—perfectly controlled environments with rows and rows of optimized plants in endless glass boxes.

– Westland striking RK and AMO as the ultimate Cartesian place turned out not to be coincidental. Underlying these very greenhouses could be the site where modern space was invented, closely entangled, then and now, with large-scale vegetable production.

H. TODAY

– the place looks strikingly inconspicuous today. A bend in a road, a small parking lot, a few industrial sheds where building materials are recycled, and further down the road, large greenhouses that Google Maps doesn't offer many details on (apart from a few 1-star reviews in Polish, probably written by former workers there).
– we are in Honselersdijk, a small residential town in the middle of Westland engulfed by steel and glass. Across the street is a massive flower auction hall built in the 1970s. Tucked away behind some modest houses is a U-shaped brick building that looks much older than everything else.
– this is all that remains—just a side building—of what once was a magnificent palace with formidable gardens. *What happened here?*

H. PALACE AND GARDEN

– after a Dutch pirate naval hero conquered a Spanish silver fleet on its way from South America to Europe, the young and ambitious Dutch stadtholder Frederik Hendrik invested a large part of the bounty in building a palace worthy of his country's global ambitions and status as an independent nation, two hours by horse and carriage from the court in The Hague. Later to be nicknamed "Versailles of the North," H. was built in the second quarter of the 17th century.

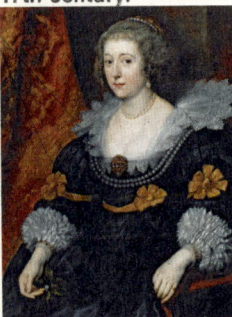

- planting season was also battle season, and with Frederik Hendrik out-and-about earning the nickname "city conqueror," his wife Amalia van Solms—in conversation with Constantijn Huygens, the stadtholder's secretary, <u>and friend, confidant, "soulmate," and enabler of René Descartes</u>—took the lead organizing the palace and laying out extensive gardens.

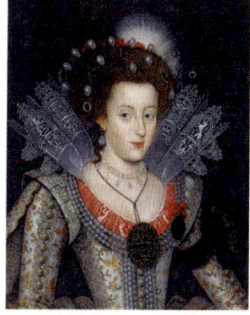

- developing a garden was central in Amalia's ambition to impress her former boss, the "Winter Queen" of Bohemia, Elizabeth Stuart, now living with her daughters and sons in exile in The Hague. Amalia had come to the Netherlands as a lady-in-waiting to Elizabeth Stuart, who had developed a famous garden next to her palace in Heidelberg, designed by her garden designer and fountain engineer Salomon de Caus. Elizabeth became queen of Bohemia. But when her husband lost a battle, within a year they had to flee (hence Winter Queen, queen for one winter).
- the proximity of the sea and abundance of sun had since Roman times made the environs of the Hague a prime spot for growing crops. But Amalia's new palace and gardens brought a new scale to horticulture, requiring intervention in the hydraulics and soil as well as planting trees, building fruit walls, and digging a canal to smooth the transport route to the stadtholder court in The Hague.
- in the 16th century, botanical gardens emerged with the systematic study of medicine, and colonial projects in which plants started to be moved across the globe. These were strictly ordered spaces that by their arrangement of plants facilitated categorization and learning.

– in the 17th century, estate gardens became sites for innovating and experimenting, leisure and sports, making money from producing crops, staging official events, framing the ambition of the nation, expressing the legitimacy of rule, projecting power onto the landscape, and exposing the divine order underlying nature.
– and whereas earlier, in Florence, Paris, and Heidelberg, geometrical renaissance garden designs followed elevations in the terrain, the flat Dutch landscape allowed for a perfect symmetrical expanse easily represented from a central perspective.

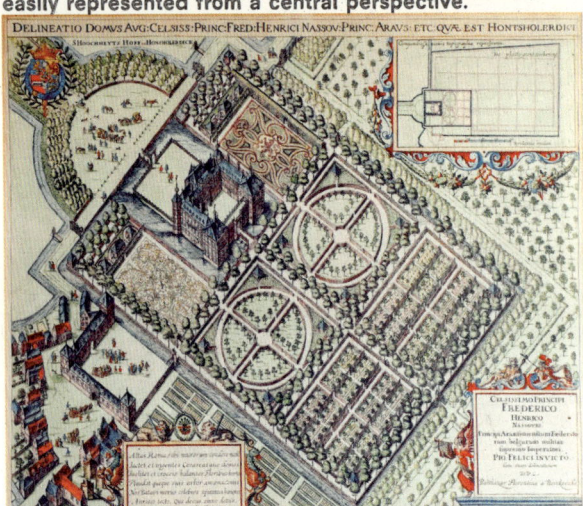

– the H. palace gardens (rendered here by Balthasar Florisz van Berckenrode, ca. 1645) became a key site for horticultural innovation: grafting fruits onto trees and producing conditions for exotic plants. Bulbs, tubers, seeds, and seedlings were shipped from the colonies run by the Dutch East India Company (VOC), extracted from indigenous cultivators and their ecologies to serve an urbanizing Dutch population.

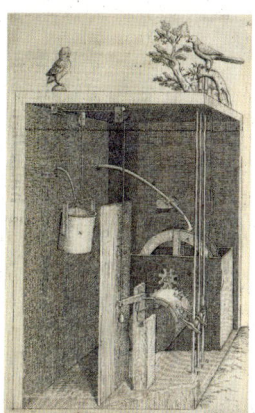

– garden designers were architects and engineers, with a special focus on hydraulics for irrigation and spectacular fountains, whose waterworks often contained mechanical contraptions that suggested independently moving mythical figures or mechanical animals: *automatons*, like the one above by Salomon de Caus, from *Les Raisons des Forces Mouvantes avec diverses machines tant utiles que plaisantes*, 1615.

RENÉ DESCARTES (1596–1650)

– a provincial French boy from a reasonably wealthy family finished school at a Jesuit college and moved to St-Germain-en-Laye, near Paris. It is there, in the geometrical gardens of St-Germain, that René Descartes experienced a garden automaton, proving to him that our senses can easily deceive us, and that the organic is actually mechanical.

"We see clocks, artificial fountains, mills, and other similar machines which, even though they are only made by man, have the power to move of their own accord in various ways."

"Those who are experienced in examining automata, since they know the use of a certain machine and observe some of its parts, easily conclude from them in what way the others, which they do not see, were made. Thus I have tried, from the sensible effects and parts of natural bodies, to discover what are their causes and insensible particles..."

— but Descartes was not a famous author/mathe-matician yet. He was drifting around Europe, trying to figure out what to do with his life. In 1618, he joined the high-tech (*avant la lettre*) army of Maurits of Orange, then the Dutch stadtholder, who was waging a lengthy war for Dutch independence from the Spanish king.

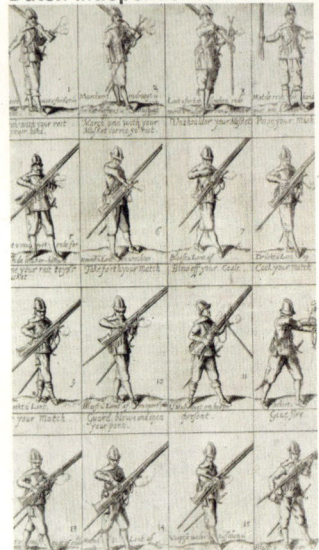 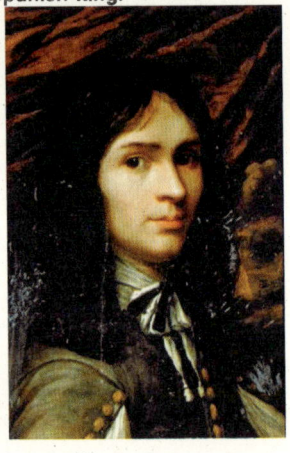

— Maurits created the first "scientific" army, with detailed prescriptions of human behaviour to optimize warfare. Maurits enlisted scientists and engineers, not just to design fortifications but also to standardize weapons, train gunners, "drill" soldiers, design battles in accordance with time-motion studies... (portrayed above in *The Exercise of Armes for Calivres, Muskettes and Pikes*, Jacob De Gheyn II, 1607.)
— upon leaving the army, still in his mid-20s, drifting through Europe, Descartes sought conditions in which to work on a new research program: to unify the sciences and base all knowledge on a single universal method, doing away with scholasticism, mythical explanations, occult forces, hidden qualities, and inherent purpose (per Aristotle's *telos*). The world that resulted would be a set of soulless material objects moving through space.

The aim: "make ourselves masters and possessors of nature"
The means: "the invention of an infinity of artifices that would enable us to enjoy, without any pain, the fruits of the earth and all the goods to be found there."
— from 1628 onwards, Descartes primarily lived in the Netherlands, where he writes most of his works. Frequently changing address, he looks for places in the countryside where he is left in peace to think and write, dissect animals and walk his dog.

NETHERLANDS

— Descartes' coming of age coincided with the emergence of the Netherlands as the "Dutch republic" in the early 17th century: an independent nation powered by self-confident merchants. International trade and colonial conquests—e.g. through the VOC, established 1602, the first ever publicly owned corporation—generated enormous profits in need of investment opportunities.

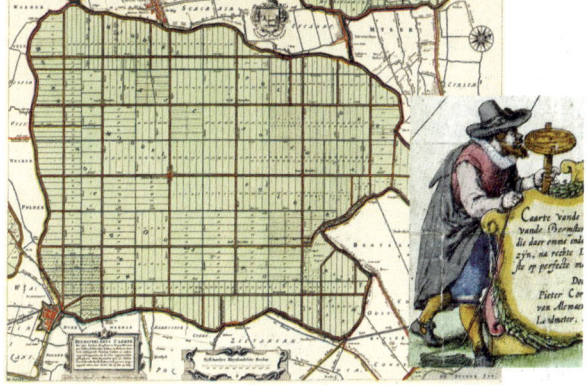

— by 1612 the Beemster lake was turned into a polder (land reclaimed from water, and protected by dikes). The rectangular grid as a principle of city planning can be traced back to ancient history, from the Indus Valley to Babylon to Mexico, ancient Egypt and Greece. Via the Roman Empire it inspired Renaissance new towns. But applied to the shaping of land at this scale, organizing space according to the grid was new.
— the Beemster occasioned the invention of the Dutch

circle: a device for the exact measurement of space based on triangulation: Adding a compass and a circle with indication of 360 degrees to a surveyor's cross facilitated the measurement of the exact angle between two straight lines to a single point. By measuring the distance between the two points of observation, the length of the unknown lines of the triangle could be calculated.

– this method reliably projected boundaries and <u>allowed for the sale of land before it emerged from the water.</u> Reclamation, together with the Dutch circle, facilitated a land-based private investment vehicle that produced a perfect grid landscape just as Descartes arrived in the Netherlands.

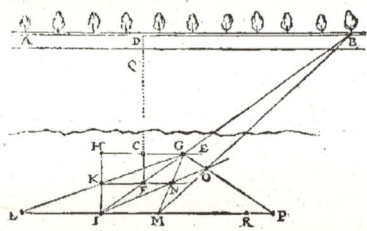

– Cartesian geometry employed to determine the distance between C and D without being able to go to A, D, or B. Drawn by Franciscus van Schooten, who made the mathematical illustrations in the *Discours de la Méthode* (above drawing from Schooten's *Mathematische Oefeningen*, 1660).

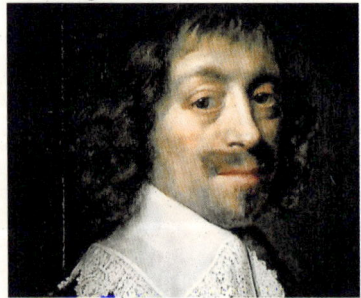

– Constantijn Huygens (1596–1687, painted here by Van Miereveldt in 1641): diplomat, composer, playwright, poet; free thinker and excited by new sciences; also still a

Renaissance man, translating Vitruvius into Dutch after a trip to Venice. Together with Amalia van Solms and palace architects, Huygens co-designed the garden at H.

- in 1632, Huygens met Descartes. After three consecutive mornings intensively sharing ideas, they wondered how it was possible to be so of one mind. Born in the same year, they are "s," according to Descartes. For the next two decades, Huygens became a key intellectual correspondent and friend of Descartes. As secretary to the new stadtholder Frederik Hendrik, Huygens could protect Descartes from orthodox Calvinist theologians worried about the overthrow of the Aristotelian system and the atheism they suspected would come in its wake.
- Huygens personally invested capital in Descartes' failed plan for an automated hyperbolic lens grinding machine, a device that would have transformed the production of binoculars, telescopes and microscopes. Huygens' son Christiaan, inspired by Descartes, would invent the pendulum clock and thereby exact time – but that was later.
- Huygens pushed Descartes to publish his ideas, especially the parts on geometry and optics. To this, Descartes adds an outline of his overarching method: the *Discours de la Méthode*.
- Huygens insists that Descartes should put images in the text (rather than on separate pages).
- Descartes' *Discours de la Méthode* comes out in 1637, at the height of the "tulip mania" gripping the Dutch merchant class: the first investment craze, it combined botanical science and horticulture with speculative capitalism.

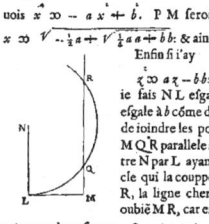

- the key innovation of Descartes was not the grid itself, which had been around since antiquity, but how (through applying algebra to geometry) the grid allowed for an embrace of complexity: curved lines that could be described by mathematical formulas, and thereby were not a sign of chaos but an expression of the divine mathematical order assumed to be underlying nature. Seeing the world through a grid produced an immensely fruitful reductionism that released the power of calculation over space. (Oddly, he invented and explained the x/y axes and coordinate system, but never actually drew these in his own work.)

– *Discours de la Méthode*, published together with volumes that applied his method to optics, meteors and geometry, sets in motion a number of interconnected transformations:

• the method of universal doubt dismissed all earlier occult accounts and traditional explanations drawing on classical ideas, myths, and superstitions, resulting for Descartes in a rock bottom individualist foundation: *je pense, donc je suis*—he originally wrote the famous formulation in French, and later published the Latin *cogito, ergo sum* (adding: "we cannot doubt of our existence, while we are doubting")

• scientific truth was equated with absolute certainty, of the kind found in mathematics and observations of causally straightforward relations between physical objects

• moving beyond Euclidian geometry based exclusively on circles and straight lines, Descartes applied algebraic formulas to describe complex geometrical figures and solve spatial problems as mathematical riddles

• to do so, Descartes invented the x/y axis and coordinate system

• and the notation of known and unknown variables in formulas of the kind $y = ax^2 + b$

• with his mathematical program to describe the world, he proposed a strict dualist cosmology: Things were either extended in space (measuring length, width, height) or things were non-spatial, such as thoughts that exist in the mind

• physical bodies of living organisms were seen as mechanical automatons

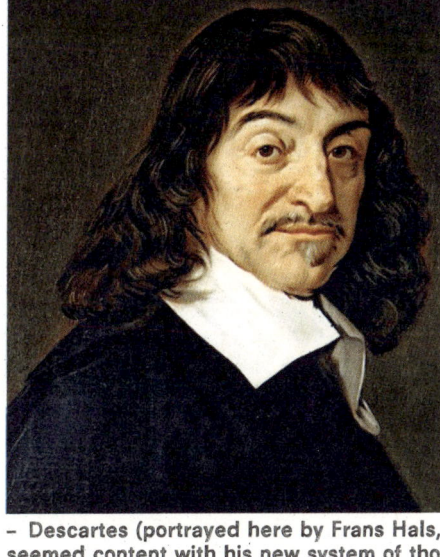

– Descartes (portrayed here by Frans Hals, 1649), seemed content with his new system of thought: "having determined as I did [in the *La Géométrie* part of the *Discours*] all that could be achieved in each type of problem and shown the way to do it, I claim that people should not only believe that I have accomplished more than my predecessors but should also be convinced that posterity will never discover anything in this subject which I could not have discovered just as well if I had bothered to look for it."

– even though many of his claims on the metaphysics of movement and gravity were quickly superseded by subsequent scientists, such as Newton, as a research program the mechanistic-mathematical approach proved extraordinarily successful for centuries to come.

– this came at a price though: radical reductionism... "There exist no occult forces in stones or plants, no amazing and marvelous sympathies and antipathies, in fact there exist nothing in the whole of nature which cannot be explained in terms of purely corporeal causes, totally devoid of mind and thought."

"The only principles which I accept, or require, in physics are those of geometry and pure mathematics; these principles explain all natural phenomena."

RAW CARTESIANISM

- lens grinding, philosophical debates, dissection of human and animal bodies, perspective drawing, mathematics, garden design, making automatons, growing vegetables, inventing new forms of government, investing in tulips, the emergence of capitalism, military fortifications, army discipline, polder design—in the early 17th century all this was intimately linked, resulting in a program combining fundamental and applied sciences; it was especially in the Netherlands that these developments coalesced.
- out of this blancmange, "Cartesian" space emerged in a particular time and place: not just a universal/timeless idea projected onto the world by a sole genius, but emerging from a culture and topography that were being ordered to reflect a certain mechanical mode of knowing and governing space, plants, and people.
- then and there, the reductionist research program started, eventually producing our contemporary situation: Land as abstract resource to measure and rearrange at will, life as mechanical, animals and plants as objects to be rendered productive in a supercharged colonial capitalism.
- in many ways we still live in this total Cartesian confidence, assuming we can and ultimately will understand in full the underlying character of every object extended in space.
- the Cartesian grid, trialled in the Beemster polder, spread over the globe, rendering space measurable and governable, without bothering about places and particularities, allowing for land to be sold before anyone had even seen it.

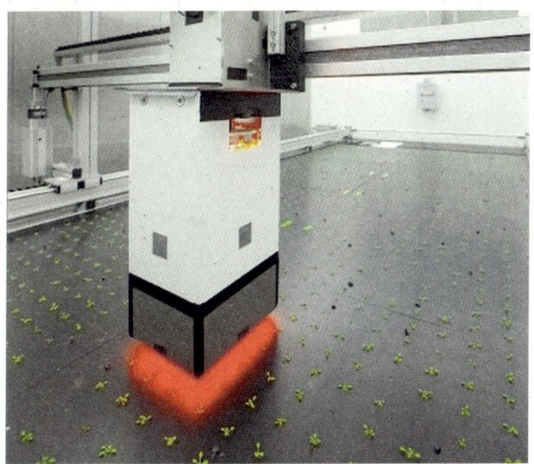

– **the Phenovator** (here operating at Wageningen University) may function as a model of the ultimate Cartesian take on plants: treating Arabidopsis seedlings as tiny mechanical beings, little suboptimal machines whose generic photosynthesis "engines" can be monitored en masse and selected for by a robot camera sensitive to a spectrum of light ranging from infrared to ultraviolet, detecting the minutest plant activity while moving randomly over a grid.

DESCARTES AND THE PINEAL GLAND

– *but is this the whole story that looking for the origin of Cartesian space can produce?*
– the progenitor, and now perhaps the villain of modernity, who rendered life mechanical, erased traditional meanings of place, instrumentalized nature—what if we get to know Descartes and the places he hung out a bit better? Not per se to sympathize with this oddly arrogant and fiercely independent character, but to reconstruct a more lively form of Cartesianism, one that may produce a richer aesthetics of Cartesian space… *a Cartesian picturesque?*
– behind Cartesian reductionism we can still find passions intimately connected to the environment, lives shared outdoors, joyful cultivation of plants, a love, of sorts, for animals. Descartes moved in wealthy merchant

circles designing gardens, while also growing his own vegetables and taking an interest in the lives of the peasants around him. He walked his dog, "Monsieur Grat," at his rural retreat in the village of Egmond. The painter Paulus Potter at the same time roamed from his house in The Hague into the countryside to draw intimate cattle portraits, elevating a young bull to the status of a powerful historical figure. We have learned to exclude such intimate, contemplative experiences from the hyper-productive, extractive, raw Cartesianism that has taken hold.
– there are several routes into complicating the Cartesian program. Let's start with a princess, and then go into the garden again, where we can witness other trajectories of Cartesian production.

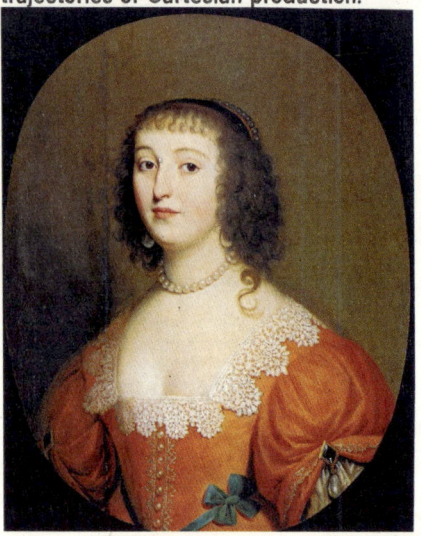

– from 1643 until his death in 1650, a special friendship emerged between Descartes and Princess Elisabeth of the Palatinate (painted here by Gerard van Honthorst in 1636), the eldest daughter of Elizabeth the Winter Queen, living in exile in The Hague. They started a correspondence that veered from mathematics to the intimate, discussing Elisabeth's depression and anxieties among other topics. Elisabeth challenged Descartes' ideas and pushed him in new directions.

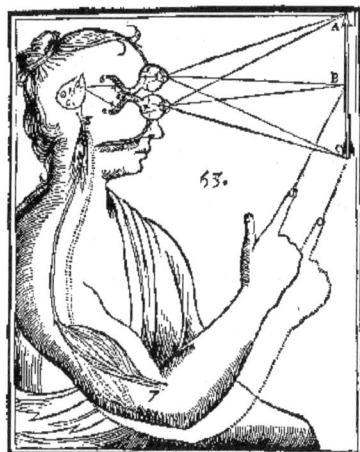

- while inspiring Descartes to discuss possible cures for psychosomatic illness and her depression, Princess Elizabeth probed his ideas for their weak spots—*how can the soul as something not extended in space influence our physical body?* Descartes claimed the interface between body and soul is situated in the pineal gland (drawn here in *Traité de l'Homme*, written 1630–1633), a gland in the brain he knew from dissecting sheep and oxen.
- Princess Elizabeth, in this correspondence, produced another Descartes: explicating a close intertwining of body and soul (rather than a "Cartesian" schism between the two), writing on the importance of embodied passions in our lives, making humans more than just a machine controlled by an independent rational mind.
- in the *Passions of the Soul* (1649), written for the Princess, Descartes acknowledges we are driven by pre-rational passions such as love, hate, desire, and curiosity, and these passions importantly indicate to us something is of interest and should spur us into action. At the same time, we should try to control these urges and make them productive:

"It's good to be born with some inclination to wonder, because that increases scientific curiosity; but after we have acquired some scientific knowledge, we should

try to free ourselves from this inclination.
We can easily make up for the loss through a special state of reflection and attention that we can voluntarily impose upon our understanding when we think that the subject-matter is worth the trouble."

WORKING IN THE GARDEN

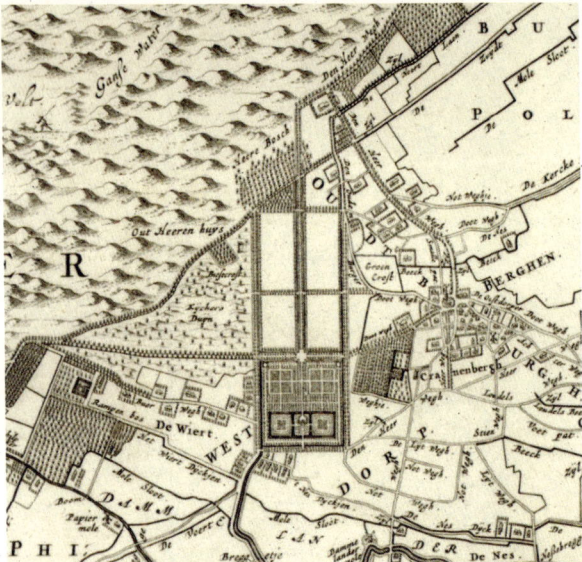

- Descartes designed a garden with his friend Anthony van Zurck (this map drawn in 1643 by Dou, son of the inventor of the Dutch circle), with ratios based on musical intervals, which reflected Descartes' early work on musical theory and mathematics.
- Huygens built his own small estate: Hofwijck, a rural retreat away from the court of The Hague. There he wrote what is still the longest poem in Dutch, celebrating his garden, not just as an ornamental space for contemplation, but also as a space of production, with zones for the tame and the wild. Huygens exuded the joy of growing his own vegetables, instilling a fashion for horticulture estates among wealthy merchants and aristocratic elites.

Daer zijn de gasten; flux, den Room-pott uyt den Polder,
De Boonen vanden staeck, de Netten vanden solder,
De Vijver in 't woel, de Snoecken inde Ly,
Jan Maertsen in de praem, en elck all even bly,
(Bly met de volle vanghst, die selden komt te missen
Van ongeroofde winst, van ongekochte vischen)
De Peeren vanden Boom, de Lijster uyt de strick;
Elck vrolicker als thuys, elck besiger dan ick

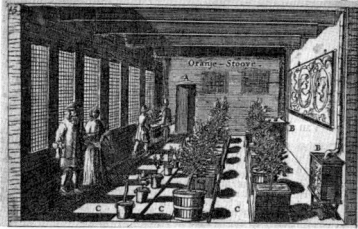

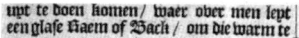

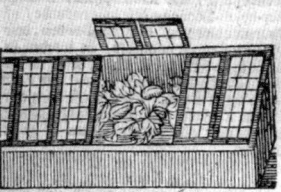

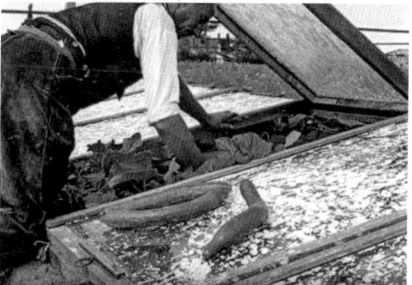

– knowledge of vegetable and fruit production developed in the garden of H. was codified and spread, including the physical structures to produce the right climatic conditions for horticulture. The head-gardener of H., in his book *Den Nederlandtsen Hovenier*, celebrated the smell of flowers and fruits contrasted with the stench of urban sewers, and described how tropical plants imported from overseas colonies were grown in innovative fossil fuel-heated spaces. He outlined growing fruit and vegetables in early greenhouses that were still in use in the 1930s.

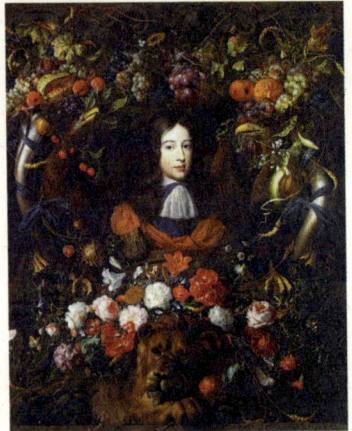

– Amalia's grandchild, Stadtholder Willem III, who would go on to become king of England in 1689, grew up on the H. estate. Here he is depicted by Jan Davidsz de Heem at age 10, surrounded by the rich produce of H., a display of wealth and promise, almost hiding from view two eagles and a reclining lion. Beyond offering symbolic references, with intertwining branches of the Stuart thistle and an orange tree, the opulent abundance of juicy produce seems intended to advertise the young boy on the European royal marriage market.

DISSOLUTION OF H.

– when Willem III died without an heir, a protracted legal battle began over ownership of the H. palace between distant royals without much interest in palace and garden maintenance. And with the end of the Dutch republic's 17th Century "golden age," when naval power and colonies were largely lost to the UK and France, the merchant class saw its wealth diminish and started investing its capital elsewhere.

— a century later, when the aristocrats associated with the House of Orange lost their positions with the arrival of Napoleon, the age of large-scale, capital-intensive production and opulent displays of wealth was over. In a great levelling, stately homes and palaces were scavenged for scrap metal, eventually sold off and torn down for the remaining building materials. Most of the big estates were cut up into parcels for independent fruit and vegetable growers. Plant collections together with the laid-off gardeners spread out over the area, where farmers on smaller plots of land continued horticultural practices. The H. palace materials dissolved into the modest structures of the Westland grape and vegetable growers.

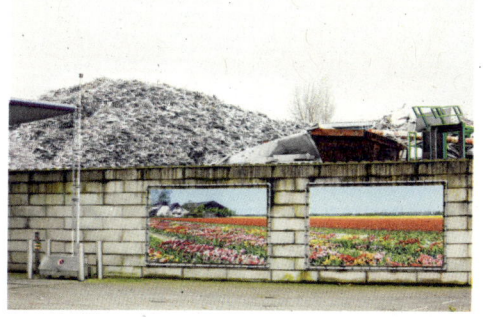

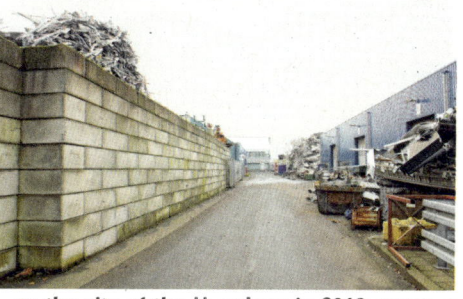

— on the site of the H. palace in 2019: scrap metal recycling for greenhouse construction.

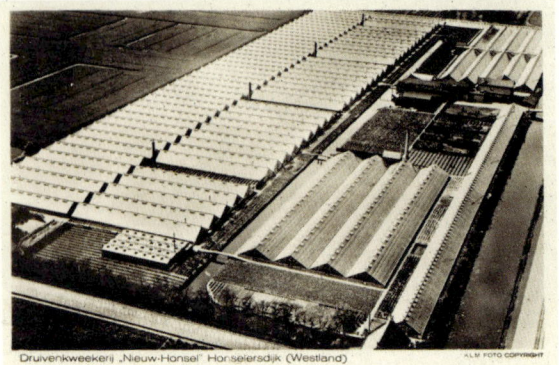

Druivenkweekerij „Nieuw-Honsel" Honselersdijk (Westland)

– at the turn of the 20th century, the scale of production started to grow again. The area still had a good connection via canal to the Hague, and a new steam-tram bringing coal to heat the greenhouses got its station right on the site of the former H. palace. When, in 1900, the first large-scale greenhouse for tomato and grape production was built by a plantation engineer returning from the Dutch colony of Indonesia, the former palace garden was the ideal site (photographed above in 1928).

AXIS

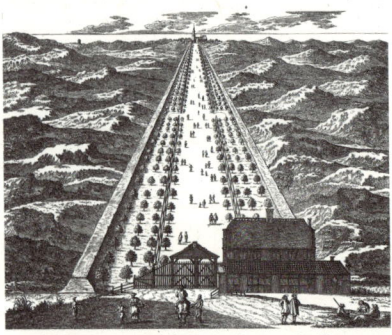

– the Zeestraat ("Sea Street") Constantijn Huygens designed in 1653 and finally realized in 1666, projecting a straight line through the ever-shifting dune landscape between the Hague and the fishing village of Scheveningen. The rational projection of engineering power onto space, it extended order onto chaotic nature and unruly humans. Where the German autobahn of the 1930s would seek to blend into and follow the natural features of the landscape, here straightforward clarity is imposed.

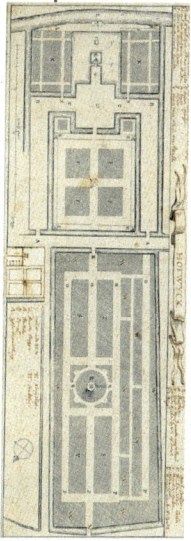
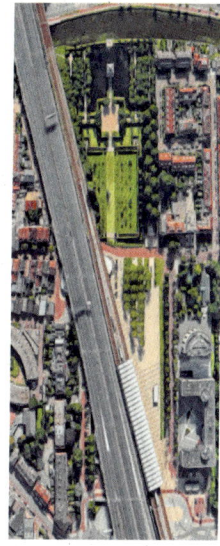

– like the Westland H. palace garden, Huygens' very own Hofwijck garden proved a fertile ground for ideas that would end up destroying it. Three centuries after Huygens' Zeestraat, the same axis was projected eastwards from the Hague for trains and automobiles. Machine-age traffic efficiency and speed overrides classicist garden design, dissecting the Vitruvian body that was the ground of Huygens' poem.
– with the cutting of Huygens' garden, his idea of horticultural space as a place of both production and leisure, combining the wild and the tame, play and contemplation, and the joy of plucking food from your own garden when unexpected guests arrive—all this also seems to have disappeared. Gardens have become ornamental, culture is deemed distinct from cultivating plants; spaces of leisure and spaces of production are separated. A Westland greenhouse is not a place where people go to hang out.

FARMBOT IN THE PIXEL GARDEN IN THE PALACE

- in the pixel farming project at Wageningen University (see page 300), the Cartesian grid has been scaled down to such a fine-grained pattern that fields give an impression of lush (bio)diversity.
- since Descartes, space defined by the grid allows for the production of certain forms of complexity, but at the same time it means the grid is everywhere, unavoidably underlying space. In the pixel farm, indigenous knowledge of symbiotic relationships is abstracted and optimized, purified of animist cosmologies and local socio-ecologies.

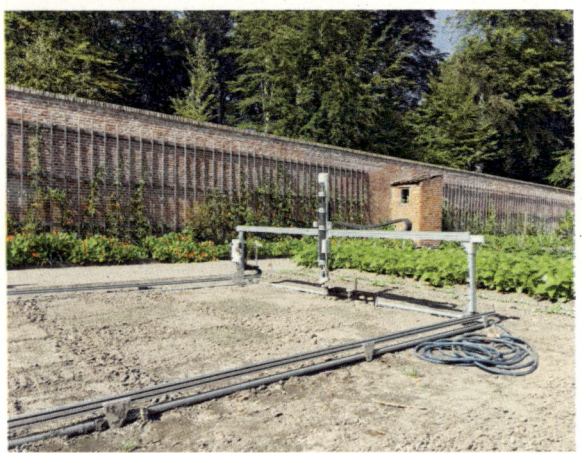

- a Farmbot XL, assembled at the Wageningen experimental farm, was transported to a recently restored 17th-century garden in 2019.
- the current owner is Jemima van Zuylestein, a direct descendant of an illegitimate son of Frederik Hendrik the designer of this space. She is glad her garden has never fallen prey to the romantic English landscape garden style, retaining its classic geometrical form. The estate maintains its gardens the way they were in the time of the stadtholder, which means not spraying weeds, etc., increasing the need for manual labor. The plan is to equip the robot with 17th-century garden tools to mimic original horticultural practice.

- the origin of Cartesian space reveals a rich array of possible directions. It may not be necessary to embrace dogma and superstition in order to undo the destructive consequences of radically reductionist Cartesianism.
- a good starting point may be to again celebrate the joy and beauty of growing vegetables in a garden, and, rather than banishing food production to distant monocultures and greenhouse conglomerations, to actually see how places of food production are central drivers of space and culture.
- the current climate and biodiversity crisis certainly suggests it would be sensible for more people to be more involved in food production, and calls for new modes of thinking, working, and creating landscapes. Would there be a way to avoid ever-larger scale production that erases everything in pursuit of passionless mechanistic rationalism? How to produce alternatives to ever more reductionist renderings of life? Maybe a fine-grained Cartesian picturesque grid will allow us to not just be "masters and possessors of nature" but also to recognize our dependencies on plants and animals interacting on their own terms.
- perhaps these future farms even have an automaton to help with harvesting, participating in a vibrant organic world rather than telling us that deep down, it is mechanical.

IMAGE SOURCES
IN ORDER OF APPEARANCE
Paleis Honselaarsdijk A. Bega, Abraham Blooteling (ca. 1683), Depot Koninklijk Huisarchief; Honselersdijk, Google, Data SIO, NOAA, U.S. Navy, NGA, GEBCO, Landsat/Copernicus (2019); Anthony van Dyck, *Portrait of Amalia van Solms*, 1631/32, , Museo Nacional del Prado, Madrid; *Unidentified painter, Portrait of Princess Elizabeth Stuart, later Queen of Bohemia, called the Winter Queen*, 1613, National Portrait Gallery, London; Balthasar Florisz. van Berckenrode, *Map of the palace Honselaarsdijk*, ca. 1645, Van Sandick archive; Salomon de Caus, *Les Raisons des forces mouvantes avec diverses machines tant utilles que plaisantes*, 1615, Smithsonian Library; Jacob De Gheyn II, *The Exercise of Armes for Calivres, Muskettes and Pikes*, 1607, Folger, Shakespeare Library; Artist Unknown, Suspected portrait of a young René Descartes, Musée des Augustins Toulouse; Daniel van Breen, Map of De Beemster, 1658, Noord-Hollands Archief; Pieter Cornelisz. Cort, *Map of Onbedijkte Beemster*, 1607 Nationaal Archief; Frans van Schooten Jr., *Mathematische Oeffeningen*, 1660 Utrecht University Library; Michiel Jansz. Van Mierevelt, *Portrait of Constantijn Huygens*, 1641, Huygens-museum Hofwijck, Voorburg; René Descartes, Discours de la Méthode, 1637 Bibliotheek Rotterdam; Frans Hals, Portrait of the French philosopher and mathematician René Descartes, 1649, Musée du Louvre; Phenovator, Wageningen University & Research, 2017; Gerard van Honthorst, *Portrait of Princess Elisabeth of Bohemia*, 1636, Koninklijke Verzamelingen; René Descartes, Traité de l'Homme, 1662, Wellcome Collection; Joannes Dou, Territorii Bergensis accuratissima descriptio, 1660, Regionaal Archief Alkmaar; Jan van der Groen, *Den Nederlandtsen Hovenier*, 1670, BioLib.de; Polygoon-Profilti, Gezicht op Het Westland in 1935, Nederlands Instituut voor Beeld en Geluid; Jan Davidsz. de Heem, Flower garland with portrait of William III of Orange, aged 10, 1662, musée des beaux-arts de Lyon; Clemens Driessen, Westland, 2019; Druivenkwekerij Nieuw Honsel 1928, KLM; Cornelis Elandt, *Scheveningse Zeestraat*, 1663–1670, Rijksmuseum Amsterdam; Constantijn Huygens, Hofwijck, 1653, Huygens-museum Hofwijck, Voorburg; Google, 2019; Renate Pekaar, Pixelfarm at Zuylestein, 2019.

5_a	4_a	4_a	1_a	4_b	4_b	2_a	3_a	2_b	4_a	4_a
5_a	2_a	3_a	2_b	4_a	4_a	1_b	5_a	3_a	5_a	2_a
1_a	5_a	2_b	5_a	3_a	5_a	4_b	4_c	4_a	1_b	1_b
3_a	3_a	3_a	3_a	5_a	3_a	4_c	1_b	2_b	1_a	2_b
2_a	2_a	1_a	5_a	2_b	5_a	3_a	1_b	2_a	4_b	5_a
1_a	4_b	2_a	5_a	5_a	1_b	4_b	2_a	3_a	1_a	4_a
4_a	4_a	2_a	5_a	3_a	2_b	5_a	4_c	2_b	5_a	1_a
1_a	4_c	2_b	2_a	1_a	1_a	1_a	5_a	2_a	1_a	2_a
5_a	5_a	5_a	4_a	3_a	3_a	5_a	5_a	5_a	1_b	2_a
3_a	1_a	5_a	5_a	4_c	2_a	5_a	5_a	1_b	2_b	1_a
2_b	5_a	3_a	5_a	1_a	1_a	3_a	2_b	2_a	5_a	1_b
2_b	1_b	4_a	2_b	1_a	4_a	4_a	4_b	4_a	1_b	5_a
3_a	5_a	4_c	3_a	5_a	3_a	5_a	3_a	5_a	2_b	5_a
3_a	5_a	4_b	4_a	2_a	2_b	4_c	4_b	3_a	4_a	2_a
1_b	3_a	4_a	5_a	4_a	1_a	4_c	1_a	3_a	4_c	5_a
4_a	2_b	5_a	3_a	3_a	1_b	3_a	2_a	1_b	1_b	4_b
1_b	1_b	5_a	2_b	4_a	2_a	3_a	2_a	1_a	1_a	3_a

The matrix: plant species, varieties, and mixtures prescribed per pixel.

3_a	5_a	3_a	2_a	3_a	2_b	1_a	1_b	2_a	3_a	2_b
1_b	2_a	4_c	1_b	3_a	4_a	5_a	1_a	1_b	5_a	3_a
5_a	5_a	3_a	5_a	5_a	2_b	2_b	3_a	4_b	4_c	4_a
3_a	2_a	3_a	4_b	2_b	5_a	5_a	5_a	4_c	1_b	2_b
2_b	1_a	4_c	5_a	5_a	1_a	2_a	1_b	3_a	1_b	2_a
4_b	3_a	1_b	4_a	3_a	5_a	5_a	1_a	4_b	2_a	3_a
5_a	5_a	4_a	2_b	2_a	4_c	1_a	3_a	5_a	4_c	2_b
1_a	4_a	1_a	4_a	2_a	5_a	3_a	2_a	3_a	2_b	2_a
2_a	3_a	4_b	2_a	4_c	5_a	4_c	4_c	4_a	4_b	4_a
5_a	3_a	1_b	5_a	3_a	5_a	1_a	3_a	5_a	3_a	5_a
2_b	2_b	1_b	1_a	5_a	4_a	2_a	1_b	1_a	5_a	2_a
5_a	5_a	4_a	4_a	1_a	4_b	5_a	4_b	4_c	1_a	3_a
5_a	1_b	1_b	4_b	2_b	4_c	1_a	3_a	3_a	2_a	1_b
1_a	3_a	2_b	1_b	3_a	1_a	1_a	3_a	4_c	4_b	3_a
3_a	5_a	4_a	3_a	5_a	3_a	5_a	3_a	5_a	5_a	5_a
3_a	1_b	1_b	2_b	1_a	3_a	3_a	4_b	5_a	5_a	1_b
2_a	4_b	2_a	1_a	4_b	1_b	5_a	1_b	3_a	2_a	1_a

1s = cabbage varieties; 2s and 4s = cereal-legume mixtures;
3s = potato varieties; 5 = clovers.

Pixel Farming
Lenora Ditzler

When I talk about pixel farming, I usually start with something like, "It's a super complicated futuristic farming system that looks and acts like nature but can only be managed by tender swarms of tiptoeing ecofeminist robots that haven't been invented yet. Are you familiar with Richter's color inventories?" I say super a lot since I moved to the Netherlands. Then I detour into a side-bar disclaimer about how I fancied myself an artist before a scientist. I think I hope that this caveat will help make the tacit and messy parts of my research less scary to scientists and the obsession with gridded order and reproducibility more appealing to creatives who don't share my fondness for Agnes Martin. Once we've got that cleared up, I pull out a pixel plot planting map.

If you follow it even loosely, you'll have noticed that current farming systems research is heavily focused on two big challenges: how to feed everyone on this overloaded globe, and how to do it in a way that doesn't render the earth uninhabitable. Researchers often group around one mandate or the other, and sometimes the two camps face off in debates that would make a bystander believe the solutions are mutually exclusive. But the whole idea behind pixel farming is that we can address *both* challenges. I work at the Farming Systems Ecology Group at Wageningen University in the Netherlands. Our mission statement as a community of researchers says we're interested in the *radical redesign* of agricultural systems. This position comes from a collective acknowledgment that the kind of thinking that got us into this mess (thawing permafrost, disappearing insects, eutrophic waterways, hungry farmers, corporate agribusiness bullies, simultaneous obesity and famine, etc.) won't get us out of it. The durability (to use a plant breeders' term) of the monoculture mentality is seemingly indestructible—we've fine-tuned the paradigm for centuries, and it's embedded into every link of the food chain. Our crops are bred to thrive in monocultures, our machines are designed to cultivate monocultures, our farmers are educated to manage monocultures, our grocery stores are organized to sell monocultures, our eating habits are adapted to demand monocultures, and our policies are developed to reward monocultures. Meanwhile, a lot of research and regulation efforts are put into trying to incrementally make less bad a system that is intrinsically bad. Pixel farming comes in at a different angle: rather than tinkering with the current agricultural system, let's totally reimagine it! Producing enough food is obviously imperative, but pixel farming asks if we can't do it in a way that also produces other things like clean water, carbon storage, biodiversity, pest and disease control, beautiful landscapes, and meaningful work, all by leveraging diversity. Depending on who you ask, you'll get a different story about how pixel farming got started. And let's be clear—anyone who tells you they invented pixel farming is full of pixelated &$#%—the concept of planting many different things next to each other in small plots as a way to mobilize natural synergies is centuries old. But pixel farming as we practice it—in a Western, industrialized, Dutch, research-oriented context—supposedly came about during a coffee break where a Farming Systems Ecologist bumped into a geek from the Farm Technology group next door and started talking about changing the world. One of them had recently flown over the midwestern United States, and upon looking out the airplane window at a perfectly tiled landscape below, had been struck by a vision of a new kind of agriculture: *What if we made these patterns on a micro-scale?* The other was a guy whose résumé claims expertise in AI, robotics, and the Internet of Things. These particular Dutch male academics, who may well be representative of the whole population, I don't know I haven't studied it, are endowed with grandiose overconfidence on par with the height of their limbs and the decibel of their egos. This annoying superpower affords them the belief that anything is possible with enough good science and bad coffee, which is something you need if your ambition is to uproot a deeply embedded and widely accepted global paradigm. A few flimsy napkin scribbles later and the Wageningen version of pixel farming was born: crop circles in miniature, tended by clever robots buzzing around the field on a radial gantry. RK has referred to it as "urbanism for vegetation," and he's not wrong: pixel farming is diverse communities of plants, packed in next to each other in small spaces, neighbors borrowing from each other, insect visitors navigating foliated avenues, colonies of uninvited but tolerated flora occupying the awkward spaces in between, all of it somehow coexisting. His interpretation is telling, both of his entry point as an urbanist and of a central paradox of pixel farming. As an urbanist, Rem recognizes complexity and symbiosis in a natural system by overlaying an urban framework—something an ecologist would never do. Anything built is arguably always going to be less complex than an ecosystem born of chance and evolution. But pixel farming isn't natural: it occupies a magnetic in-between state of being both planned and anarchic, a nuance that's perhaps more detectable when you've spent your life interrogating cities. Pixel farming as a research phenomenon wasn't immediately (and still isn't) embraced. An interdisciplinary team of star Wageningen scientists including plant ecologists, soil biologists, farm technologists, agronomists, entomologists, and agroecologists submitted a grant proposal to the Dutch Research Council to get funding for a large-scale pixel farming experiment in early 2017. A recently-published meta-analysis had shown that crops grown in narrow strips produced up to 25 percent more yield than those grown in large monocropped fields, and the proposal built on this finding, hypothesizing that if you cut the strips into even smaller pieces (pixels!) you could get even better yields, and other ecosystem benefits as well. What made the proposal unique—and perhaps precipitated its demise—was that the team acknowledged the essential role of technology in facilitating agriculture, but flipped the normative framework. Rather than designing farming systems to control ecological processes in favor of mechanization and efficiency, they argued that farming systems, and the technologies built to enable them, should be designed to support and enhance ecological processes. The pixel farming narrative put ecology first, and other outcomes (like food production) second: if you take care of the ecology, even with machines, the rest will take care of itself. Despite its robust scientific foundations, stellar team, and timeliness, the proposal was flatly rejected. The fact that our experiment exists now is purely the result of passionate people believing so much in the concept that they are willing to work on it unfunded. With a brilliant and tireless team of researchers, farmers, and students, I co-manage the pixel farming experiment on the Droevendaal Organic Experimental and Training Farm in Wageningen; this is usually where I'm standing when I talk about pixel farming. Our experiment is especially interesting (read: anxiety-inducing) to other scientists because it follows accepted protocols for experiment design (randomization, replicability), but the outcome looks like something totally different than your standard agronomic field trial. Ok, it looks like a mess. At the start of the experiment it looked sterile, as if an OCD scientist went out to the field with a T-square and an R script to plant 1,000 blue plastic stakes (which she did). The plots were set up on a neatly planned grid of squares, each plant allotted its own equal share of the space. But the crops we planted quickly emerged and outgrew the right angles, squatters moved in, and the pixels took on lives of their own. The grid is still there but it's become hard to see.

The non-linearity of interactions in a complex living system like a pixel plot makes them difficult (and probably undesirable) to optimize. In systems research, we get more excited about emergent properties—the ecological checks and balances, the feedback loops, the unexpected interactions—that appear when you throw a bunch of plants together and watch what happens. But because it's agriculture and one of our objectives is to produce extractable resources (food), we impose some measures to direct the system toward our desired outcomes. The plants we grow are randomly allocated within the plots, but they have been carefully chosen to be there because we expect them to behave in certain ways. We use design principles that draw on decades of classical agronomy and ecology, and centuries of farmers' innovations and indigenous knowledge.

Some of the plants are there to provide food for humans: we plant cabbages, potatoes, cereals, and sugar beets because we're in the Netherlands and that's what the superlatively sophisticated and wildly adventurous Dutch taste buds demand. Others are there to provide services beneficial for the agro-ecosystem. Cabbages need a lot of nitrogen, so we also plant clovers, which are leguminous and fix nitrogen through a symbiotic relationship with soil-dwelling bacteria. Cereals need nitrogen early in the season, so we plant them in simultaneously sown mixtures with fava beans and peas (other nitrogen-fixers). The fava beans are extra cool because they also help out with controlling invasions of cabbage-eating caterpillars by providing nectar to tiny parasitoid wasps whose offspring eat the caterpillars from the inside out (gnarly, right?!). Between food crops we plant green manures that protect and build the soil while providing resources for beneficial insects. Each pixel follows a standard organic arable rotation, which alternates root crops with leafy crops and cereals to avoid soil degradation, separates species that share soil-borne pests and diseases, allows regeneration of soil nutrients, and keeps the ground covered year-round. We take an intentionally hands-off approach to managing weeds, because these uninvited flora also have something to offer the system: many provide root exudates that feed soil life, some are deep rooting and transport valuable soil nutrients up to the range where our food crops can reach them, others provide shelter to aphid-eating ground beetles, and still others are bio-indicators of nutrient deficiencies or soil compaction. These services and signals help us understand how the system is functioning and how to design it better in the next iteration.

There are biodiverse agricultural systems all over the world that resemble pixel farming, each of them with indigenous roots and localized functionalities: Central American home gardens, the Chinese tradition of intercropping, the iconic Three Sisters practiced in Mexican milpas and across the Americas, California's Alan Chadwick-inspired biointensive farms, Dutch *voedselbossen*, "square foot gardening," French intensive gardening, Cuba's *organopónicos*, Ernst Götsch-style syntropic farms, even allotment gardens around Europe. Although contextually quite different, these systems share foundational principles that make them robust—even antifragile—in the face of disturbances like a pest outbreak or a drought. A diversity of species creates both a diversity and redundancy of functions within the system. Diversity helps to make sure all your bases (food production, soil quality, pest and disease control, etc.) are covered, and redundancy is like insurance in case one of your functions fails. These systems also intentionally combine species that have synergistic (complementary, facilitative) relationships. The Three Sisters is a banner example: corn grows into a tall and strong stalk upon which climbing beans can gain purchase; squash vines its wide leaves across the soil surface, suppressing weeds and retaining moisture; beans fix nitrogen, which feeds the corn and the pumpkins; and all three plants provide food for humans and the soil. The pixel farm we're prototyping is very much inspired by these high-resolution systems, but the context we're designing for is decidedly different. Small-scale, subsistence farms tend to already be more diverse and less environmentally problematic than large-scale industrial farms. That's not to say that there aren't challenges to be solved on smallholder farms, but those often have more to do with nutrition, hunger, power structures, access, poverty. Instead, our imaginations are trained to the vast industrial monocultures of the West, acres and acres of single crops planted in neat rows that rely heavily on fossil fuels and agrochemicals to enforce a tenuous (albeit productive) state of homogeneity. We're interested in taking pixel farming to an industrial scale because industrial-scale agriculture—in its current form—is the most ecologically problematic kind of farming. Hunger, power struggles, and poverty are by no means absent from the industrialized parts of the world, but these issues are usually not caused by a lack of bulk food production. The global North is not where we need to produce more food—it's where we desperately need to produce food in a better way.

This would be a good moment to say something about privilege—mine, that is. I don't usually talk about it when I talk about pixel farming, but I think about it a lot: how privileged I am to get paid to spend my time thinking, writing, reading, asking questions, dreaming about a better kind of farming, fueled by a lunch I made of locally raised lamb and organic kale, sitting in my carbon-neutral office, drinking clean tap water, playing with my iPhone. Choosing to study the diversification of European industrial farming systems was a turning point in my career in agricultural sciences: it was a conscious choice I made to move away from projects working with smallholder farmers in developing countries and instead carve out my contribution in a context in which I felt better equipped and more deeply obligated to make a positive difference. I often wonder about access, ownership, equity—if this vision of agriculture I'm promoting is inherently designed for some and not for others—but I'm convinced that I'm asking those questions in the right place, one where my privilege positions me to make a tangible impact. Lately there's been a rejuvenated interest in farming systems that support and enhance biodiversity, so intercropping (planting more than one crop in the field at once, usually in alternating rows) is getting a lot of attention in the research world. A large part of my own research on crop diversity is focused on strip intercropping, the practice of growing two or more species in alternate, multi-row strips wide enough to allow independent cultivation but narrow enough to support ecological interaction. Strip cropping is interesting

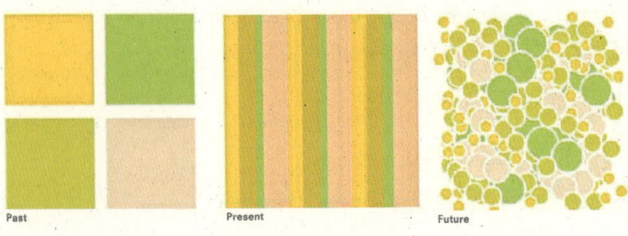

Redesigning the agricultural field: from monocultures, to strips, to pixels.
(Dirk van Apeldoorn & Rogier Schulte)

Farming in strips next to pixel plots. (Peter van der Zee)

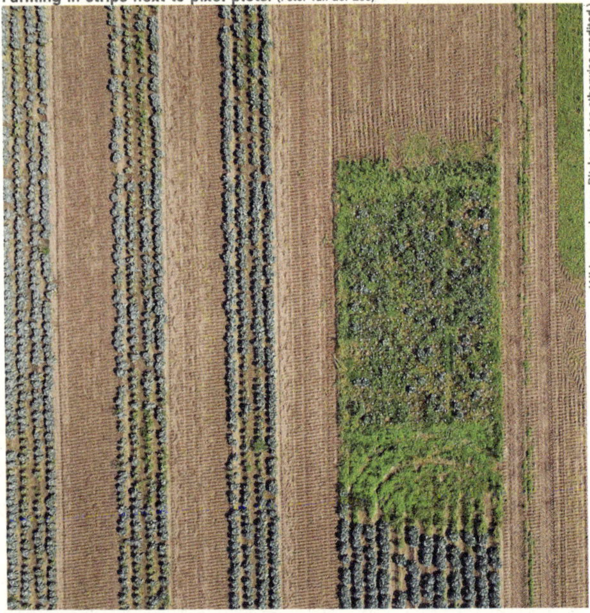

(All images: Lenora Ditzler, unless otherwise credited.)

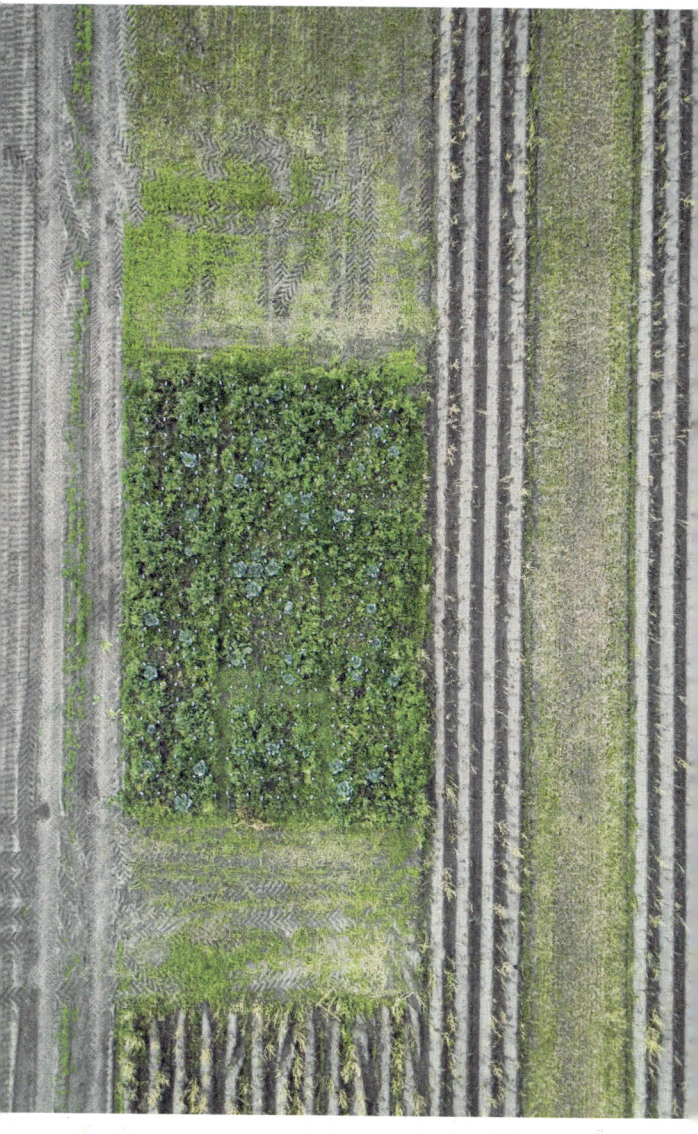

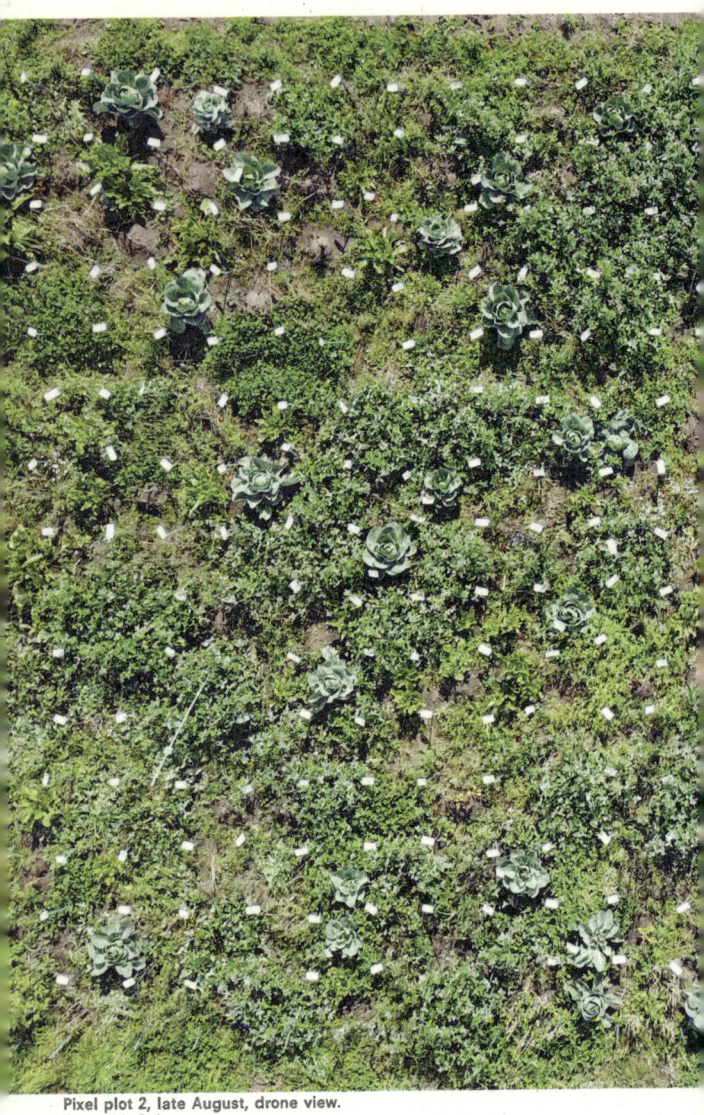

Pixel plot 2, late August, drone view.
(Peter van der Zee)

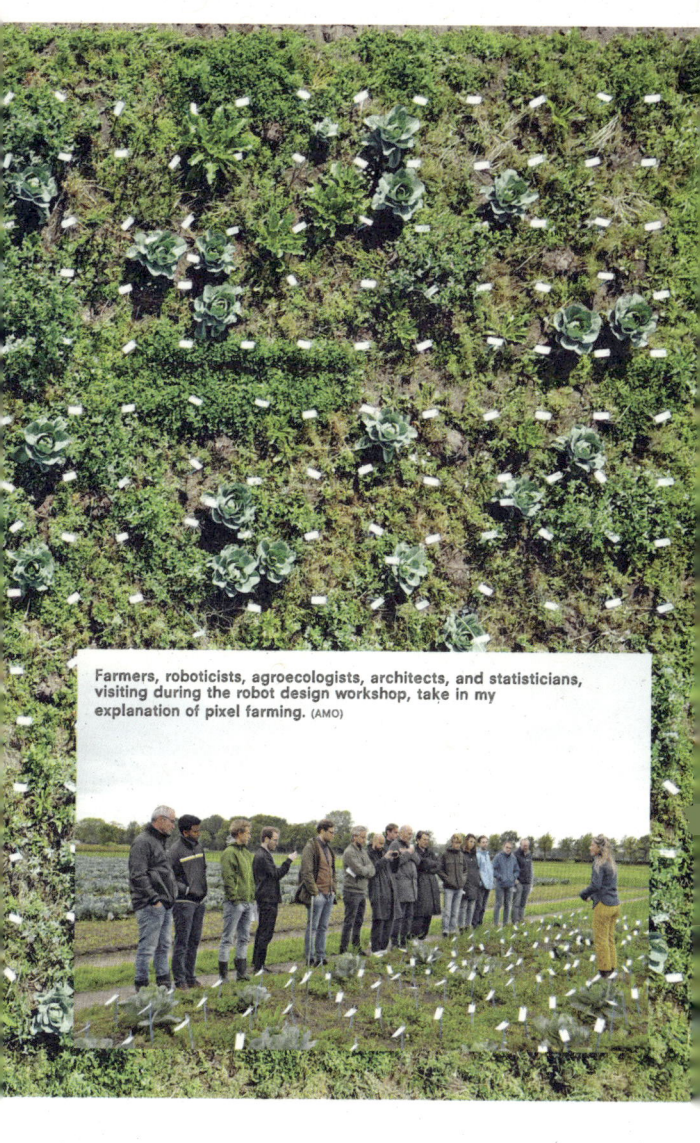

Farmers, roboticists, agroecologists, architects, and statisticians, visiting during the robot design workshop, take in my explanation of pixel farming. (AMO)

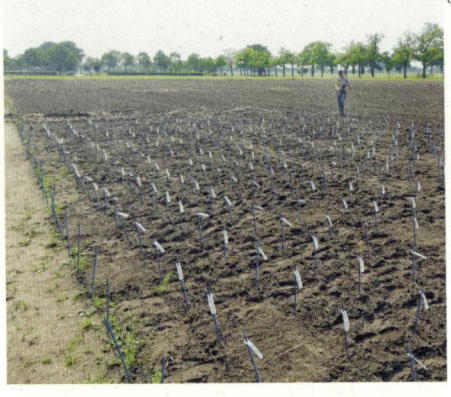

Setting up pixel plots: working from opposite corners of the outer rectangle inwards.
(Lieneke Bakker)

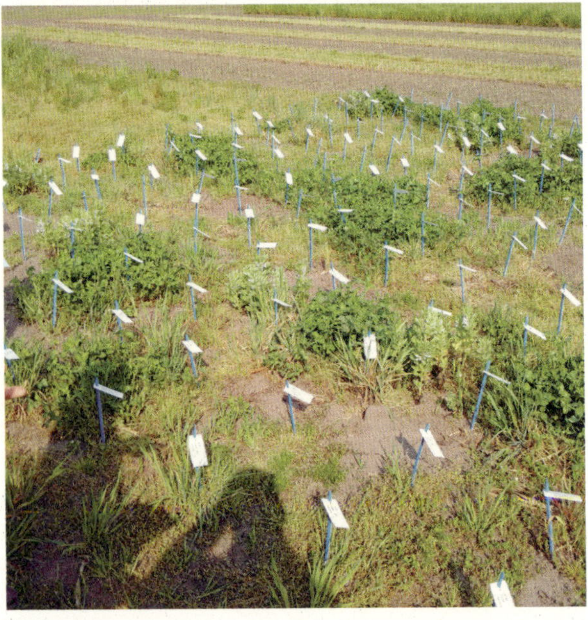

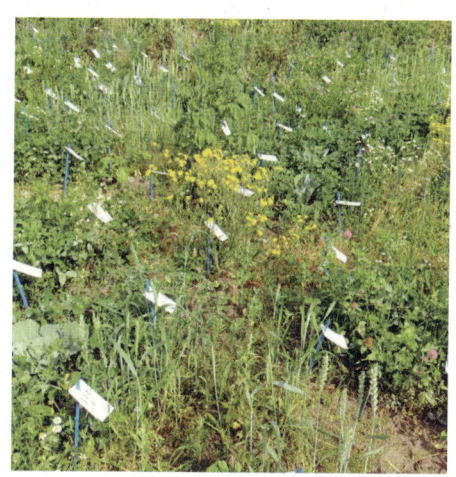

Pixel plots from spring to summer.

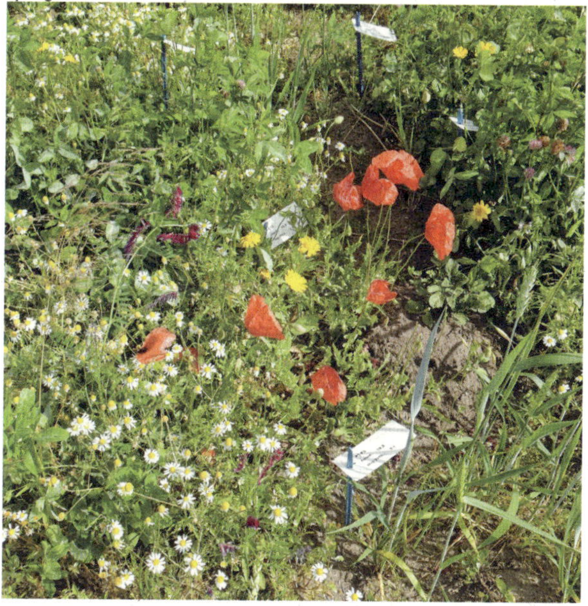

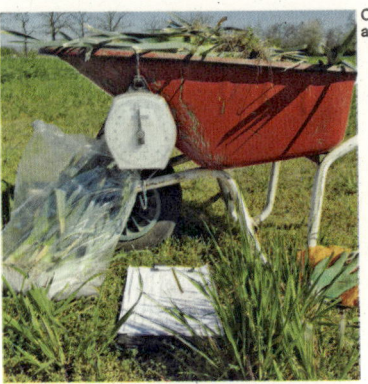

Crop harvests measured and recorded per pixel.

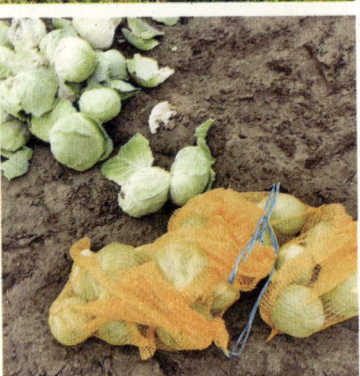

Sorting marketable (orange bags) and non-marketable (Christmas Drumhead) cabbage varieties.

Decoy: Christmas Drumhead cabbages, planted intermittently as a sacrificial trap-crop to lure pests away from the other (tastier) cabbage variety. There's no real market for Christmas Drumheads so they usually end up becoming compost.

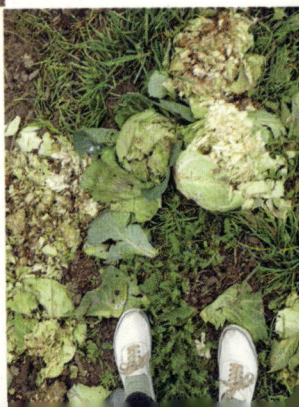

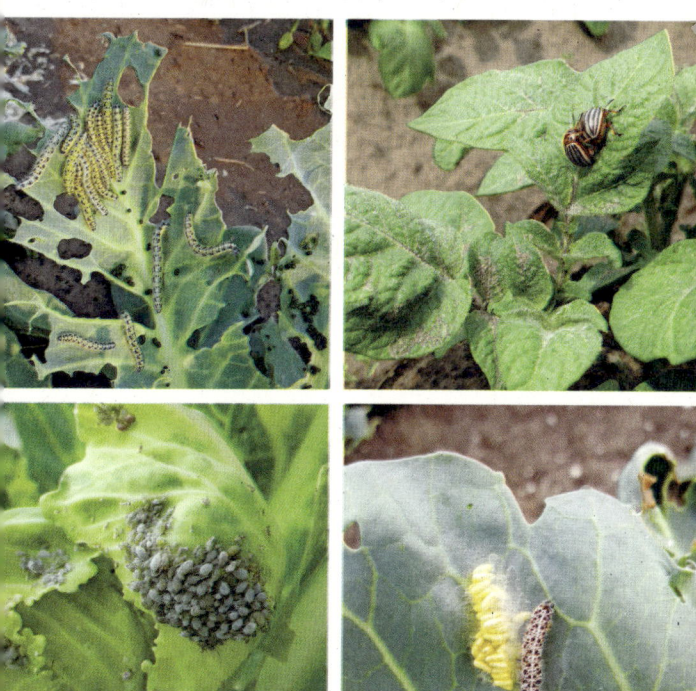

Pixel plot insect inhabitants: *Pieris brassicae* caterpillars; adult Colorado potato beetles (*Leptinotarsa decemlineata*); *Cotesia glomerata* cocoons near a parasitized *Pieris brassicae* caterpillar; cabbage aphids (*Brevicoryne brassicae*) feasting on cabbage. Tolerating a few pests is necessary to support the natural enemy populations that provide biocontrol.

(Caterpillars, coccoons, aphids: Mirthe Jansen)

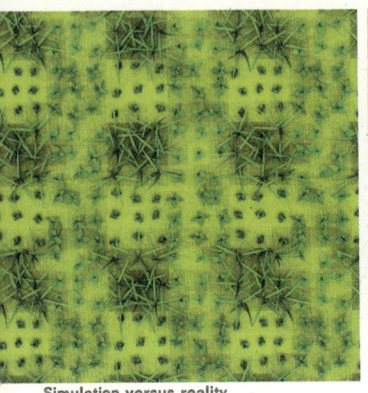 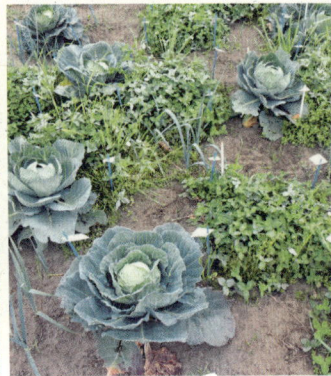

Simulation versus reality.
(Left: Jochem Evers)

right
Combining information fro[m]
field measurements and
underground filming, plan[t]
growth models capture ro[ot]
interactions with the grea[t]-
er precision of predictive
rendering. (Jochem Evers)

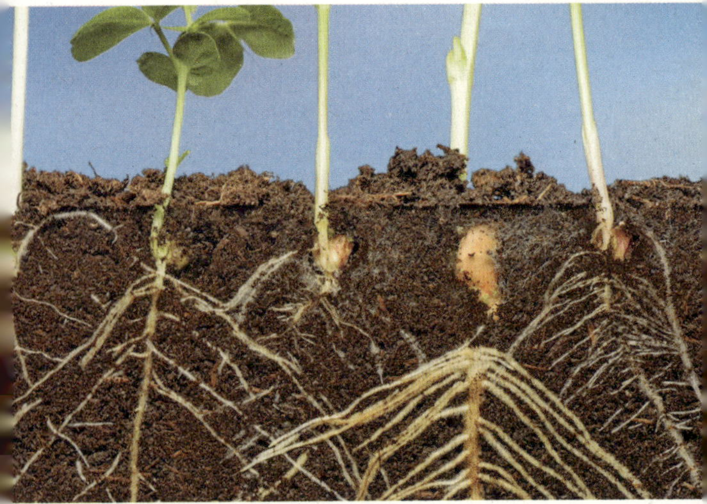

Roots intermingle in a complex plant mixture.
(Gerlinde de Deyn & Wim van Egmond)

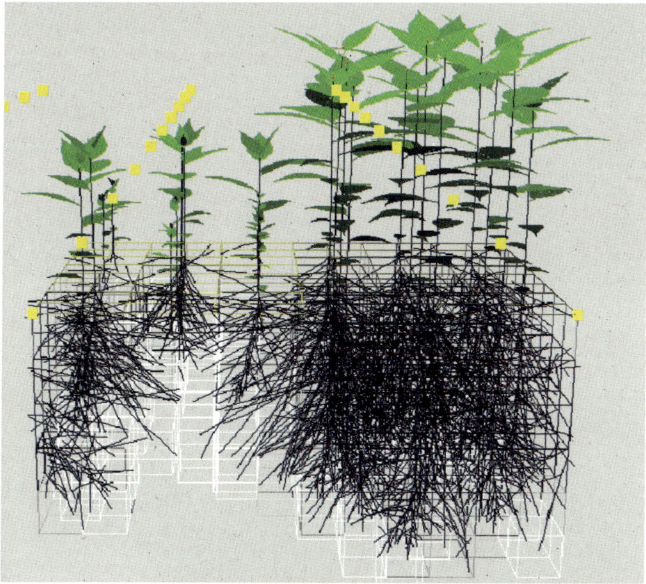

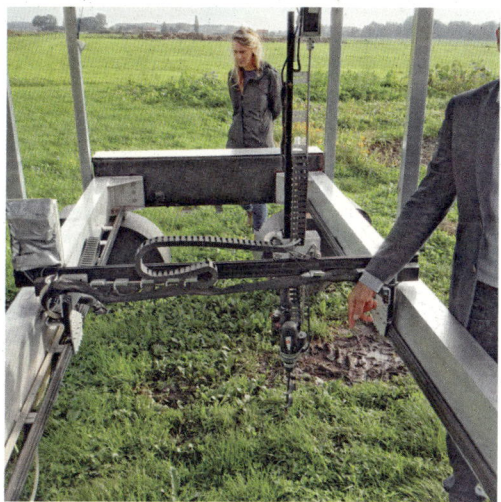

Judging a not-so-eco-feminist robot.

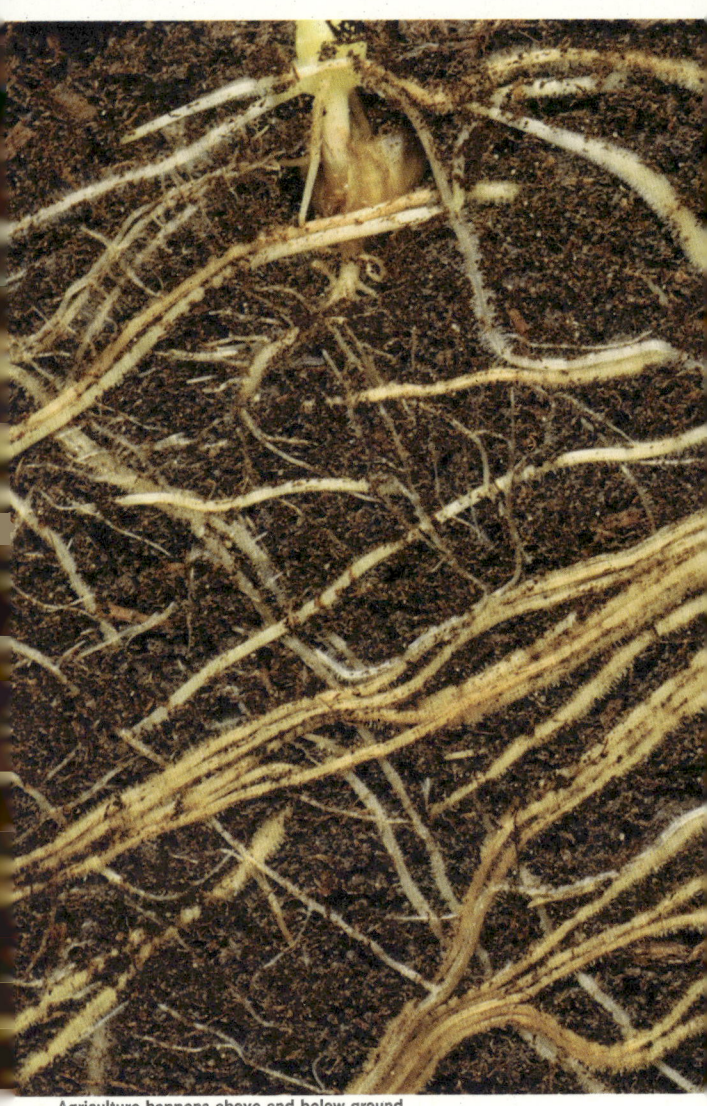
Agriculture happens above and below ground.
(Gerlinde de Deyn & Wim van Egmond)

because it affords the opportunity to bring biodiversity into the standard arable field—and gain the yield and ecological benefits of doing so—while still using standard farm machinery. Strip cropping can be seen as a necessary intermediary step between monocultures and something more radically diverse, but it clings to the Western conventional ideal of long straight rows that can be uniformly managed with heavy, fuel-guzzling machinery. Imagine if instead of one or two crops in rows, you saw clusters of different sizes, shapes, and colors daubed across the landscape. What we're doing with pixel farming —breaking out of the linear confines of a monoculture mentality—has huge potential but also presents whole new challenges for how to design and manage diversity at an industrial scale. Pixel farming big fields is not possible yet: the machinery just doesn't exist. Maybe more importantly, we don't have the scientific knowledge to design successful pixel cropped fields. Acquiring this knowledge would require conducting endless field experiments in which the complexity of the experimental setup is incrementally amplified to accommodate all possible neighbor and pixel size (and shape) combinations for all possible crops. This is frankly more than our little team of researchers can handle in one lifetime; that's why we started by implementing superficial design rules, limiting the number of crop species we grow, and allocating all plant communities to a uniform pixel within a fixed grid. Fortunately, there are other ways besides in-the-field experimentation to inform pixel farm design.

A major design—knowledge hurdle we're exploring now is what plants make good and bad neighbors. To understand these complex inter- and intra-specific interactions, we've been teaming up with functional—structural plant modelers and statisticians. There are treasure troves of information about so-called "companion planting" in non-academic spheres (local ecological knowledge, garden clubs, permaculture handbooks), but little of it has been formalized in a way that can be used for developing design rules. We come to pixel farming with the assumption that more diversity is better, but it may be that some plants exhibit a kind of botanical xenophobia. We've seen evidence of this already in our field experiments: the cabbages are always bigger when they're next to other cabbages than when they're next to a potato or a clover patch, although this probably says more about how the cabbage variety we grow has been bred for monocultures than it does about the inherent bigotry of the cabbage species. With our plant modeling friends, we've been working on creating simulated pixel plots; these offer a platform to explore planting patterns and crop interactions out of the field. We can use virtual pixel plots, validated on real plants, to answer both fundamental science questions (*How do plants bred for monocultures respond to being grown in heterogeneous communities? Which particular plant traits make a species suitable for pixel farming?*), and practical design questions (*Which crop combinations make good and bad neighbors? What is the optimal pixel resolution for each crop?*). In a triangulation process, we bring our empirical data to our statistician friends[1] who use mathematical models to explore the effects of implementing different design rules on outcomes like yield or pest damage. Eventually, we'll take these theoretical findings back to the field to design new pixel neighborhoods, and with the help of ecologists and entomologists, find out if the intentional plant communities behave the way our models predicted. But back to the issue of machinery. No matter what I start talking about, I always end up coming back to machinery. More than other design choices, pixel shape and resolution will direct the technological demands of large-scale pixel farming. Currently, our experimental plots are managed entirely by people (*moi*). Tending the quilt-like layout requires excessive manual labor, because the tractors we have cannot accommodate such diverse and small resolution "fields." Preparing the soil, planting, fertilizing, weeding, harvesting, it's all done by hand. It may well be that creating more work on farms is something Western society will one day demand, that we'll realize what we want is actually a lower-tech future, but at the moment we are occupied with relieving people of the drudgery of farm labor. To make pixel farming viable at scale without overburdening humans, technological advances—and automation—will be necessary. The real question is what kinds of technologies we should develop, and how. The world of agricultural robotics is a weird place that appears to be occupied almost entirely by men who mostly operate in the familiar comfort of the patriarchal and monocultural paradigms. There are some exciting initiatives to develop autonomous machines built to navigate heterogeneous field conditions and tend complicated crop layouts, but the progress toward getting these robots on the market seems to be painfully slow, especially when you compare it to the other radical feats of engineering, AI, and machine learning that have already become mainstream. I see one of the obstructions to acceleration as rooted in the fundamental error that we are trying to adapt our farming systems to the machine parts we already have, and not imagining radical new machines that fit the demands of radical new systems.

I recently tried to get a bunch of robot dudes to talk about this issue in a workshop I titled "Automating agroecology: how to make an ecofeminist pixel farming robot?" At the start of the workshop, in a strident interruption of the presentation in which the conceptual framing of the project was about to be justified, I was loudly informed by a Dutch white cis man in a position of high academic standing (who, it turns out, I had in fact not invited—he invited himself) that the term ecofeminism was offensive and divisive, and that if I wanted to successfully continue with my research I would have to drop it. Rather than smoothly sliding into a metered *"You know what, you're totally right. We've made a huge mistake and I thank you for enlightening me. As I'm sure you agree, we should really be talking about 'new materialist' robotics instead,"* I found myself paralyzed in a subservient response you might expect from the physical manifestation of Siri or Alexa: gently smiling and slow-motion nodding. Fortunately, a colleague came to the rescue and attempted to explain why we think ecofeminist theory is a useful framework for interrogating the implications of design choices on the identity and functionality of new technologies meant to enable a kind of farming that boldly claims to resemble nature.   We started discussing the idea of ecofeminist robotics in the context of pixel farming as we noticed that things often got heated when we talked about automation with value-driven farming systems experts. I had been focused on the technical challenges of automation, but other people wanted to talk about labor, meaningful work, communal relations, access, ownership, promoting particular forms of farming knowledge and experience... *are you saying farmers will be obsolete?* Ecofeminism gave us a theoretical framework to position pixel farming's practical issues in a longer-standing debate about the entangled tacit and socio-political relationships between nature, (agri)culture, and humans. Obviously, it's not undeserving of critique (and it's arguably out of date), but ecofeminism offers an interesting way to rethink automation and robots in agroecological terms: can we make a tool that is place-based, enables complexity, fosters relations, doesn't scare the birds, rejects binary thinking, collaborates with ecological processes, provides meaningful work, promotes indigenous knowledge, invites community, and looks cool?

During our workshop we asked mixed teams of agro-eco-socio-techno experts to design the pixel farming robot of their dreams, keeping our ecofeminist demands in mind. The disappointing—although in retrospect unsurprising—outcome was that all the design teams reinvented the same robotic machinery that already exists (and has been consistently found to malfunction). Apparently, the monoculture mentality runs even deeper than I thought.

Speaking of deeply engrained paradigms, it's worth taking a moment to talk about the digital metaphor of the pixel. Earlier I claimed that we were breaking out of linear confines with this futuristic farming system that looks like miniature crop circles. But if you're paying attention, you'll remember the Richter/Martin reference. Right, our pixels are squares. And plants don't grow in squares (something our permaculturalist friends like to remind us of... *also, where are the chickens?*). In digital image vocabulary, a pixel is the smallest controllable element on the screen. We use the word in the same way: the pixel is the smallest unit of control in our experiment. In our case, it's a 1.5 x 1.5-foot crop cell, which is scaled to fit the largest individual plant in our field, the cabbage. It's an unavoidable paradox that in our pursuit of the pixel arcadia, we impose order to get rid of it. We do this because, Science. By breaking up the agricultural field into tiny units fit neatly into a grid, we claim we're achieving a kind of native agriculture. In some ways, this might be true (*If you make the squares small enough, could you not arrive at a state where Cartesianism becomes natural again? Or are we still stuck in a reductionist, Dutch, right-angle world?*). But really what we're doing is making the system experimentable. There are so many possible ways you could arrange plants that the experimental factors are literally endless, and practically speaking we have to impress limits in order to take measurements and conduct statistical analyses. Pixels are convenient. They also make the idea of radical farming more palatable to digitally minded people, like the IT folks whose help we desperately need to make the system plausible. The digital metaphor makes it easy to talk about diversity and complexity in terms of resolution and pattern. It also gives me a convenient segue into bragging that I'm really good at Tetris. Like, way better than you. In general, I try to avoid talking about the concrete outcomes of our pixel farming experiment thus far. I'm hesitant to make conclusions about what our system produces—in terms of yield or any other ecosystem service—because it's a long-term experiment and it's still in its infancy (year two at the time of writing). Switching from a mono-cropped system to a complex and self-regulating one presumably requires time to settle in and evolve. We see it on real farms that management transitions, say from conventional to organic, take time before benefits can be realized. What we're creating is not an agricultural field as we know it, but a living ecosystem, and new dynamic equilibria must be established. I can tell you that what we have observed so far is promising: our pixel plots seem to attract more functional biodiversity, the plants seem to have less pest damage, and the crop yields appear to be, for the most part (*I see you, cabbages*), comparable to our monoculture references.

I talk about a lot of stuff when I talk about pixel farming, but ultimately the claim I make is simple: if we just put the right plant in the right place at the right time and in a community of the right resolution, we could produce enough food for everybody, including the soil biota and the pollinators and the parasitic wasps, and we could do it without relying on agrochemicals or fossil fuels, because diversity works. It's a big claim for a postage-stamp-sized experiment in a postage-stamp-sized country, but I've lived in the Netherlands long enough now to believe it's possible. Bring on the bad coffee.

[1] This may be the biggest triumph of my PhD so far: that I can say with a straight face that I have "statistician friends." Richard Lautze, you understand.

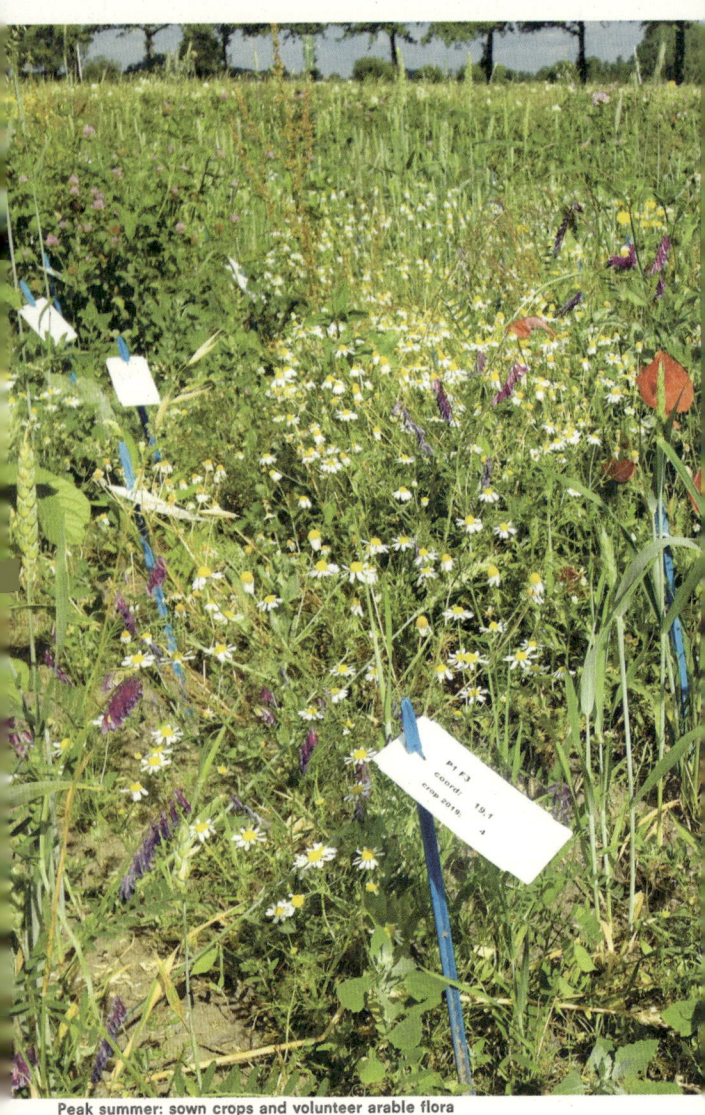

Peak summer: sown crops and volunteer arable flora (aka "weeds") almost indistinguishable.

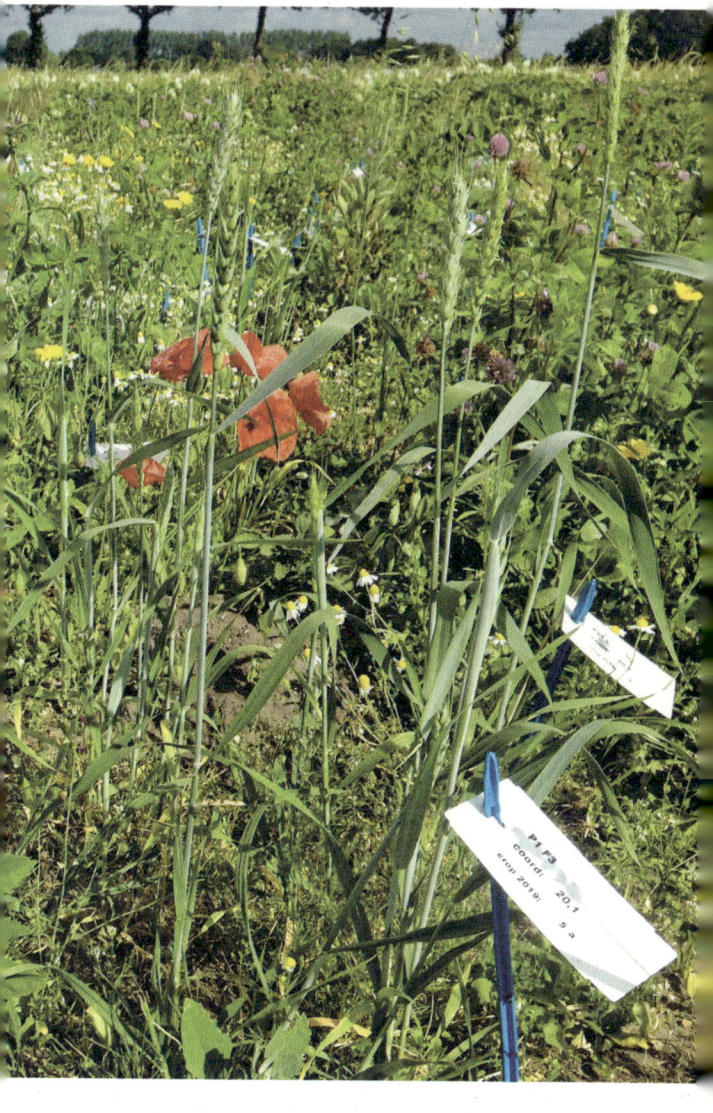

?
RK

Where did the cows go?

And when did they leave?

Could we no longer tolerate the smell ?

Did China find a way to exploit the connections of internet also in a physical way ?

325 ?

The sound of their bells filled the valley like a tangible substance ?
When did "old" disappear ?
Why did the nuclear scientist become a farmer ?
Where are the inhabitants ? Do they live elsewhere ?
Are there inhabitants ?
Why are the gardens unused ? When was the last barbecue ?
Who maintains the unused ?
Does grass always need cutting ? Why don't they invent grass that doesn't grow ?
Is hay still relevant ?
What happened in the last 100 years ? How did we evolve from costume to jeans ?
Definitive clothing ? The outward sign of a new me ?
How did the Romans live in the countryside ?
And their contemporaries, the Chinese ? What made them happy ?
Who thought of free time ?
Singing in the stream, reciting poetry...
Since when did we sell entire villages ?
Work or Wellness ? Can tourism be real ? Is massage a new duty ?
Dung or Design ?
How close to heaven are satellites ? Do they reach heaven ? Do they know everything ?
Can we hide ?
What happened between the moment when everyone knew their place and now ?
Did they stop suffering in silence ? Was the countryside unbearable ?
Was mankind once better ?
Why did we produce whole generations that have never touched the teat of a cow ?
That only know milk ?
That have never stepped on a shovel, don't know the scale of a pig, the strength of a sheep ?
Who ordered this exodus ?
Was it a plan or did it just happen ?
Could they have stopped it ?
Was it under duress ?
Where did they go ?
Where did they recruit the replacements ?
Did the new ones meet the old ones ?
When did they abandon their costumes ?
Yesterday ? Did they wear veils ?

What did the men wear ?
Can you recondition / rehabilitate / remodel / refurbish / rebuild / repair history ?
How do you learn farming ?
Why do they always convert what is abandoned ?
Should architects design for disoccupation ?
Can only what is abandoned be converted ?
Why do new occupants use interior designers ?
Who produces the cushions ?
Locally ? Internationally ? Internet ?
Did anyone regret leaving ? Come back ?
Do they still communicate now that they are dispersed ?
Did they sell or rent ?
Do they own or rent ?
Does renting mean a potential return ?
Is selling definitive ?
When are they there ?
12 days a year ?
What percentage of the days are they there ?
Are they all from one big city ?
Milan ? Paris ? Riyadh ? Amman ?
Can you base a culture on absence ? Or is it the new culture of absence ?
Are their children still rural ?
What binds them together ?
Nationality ? Politics ? Dissatisfaction ?
Is there a connection between satellites, the sky, and the beyond ? Are they the beyond ?
What is the difference between the Cassini Orbiter and God ?
Can they see everything now ?
Is everything seen ?
Is seeing believing ?
Are we a new cast performing the same old play or does every cast imply a new play ?
What happens when the snow melts ? Disappears ?
Dark Swiss or white chocolate ?
Will white Xmas turn into brown Xmas ?
Can we order snow like a carpet ? Roll it out ?
Should we remove white from all paintings ? To visualize what is going to happen ?
Is architecture always for humans ? Can architecture serve other species ?
Animals ?
Robots ?
Do objects have something to say to each other ?

Do architects know how to address things that are
not alive ? Know how to please "things" ?
Do we have to find a new name for emptiness ?
A new form of policing ? What happens to an alarm
that nobody hears ?
How should we "clad" it ?
Vegetation ?
Do we bother to mow, trim, cut... the landscape ?
Or tile it ?
Asphalt ?
What do you call a public domain from which the public
has been drained ? A domain ?
Can a condition be urban without people ?
Who will control the animals ? The wild horses ?
Beyond the factory, the safari ?
Does living require courage ?
Will it make sense to abandon time in the future ?
Night and day ?
Will robots keep us from sleeping ?
Should we adopt a new system to meet the needs of
machines ?
To plan when to coincide ?
What is their measure of achievement ? Not to break
down ?
Will they produce equally ? Maintain it ?
Where will one machine end and another begin ?
If machines take care of animals, infrastructure, the
world—on whose terms ?

Could there ever be a new anarchy ?

Was the world safer ?
When China represented 1/3 of humankind ?
Would you say no if China offered to pay for your
infrastructure ?
To connect the coast and the most remote places inland ?
Or to create a Y shaped system that, opens up your
entire country like a crowbar ?
Is it helpful that they not only loan, but that they also
construct ?
If this is not "aid," is it help ? Post-colonial
collaboration ?
Are their train stations Chinese ? Welcome to your own
country ?
Chinese TV shows interaction between two populations,
even the outbreak of love... where is the equivalent on
the African side ? Is there love ?

In media, on the ground ?
Is it fun being Chinese in Africa ? All you see are sterile encampments covered in slogans—"Don't violate regulations is equal to cherish your life" or "cherish your life, say no to violations" ?
Just another challenge ?
Globalization is sharing ? And now we forgot how to share ? Since when are we against sharing ?
Is humankind's interest in knowing each other distributed equally ? Is curiosity about the other a given ?
Or is curiosity a one-sided aspirational claim ?
Is the airline system a symbol of our constantly expanding curiosity, or a never ending search for ownership ?
Why are African countries barely connected to other African countries ? Self-sufficiency ?
That you have to fly via Paris if you want to go from Kenya to Nigeria ?
Would that attitude, exported to the rest of the world, lead to a significant increase in global serenity ? Or exacerbate tensions ? Gains for sustainability ?
How paralyzing is our current connectedness ?

Re: vanishing cows: was it a plan or just a result ?

For every cow that disappeared, a new second home ?
Suddenly new, ungraceful cows appeared from the mists... new species, emphasizing meat at the expense of their heads ? The bovine equivalent of microcephaly, imported from where ?
Can art replace life ?
At what scale ?
How much art does Switzerland need to remain "alive" ?
Four artists per village ?
If artists show in former farms, should farmers show in museums ?
Can our schools produce enough artists ?
To fulfill the quota ?
Does A.I. offer help ?
Will Artists recognize AI.tists ?
Will they compete or collaborate ?
Will the profits of AI.tists be shared with poor Artists ?
How will we recognize AI.tists ?
Can there again be art without CV, biography, context ?
As in Lascaux ?
Do good intentions count for sustainability ?
LEED ? BREEAM ? DGNB ? HQE ? GBL ?

Can acronyms save the world ?
Bronze, silver, gold, platinum ?
What is beyond ? Holiness ?
Would it be exciting to try holiness ?
And for After ?

Is it me or are sections of Switzerland—and maybe much larger sections of the world—living a new form of afterlife ?

Manicured like a cemetery ?
Maintained by newcomers—artists, expats and owners—
that can only focus on "essence," on how it was, once ?
Is *now* still the same ?
What did they mean by afterlife ?
Who thought of the word ?
Could we dwell on it for a moment ?
Dwell in it ?

Can we liberate art from the obligation to remember ?

To fabricate non-existent pasts ?
Do people realize that certain parts of countryside died ?
Do we even remember it was alive ?
Stinking, messy, chaotic, unfriendly ?
Will we find an alternative to death ?
Why do we avoid death ? Can we celebrate death ?
Is it ironic that Switzerland needs to be kept alive
artificially while its elevation alone is its most effective
defense against heat ?
After the winter onslaught of skiing, orchestrate a
summer offensive of mountain bikes ?
Will there be a huge confrontation between what is flat
and what is sloped—flat for machines, sloped for
humankind ?
Will entire populations be adopted officially by cold
climates ?
Twin countries ?
Can nations be doubled ?
A winter and summer population ?
Are we only experiencing the beginning ?
Will they have to pay ?
Or rent ?
Will flat and sloped combine ?
Japan with the Midwest ? Chile with Holland ?

Does anywhere layered—like a city—need sensors ?

And anywhere open air—like countryside—
need satellites ?
Because it can be inspected only from above ?
The city is sensored, the countryside supervised...
god-like from the sky ?
Culture = sensor ?
Nature = satellite ?
"We" = sensor ?
"It" = satellite ?
Are satellites for viewing the spaces that are natural,
uninhabited, sparsely populated ?
If you feel God is following you, you are a believer; what
are you if you know that satellites are following you... an
actor ?
Is each of us (inadvertently) the subject of a movie ?
If a panopticon is an all-seeing eye that surveys, from the
center—is earth now itself the captive of a surrounding
Sensorsphere that captures any event on its surface ?
Is it a coincidence that, at the very moment surveillance
techniques have reached a superhuman precision, "fake"
has become the category we obsess over ?

When the UN launched its famous 50/50 subdivision of humanity into urbanites and remnants in the countryside, was it actually true ?

Did they amalgamate as many definitions of "urban"
as the UN itself has members ?
Equate Denmark's density with China's ?
Can we begin to correct it ?
Was it premature ? Self-fulfilling ?
50/50 sounds reassuring; did it mask a massive imbalance ?
Was it a warning, a reassurance, science or a polemic ?
If they were only indicating a trend, are we doomed
to obey ?
To what point ?
70/30 ?
80/20 ?
Even 90/10 ?
Did the UN condemn the countryside to perpetual
(and ever-increasing) backwardness, emptiness, by not
defining the meaning of its statistic ?

Would you still recognize cities if everyone lived there?
Beyond recognition?
If the UN's announcement just pre-dated the ubiquity
of the digital, does digital only accelerate urbanization?
Or potentially slow it down?
Do we really want Total City?

What will be the relationship between the "total" city and the "smart" city?

After working in the city, did Romans come alive in
the countryside?
Where will we come alive?
Is Otium with mobile phones still Otium?
Is Canada as a whole the new low key Otium?
Otium diluted to a homeopathic dose?
Do you also have friends who live in houses without any
books?
Do you feel old then?
(Or did reading keep you young?)
Do those friends read *Wallpaper*? *Monocle*? *The Good
Life*? *Home and Gardens*, the new *Playboy*?
Did you see the issue on the "Smart City"?
Sidewalk's new global HQ in Toronto?
How smart is it to build the first prototype of your "Smart
City" in the most generic version of the West?
In anticipation of its eventual "roll-out" worldwide?
Can we guess in which sequence?
Netherlands? Zimbabwe? New Zealand? Bhutan?
Is Google a microcosm of the world or has it belittled the
world?
If it covers the entire spectrum from mysticism to
science, what is still lacking?
Can religion be far behind?
Is it smart to insist that the total city will be totally
middle class?

To bet on white bread?

That the smart city does not need "stringent" geometries
anymore?
That it can be informal?
That we can all have a balcony?
Will Warming be mitigated, like everything else in Toronto?
What does it mean that the same organization that
promises a future of informal geometries, requires acres
and acres of meticulous three-dimensional orthogonality
to store the data generated by our post-orthogonal lives?

With the return of wood, what will architects have to unlearn?
What will be the New Style?
Holistic righteousness?
Apple Flintstone, if you're lucky?
Are we facing a golden age? (in the rear view mirror?)
Can architects give up Sir and Lord in favor of new equalities?
Why was the metaphor of the treadmill abandoned?
Since when did we overcome boredom?
Is the implication of data that ultimately their storage will require more energy than our actual lives?
Can our cities become village, or souk-like, like the places where the refugees that we refuse came from?
That you can wear anything, be everything, go everywhere?
Which political system could deliver that promise?
Since when did the word vision apply only to cities?
To urbanization? To development?
When did planning abandon the countryside?
Does living in cities promote ignorance?
Of the countryside, if not in general?
Of other species?
Of the world?
Of ourselves?
Of our needs?

Would it be possible to replace the question mark— with its implied hesitation...— by another sign?

A hybrid of exclamation and question?
And could you vary its size to reflect the depth of uncertainty?
What does a question mark express beyond uncertainty...?
Why are there so few of them now? you'd expect each printed page dominated by forests of them?
Are they derived from the sickle?
Was that the tool most unthinkingly derived from an arm?
Its strength and authoritative movement?
Hammer and sickle... is the symbol of communism deep down a combination of exclamation mark and question mark?
Can you describe a situation through the questions it raises?
Is there any other way if you're not really familiar with it?
Is urgency reason enough to introduce a new subject?

Even if it is not digested ?
Can you choose samples in such a way that together they imply the whole ? Or can you not generalize ?
Is it that cities are the same and countryside isn't ?
Is "pointillism" the only way to depict countryside ?
Subjects too rich, too unrelated, too subtle for harsh polemical statements ?
Is a text based on question marks a one-sided dialogue ?
Can you say yes or no to any question ?

Why did we embrace the Market Economy at the exact moment that science knew Climate change was upon us ? That science was certain ?

Did we embrace the Market Economy because we did not want to hear the Big Story ?
Is Warming too Big a Story ?
Or did we stop wanting what was needed after an entire generation had been exposed to the Market Economy ?
Is the point of the Market Economy to undermine the credibility of all intellectual speculation – to make any hypothesis look irresponsible compared to the certainty of the algorithm ?
Will we try communism one more time ?
Can only dictatorship address sustainability ?
Is democracy our undoing or our redemption ?
Will A.I. restore the *Grand Récit* (to its rightful place) ?
A.I. or dictatorship ?
A.I. = dictatorship ?
A.I. + dictatorship ?
A.I. ≠ dictatorship ?
Will A.I. offer us an alibi to be done with humanism once and for all ?
Good riddance or irretrievable loss ?
Is a flight forward also a plan ?
Why are we waiting for confirmation ? From whom ?
If we can verify every day that science is right ?
From different scientists ?
Did the market cause Warming and then make it impossible to undo it ?
What is in store ?
We believed in science, we believed in politics; both were replaced by the market, but the market has no plan, no program, no manifesto, no story... who helps us out of this impasse ?

Are we lost or found ?
If we are lost, who will find us ?
Will Warming make us believe in God ? Help !
Someone like Albert Schweitzer again, behind his organ in Lambaréné ?
There was always an air of unreality in realism; it was a "position," an ideology—what is it today ?
A depression ?
Is the intermittent habitation of (Gulf) cities a response to Warming that could become universal: leave the city when it overheats ?
Why were cities presented as a condition for mitigating Warming ?
By scientists ? Developers ? Architects ?
Is the earth anything but a homogeneous system ?
Even the sea not a plane but a relief ?
Are we ready, are we not, to welcome our unlucky brothers and sisters... ?
Are we clueless about climate ?
Because we're too smart for big stories ?
Has our own skepticism destroyed the way out ?
Do we know so much that nobody knows ?
In what sequence should we take what steps ?
Which are the low-hanging fruit ?
Is there a method or is hope fading ?
Is it too late to learn from the peoples we murdered ?
"Nomad" was a very fashionable term... why did it disappear ?
Were people on a treadmill not supposed to be susceptible to the call of the nomad ?
Did they not take care of the countryside, their movement subtly coordinated with seasons, growth, ecologies ?
Were there not human beings, hunters, herders, shepherds, even cowboys, that could live without leaving a trail of destruction ?
Or is the countryside a figment of the urban imagination ?
Did they also move to the city ?
Did they stop introducing their children to their traditions ?
Were hippies right ?
Is the commune the future ?
Can we relearn how to play ?
Why did play disappear ?
With the digital ?

Is the Market Economy slavery ?
Did slaves play ?
Do we now ?

Who would have guessed that the future is wood ?

How can we rediscover wood as a building material if we are told at the same time that forests are the most robust response to Warming ?
Will there be any wood left if we start to build with it ?
Is wood our collective security blanket ?
Did countryside have one line
of defense, the regional ?
Does "regional" offer a righteous alternative to the city ?
More serious ?
Less fashionable ?
Slower ?
Did critical regionalism suggest a respite, a place for thinking and resistance ?
Can a €4 million renovation be "critical" ? The remote, luxurious spa ?
Can rich people no longer be right ?
Has the "critical" moved to the wrong side ?
Can we still afford minimalism ? Signifier *par excellence* for a pampered elite ? From the monk to the CEO ?

Is the preservation of culture and of nature having similar effects on both ?

Should we even use the same words for both the protection of nature and of culture ?
Preservation, conservation, reservation... what is the difference ?
Is the first an ambition, the second a procedure, the third a precaution ?
How much meaning do *preserve* and *sustain* share ?
What is the difference ?
How did two mere verbs each become a movement ?
Does each act of preservation imply the sacrifice of another condition ?
Because it has to absorb the pressure to change that has been averted in the first case ?
As we preserve more, do we sacrifice more ?
Preservation = change (of another site) ?
As shown by the ring of lodges, resorts, motels, shops, crafts, police, guides, NGOs, guards—along the perimeter of the nature reserve ?

Does each impulse to stop change inevitably trigger more change ?
For whom do we preserve ?
Who do we sacrifice ?
How many reserves do we have in the world ?
Is it enough ? to save us ? or the world ?
Is the number of species we exterminated, inversely proportional to the number of reserves we have created ?
What is their impact ?
Will they stop the extinction ?
Create privileged species ?
New imbalances ?
Good and bad species ?
Will NGOs propose face recognition for animals to better protect them ?
Social credits ?
What we resent in China, we apply to animals ?
What is the collateral damage of good intentions ?
If crisis is any NGO's reason for being, can they still have a real vision ?
What if the crisis disappears ?
Would any NGO be viable if it tried to deal with too many, not too few, with overpopulation instead of extinction ?
Might the *Gorilla Doctors* on call in the jungle begin to hand out contraceptives ?
What if the preserved areas flourish ? augment beyond their allocated footprint ? evolve beyond their original identity ?
Can preservation save what is average, even in nature ?
Generic nature ?
A cross section, not the exceptions ?
If half of the world—urban, countryside, wilderness— would be subject to preservation, what happens to the other half ? A new 50/50 ?
Is the "whole world" a thing of the past ?
Will the current—random—patchwork of preservation turn out to be too complex, impossible to administer? Will it be simplified ? One half of the world ? A quarter ?
Gridded or pixelated zones for convenience ?
A barcode ?
Not impossible if you note the growth of countries undergoing regime change ?
Can we please preserve Europe ? (even as a theme park ?)
Will the future world be a patchwork of arrested and accelerated development ?

Of frozen and melted ?
Is the reserves a prototype for civilization 3.0 ?
If more than half our territories—both inside "civilization" and outside of it—will be preserved, will the residual become essence ?
What do we call the land between reserves ?
Countryside ?

How to think about Africa ?

Do we first need to admit our own role ?
Or can we look at it as a current reality ?
How did it evolve ?
Does our own current confusion enable us to look at Africa not as "parents" but as equals ? As an example ?
Can you be urban and rural at the same time ?
What does it mean if a brand new Chinese railway lands in an African village ?
Whose interest is served ?
Are China's abstract encampments in the Kenyan countryside a sign of ultimate rigidity or enviable determination ?
Does the new railway create new potentials or does it complete a plunder launched by the colonizer ?
Does it establish a communication between capital and remote hinterland that enables a young urban elite to maintain a relationship with their rural communities ?
Does each country need to be accessible ?
Will the tourists it distributes affect delicate balances, stand offs, traditions ?
Can you do good and do bad at the same time ?
Why is European infrastructure typically planned on the ground and Chinese infrastructure propped up on stilts ?
Domination vs disconnect ?
The first excludes alternatives, the second can coexist with anything—is it therefore more contemporary ?
Is avoiding disaster the last mission of humankind ?
Is the apocalyptic the only rhetorical mode left ?
Is each observation inevitably a fragment of theory ?
Could a situation emerge where there are more theories than species ?
If leapfrogging is skipping seemingly inevitable phases of civilization, will Africa avoid total urbanization ?
Develop a new prototype of the countryside ?
By the sheer diversity of its conditions, make the countryside more desirable than the city ?

What features could we adopt from Africa ?
What would be the equivalent of loyalty to a tribe ?
Can we still imagine unquestioned loyalty ?
Why did we shed that kind of loyalty as a burden ?
Where did that get us ?
Would it make us feel better if we could reintroduce it ?
Is populism a nostalgia for the same loyalty or a compensation for its loss ?
What if friendship, support and affinity were a given, not an effort ?
What if all urban citizens were also citizens of remote areas, not as a form of schizophrenia, but as a way of balancing different obligations, needs and pleasures ?
Would we know the world better ?
Understand what to do ?
How do you abort a flight forward ?

Can we relearn romanticism ?
Is a romantic someone who sees beauty even where it doesn't exist ?
Can you reframe situations with your brain even if you know "reality" is stubborn and resistant ?
Should you be dressed beautifully in the countryside ?
Is sophistication by definition inauthentic ?
Is the point of education to discover who you are or to create an improved version ?
Can you imagine Jane Austen describing a datacenter ?
What would Goethe think of a tractor ?
How far can elective affinities be stretched ?
Or are they possible only between similar, minds, cultures, environments ?
Do they exist between species ?
Can we relearn to idolize ? Collectively ?
Is beauty a decision ? Does it involve willpower ?
How can we resurrect the picturesque and the sublime ?
The first because it consoles us, the second because it makes us feel humble ?
Do you have to be alone to realize what you feel ?
Are we never alone anymore ?
Is the Sublime a way to combine good and bad ?
Incomprehensible dimensions, contrasts, intensities, the most exceptional ?
Is the contemporary countryside on its way to the Sublime ?
Wind farms, solar farms, storage and distribution centers, factory farms, greenhouses, airports, highways, nuclear

test sites, colossal art works, dams, nature reserves—is their advance a good sign ?
Why are they impeccably organized while we are stuck in a perpetual muddle ?
Why does perfection only exist in domains to which we don't seem to have access ?
Could a political party that proclaimed this new world ever win ?
Is nostalgia permanent now ?
Can harsh compounds in lush nature become attractions ?
Are the wild horses in Google's backyard tragic ?
Beautiful ?
Should we plan hotels in our most alienated landscapes ?
Wellness ?
Pools ?
Supervised by anthropologists ?
Is it too late ?
Is the destruction of the world doomed to remain a minority taste ?
Will the beauty of China's countryside survive our interest ?
Can we invent a minority tourism ?
Why is the poolside lounge chair the emblematic furniture type at the moment of humankind's greatest crisis ?
Did Baudelaire write that the charms of the "horror" only excite the strong ?
Can we enjoy what the countryside no longer is without the hospitality industry to maintain the illusion of what it was ?

When did we cease to meander ?

Why do we only bisect spaces now, not turn off or reverse ?
When did the countryside stop being romantic ?
Was the countryside ever romantic ?
Or was that a need we projected on it because we never really knew it ?
You can know a city… can you know the countryside ?
Is the countryside unknowable ?
Does that explain our neglect ?
Have all new typologies emerged from the countryside ?

What is more important for

humankind: the Tesla GigaFactory, the Thermae at Vals, CCTV, or a refugee camp ?

Most of it is rectangular ?
What happened to the blob ?
Do blobs need a public ?
Why is the computer's versatility used in the countryside only to produce repetitions of the right angle ?
Is the countryside shed becoming a model for *all* construction ?
Are boxes triumphant in countryside because there is no one left to impress ? Have we denied the countryside its own evolution? By introducing cheaper workers, ingenious technologies, a new scale ?
What did we erase ?
Did you ever look from the air at the periphery of any city ?
All you saw were boxes, packed closely together ?
Do those boxes need more space now ?
Are we witnessing the emancipation of the box in the countryside ?
Can we imagine a city of boxes ?
What kept them close to the city ?
Workers ?
Why were those huge parking lots always half empty ?
Do boxes move to the countryside when workers are not needed any more ?
By how much did human density decline in factories, databanks, distribution centers... ironically mostly in "centers" ?
Do you remember seeing the masses on film, in documentaries, in fiction, move in and out of boxes, exploited, ready at any time to revolt ?
Where did they go ?
To Bangladesh ?
Where did revolt go ?
If factories are now barely inhabited by workers, how many "human" concerns can we abandon ?
Disabled access ?
Beige ?
Welcome ?
Hygiene ?
AC ? Ventilation ?
Light ?

Can robots work in the dark ?
Can robots function in overheated facilities ?
Could we devise "suits" that provide workers with their own individual needs: heat, cooling, food, air, so he or she can "share" space with robots ?
Like divers or astronauts ? Nuclear maintenance crews ?
Could architecture start from scratch ?
Is a futurist someone who forgot history ?
Shouldn't everyone have a future ?
Or do we count on the algorithm ?
Will the countryside prove that there is no inherent connection between population and size ?
That you can have a second Los Angeles but with a fraction of the people ?
A size like Manhattan but with 50, 250, max 1250 inhabitants ?
Is emptiness exciting ?
Will it need a new name?
Inhabited by a race of maintenance people ?
A new name for inhabitants ? *Can* they be inhabited even ?
Will weather still matter ?
Color ?
Smell ?
Health ?
Survival ?
Where are they recruited ?
What skills do they need to develop ?
Intervene each time algorithms fuck up ?
Obey algorithms ? What is IT anyway ?
Who do they work for ?
Humankind or the otherside ?
Will mathematics still matter ?
Will they want to move to the remote constellations of boxes—or are there too many boxes ? Or are the boxes too big ?
How do you design space if it no longer is for human interaction ?
Does the new "condition" require its own discipline ?
Will architecture schools die of irrelevance at the moment a new architecture is born ?
How do you imagine a new world when it's already there ?
Can we still outrun it ?
Can you leapfrog to a really new vision ? Or are we stuck in evolution... ?
Do we really want slow architecture ?

Were the Baths of Caracalla in Rome as big as Tesla in Reno ?
Are we capable of embracing a new beauty ?
What if we loved more of what we saw ?
Can you will love ?
Why do we accept disappointment ?
Is it easier than love ?
Could we exile humankind to the countryside?
Condemn ourselves to paradise ?
Dismantle the cities and let machines take care of everything else?

Did TED kill innovation ?

Is innovation equal to progress ?
Is failure endemic to vision ?
Will Warming kill Democracy ?
Can it only be stopped by authority ?
Could Democracy kill Warming ?
Who will beg citizens who don't understand ?
For what breakthrough were we waiting ?
Or did it happen already ?
How did we miss it ?
Will women have answers ?
Did strong men have answers ?
It always ended in tears ?
Why did earlier generations take risks ?
Were their risks more monumental than ours ?
Can a risk-averse generation handle the largest dilemmas ?
Would we have been more alert if we had been more afraid ? To address the accumulated risk of all generations before them ?
Now that we can separate plants from the ground, isolate them from the sun and other, "natural" givens, can we not proceed beyond plants ? Why do we still bother with plants ?
With potatoes, tomatoes, spinach ?
Could they merge, become "veg" ?
With milk ?
Does countryside not equal nature ?

Does nature now live in universities ?

Laboratories ?
Bunkers ?
Will it perform better there ?
By eliminating the irregularity of the sun ?

The dirt of the earth ?
Compensate for the absence of bees ?
Treat each plant individually ?
Manipulate light ?
Monitor their efficiency, happiness ? Introduce
overwork ? (Burnouts ?)
Avoid jetlag ?
Analyze individual stress ?
Should plants live in the equivalent of the smart city ?
Can a plant have its own life in an incubator ?
Can they still exist outside ?
Is Warming also creating new territories and new species ?
While it's wiping out many others ?
Can you be natural and artificial at the same time ?
Do the "new" plants grow best when they have fewer
experiences, less memory ? Are used to perfection ?
Or do they need challenge ?
Or should they grow next to each other ?
Is there mutual, interspecies benefit ? Is there urbanism
for plants ?
Can plants be maintained by swarms of miniature
robots ?
Is a gardener nature's helper or tormentor ?
Is a hunter an animal's friend or an enemy ?
Did we ever resolve this dilemma ?
If we want to eat, are we the tormentors ?
Or can helpers produce more and better food ?
Is it because we don't go to the countryside (anymore) ?
Can we still go there, unobserved ?
Do those who transformed it beyond recognition not
want you to go anymore ?
What do they hide or defend ?
Their patents ?
Their copyrights ?
Their scale ?
Their dominance ?
Their impunity ?
Their crimes ?
Their privacy, after they stole yours ?
Is the countryside the last hope for privacy ?
Is the countryside now a resort for everything that
is not public, not intended to be public, wanting to
become public ?
What explains the appearance, in the 60s and 70s, of
suburban HQs—IBM and General Life in Connecticut,
John Deere in Illinois—were they the first to escape ?

We can fish on land, grow salad on the 10th floor, create single plants that grow potatoes underground and tomatoes above, we can measure each leaf... Why do our achievements happen in secret ?

Are we embarrassed about our inventions at the moment we most depend on them ?
Do patents and copyrights interfere with the proclamation of our most radical successes ?
Is the code of the start-up the source of our craving for secrecy ?
Do patents hide large sections of intellectual life from view ?
By introducing the notion of intellectual property, did we corrupt intellectual life ?
Secrecy to enable manipulative, market-driven revelation ?
How compatible are science and copyright ?
Shall we copyright the countryside ?
What can you copyright in the countryside ?
Can the farmer copyright the farm ?
Why do farmers have to pay for their own data ?
Their own seeds ?
Does that explain why the countryside feels uncanny now ?
Too many opaque deals ?

What is the most plausible relationship between intellectuals and the countryside ?

The back and forth of Otium ?
Agritourism in Tuscany ? To be "sent" by Mao... ?
What did countryside natives think of the city dwellers visiting their domain ?
How did the import of the intellectuals strike the average villager ?
Were they even told why these visitors came ?
To help harvest or to educate their children ?
What was the real attraction ? Mao ? Revolution ? Authoritarianism ? Rice ?

Could the current countryside produce another Mao ?
Are there still schools, libraries, mentors, books in the countryside ?
Do we know recent intellectuals that have emerged from the countryside ?
Should an intellectual take risks or be smart enough to avoid them ?
Was any time ever better ?

Did the Romans propose an ideal model to shape the difference between city and countryside ?

The city for business, the country for thinking and feeling ?
You worked in the city, and came alive in the countryside ?
Countryside offered you a model for a deeper fullfillment ?
Friends, farming, meditation, and writing as the foundation for happiness ?
Among locals and slaves ? Did they have any choice ?
Did the Chinese believe in a similar model ?
Was civilization launched from the countryside, not imported from the city ?
Was countryside once flooded with poetry, agricultural knowledge, (terrestrial) music, mandarins, stories ?
Epicurean bureaucrats ? Literate hedonists ?
What is the regimented opposite of decadence ?
Refinement in the country, provincialism in the city ?

Does anyone still like cities ?

Gentrification, inequality, unaffordability, insecurity, pollution, garbage, too many problems ?
Or is it too late to critique ?
What comes first, unpleasantness or indignation... ?
Are we destroying the pinnacle of civilization with our apps ?
City of users ?
All of us users ?
Did we spoil it ?
Did we underestimate what it takes ?
To be a citizen ?
How did we become so ungenerous ?
How did we unlearn to coexist, at the exact moment we all live in cities ? Coincidence ?

Why is the countryside passive, waiting for plans

elaborated in the big centers, by dysfunctional governments at the moment democracies and other regimes seem equally stumped ?

Can it make its own plans ?
Or are there not enough people left ?
Where is the MIT for the countryside ? Yale's agrarian studies ? Wageningen University ? Why are they not more in the foreground ?
Is the countryside reduced to a populist base, a free-floating reservoir of indignation, there for the taking ?
We already blame it for Trump, Brexit, AFD, Salvini, Putin... ? Will "bad" politics make it even more inaccessible ?
Could you connect politics and territory in a new way ?
Not city or countryside but fake or real ?
Communism thought about countryside, the Welfare state too—did neoliberalism simply delete it ? Can it still be found, under "trash" ?
Can we rehearse some what-ifs ?
The car industry had solved the issue of cars ?
Why did they invest all that competence merely in cheating ?
Could they have saved us ?
Is the selfdriving car a car programmed only by everything it should not do ?
That it shall not kill ?

Since when did we believe that architecture always was about welcoming humans ?

Make them cohere ?
Since the Renaissance ?
And since when do we accept that it is just as much about exclusion and separation ?
Since Clinton ? Neoliberalism ?
Since Obama ?
When did the "reception" change character ?
How did the "reception" become the ultimate symbol of the urban: pretending to welcome, geared to reject ?
Turn into a mini-investigation ?
Facial recognition, the essence of the city today ?
Are the keycard, the iris scan, the finger print, the face,

the current equivalents of the moat, the drawbridge, the fortification ?
Has military isolation become the model for the coexistence of data, machines, robots and humans ?
Are Nevada's nuclear, military, and digital exclusion zones, a new global prototype ?
Are the guards "manning" the elaborate control rooms, the elaborate fencing, the tiny openings in the perimeter walls, a new language ?

Their scowls a form of 21st century mask ?

Or is it simple decoration ?
The illusion of security projected by those who undermine it for all ?
A massive collusion between State & Tech where the paranoid demands of the first increase the scale of the second in a mutual escalation ?
In the city, we work and live in welcoming, shapeless, undemanding spaces, preferably old, only to produce the harshest, inhuman typologies outside the city ?
Is the demise of WeWork a good sign ?
Will they dominate the countryside ?
Will farmers have to identify themselves with fingerprints ? For animals ?
Will urban citizens in the future be "missed" by their smarthomes when they venture into uncharted territory, beyond the last sensor ?
Is the countryside uncharted territory ? Can it become uncharted again ?
Will ultimate surveillance be possible only in cities, because only density makes it affordable ?
Does that offer respite for the countryside ?
Will surveillance be defined by X sensors per person ?
Will the ultimate division of the world be defined by two types of surveillance, from the air or on the ground ?
Do both impose their own values, blindness, systems ?
Their own crimes, dystopias, crises... ?
Is our environment defined by sensors that feel or satellites that see ?
What about the other senses; will they soon smell and taste ?
Will artificial organs dictate further differentiations— more radical than the current distinction between city and countryside ? The smell zone ?
Could they lead to new identities ? Separate worlds ?
How disconcerting is it to drive through the definitive

"absence" of the Saudis' Empty Quarter and realize it's made inaccessible by barbed wire... ? Is that the future ? To be excluded from emptiness ?
Should we anticipate a new world order based on more radical divisions ?
Between human and machine for instance ?
Can we think of something more intelligent than the current flourish of neglect euphoria ?
Can we reverse the movement's priorities ?

Does big data + A.I. equal infinity ? Or its opposite ?

When did they invent multiple choice in exams ?
Is the name alone a form of indoctrination ?
Did it coincide with Einstein ?
A form of relativity ?
Does multiple choice emphasize choosing over knowing ?
A sign of consumerism ?
The end of decision making ?
Did it prepare us for the Market Economy ?
Is fake news the consequence of a culture of multiple choice ?
Can being wrong be a lifestyle ?

Are data centers more impressive than pyramids ?

Are more secrets buried in their chambers ?
Are we buried alive in them ?
Are our lives buried in them ?
We don't know the blueprints of either ?
Is it true that the architects of pyramids were killed ?
Buried in their own creations ?
How about the millennials that entomb whole generations ?
Do they contain treasure chambers ?
Will later archeologists ever unearth them ?
Will they understand ? Develop conflicting theories about their geometries ? Their purpose, their dates ? Will current materials last that long ?
Will they be unearthed by robots and deciphered by A.I. ?
Will there be competing theories about how they worked ?
Or just one ?
Who will name it ? Or will it just have a QR code ?
How soon will Reagan, (Clinton ?) Bush, Obama, Trump seem remote as Egyptian dynasties ?

Did the enormity of the countryside trigger the car?

Could mobility be reversed? Where you would not have to go out, but "out" comes to you? Delivered by self-driving cars?
Will travel be rationed soon?
Is the self-driving car a car full of MCAS?
When travel is rationed, who will be allocated to the countryside? to the city?
Will it still be cheaper? cleaner? freeer?
If the greenhouse turns vegetables into artifacts, will they become more expensive in the places where they were once grown in abundance for free?
If robots rule, what will happen with disobedience?
Will there still be fences?
Will a chip tell us where and where not to go?
Will chip implants be as natural as vaccines now?
Will you be able to doubt?
Who will maintain the robots that maintain the land?
Will you be excluded, unless you are included?
Will exclusion be the default condition?
The world as a gated community, everybody protected against everybody else?
With whom will you argue?

Was Chernobyl a prototype?

Did the Soviet Union bestow to the world a preview of its final condition?
A combination of unplanned preservation and accidental destruction?
Was the disaster good for nature? And for us?

Can words decay? Why has the word "visionary" become so banal?

Can it still accommodate radical insights?
Why do we cling to modernity when we face something utterly new?
Can you stop a tradition abruptly?
Start a new one from scratch?
Judeo-Christian, Islamic, Confucian... What do they say about current conditions?
The last one the most?
Why did religion not simply disappear?
Delete all that is dysfunctional?
Could we try to connect them, throw out everything that

does not work, and generate a meta-collage of concepts in each that do offer solutions ?

What are we afraid of ?

Is fake news not a new phenomenon but the realization of a black hole in society ?

Do we need 400 monks ? To withdraw until they are done ?

The doors of their cloister cemented ?

Mobiles destroyed ? Only one left, for a single text when there's been breakthrough ?

What if there is no contemporary issue that has an adequate description, understanding, solution ?

A great simultaneous unraveling—each side equally spent, a dump of ideas ?

How should we think about earth ?

As a precious ball that should be preserved at all cost, or as a dysfunctional sphere that will not survive without our intervention ?

Are we confusing preservation with sustainability ?

Can we pursue sustainability and preservation at the same time ?

Is sustainability sustainable ?

Why have we imposed intolerable complexities on ourselves ?

Why did we abandon the idea of a way out or a way back ?

Did we colonize the countryside to better abandon it ? Are nature and its most powerful adversary, corporations, engaged in a final confrontation in the countryside ?

Could the corporate switch to repair the earth, when it becomes profitable ?

Will we pay for it ourselves ?

Why don't we pay for it ?

What perverted genius thought of the name fulfillment center ?

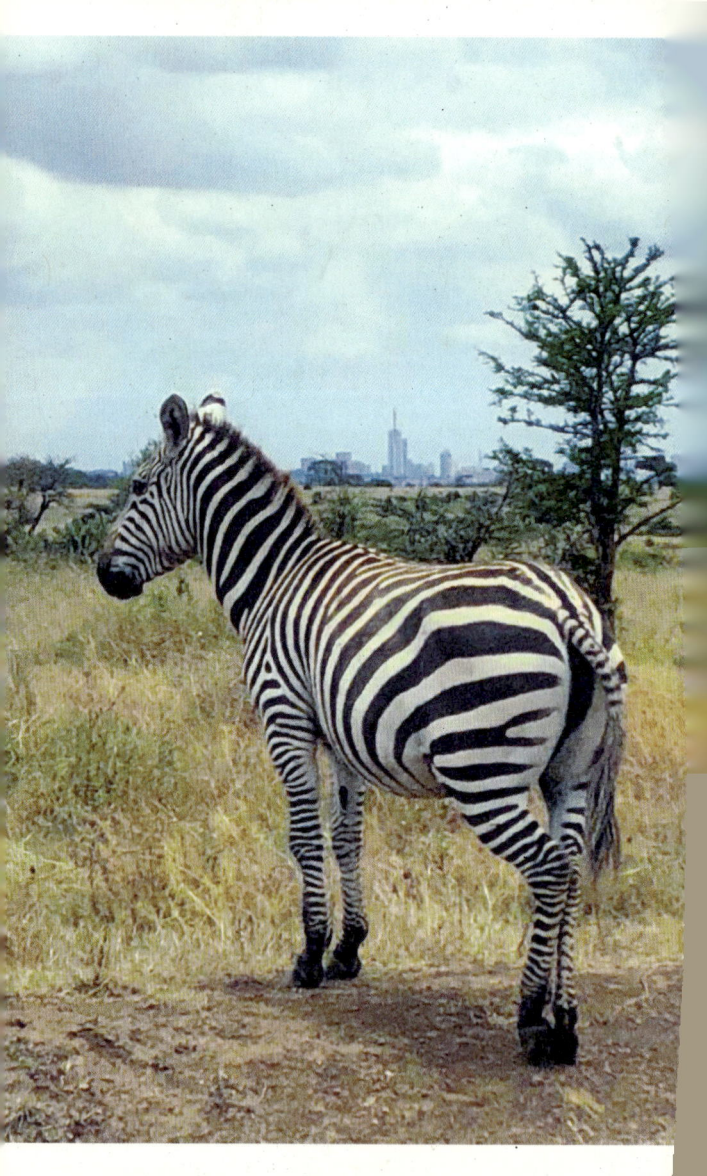